Editing Economic History

European University Studies

Europäische Hochschulschriften
Publications Universitaires Européennes

Series XIV
Anglo-Saxon Language and Literature

Reihe XIV Série XIV
Angelsächsische Sprache und Literatur
Langue et littérature anglo-saxonnes

Vol./Bd. 420

PETER LANG
Frankfurt am Main · Berlin · Bern · Bruxelles · New York · Oxford · Wien

Mike W. Malm

Editing Economic History

Ezra Pound's *The Fifth Decad of Cantos*

PETER LANG
Europäischer Verlag der Wissenschaften

Bibliographic Information published by Die Deutsche Bibliothek
Die Deutsche Bibliothek lists this publication in the Deutsche Nationalbibliografie; detailed bibliographic data is available in the internet at <http://dnb.ddb.de>.

Zugl.: München, Univ., Diss., 2003

D 19
ISSN 0721-3387
ISBN 3-631-54209-7
US-ISBN 0-8204-7752-4

www.peterlang.de

Table of Contents

Others will go that stony road whose end is unpredictable, that road into a darkness full of pitfalls, full of forebodings, uncertainties, and errings. We should let them go, and we should hope for their return.

(Hans Werner Henze, *Essays*)

Acknowledgements

Thank you – to my parents, Gerhard, Hanna and the rest of my family for their warm support, and to my friends for their encouragement and patience.

On the professional side, I am indebted first and foremost to Prof. Dr. Hans W. Gabler (Munich) for accepting my PhD project and for being an exemplary, tireless supervisor in both practical and theoretical matters; and to Prof. Dr. Goetz Schmitz (Bonn) for his encouraging guidance and quiet presence at many times. I want to thank Prof. Dr. Richard Taylor (Bayreuth) for granting me invaluable insights into many years of Pound scholarship; Jürgen Schenkelberg of Schenkelberg Software; Prof. Dr. Werner von Koppenfels; the University of Munich, the DAAD and the DFG for funding my research; the Beinecke Rare Book and Manuscript Library (Yale University), especially curator Patricia Willis and the committed members of the desk staff; the Harry Ransom Research Center (University of Texas at Austin), especially research librarian Tara Wenger; New Directions Publishing (New York); Barbara Fischer and Bruno Jahn; Prof. Dr. Jörg Jantzen; the fellows of the graduate program "Textual Criticism" at the University of Munich, especially my "computer companions" Ulrike Wolfrum and Harald Saller; PD Dr. Anne Bohnenkamp-Renken, Prof. Dr. Wieland Schmied; Dr. Paolo d'Iorio; Dr. Norbert Ott; Prof. Dr. Christoph Kampmann; Dr. Peter Robinson.

I would also like to thank Jane, Peter and Christian for their hospitality at different times and different places, and Julia for her magical place at the lake.

Bring us back soon the plants of Your vineyard,
Redeemed into Zion with joyful song.
Next year in Jerusalem!

(from the *Haggadah*)

Abbreviations

Editorial Abbreviations

BL . . . . Beinecke Rare Book and Manuscript Library, Yale University. Quotations from BL material are given in the following format: BL 43 / 72 /3245, that is, Beinecke Library call number 43, box 72, folder 3245.

HRC . . . . Ezra Pound Collection of the Harry Ransom Research Center, University of Texas at Austin. Quotations from HRC material are given in the following format: HRC 1 / 1 / 9, that is, series 1, box 1, folder 9.

Lilly . . . . Lilly Library, Indiana University, Pound MSS.

add. . . . . Addition(s), e.g. lines added to a draft.

cc. . . . . Carbon copy.

ls. . . . . .Letter-sized sheet.

pc. . . . . Pencil.

rev. . . . . Revision(s).

ts. . . . . .Typescript.

* * *

BL or HRC papers featured in the item list at the end of this book are quoted with the item number used in the list. Roman numerals as in "BL Rudge I" or "Lilly Pound II" are the numbers of the general archival series referred to.

* * *

For the sake of brevity, individual Cantos are referred to in short form as "Cxx." E.g. Canto LI is called C51.

* * *

Quotations from "The Cantos of Ezra Pound" are given in the following format: C36.179, that is, Canto 36, page 179 of the 1995 New Directions edition.

* * *

Line breaks in quotations from poems are conventionally indicated by a slash ("/"). Because of Pound's frequent use of the slash symbol, line breaks in texts by Pound are indicated by a slash in square brackets ("[/]").

Bibliographical Abbreviations

The following abbreviations are used for titles frequently cited in the study or the edition. Full records of all other titles can be found in the bibliographical appendix to this study.

ANB .... American National Biography, general eds. John A. Garraty / Mark C. Carnes, 24 vols., New York 1999.

Centenario ... Sorosina, Amedeo, Il Monte dei Paschi di Siena: Per il terzo centenario, Siena 1925.

Companion ...Terrell, Carroll F., A Companion to the Cantos of Ezra Pound, 2 vols., Berkeley / Los Angeles / London 1980.

EB ....Encyclopaedia Britannica CD 99, [s.l.] 1999.

GK ....Pound, Ezra, Guide to Kulchur, London 1966 [1st ed. 1938].

J/M ....Pound, Ezra, Jefferson and/or Mussolini: L'Idea Statale, New York: Liveright / London: Stanley Nott 1935.

LE .... Pound, Ezra, Literary Essays, Norfolk (Conn.) 1954.

Monte .... Mengozzi, Narcisco (ed.), Il Monte dei Paschi di Siena e le Aziende in Esso Riunite, 9 vols., Siena 1891-1925.

OED .... Oxford English Dictionary 2 on CD-ROM, Version 1.13, [s.l.] 1994.

P&P . . . . .Pound, Ezra, Ezra Pound's Poetry and Prose Contributions to Periodicals, eds. Lea Baechler / A. Walton Litz / James Longenbach, New York / London 1991.

Paid . . . . *Paideuma.*

Pauly . . . . .Wissowa, Georg et.al. (eds.), Paulys Realencyclopädie der classischen Altertumswissenschaft (+ suppl.), Stuttgart 1893-1978.

SP . . . . Pound, Ezra, Selected Prose 1909-1965, ed. William Cookson, London 1973.

Zobi . . . . .Zobi, Antonio, Storia Civile della Toscana dal MDCCXXXVII al MDCCCXLVIII, 5 vols., Florence 1850-53.

I. Mnemosyne 1 – Approaching the Text

Can you describe *history I'd like to know?*
Isn't it a fiction that pretends to be fact
like A Journal of the Plague Year*?*

(Tom Paulin, *Martello*)

I.1 Introduction

The Fifth Decad of Cantos*: A Primer on Economy?*

Let us begin where there is no point to begin with: in a Heraclitean space of ever-changing forms, a space of individual elements that mix or separate, diversify or lose themselves in multiple ramifications before returning to fragile unities. In history, territories are united, stabilized and transformed into political entities, only to be conquered and lost again, as in the case of Tuscany. In literature, some author hastily scribbles a number of lyrical sentences on a sheet of paper, writes down excerpts from a book about, say, Tuscan history, then combines the two elements, adds references to other places, other times, and finally forms one text out of a diversity of sources. All this: the transience of political entities, the myriad figures of economic history, an ancient Asian past of dynastic dignity – all this diversity has been condensed into historiography and finally poetry in the text of Ezra Pound's *Cantos*.

Diversity and condensation govern Pound's modernist epic as a whole. Together, they create a typically modernist and at the same time highly original complexity that contributes strongly to the unique character of the *Cantos*. Their broad, pluralistic scope of literary references and historical sources integrates European and Asian literature, western and eastern history. Although deeply rooted in Dante's *Divine Comedy* and the European Middle Ages, the *Cantos* go even further back to Homer and Confucius. Few limits in terms of space and time seem to exist, as the poem moves from the dynasties of ancient China to Pound's own mundane experiences. But although Pound confronts his readers with multiple histories, references and subjects, the *Cantos* are not without recurring subjects, e.g. good government, economic power and the corruption of man by money.

Those subjects are present throughout the *Cantos*, but prevail in particular passages of the poem. Among them is *The Fifth Decad of Cantos*, which was published in 1937 and is the subject of this study. The featured Cantos (C42-51) are usually included among the so-called "Middle Cantos," because they belong to the middle working period of the then 52-year-old Pound. In the *Fifth Decad*, the broad spectrum of Pound's interests is developed in full. Subjects and motifs are fluently connected and transformed into a symbiosis of historical, literary and economic references. Among them are the foundation of the *Monte dei Paschi* bank in Early Modern Siena, the reforms of Duke Pietro Leopoldo in Tuscany and the condemnation of usury as an unnatural form of economic greed. The *Fifth Decad* gains a particularly controversial direction by Pound's fascist allegiances, which had reached their full peak by 1937.

In the years before he published the decad, Pound was deeply immersed in the economic theories of Silvio Gesell[1] and in the eventful history of Tuscany, where, during the reigns of Pietro Leopoldo and Ferdinando III, a perfect balance of political and economic innovation seemed to have been achieved. This sane side of Pound's economic obsessions had a darker counterpart that also came to the fore during the 1930s and found its expression in Pound's essays and in many passages of the *Fifth Decad*. In one and the same collection of Cantos, Pound not only praises the wisdom of enlightened rulers, but also warns his readers of an alleged conspiracy of international Jewish financiers and laments the global prevalence of usury as the symptom of a perverted monetary system. Even if, as Makin states, the *Fifth Decad* was written in "serene circumstances," that serenity was virtually reversed by Pound's nervous polemics about economic issues.[2] In fact, Pound himself acknowledged the strong influence of economics on his thought when he claimed in 1935 to lead a "constant life in econ/ at present, hardly elsewhere."[3] It should therefore not be surprising to discover an extreme amount of "econ/" in the decad.

In general, the economic emphasis of the *Fifth Decad* has not damaged the reputation of the poem. One of its earliest reviewers, Edwin Muir, even praised its universal appeal when he said: "Everything is brought immediately before us; the seventeenth century is just as close as the present, and China as near as London; the resulting world is the world of this poem."[4] A more recent critic called the *Fifth Decad* "one of the more notable poetic and structural successes" of the *Cantos*.[5] As to its place among the other Cantos, the *Fifth Decad* is now often regarded as an intermediate passage. It is preceded by *Eleven New Cantos*: The "American Cantos" 31 to 34 praise the nation-building Jefferson. Then "Mitteleuropa" (C35) is introduced as a contrast to the U.S., followed by the Cavalcanti Canto (C36) as a model of intelligent passion, whereas C39 celebrates natural fertility and the final C41 expresses Pound's admiration for Mussolini. Love, statecraft, order, precision of thought, fertility and money are some of the section's major subjects, most

---

[1] On Gesell's influence on Pound see e.g. Tim Redman, Ezra Pound and Fascism, passim. On Gesell's life and work see Frances Hutchinson / Brian Burkitt, The Political Economy of Social Credit and Guild Socialism; Werner Schmid, Silvio Gesell: Die Lebensgeschichte eines Pioniers, Bern 1954; Siegbert Wolf, Silvio Gesell, Munich 1983.

[2] Makin, Peter, Pound's Cantos, 196.

[3] Letter of 12 March 1935, in: Gordon, David M. (ed.), Ezra Pound and James Laughlin, 41.

[4] Muir, Edwin, Review: *The Fifth Decad of Cantos*, 149.

[5] Bacigalupo, Massimo, The Forméd Trace, 67.

of which are revisited in the *Fifth Decad*.[6] The latter decad is followed by the "Chinese Cantos" (C52 and following), whose rich tapestry unfolds centuries of China's dynastic history. Situated between the multiple events of American-European history and the more stringent thread of Asian imperial history, *The Fifth Decad of Cantos* functions as a transitional sequence which "leads us out of the unchronological muck-raking cantos into the great chronological unfolding of Chinese history."[7]

Maybe due to its transitional character, *The Fifth Decad of Cantos* has not yet been subject to comprehensive research. The present study is the first thorough analysis of the section as a whole. Interpretations of the decad have only been attempted in a number of brief studies that mainly focus on well-known Cantos like the Usura Canto (C45).[8] Kimpel and Duncan Eaves have written several helpful essays on Pound's use of historical documents in *The Fifth Decad of Cantos*.[9] And by its lyrical adaptation of Asian poetry, the Seven Lakes Canto (C49) has gained attention as one of Pound's most excellent poems.[10] But an in-depth analysis of *The Fifth Decad of Cantos*, one that would consider not only the published text but also the pre-publication manuscripts,[11] is still lacking, although *The Fifth Decad* is hardly less complex than other parts of Pound's epic.

But why analyze Pound's often hardly legible autographs? One reason is the unreliability of the existing editions. Their textual faults and complicated publication histories have become commonplaces among Pound scholars. Indeed, Pound readers have been confronted for decades with two official, but textually different editions of the *Cantos*, published by Faber & Faber in the U.K. and by New Directions in the U.S. – not even to mention the many Cantos Pound published in periodicals and anthologies.

This uncertainty towards existing editions of the *Cantos* has given rise to several projects that concentrate on analyzing the genetic aspects of text and publication process. Richard Taylor has started working on a Variorum Edition of the printed versions of the Cantos.[12] Then there is Peter Stoicheff's study on the late *Drafts and Fragments*, which opened new perspectives on

---

[6] Comp. the synopsis in Kenner, Hugh, The Pound Era, 424.
[7] Dekker, George, Sailing After Knowledge, 179.
[8] E.g. Christine Brooke-Rose, A Structural Analysis of Pound's Usura Canto.
[9] For a list of their essays see Ricks, Beatrice, Ezra Pound: A Bibliography of Secondary Works, 49.
[10] Comp. Kenner, Hugh, "More on the Seven Lakes Canto;" or Palandri, Angela J., "The 'Seven Lakes Canto' Revisited," in: *Paideuma* 3.1 (1974), 52ff.
[11] As Rainey does for the Malatesta Cantos. See Rainey, Lawrence S., Ezra Pound and the Monument of Culture.
[12] Until now, only a prototype has been published; see Taylor, Richard, Variorum Edition of "Three Cantos" by Ezra Pound.

the publication process of the final Cantos.[13] In 1984 Christine Froula published a complete edition of C4 from the manuscript drafts to the printed versions.[14] As to the pre-publication documents, her book contains a sequence of diplomatic transcriptions, while the published versions are provided with a critical apparatus. Eva Hesse's book on Cantos 45 and 51[15] was a first attempt to present selected Cantos from the *Fifth Decad* in a genetic perspective. The selection not only provides photographic reproductions and transcriptions of drafts directly related to C45 and C51, but also includes fragments thematically related to *The Fifth Decad* and excerpts from Pound's reading notes. Hence, readers gain insights into the poet's working methods and his approach to source texts. Textual genesis and content analysis are combined, because they complement each other.

My study will continue this two-fold approach, as content and composition cannot be divided when studying *The Fifth Decad of Cantos*. The work contains a highly original mixture of eclecticism, conspiracy theories and economic obsessions, which may make it seem surprisingly modern to today's readers. This syncretism of thought, which mirrors Pound's intellectual condition during the 1930s, not only manifests itself in the free-verse, collage-like form of the Cantos, but also in Pound's writing and composing. Pound's notes, drafts and letters in the libraries bear material witness to his wide-spread interests and his condensing method of writing, by which he transformed vast quantities of source materials into brief, if not elliptical, Cantos. Pound's manner of composing was so characteristic that, for many Cantos, unique stories could be told. For instance, about how Pound went to the Sienese *Archivio di Stato* to read historical documents on the 1602 foundation of the *Monte dei Paschi* bank. We could mention his silent wrestling with the old source manuscripts and his attempts to decipher their handwriting. We could also remember how Pound, sitting on his balcony in Rapallo, had a Chinese teacher translate to him some Asian poems from a book he had inherited from his parents, poems he later transformed into one of his most widely acclaimed Cantos, C49.

At a first glance, those are merely stories, but beyond their anecdotal contents, Pound's highly characteristic attempts of absorbing different subjects hint at a crucial structural element of the Cantos. Only few passages of the text are "pure" poetry. Rather, the text consists of a large number of excerpts: First, *conceptual excerpts*, e.g. from the philosophy of Confucius, the economic theories of Douglas and Gesell or the anti-usury writings of medieval thinkers. The conceptual excerpts are supplemented by shorter, often fragmentary or abbridged, *textual excerpts* – quotations from books (e.g.

[13] Stoicheff, Peter, The Hall of Mirrors.
[14] Froula, Christine, To Write Paradise.
[15] Hesse, Eva (ed.), Ezra Pound: Usura-Cantos XLV und LI.

Zobi's history of Tuscany), archival documents (e.g. the founding instrument of the *Monte dei Paschi*), newspapers and letters, oral remarks, pieces of conversation and reminiscences. The interaction and step-by-step structuring and condensing of those constituents took place in Pound's manuscripts and typescripts. In them, Pound worked on the material level, by *writing*, and on the structural, or content level, by *composing*. He composed by combining pieces of text, shaping them into blocks and sequences, sometimes by association, sometimes by constructing almost contrapuntal parallels. *The Fifth Decad of Cantos* can hardly be imagined without its sources, from which Pound proceeded through several layers of writing to form an increasingly condensed patchwork of elements. Given the multiple layers and intertextual nature of the *Fifth Decad*, it is necessary to find an approach that suits their complexity.

Setting the Scene: History, Methodology, Genesis

Any analysis of *The Fifth Decad of Cantos* must pay attention to economics and history, as both determine the form of the text. Although, in 1944, Pound claimed not to have written an economic history in the *Cantos*, he actually came very close to doing so when he based many Cantos on economic sources or devoted them to economic subjects. At one time, he was mainly interested in creating a modern epic that would range from the "Dark Forest" of human error to divine perfection, without paying too much attention to individual instances of economic malpractice.[16] Many Cantos, however, confront readers with myriads of economic-historical facts from past and present. We read about armament deals (C38.187), the Bank of England (C46.233) and the socio-economic condition of the U.S. in 1935 (C46.235), to name but a few examples. While such references may seem exotic subjects for a poem, Pound himself never considered his broad interest in economics and history to be very original. He believed that, among non-economists and novelists, Henry James had already developed a sense of money as the most crucial element in modern life.[17] Nor did Pound regard economic history as something very obscure. Rather, he saw economics as a substantial element of historical studies: "I don't see that anyone save a sap-head can now think he

---

[16] Pound: "For forty years I have schooled myself, not to write an economic history of the U.S. or any other country, but to write an epic poem which begins 'In the Dark Forest'[,] crosses the purgatory of human error, and ends in the light, and 'fra i maestri di color che sanno'. For this reason I have had to understand the NATURE of error. But I don't think it necessary to refer to each particular case of error." See "An Introduction to the Economic Nature of the United States" (1944, orig. Italian), in: SP, 137. For a comment on this statement see Brooke-Rose, Christine, "Lay me by Aurelie," 243.

[17] "The Individual in his Milieu" (1935), in: SP, 242.

knows any history until he understands economics."[18] In 1935 he raged at "young idiots who can't see that history does not exist without economics."[19]

That Pound took economic history so serious was not simply one of his peculiarities. For him economics possessed a deeply moral dimension, as he emphasized repeatedly during the 1930s. First, it allowed him insights into a history of manners as H. James and French novelists like Flaubert had written it. In a letter to John Drummond of 16 June 1936, Pound stated: "Without study of econ/ motivations NO *histoire morale contemporaine* can be written."[20] This is the socio-historical aspect of Pound's idea of history. Second, the study of economic history served to analyze the connection between politics and power. In 1935 Pound claimed that the study of history was impossible without a thorough analysis of economic conditions, and that pacifists who neglected economics would not be able to realize the true causes of war.[21] As we will see later, Pound held a deep conviction that economic history would reveal a secret history of conspiracies, in which economic forces and interests played a major role.[22] Knowledge of historical facts would help to make readers immune against those powerful bankers and financiers who were allegedly interested in keeping the public ignorant of economics.[23] Pound, on the other hand, fought that ignorance and promoted an urgent didacticism, which may not have improved his poetry, but served to render his texts useful "to instruct the pore god damn bloody pubk/ in history and economics," as he said about his *Eleven New Cantos*.[24] On 16 February 1935, Pound wrote in a letter to Eliot that the last eleven Cantos had been intended to teach readers history and economics.[25]

Obviously, Pound believed that we would simply have to study economic history to understand the reasons for wars and to discover the vested interests behind politics. Was Pound, then, yet another adherent of the traditional conspiracy theories, and was his interest in denouncing the rich and powerful not simply a reaction to his own difficult financial situation as an avantgarde writer? At least Pound himself claimed that the unemployment problem he was concerned with was that of T. S. Eliot, Wyndham Lewis, Henri Gaudier-Brzeska and himself – "Whatever economic passions I now have, began *ab infinitio* from having crimes against living art thrust under my perceptions."[26] And is it not possible to define Pound's idea of history in such

[18] "Date Line" (1934), in: LE, 86.
[19] "Jean Cocteau Sociologist" (1935), in: P&P VI.238.
[20] Quot. in Redman, Tim, Ezra Pound and Italian Fascism, 172.
[21] "History and Ignorance" (1935), in: SP, 237.
[22] For Pound's definition of "secret history" see GK, 264.
[23] Comp. Pound, Ezra, "American Revolution" [n.d.], BL 43 / 67 / 2911, 7.
[24] Gordon, David M. (ed.), Ezra Pound and James Laughlin: Selected Letters, 36.
[25] Quot. in Redman, Tim, Ezra Pound and Italian Fascism, 156.
[26] "Murder by Capital" (1933), in: SP, 200f.

commonplace categories as "the degenerative, the progressivist, and the cyclical"?[27] These are the questions this study seeks to answer.

If Pound's idea of history is as complex as we claim, then a naïve or simplifying approach will not be sufficient to understand the layers of meaning encoded in the *Cantos*. If we want to understand fully the interdisciplinary implications of Pound's work, we are forced to bridge the gap between economics and literature. In recent years, this has been undertaken chiefly by New Economic Criticism.[28] Some scholars involved in this movement concentrate on the economic conditions of writing, such as writers' incomes, showing to which extent modernist writers depended on wealthy patrons.[29] Others analyze how economic facts and perceptions are represented in literature.[30] These scholars are not economists who turned into literary scholars at some point. Rather, recent interest in the relation between economics and literature emerged from the broad background of Cultural Studies and one of its branches, New Historicism.[31]

Its preoccupation with economics has its place within a set of general theoretical assumptions of New Historicism, some of which are useful for our purposes. First, all forms of signs and rhetoric – not only public discourse – can be subject to historical analysis. This includes, for instance, personal diary entries or, in our case, pre-publication documents.[32] Second, "every expressive act is embedded in a network of material practices," as literary and non-literary "texts" are inseparable.[33] These two theorems show an awareness of the historical specificity of the literary work. As opposed to the perspective

---

[27] McGann, Jerome J., "History, Herstory, Theirstory, Ourstory," 196.

[28] For an introduction with a representative number of case studies, see Woodmansee, Martha / Osteen, Mark, The New Economic Criticism. Other interdisciplinary titles include substantial contributions by pioneer Marc Shell and others: Marc Shell, The Economy of Literature, Baltimore 1978; Marc Shell, Money, Language and Thought: Literary and Philospohical Economies from the Medieval to the Modern Era, Berkeley 1982; Walter B. Michaels, The Gold Standard and the Logic of Naturalism: American Literature at the Turn of the Century, Berkeley 1987; Cedric Watts, Literature and Money: Financial Myth and Literary Truth, New York et.al. 1990; Richard Godden, Fictions of Capital: The American Novel from James to Mailer, Cambridge 1990; Marc Shell, Art and Money, Chicago 1995; Willie Henderson, Economics as Literature, London 1995.

[29] For a brief, but excellent account of modernism and its necessarily close relation to the problem of funding, see Paul Delany's "Who Paid for Modernism" in: Woodmansee, Martha / Osteen, Mark, The New Economic Criticism, 335-351.

[30] Watts and Godden, in their works mentioned above, are two proponents of this approach.

[31] This connection is emphasized in the editors' preface in Woodmansee, Martha / Osteen, Mark, The New Economic Criticism, 4, which also mentions reasons for this development.

[32] Veeser, Harold A., "The New Historicism," 8. Also comp. Wilentz, Sean / Cannadine, David (eds.), Rites of Power: Symbolism, Ritual, and Politics Since the Middle Ages, Philadelphia 1985, 4f.

[33] Veeser, Harold A., "The New Historicism," 2, and, more detailed, in 14-19.

of New Criticism, the work no longer figures as an autonomous being, but loses part of its hermeneutical significance to the preconditions under which it was created. The new interpretational space opened by the epistemological expansions of New Historicism is vast enough to embrace not only a broader study of contexts (biographical, mental etc.), but also to encourage a closer reading of the text itself. With the arrival of what we uneasily call poststructuralism, scholars began to concern themselves with, first, the historicity of texts and, second, the textuality of history.[34] The second aspect, although important, has little relevance for this study. It postulates a textual bias of historical transmission, as our knowledge of history is mainly based on textual evidence. The first point is more crucial for our study: The historicity of texts denotes "the historical specificity, the social and material embedding, of all modes of *writing*" and *reading*.[35]

In this study, the specificity of writing is primarily analyzed in two areas – in the *material* writing space (textual genesis) and in the *contextual* writing space, in which the author constitutes a biographical object within a cluster of historical and mental-intellectual conditions. Part II of this study will cover both aspects. Starting from the micro-level and taking into account our genetic-historical interest, we will first concentrate on the Pound papers as chief witnesses of the poem's development, and then describe aspects of its composition: Pound's use of literary and non-literary sources, structural principles that govern the text, the interaction of motifs and subjects. Combining the genetic and the hermeneutical, an outline of the poem's genesis follows.

Moving on to the macro-level of the contextual writing space in part III, we will reconstruct a portrait of fifty-year-old Pound and his intellectual world, a portrait intended to enhance our understanding of *The Fifth Decad*. Pound's ideas about the power of greed, his situation as an American intellectual in fascist Italy, and his reading of sources on the economic history of Italy are all keys to an interpretation of *The Fifth Decad*, as they help to locate the individual in the context of his time. We will unfold Pound's life in fascist Italy and his positions during the 1930s, as far as they can be deduced from his reading, letters, notes and drafts. Our aim is to bring to life a time when Pound's activist poetology formed a sinister alliance with Italian fascism and lured Pound into a deep reverence for the political "doer" Mussolini, a reverence which left its traces in the poetry of the *Cantos*.[36]

[34] Montrose, Louis, "New Historicisms," 410.

[35] Ibid. The term "specificity" is also used and explained in more detail in the introduction and chapter I of James Chandler, England in 1819. The Politics of Literary Culture and the Case of Romantic Historicism, Chicago 1999.

[36] As emphasized by Rainey, Lawrence S., " 'All I Want You to Do Is to Follow the Orders' ," 88f.

Based on our contextual findings, we will finally analyze the poems included in *The Fifth Decad* in detail, will comment on Pound's structural strategies and his historical method, and ask whether Pound merely presented, or deliberately instrumentalized, economic and political history. To have unfolded the complexity of Pound's thought will help us to discover the preconditions and non-literary interests involved in the creation of the text and to give a general account of structural aspects and models that are relevant for the poem, ranging from musical structures to the literary traditions of China.

While economic relations and market mechanisms are often at the core of New Historicist studies, e.g. when they discuss money and prestige,[37] we are not interested in Pound as an actor within an economic system, but on his perception of economic aspects of history. This objective is of course supported by Pound's obvious focusing on the subject in *The Fifth Decad*, so we hardly have to justify our emphasis on economics and history. Other, more ambiguous literary works make such a justification more difficult. For instance, a New Historicist reading of Hawthorne's *The Scarlet Letter* in economic terms regards the witch-hunts not as expressions of a mass psychosis or of religious outrage, but of economic interests related to real-estate deals.[38] This interpretation is based on hermeneutical evidence which could be challenged by other scholars. In other words, an economic reading of the Hawthorne text seems optional, not obligatory. The synopsis of Sienese banking presented in C42-44, however, is different, as is the more fragmented panorama of C48, because in *The Fifth Decad* the economic is omnipresent. We cannot avoid an interdisciplinary reading of the text, given its strongly non-literary systems of reference. At the same time, though, we should not forget that each economic source, once it has been integrated into the poem, is transformed into an element within a literary structure, even if directly copied from the source. Our starting point will always be *The Fifth Decad* as literature, not as a study in economics.

In terms of interdisciplinarity, Pound scholarship has undergone several waves and shifts of interest. Some major tendencies are useful for our purposes. Starting from early, but still valid, cultural-historical readings of Pound,[39] some scholars have concentrated on the economic aspects of the *Cantos*, particulary on Pound's relation to C. H. Douglas, the Social Credit movement, Gesell and Odon Por, who wrote a book on *Guilds and Co-operatives in Italy*. The same scholars are often concerned with a contextualization and historization of Pound and his work, i.e. they emphasize

[37] Veeser, Harold A., "The New Historicism," 3f.

[38] Walter B. Michaels, "Romance and Real Estate," in: Veeser, Harold A. (ed.), The New Historicism Reader, New York / London 1994, 186-205.

[39] Mainly: Hugh Kenner, The Pound Era, Berkeley / Los Angeles ^{2}1973.

his strong ties to Italian fascism and thus connect Pound's political and economic ideas.[40] The contextualization of Pound is taken further by scholars with a broad interest rooted in cultural studies, who seek to explain Pound'a deeper obsessions by linking them to the general intellectual history of his time. They are interested in subjects such as anti-Semitism, American populism and conspiracy theories.[41] Finally, we should not forget scholars with a more bibliographical interest in Pound, who look for ways to gain a better understanding of the *Cantos* by analyzing their textual history.[42] The mentioned groups of scholars are not working in total autarchy, nor do they represent factions divided by hostility. Each of them has benefitted from the work of the others. Accordingly, the present study seeks to take their perspectives into balanced consideration. The impressing complexity of *The Fifth Decad* calls for a comprehensive approach that encompasses both dry economic figures and the irrationality of conspiracy theories.

One of the objectives to guide us through this study is neutrality. We will not comment upon the "truth" or "factual validity" of Pound's views on contemporary economics. We are neither concerned with mere statistics, nor with economics proper. We are moving entirely in the realm of opinion, not in the empire of fact. What Pound uttered as an amateur economicst was opinion, and much of the information he digested was acquired from non-academic sources – such as journalists, reformers, politicians and populists. It is true, there were some scholars among them, like professor Irving Fisher, one of Pound's favorite economists. Yet what found its way into the *Cantos* was mostly not the theory, but the polemics. In the poem, as will be discussed later, Pound used facts to support the points he wanted to make, rather than to construct a systematic theory of economics. We should not be deceived by the seemingly objective "case" presented by Pound in the persona of an inquisitive inspector-prosecutor in C46. We should bear in mind from the beginning the importance Pound attached to the *message* he wanted to convey. He tended to adopt such economic theories and models as fitted his message. It should not be supposed, however, that the aim of this study is to belittle Pound's interest in economics as mere dilettantism. Because, in the case of the *Fifth Decad*, the medium is inseparable from the message, we had better take his economic opinions serious in order to understand the form of the included poems. In short, we seek to identify structural components,[43] not to judge Pound's economic expertise.

---

[40] Like Redman, Tim, "Pound's Politics and Economics," 249-263; or, with an emphasis on politics, Morrison, Paul, The Poetics of Fascism.

[41] E.g. Robert Casillo, The Genealogy of Demons; Leon Surette, Pound in Purgatory.

[42] E.g. Christine Froula, To Write Paradise; Lawrence S. Rainey, Ezra Pound and the Monument of Culture; Peter Stoicheff, The Hall of Mirrors.

[43] White, Hayden, Metahistory, 3f.

We have so far discussed history as a factor that determines the content of the work, but have mostly ignored the textual level, which is as dynamic as any historical process. In fact all text is historical – stained by error, distorted by biographical accident and as imperfect as the course of real-life events. The work itself has a historical dimension and bears witness to the passage of time. This dimension not merely constitutes a one-dimensional chronology. While it is obvious that writing always precedes publication, we can hardly cover the complete genesis of a work in such simplifying terms, or establish a simple thread from one starting point (like a key sentence) to a clear-cut, neatly printed *Finis*. In fact we may find no point to begin with at all. At what point does a "work" start to exist? When an author types the first letter of the first draft, not yet knowing where the writing will take the writer? Or much later, when the typewriter has fulfilled its purpose, the proofs have been corrected, and a book is published? Maybe the origins of a work lie in the obscurity of accidental notes, untitled sketches and hastily scribbled phrases, or in a conversation overheard by chance, the memory of some trivial experience never quite forgotten. The work is usually not rooted in one incident alone, but grows from many sources.

The writing process itself is hardly less complex than the development of the poet's initial ideas, as writing consists of corrections and additions, re-reading and re-writing, a constant dialogue between the author and the text. As Hugh Kenner acknowledged, a poem is not an ultimate end product, but only a "controlled transformational process."[44] And Gabler stressed the "continuous play of authorial writing and authorial reading that characterizes composition and revision in acts of writing."[45] On a more abstract level, McGann regards textual history as a history of social interactions between individuals.[46] He postulates "textual moments," including the author; other persons or groups involved in the intial process of production, e.g. editors; phases and stages in the initial productive process; finally materials, means and modes (physical, psychological, ideological) of production.[47] To oppose a modern tendency, grounded in hermeneutics, to imagine texts exclusively as scenes of reading and interpreting,[48] they can also be regarded as scenes of writing. Production is not strictly dependent on the product; and as Hay

---

[44] Kenner, Hugh, The Pound Era, 171.

[45] Gabler, Hans Walter, „Genetic Texts – Genetic Editions – Genetic Criticism," 70.

[46] McGann: "Textual criticism investigates the history, deposited in literary works, of the specific interactions which took (and are taking) place between determinate individuals in determinate social circumstances." In: McGann, Jerome, "Interpretation, Meaning, and Textual Criticism: A Homily," 57.

[47] McGann, Jerome, "Interpretation, Meaning, and Textual Criticism: A Homily," 58.

[48] McGann, Jerome, The Textual Condition, 4.

emphasized, the writing habits of a poet do not depend entirely on the text, but follow their own laws.[49]

While the latter point yet has to be proven, we can, for the moment, agree with Gabler's notion of textual processuality and McGann's concept of textual history as a dynamic interaction between human and material elements in a social context. Starting with these notions, a genetic perspective is adopted in both parts II and III of this study. On the hermeneutical level, the motifs and subjects in *The Fifth Decad* will be analyzed in the contexts of Pound's thought (intellectual) and of his notes and drafts (textual). This double perspective prevents us from adopting too narrow a focus and allows us to explain obscure parts of the text with the help of discarded drafts. In addition, a genetic approach is appropriate for emphasizing the unique character of the *Cantos* as a dynamic poem whose writing parallels the life of its author, including his errors.

As explained above, part III of this study is concerned with the historical-hermeneutical dimension of the poem's genesis. Specifying the genetic perspective of this study, part IV then takes the conclusions gained from the analysis in parts II and III and puts them into an editorial context. Part IV will isolate the essential requirements of the Pound papers, as based on their physical properties and Pound's individual writing habits. It will then proceed to a more general consideration of theoretical options suitable for a genetic criticism of *The Fifth Decad.* Our goal is to outline principles of a possible genetic edition of the decad: Which medium should such an edition use, how should it structure and present the Poundian documents?

In brief, this study *The Fifth Decad* wants to cover the historical dimensions of writing, as outlined by Espagne. This includes biographical aspects (the author as a reader of source texts, as a witness of events which lead to a literary work, etc.), the semantic relations between the work and its historical context, documents as historical evidence of the writing process, and the reception of the work.[50] Our general objective is the reconstruction, not the deconstruction, of Pound's poem. In isolating the pieces it consists of, we will anatomize the complexity the work embraces and emphasize the metamorphoses it underwent. Our aim is to isolate the elements – and their revisional metamorphoses – that govern Pound's journey from Ancient China to modern Italy and render the poem complicated, but coherent in an innovative way. The study of genetic processes can support our seemingly paradoxical attempt to isolate diverse layers of textual historicity and, at the same time, re-enact the creation of a coherent whole. Therefore we will not make a choice as to the validity of Karl Popper's statement that studying the

---

[49] According to Hay, "the *method of writing* is not dependent on *what is written*, and the genesis of a work is not a function of its text." See Hay, Louis, "History or Genesis?," 207.
[50] Espagne, Michel, De l'archive au texte, 169.

products is more essential than studying the production, even for an understanding of production itself: We will employ both flux and stasis for our purposes.

I.2 Terminology

The following working definitions are used throughout this study. They are not intended as final definitions applicable to other than genetic or even editorial purposes.

Work

The work of an author is conventionally defined either by the criterion of publication, by the existence of a title, or both. Hurlebusch, for example, states that a work is a text which can be defined or marked by a title.[51] However, an unpublished, yet finished novel can be called a work, too, even it has never been given more than a working title, as the title is certainly *one*, but not the only crucial element to turn a text into a work. The argument that the text is unrevised, therefore unfinished and not to be defined as a work is not valid in this context, because even published texts are often revised by their authors and still bear the label "work."

According to Scheibe, the work is that form of a text ("Textgestalt") on which an author is currently working.[52] Publication or non-publication, as well as the finished or unfinished state of the text, do not play a central role in this definition. More important is authorial intention. Scheibe defines the work as a text intended, by the author, for publication, transmitted to posterity in the form of authorized documents or other traceable evidence.[53] Given deficiencies in transmission, however, authorial intention is often likely to be buried with the author. I therefore propose an alternative definition of the term "work":

1) The term "work" functions on a socio-cultural level. It denotes an *act of canonization* that creates a set of texts associated with, in most cases, an authorial instance. Canonization can be achieved by the author, but at the same time requires additional agents to affect the inclusion of a work into cultural memory. Hence, a work is established by the author *and* posterity; no single instance can assume full responsibility for establishing a work.

---

[51] Martens, Gunter / Zeller, Hans (eds.), Texte und Varianten, 127.

[52] Kanzog, Klaus, Einführung in die Editionsphilologie der neueren deutschen Literatur, 134.

[53] Scheibe: "Texte, die nach der Intention des Autors für die Öffentlichkeit bestimmt und entweder in autorisierten Zeugen oder deren Stellvertretern oft in verschiedenen Textfassungen überliefert oder durch Zeugnisse belegt sind." From Scheibe, Siegfried, "Editorische Grundmodelle," in: Siegfried Scheibe (ed.), Zu Werk und Text, Berlin 1991, 25.

2) A text becomes a work if *published*, even if unfinished and / or without title. Hence, Kafka's novels and fragments, after their publication by Max Brod, are now the author's "works," because they have been canonized in this form.

3) A text also becomes a work if *finished*, even if forever unpublished and / or left without title. An author may call the finished epic in his drawer a work, as may the scholar who discovers the manuscript after the writer's death and refers to it in a published article.

4) Only the *unfinished and unpublished* text is clearly not a work. For instance, the unedited fragment of a poem in an archive.

Once defined, a work comprises all genetic stages, drafts, fragments and paralipomena for which a relation to the finished / published text can be established.[54] Note that those *avant-textes* are not necessarily part of the *text* of the work. An early chronology or sketch for a novel are merely notes and not part of the textual genesis. Still, they have to be read as genetic sub-units within the context of the work.

Text

Although the name-label of textual criticism, the term "text" remains its most opaque chimera. A universal understanding of it does hardly exist, as most definitions are instrumentalized for particular purposes. Hence the danger of assigning too broad or too narrow a definition to the term. For instance, understanding text as "a system of signs characterized by the functional interrelations of its components"[55] formulates an extremely broad notion of text which could well be applied to non-literary arts like painting or architecture. We do not endorse an extended definition of text which covers other than literary arts by defining them as "textures" of elements.[56]

In a more specific definition, Shillingsburg understands text as "the sequence of words that constitute the novel as it appears in a particular publication, like the first edition, or in a manuscript."[57] This strong focus on the word as the genuine, constituting element of text is very common and

[54] In McGann's words, the work "comprehends the global set of all the texts and poems which have emerged in the literary production and reproduction processes." See McGann, Jerome, The Textual Condition, 31f.

[55] Zeller, Hans, "Structure and Genesis in Editing," 106.

[56] As defined by Tanselle: "All works of art have texts, whether usually called by that name or not, for they all consist of arrangements of elements; and all can be the objects of emendation, for those elements (or their arrangements) can always be altered, producing different textures." See Tanselle, George Thomas, A Rationale of Textual Criticism, 18.

[57] Shillingsburg, Peter L., Resisting Texts, 106.

conceives of the text as a lexical event.[58] It distinguishes the diplomatic from the textual understanding of a work. Whereas the diplomatic contents of a document comprise single letters and signs, textual errors and corrections, the textual contents only include the proper words of a document.[59] Hence, a sequence of obviously meaningless, single letters would usually not be regarded as text. Unfortunately, this definition does not cover the idiosyncratic abbreviations and signs so often used in manuscripts. It is therefore not completely useful for a genetic study.

Scheibe provides a more suitable definition. It avoids Zeller's broad approach, makes no distinction between letters and signs, and at the same time includes the genetic dimension of a work: "The text of a work in the editorial sense consists of the texts of all versions produced in the course of the process of development of a work by the author or under his or her instructions. It reflects the entire development history of the work."[60] This definition excludes, for instance, reading notes or chronologies, which are part of the work, but not of its text.

The text of a *version* is the subordinate unit to the text of a *work*. It is the most basic level of text. As I define it, it consists of all those letters and signs which can be encoded typographically. This definition has three consequences:

First, text can be defined for any recognized regional typographical code, whether Latin, Japanese, Arabic or other.

Second, single letters, fragmented words, corrections etc. have to be included in the text.

Third, if a manuscript contains a sign that was invented by the author, but is used consistently throughout the manuscript and can be translated into a lexeme, then the translated word becomes part of the text, as it can be expressed in typographical code. For instance, a manuscript reading "law [sign] order" contains the text "law and order," if "[sign]" unequivocally signifies "and." On the other hand, a sign denoting a semantic concept, like "subordinate to" (" ↳," for instance), does not possess a textual meaning and should therefore not be incorporated into the text.

Notes

Notes are the marginalia of textual genesis. They often record the first outline of a plot, personal experiences, conversations or the results of research (reading notes, excerpts). Written at a later point of a work's genesis, they can

58 McGann, Jerome, The Textual Condition, 31f.

59 Kanzog, Klaus, Einführung in die Editionsphilologie, 51.

60 Scheibe, Siegfried, "On the Editorial Problem of the Text," 207.

include advanced sketches or chronologies. They do not necessarily possess a literary / artistic form comparable to the finished work, but may include single words or lines later incorporated into the text – or even such as have *never* been used any further. In fact, notes may exist without later textual stages derived from them. Whereas drafts need to be complemented by subsequent stages, notes are not necessarily related to drafts, fragments or achieved texts.

Draft

De Biasi places the draft between the conception of a work and its preparation for publication. Microgenetically, the term "draft" receives an expanded definition, including research documents, initial workplans and final adjustments. Macrogenetically, its definition is much more restricted, denoting merely the compositional space, not supplementary documents.[61]

Like the fragment, the draft has a literary form (as opposed to notes). What distinguishes the fragment from the draft is the latter's partial character – the draft only exists as the pre-form of a later stage. As De Biasi states, it can only be defined in functional relation to other elements.[62] A draft might not only be the early form of a published text, but also of a fragment. Several drafts leading to an obviously unfinished text are regarded as parts of one fragment. A potential draft, of which no later stage exists, is not an actual draft, but a fragment.

Fragment

The fragment shows attempts at artistic form, but remains unfinished. The unfinished state of a fragment can be deduced from *intrinsic* characteristics such as blanks in the text, broken-off sentences or the lack of a title. If no fair copy of a draft exists, that draft is a fragment. Publication does not alter the status of a fragment – the published fragment might be called a "work" in terms of canonization, but, on the genetic level, remains a fragment.

Variant

In genetic criticism, the term "variant" is only used in a restricted way. Bellemin-Noël proposes to employ the term to describe differences between several editions of a work, as well as between the working manuscript and the

[61] De Biasi, Pierre-Marc, "What is a Literary Draft?," 27, 29f.
[62] De Biasi, Pierre-Marc, "What is a Literary Draft?," 32.

printed work. Within one manuscript, he would rather speak of "substitutions." Within these limits, the term "variant" can only be applied in cases "dans lesquels on a de bonnes raisons de considérer qu'il existe un texte de base unique dont on peut reconstituer la lettre à travers une série d'incarnations présentant entre elles des variations qui, correctement analysées, permettront de remonter vers le texte source."[63] For instance, when an authorized copy of a work exists, but the edition shows non-authorial interventions.

Grésillon defines the variant not as a deviation from a constituted text, but as the difference between two genetic stages.[64] Typical textual alterations constituting a variant are immediate corrections (unfinished words, deletions in a line while writing etc.) or later revisions (corrections within a word, replacement of words in the margin, insertions.[65] In this study, I will use Grésillon's definition, because it suits the purpose of my approach, which divides Pound's drafts into genetic stages.

Genetic stage

A genetic stage is any document or set of documents, or layer within one document or set of documents (a single document in the case of a one-page poem, for instance; a set of documents for any text consisting of several pages) which is textually different from the other states of a text collected in a genetic dossier and can therefore be located at a different chronological point in the genesis of a text.[66] Textual difference is constituted by variants, as defined above. Strictly speaking, the first, typed layer on a typescript sheet belongs to another genetic stage than any corrections added on the page. Carbon copies showing no textual deviation from their top copies, however, are part of the same genetic stage as the top copies. They differ physically, but not textually.

Note that each version of a text constitutes a genetic stage of its own (because created at different times), whereas genetic stages do not have to be versions. A drafted, but afterwards discarded part of a poem is not a version, but a genetic stage – and paralipomenon – of the work. An example: A sheet contains a single stanza which, by its title, can be identified as part of a larger poem. Yet the stanza has been written on a separate sheet, has then been discarded and cannot be assigned an exact position within the poem. Thus it

---

[63] Ferrer, Daniel / Lebrave, Jean-Louis, "De la variante textuelle au geste d'écriture," 15f.

[64] Grésillon, Almuth, Literarische Handschriften, 101.

[65] For these and more examples see Kanzog, Klaus, Einführung in die Editionsphilologie, 111ff.

[66] Similarly: Zwerschina, Hermann, "Die editorische Einheit 'Textstufe'," 182.

does not constitute a version of the poem, but a genetic stage by itself. The term "genetic stage" is more comprehensive than "version."

Version

A version is that state of a textual unit which deviates from other states by its textual variants. The number of variants necessary to constitute a version is subject to discussion. One of the strictest definitions can be found in Zeller, who argues that as little as one variant is enough to create a new version.[67]

Note that a version is a state of *one textual unit* and that a finished text may comprise several textual units for which versions exist. Each version is at the same time a genetic stage.

Paralipomena

Paralipomena are units of text which are not included in the published, canonized work. They are not regarded as discarded, but as complementary.[68] They are not identical with textual variants, as their connection to the work is not established by textual identities or variants, but by correspondences in structure and content. Scenarios, workplans, excerpts and chronologies (in short: notes) are often paralipomena, as are such units of text that cannot be linked exactly to one part of the finished work. In common editorial practice, paralipomena comprise those textual units whose relation to a certain passage in the work is doubtful or difficult to prove.[69]

Dossier Génétique

De Biasi defines as a genetic dossier "the whole body of known, classified, and transcribed manuscripts and documents connected with a text whose form has reached, in the opinion of its author, a state of completion or near completion."[70] The weak point of this definition is its reliance on authorial "opinion." In the case of an unpublished text left after the author's death, any predictions about possible further revisions of the text are questionable. Still, a dossier can be created.

---

[67] Zeller, Hans, "Structure and Genesis in Editing," 106.
[68] Bohnenkamp, Anne, "...das Hauptgeschäft nicht außer Augen lassend," 58.
[69] Kanzog, Klaus, Einführung in die Editionsphilologie, 106.
[70] De Biasi, Pierre-Marc, "What is a Literary Draft?," 31.

A broader definition by Grésillon understands the dossier as a file comprising all pieces of writing related to a textual genesis, as long as they are autographs, authorial typescripts, corrected page proofs or authorized prints with authorial corrections. In addition to textual witnesses that constitute the internal genesis of a text (mainly drafts), the genetic dossier also documents the text's external genesis by including "péri-avant-textes," i.e. diaries, interviews, letters and similar documents.[71]

[71] Grésillon, Almuth, Literarische Handschriften, 97, 131.

II. Mnemosyne 2 – Writing the Text

II.1 Pound's Bibliographical Muse: Writing and Composition

II.1.a The Writing Process: Material Aspects

It is a long way from Torquato Tasso's *ottava rima* to the *vers libre* of Pound and his fellow modernists. What had once been the regular meter of the traditional epic was dissolved into unpredictable collage when old and new rhythms and forms mixed in the melting-pots of modernism. Book pages no longer showed the neat blocks of text that readers had known for so long. New methods of composition changed the face of poetry, which now looked irregular, if not exotic. Even Chinese ideograms and Egyptian hieroglyphs found their way into Western poetry, announcing a thorough change of literary paradigms. Some changes, however, were not as thorough as one might expect, as a look at literary manuscripts reveals.

This particularly applies to the working methods of poets. The manuscript of Tasso's *Gerusalem conquistata*, for instance, shows generic similarities to drafts by later poets.[1] The first layer of text is written in almost regular lines, but subsequent corrections distort the face of the page: Whole lines have been crossed out, words have been replaced, additions and corrections been written into the margins, their appropriate place designated by signs. The corrections themselves have been partly revised or deleted. In short, the Early Modern manuscript page, despite the poet's attempt at epic unity, represents a complex system of references and successive layers. This also applies to prose drafts, as in the case of Flaubert.[2] Typical drafts by the French novelist include basic layers of regular handwriting with interlinear corrections, plus additional text blocks in the left-hand margin to be inserted into existing paragraphs. The destination of the marginal notes is signified by lines, their sequence by capital letters. Even though literature itself had changed, Flaubert's writing habits were in some respects hardly different from Tasso's.

The introduction of the first mass-market compatible Remington typewriters after 1874 made writing even more uniform. Thousands of people bought the same typewriter models, the same ribbons and identical paper. Soon criminologists would have to search for irregular types in anonymous letters to establish at least the individuality of the typewriter, if not of its owner. It was on those uniform machines that Pound created some of the most original poetry of the 20th century. But even if Pound the poet is distinguished

[1] The manuscript, now in the *Biblioteca Nacionale* (Naples) is partly reproduced in Hay, Louis, "History or Genesis?," 196.

[2] See Grésillon, Almuth, Literarische Handschriften, images 35-37.

by an individual profile, the same does not necessarily have to apply to Pound the "writer," in the literal sense. Hence, this chapter seeks to establish a specific profile of Pound's writing habits on their most material level. Mary de Rachewiltz has provided us with a lively account of Pound's working methods: "A hasty scribbling on a piece of paper, a tearing off of newspaper clippings, a frantic annotation in a book."[3] Such are the traces the author leaves behind; with them, our archeology must start. As Scheibe recognized, you can only achieve a precise representation of the genesis of a work when you know the writing habits of your subject.

Scheibe also outlined some typical writing habits we should analyze in order to be able to read the Poundian documents properly:

> use of different kinds of paper at different stages of production of a work [...] different ways of using this paper (as individual sheets, in quires, or in a combination of both, or the preference for specific sizes in individual preliminary stages), the way in which the author covers this paper with different writing instruments, the manner of corrections (again with different writing materials).[4]

I will readily follow Scheibe's guidelines, although Pound's writing habits can hardly be called systematic. If the following seems at times like a random collection of evidence, it is because of the irregularity of the documents. Irregularity, however, is the hallmark of individuality. It may be caused e.g. by exterior circumstances – during the years 1922 and 1923, for instance, Pound used graph paper because he was travelling extensively, was therefore not able to use his typewriter and had to rely on handwritten notes.[5] Sometimes the individuality of writing seems like mere chaos. As Taylor says, Pound's documents are "maddeningly idiosyncratic in format, spelling, and punctuation."[6] But despite the danger of generalizing what is individual, we will hint at some overall aspects like paper properties, typical writing instruments, page layout and revisions.

Paper

The standard paper used by Pound possesses few distinct qualities. The general properties of the sheets are mostly identical (pale white, letter

[3] Rachewiltz, Mary de, Discretions, 47, also 156.
[4] Scheibe, Siegfried, "Theoretical Problems of the Authorization and Constitution of Texts," 171f.
[5] Rainey, Lawrence S., Ezra Pound and the Monument of Culture, 231f.
[6] Taylor, Richard, Variorum Edition of "Three Cantos" by Ezra Pound: A Prototype, 2; also comp. Pound, Ezra, "I Cease Not to Yowl," xxvi.

format).[7] What distinguishes them are the watermarks.[8] In about 1915, Pound worked with paper watermarked "Imperial Strong III," whereas in 1919 he used "Bilston Extra Strong."[9] Pound's standard paper used during the mid-1930s is mostly watermarked "Extra Strong," followed by "Papel Fluminense" and a smaller number of sheets watermarked "Extra Strong CCCM." and "Extra Strong LJC." "Extra Strong" and "Papel Fluminense" are used for both top and carbon copies, manuscript and typescript pages. No system is discernible in their use.

Pound often used an orange-colored type of paper with a lily as its watermark for advanced versions and setting copies of Cantos, like most of items 248-276 (a group sent to Olga Rudge) and 329-359 (HRC setting copies). Although Pound is fairly systematic in his use of the lily paper, we find some exceptions among the documents. Item 56 is a fragment from the genesis of C45 and contains some discarded lines, which make it likely that it was written at an early point of the creative process, an unusual use of the lily paper. Items 71 and 78 combine elements from C36 and C51, and, like them, are not part of advanced genetic stages. Here we encounter an irregularity typical of Pound's autographs.

As far as paper types are concerned, the Pound documents contain some special cases. Two notes (items 109, 110) are written on striped paper, a translation of Guinizellis poem "Al Cor Gentil" on paper watermarked "In Tritico Vis et Vita" (item 215). Item 282, a brief passage from C46, uses the letter-paper of the "Albergo Bristol" (Rapallo). Item 126 bears Pound's letter-head (Gaudier-Brzeska's drawing of Pound's profile) and is watermarked "1902 Extra Strong." Pound's letter-paper carried the drawing in the middle of the letter-head from March 1932, had no artwork from 1934 to 1936, then bore the profile again, now printed on the right side of the paper. The 1937 letters by Pound carry the printed motto "A tax is not a share A nation need not and should not pay rent for its credit." in their upper left-hand corner.[10]

---

[7] Subsequent descriptions of colors in Pound's tss. and mss. will largely follow the color terminology in Tanselle, G. Thomas, "A System of Color-Identification for Bibliographical Description," 154, from: The ISCC-NBS Method of Designating Colors and a Dictionary of Color Names (= NBS Circular 553), 1955; and the ISCC-NBS Centroid Color Charts, 1965 (NBS = National Bureau of Standards). The charts include colors like blue, bluish, red, violet, black, blackish; also value modifiers (lightness): dark, light, medium, very; plus chroma modifiers (saturation): grayish, moderate, strong, vivid; value and chroma combinations: brilliant (light + strong), deep (dark + strong), pale (light + grayish). For a bibliography on color identification see Tanselle, G. Thomas, "A System of Color-Identification for Bibliographical Description," 165-170.

[8] For remarks on the traditional description of watermarks see Tanselle, George Thomas, Selected Studies in Bibliography, 222.

[9] Froula, To Write Paradise, 65ff.

[10] Pound, Ezra, Pound/Zukofsky, xxiv.

The note may have been written between 1932 and 1934, but we must at the same time consider the possibility of Pound using an old sheet as late as 1936 or 1937. Items 181-185 consist of light brown note-pad sheets in letter format and contain excerpts from a book.[11] Items 246 and 247 (note-pad paper, too) contain an unattributed fragment which, like the previously mentioned excerpts, testifies to Pound's random use of paper for notes not used in the *Cantos*. Accordingly, the text of item 3 (facts from Zobi's history of Tuscany) is written on a bank cheque. For extensive reading notes, Pound often used notebooks, but not consistently. He wrote into small-sized ones when studying Cavalcanti (1928-31), used larger ones for his library research in Siena (1936; items 301-305) and letter-sized ones for De Mailla (1937/38) and John Adams (1937/38).

As rust traces show, many BL sheets were once clipped together, but we can neither state when, nor by whom. Common properties of sheets, like traces of rusty clips, are therefore not a feasible criterion for the establishing of genetic groupings.

Writing Instruments

A major part of the Pound papers consists of characteristic typescripts of which facsimiles can offer only a faint reproduction. Pound's typing was infamous. While his daughter mentions Pound's "discarded old portable Corona typewriters,"[12] Laughlin has left us with a lively description of a writer at work: "He would assault his typewriter with an incredible vigor. In fact, he had to have two typewriters, because one was always at the repair shop." Laughlin comes to the conclusion that Pound "was trying to destroy his typewriter."[13] Although he may have typed ferociously, however, his use of the typewriter was not without system.

The material process of writing (sequence of writing instruments) complements the process of composition (sequence of fragments, drafts and versions). Pound recorded early notes in black ink. More advanced drafts were written, in consecutive stages, on the typewriter. An example of this method is C45: the first draft is a manuscript, whereas the second draft and all subsequent drafts are typescripts. This does not imply, however, a greater textual stability of the typewritten stages. They, too, were subject to

[11] For a definition of the note-pad / notebook see Anis (*carnet* versus *bloc*): "Le carnet est un cahier de petit format, destiné à être emporté dans un sac ou placé dans une poche [...] Le bloc est en règle générale un simple réservoir de feuilles, il n'a pas de structure ni d'autonomie," Anis, Jacques, L'écriture, 183.
[12] Rachewiltz, Mary de, Discretions, 156.
[13] Laughlin, James, Pound as Wuz, 7, 168.

substantial revisions. Pound merely shifted his compositional work from handwriting to typing. In some cases, the typewriter was not only used for advanced stages. Item 293 is an early draft, as can be learned from the atribution of some lines to Cantos "43" and "44," which later became C48 and C49. Item 292 shows a piece of text later incorporated into C48.

Pound's typescripts are discernible by several characteristic properties, including irregular indentations, frequent typos and other errors, on which we will comment later. Another important feature are the ribbon colors. Typescript top copies are, for the major part, written in blue type, while some single notes (e.g. items 56 and 57) are in black type. The typescript color of the carbon copies is mostly purple or black. As Anis remarks, black and blue have always been among the standard colors used by writers because of their contrast to the background color of the paper.[14] Pound preferred blue for his typescripts and black for the ink he wrote with. The writing instrument he used was presumably a Waterman pen.[15] Pound used ink for handwritten notes like historical facts (item 3) or excerpts from books (items 294-300). He also wrote drafts of complete passages in ink (items 31-37 for C47, items 50-55 for C45). Ink was used for drawings, like a cross (item 5), the symbol of the *Monte dei Paschi* (item 10) or other sketches. It also served to connect elements dispersed over the page, like a typed part on the top and additions on the bottom part of the page (item 132). Except for corrections and additions, the gray standard pencil was used for the structural sketch (item 1), the translation (item 215) or the quick draft (items 109-110). Pencilled additions usually occur together with ink revisions, but also without them (item 287).

We can establish different uses of writing instruments in Pound's numbering of the Cantos: red pencil for numbers within the decad (a "III" on item 84), ink for the final number of the Canto (the "XLIII" on the same item). But this is difficult to generalize, because in some cases the number was only typed (item 93). A red pencil was also used for general revisions, like the deleting and structuring of passages of text (items 123, 208). We find it as the chief writing instrument in the De Mailla and Adams notebooks (1937/38), but not in the Siena notebooks. The latter represent an interesting case, because, although Pound generally used a pencil in them, some passages were nevertheless written with ink. Whereas pencil denotes excerpts from historical documents and studies, or immediate remarks on what was excerpted, ink signifies Pound's own, genuinely "poetic," additions (comp. item 301, [51-56]; item 304, [31-38], [71-74]). As always, Pound managed to

[14] "Le texte étant écrit normalement en noir ou en bleu, couleurs qui permettent un bon contraste par rapport au blanc du papier, les autres couleurs, notamment le rouge, peuvent être utilisées pour les titres et pour les mises en relief," Anis, Jacques, L'écriture, 179.

[15] This conclusion is based on a complaint he uttered in 1937: "Impossible to write ideogram with a Waterman pen," see Pound, Ezra, Ezra Pound and Japan, 39.

create exceptions to the rule (see item 302, [52-60]). One possible reason for the repeated switch of writing instruments is suggested by Pound's working conditions. Pound was then researching in the *Archivio di Stato* (Siena) and maybe was only allowed to use a pencil. This means he would have added the ink passages in the evenings, after returning from the archive.

As regards the actual handwriting, it seems legitimate to speak of a distinctly Poundian style. The scope of Pound's handwriting ranges from clearly legible to almost illegible. Purely handwritten drafts of longer passages (like items 50-55) are mostly more legible than many of the additions in typescripts. As Froula has noticed, Pound's handwriting often omits or elides letters.[16]

Another particular feature of the Pound papers is the use of signs, like "z" and two signs signifying "and." First, the "z." It occurs in two forms, the smaller of which – about 2-3 mm in length – marks the ending of a small unit of composition, a single line or less. The larger version – 5-6 mm – appears near the left margins of the sheets, located between two lines and with a larger amount of interlinear space preceding and following. It represents "the completion or the new beginning of a larger unit of composition, most typically some five to six lines, or something resembling a stanza."[17] When moving on to typewritten drafts, Rainey states, Pound deleted the larger marks and most of the smaller ones, transforming the rest into commas. This finding, however, may only be verified to a certain extent. In the case of *The Fifth Decad*, the early typescripts are never identical with their preceding drafts. The ink notes beginning the genesis of C45 are not in a 1:1 relation to the subsequent typescript drafts, as Pound changed or omitted lines and passages. It is therefore difficult to speak of a translation of the "z" signs into commas, when what actually took place was also a structural transformation.

Pound's use of the "and" signs is less complex. Either taking the shape of a "+" (e.g. item 31) or a "&" (item 37), the signs are interchangeable and not placed systematically. An intermediate position between manuscript and typescript is occupied by italics, which are indicated by underlinings, either in handwriting (item 86) or in typescript (item 87).

Forming the Text

The *Cantos* are a "poem to lie on the page."[18] Interspersed with ideograms, musical scores and drawings, the work represents a challenge to editors and printers. Whereas the first editions of the early Cantos contained colored

---

16 Froula, Christine, To Write Paradise, 62.
17 Rainey, Lawrence S., Ezra Pound and the Monument of Culture, 23.
18 Pound, Ezra, Instigations, 35.

drawings by Dorothy Pound and conjured up reminiscences of William Morris,[19] later printings introduced a more sober black-and-white style. If modernists hoped to support the meaning of their texts by a particular typography,[20] Pound participated in this aim by extending the boundaries of layout and typography. *The Fifth Decad*, however, seems conventional if compared to C75 with its musical score or to C85 with its Chinese ideograms. Hence, the pre-publication papers are not rich in individual intricacies, but rather offer insights into generic aspects of how the text was formed.

Anis stresses the innovative use of spacing in Mallarmé's "Coup de dés," where the blanks assume a central role in constituting the poem.[21] In the Pound papers, spacing is a specific element in two respects: as spacings between words and as indentations. On the most basic micro-level, we notice Pound's use of double spacing in typescripts as a constantly recurring feature. He left double spacings between words and before punctuation marks. As McGann points out, this was a pre-publication habit and not always continued in the printed text.[22] Double spacing is used regularly throughout the drafts, both in earlier and later stages of the text. In some cases, Pound even extended it to triple or quadruple spacing (item 230) which was not used for corrections. If a line seemed to become too long, Pound reduced the spacing while approaching the right-hand margin of a sheet (item 230).

Traditional poetry is structured by using certain signals. Stanzas are recognizable by the blank lines between them, which often goes together with an oral hiatus and the end of a grammatical unit.[23] In addition to blank lines, indentations are another means of dividing text. Usually used deliberately, this device seems to have become accidental in Pound's hands. As Laughlin remembers, "in the fury of composition, he couldn't always take time to go all the way back to the left margin; he would slap the carriage and wherever it stopped that determined the indent."[24] The statement is partly justified. On the one hand, the Pound papers contain drafts with intricate layouts. Item 218 shows a systematic use of indentations as structuring devices. They serve to maintain the individual character of a quoted letter by imitating the special position of the signatures following the main text. In other cases, they mark the beginning of new units. On item 41 indentations mark the final sentence of a textual unit. On item 22 they emphasize a single sentence by setting it off

---

[19] For the design of early Pound books see the facsimiles in: Christie's New York, Masterpieces of Modern Literature: The Library of Roger Rechler, New York 2002, 298-301.

[20] Albright, Daniel, "Early Cantos I – XLI," 62.

[21] Anis, Jacques, L'écriture, 212f.

[22] McGann, Jerome, The Textual Condition, 155; on spacing also see Gordon, David M. (ed.), Ezra Pound and James Laughlin: Selected Letters, 16.

[23] Anis, Jacques, L'écriture, 205f.

[24] Laughlin, James, Pound as Wuz, 7.

against the following sentence. Thus, indentations are used to emphasize textual and grammatical units in the text. At the same time, though, Pound's page layout has random elements for which no purpose can be stated. On item 45, it is much more difficult to establish an intention behind the indentations. A procession (later in C44) is described in one single block of text, into which only three indentations have been inserted. While the first one may indicate the break between morning and afternoon ("thus ended the morning"), the other two were placed where they interrupt the continuity of the poem. The dances at sundown and the masked people appear at the same time and belong to the same celebration, which is why the indentations can be interpreted as accidental.

Among the most complex aspects of writing are errors and revisions. We will not psychologize about errors, as did the Swiss psychiatrist Eugen Bleuler, who used his typewriter to record dreams and assciations and regarded typing errors as symptoms of inner complexes which appeared on the surface of consciousness while writing.[25] Rather, we will simply point out Pound's habit of quoting from memory, which naturally inheres a chance for error. Other errors had the philological reason that Pound relied too closely on his sources. Sometimes he falsified an originally correct spelling by adapting a misprint from a dictionary. When he used a French source for Chinese names (De Mailla's history of China), his spelling was influenced by the French transliterations.[26] When working with historical documents, as he did for the Siena Cantos, Pound sometimes had difficulties reading the old manuscripts. To summarize, Pound's errors in connection with sources include errors of fact (misremembered names and dates), misquotations, mistranscriptions, misspellings and transliterations adhering to local or otherwise nonstandard principles.[27] The Pound papers include many accidentals of which only some occur repeatedly, like the typing of an "m" for a comma or missing punctuation marks. In other cases, Pound himself was aware of what an editor might call error: "I DO want the misspellings in the documents, letters, etc. kept VERY carefully. Also the abbreviations."[28]

Bearing in mind the concept of a "writing profile," as outlined above, we will offer some remarks on Pound's most characteristic revisional strategies. As noted earlier, Pound's usual revisional sequence was: typescript, black ink, pencil. Pound added handwritten parts to both top copies and carbon copies. Additions are often associative, i.e. they show no immediate link to the earlier layers of text on the page. Other additions are

---

[25] Bleuler is mentioned in: Giuriato, Davide / Stingelin, Martin / Zanetti, Sandro, "Eigensinnige Schreibwerkzeuge," 8.

[26] Kenner, Hugh, "Notes on Amateur Emendations," 24f.

[27] Froula, Christine, To Write Paradise, 140.

[28] Sutton, Walter (ed.), Pound, Thayer, Watson, 255f., letter of 4 Jan 1923.

corrections of already written text, but are not applied in the next genetic stage. On item 2, for instance, we find additions which belong to the same thematical context (Tuscan history), but are neither integrated into the already existing draft text, nor used in the subsequent draft. We also discover additions of non-Latin, and therefore non-typable, signs, like Greek symbols. In many cases, Pound simply added missing commas, question marks, periods or other signs. The same applies to mistyped or weakly typed letters.

Pound used different forms of substitution, all of which can be found on item 26: substitutions over or immediately behind a deleted passage, interlinear or marginal, by re-formulation. Substitution itself can be divided into replacement, deletion, extension and regrouping.[29] Regrouping is usually achieved by a square serpentine line (item 26).

Another element of revisions are deletions. While typing, Pound often executed deletions immediately by typing. We also find double deletions, when a word was first typed over and then deleted by ink. Among the more extensive types of deletions used are the crossing out of whole paragraphs by diagonal lines, or of several lines of text by drawing a serpentine line over them. In some cases, Pound combined both types or performed multiple deletions, first of individual lines, then of a whole paragraph (e.g. item 102).

Finally, a remark on Pound's Siena notebooks (items 301-305). One might assume that, because of their copied contents, they differ from the "original" papers, the fragments and drafts. But the general profile of the notebooks is similar to that of the other Pound papers. Apart from structuring elements, like single and double underlinings, separating lines between parts (short and long lines), brackets, frames and circles, they include conventional techniques of emphasis (important words in capital letters), tables of dates (e.g. to calculate the date of birth of a ruler) and, due to the difficult nature of the historical sources, sometimes several attempts of translating or rephrasing an expression. These were executed with the same revisional strategies as outlined above.

In total, Pound's profile as a *scriptor* is less individual than his profile as a poet. Using mostly the same means of revision like earlier writers, whether Tasso or Flaubert, we find only some noteworthy features. What strikes us as individual are:

- main types of paper used, especially the lily paper.
- standard combinations of genetic layers, i.e. blue ribbon plus ink corrections, partly with additional pencilled corrections.
- extensive use of indentations, rather than blank lines, to separate textual and grammatical units.
- special typographical signs, like Pound's "z."

---

[29] Typologies according to Grésillon, Almuth, Literarische Handschriften, 94f., 184.

As should be noted, we do not complain about a lack of individuality in the Pound papers. In fact, few scholars who have seen the originals will ever forget those yellow sheets with their traces of ferocious typing and black ink lines, seismographic marks of creativity.

II.1.b Policies of Borrowing: Units of Reference

Pound is that curious thing, a person without a trace of originality of any sort.

(Wyndham Lewis, *Time and Western Man*)

Only an inventor knows how to borrow.

(Ralph Waldo Emerson, *Quotation and Originality*)

Despite the originality of his poems, Pound borrowed extensively from other, literary and non-literary works. Pound's frequent use of obscure quotations challenged even a well-read scholar like F. R. Leavis into confessing his ignorance of their intended meaning: "But even when one is fully informed about Mr Pound's allusions one's recognition has no significant effect: the value remains private to the author."[30] But even if many of Pound's allusions seem cryptic to his readers, their importance is not to be denied. A substantial part of the originality of the *Cantos* derives exactly from Pound's selection of sources. Pound used borrowing not simply as a conventional tool, but as an overall strategy that formed the structure of his work. This includes both overt references to certain sources and more sublime, if not hidden forms of borrowing.

In order to analyze Pound's policies and strategies of borrowing, this chapter will provide a closer look at the use of referential units in *The Fifth Decad*, i.e. units that refer to sources outside of the *Cantos* themselves. Focusing on the micro-level of the text, the present chapter is concerned with both individual elements and general types of references, especially intertextual references. This includes miscellaneous examples from different parts of the poem, as well as some important quotational clusters in *The Fifth Decad*, like the Siena Cantos and C49. To maintain the genetic perspective of this study, we will give particular attention to Pound's transformation, during the writing process, of borrowed elements into parts of the *Cantos*.

The use of quotations in modern literary texts has long been recognized as an important subject.[31] Accordingly, the term "quotation" has received a

---

[30] Leavis, Frank R., New Bearings in English Poetry, 155.

[31] For studies on quotations in literary texts see Rainey, Lawrence S., Ezra Pound and the Monument of Culture, 263, n. 71.

variety of definitions, ranging from the pragmatic approach of standard dictionaries to the intricacies of structuralist theory. The *Collins English Dictionary* (1998) defines "quotation" as: "1. a phrase or passage from a book, poem, play, etc., remembered and spoken, esp to illustrate succinctly or support a point or an argument" and "2. the act or habit of quoting from books, plays, poems, etc." The *Cambridge Dictionary of English* (2001) calls it "a phrase or short piece of writing taken from a longer work of literature, poetry, etc. or what someone else has said." The OED (s.v. "quote," v.) defines "to quote" as to "copy out or repeat a passage or passages from. Also, to repeat a statement by (someone); to give (a person's name) as the authority for a statement" and to "copy out or repeat (a passage, statement, etc.) from a book, document, speech, etc., with some indication that one is giving the words of another."

Standard definitions are of course text-centered, although quotation may also be defined to embrace the general derivation of thought from others. Ralph Waldo Emerson, for instance, takes quotation in an extremely broad sense, including, for instance, thoughts picked up in a conversation. Hence his fairly general statement: "Our debt to tradition through reading and conversation is so massive, our protest or private addition so rare and insignificant […] that, in a large sense, one would say there is no pure originality. All minds quote." He applies the term to everything from proverbs to architecture, inventions that have been "many times found and lost, from Egypt, China, and Pompeii down." In literature, Emerson establishes a line from Homer, over Virgil and Tasso, to Milton; from Heraclitus and Parmenides to Proclus and, later, Hegel.[32] As this comes dangerously close to an over-extension of the term, we may certainly wonder whether Emerson did not confuse quotation with tradition.

Among modern scholars, Barthes extended the concept of quotation by placing the writer within language structures that he assumed to constitute the text, which now becomes a conglomerate of elements derived from multiple external (i.e. not originally authorial) discourses. In the case of Mallarmé, for example, Barthes states that language, not the author, speaks in texts nominally written by the poet. Barthes conceives of the scriptor as "a timeless, placeless, authority-less aggregator of quotations from the web of language."[33]

In this study, I will not go so far as to make the writer a subject of the language he uses, nor will I attribute all his ideological faults to his biographical background. To cut a profound anthropological matter short, I understand the author as a biographically defined, textual agent who separates, moves and concentrates units of authorial or extra-authorial

[32] Emerson, Ralph Waldo, "Quotation and Originality," 170ff.

[33] Shillingsburg, Peter L., Resisting Texts, 14.

discourse. This definition avoids both the danger of a purely "biographistic" hermeneutics (author-centered) and the discourse-dominated relativity of strucuralism (language-centered). It allows for a socio-genetic criticism of Pound's texts without having to give one-sided preference to either of the two alternatives.

Adopting a genetic perspective towards the use of quotations by Pound, we are less interested in the exact influence of one particular source on Pound, but rather in the *production value* of that source – i.e. in Pound's extraction of certain discursive units from it, and their subsequent transformation and adaptation by the author during the interaction of reading and writing.[34] Thus we extend the poem's historicity to not only include the process of writing, but also reach beyond the actual text and its historical context in order to include the historical paradigms of those periods from which the text borrows. "Historical paradigm" will be used here as an umbrella term to denote the specific properties of a given period, including its linguistic discourses, technical inventions, epistemological foundations and all other factors that help us to describe the individuality of a point in time.

A genetic approach to literary analysis will always have to be aware of individual paradigms: The closer we come to the source of a textual reference, the more we leave the authorial paradigm and approach other paradigms that have been woven, consciously or unconsciouly, into the text. For instance, we start with the written description of a place, then identify the photograph of the same place on which that description is based, and finally travel to the place itself. In this ideal sequence, we move from one paradigm to the next, and each time encounter a new historical context. In Pound's case, the original "place" is of course lost in time, as the founding fathers of the *Monte dei Paschi* have long vanished and left only documents as witnesses of their acts. However, we should be aware of the new spaces of historicity a genetic approach to a multi-referential text like the *Cantos* can open.

Although Pound may to some people appear like a universal, timeless scholar, he clearly moved within one of those historical paradigms himself. Each paradigm creates relativity through specificity, and Pound's language, for example, was specific in its reference to the American idiom, like in the persona of "Uncle Ez," the impatient village-explainer whose voice appears even between the dry Sienese documents (C42.209: "damn good bank, in Siena"). Thus, Pound's language disrupts any reader's illusions about an objective representation of facts in the text.[35] Where many historical novels try to simulate, as detailed as possible, the conditions of past paradigms, Pound has a different relation to them, as we will analyze later on.

---

[34] We follow Grésillon, Almuth, Literarische Handschriften, 132.

[35] Comp. White, Hayden, "Historical Emplotment and the Problem of Truth," 392.

Pound's own historical paradigm includes the context which made the *Cantos* possible as a texture of borrowed or original micro-discourses within the limits of authorial specificity. At the same time, though, it comprises the genesis of textual units. We emphasize textuality here in order to contradict the at a first glance realistic, but actually limited perspective of some New Historicists. Rainey provides an example of it when he claims: "The routes of quotations are not governed by the infinite play of 'textuality', but are regulated in configurations of literacy, schooling, the distribution or prohibition of texts, and in axes of class, power, and property."[36] Of course, quoting a controversial text might be understood as an act of resistance to a governing political power. But it would be wrong to denigrate textuality and over-emphasize historical-political backgrounds. Textual transformations often follow their own laws. They may be among the smaller gears of history, but are gears nonetheless.

Poundian Concepts of Borrowing

We are not able to judge whether Pound's preference for quotations stemmed from psychological reasons[37] or was inspired by a work like Joyce's *Ulysses*.[38] Generally, Pound held that readers were to be provided with facts, which Pound understood as "concrete details." As he stated in an essay: "Bad writing, or a great deal of it, drips down from an abstract received 'idea' or 'generality' held with fanaticism [...] by men who NEVER take in concrete detail. Men are good or bad in the year 1935 in proportion as they will LOOK AT the facts, new facts, any facts."[39] These facts include significant details, which serve to illuminate the deeper meaning of a historical period.

To provide, in poetical form, an objective documentation of the past was one of Pound's earliest objectives. In 1911/12 he demanded that the artist "seeks out the luminous detail and presents it. He does not comment." Luminous details are independent from historians' findings and remain unaltered, as they represent the total spirit of a period.[40] While Pound never fully adhered to his claim that a poet should not comment on the facts, he remained committed to the image of the poet as a collector of evidence, like the prosecutor in C46. For Pound, knowledge resulted from the assembling of

---

[36] Rainey, Lawrence S., Ezra Pound and the Monument of Culture, 60.

[37] Hesse: "In fact his deep-rooted distrust of alleged artistic creation 'ex nihil', which he places on a par with moneys created 'out of nothing' by the bank, may be traced throughout his writing, where it assumes increasing proportions with the years", Hesse, Eva, "Introduction", in: Hesse, Eva (ed.), New Approaches to Ezra Pound, 23f.

[38] See Bush, Ronald, The Genesis of Ezra Pound's Cantos, 225f.

[39] Pound, Ezra, Polite Essays 51.

[40] "I gather the limbs of Osiris" (1911-1912), in: SP, 23.

facts or of units of information.[41] This explains the newspaper clippings found among the Pound papers (comp. item 116) and also the excerpts from historical works in Pound's notebooks. Pound defined the artist as an archeologist who steps down into the vaults of history, discovers important artefacts and brings them back to light. Some may criticize this notion as a limitation that confines the artist to working with secondary materials, but in fact Pound thus proved how far ahead he was of his time and of post-romantic ideas of originality. Pound is often quoted as the inventor of the motto "Make It New" in a conventional sense: as a brilliant inventor of totally new forms of expression in poetry. But what is important to emphasize is Pound's broad understanding of his motto. For him, it would not only include invention, but also the rediscovery of forgotten treasures. Unearthing the lasting remains of the past can therefore become an act of substantial re-creation, as Pound stressed in "Arnold Dolmetsch" (1917): "There are times when archaeology is almost equal to creation, or when a resurrection is equally creative or even more creative than invention."[42]

This creative concept of borrowing may also be extended to include Pound's poetics of translation. When Pound translated, he concentrated less on the exact reproduction of rhythmic patterns, but rather on the transformation of content and subject matter from one national poetry to the other. He did not merely move poetic content between two completely different areas. Pound's aim was the highlighting of correspondences, as in the *Classic Anthology* – "the use of a full range of Western forms and genres to suggest parallel or equivalent poetic structures of feeling and response."[43] When Pound discovered Confucius, Mencius or the Provençal poets, he committed himself to the type of archeology we described above. Invention was only a marginal goal, compared to Pound's interest in re-discovering buried connections and facts. When he approached China in the context of the China Cantos, it was mainly through De Mailla's *Histoire de la Chine*, i.e. through a specific historical (because European) paradigm which served to connect China and Europe. When the poet reconstructed Tuscan history for C50, it was through the eyes of *Risorgimento* historian Antonio Zobi, whose freedom-loving attitude was a paradigm Pound adopted by using facts and quotations from Zobi's history of Tuscany. Pound then executed textual transformations to isolate those pieces which seemed to be prime witnesses of historical continuities.

Pound read many of his sources as historical documents, i.e. witnesses of certain periods and collections of "luminous details." That he often kept the particular spelling of a word, as used in the source, shows his tendency to

[41] Stock, Noel, The Life of Ezra Pound, 325.
[42] Pound, Ezra, Ezra Pound and Music, 46.
[43] Xie, Ming, "Pound as Translator," 214.

maintain historical contingency. Of course, errors in quotations are also due to flaws in Pound's method of composition. Laughlin claims that the Cantos were largely written from Pound's memory. He would often include a quotation without checking its source, except in some cases, as with old manuscripts.[44] However, we cannot generalize this notion. Pound's bibliographical policies of borrowing ususally aimed at exactness. Especially his notebooks are a first-hand source for an analysis of his practices. When gathering facts and excerpts from a source like Zobi's Tuscan history, Pound included page numbers among his notes, pointing out the exact source of an information or quotation (e.g. item 304, [6]). When Pound discovered an interesting reference in the footnotes of the volume he was working on, he also reproduced bibliographical details (item 304, [6]; item 304, [14]). Dates are important, too – when a source gives an exact date, Pound usually adds it to his notes (item 303, [26]; item 303, [37]). This exactness also applies to quotations in pre-publication documents other than the notebooks. Item 122 includes a quotation from Crevel's *Les pieds dans le plat* identified by its page number (p. 291). Pound's use of sources varies in adherence to the sequence of facts presented in a source. The Mailla notebooks for the China Cantos (BL 43 / 115 / 4900ff., starting in 1937) proceed in the order of the source pages and in accordance with the chronology established by De Mailla. Pound followed the same procedure in his work with the Sienese sources, moving from volume to volume. On the other hand, Pound would sometimes change the sequence of references, as we will see when discussing C49.

Pound's close work with sources has never been appreciated by all scholars. One of the more controversial sections in terms of quoting are the Adams Cantos (C62-71), which strongly rely on John Adams's *Life and Works*. In fact Surette even accused Pound of slavishly following the sequence of texts in the Adams edition: "He has printed marginalia, and called it poetry. For *him*, the marginalia convey, in an abbreviated and intensified form, the image of Adams that emerges from the *Life and Works*."[45] Pound randomly selected pieces from the Adams edition, without paying due attention to the really essential events. Instead, Surette claims, he bores the reader with details about the weather and other trivia. Surette regards the Adams Cantos as a failure, because they neither condense American history, nor Adams's career, but merely the *Life and Works*. In other words, they are a bibliographical fata morgana. This position was challenged by other scholars. A. D. Moody, for example, concedes that Pound reduced 8,000 pages of Adams to 80 pages of poetry and borrowed pieces of text exactly in the sequence in which the pieces appear in the Adams edition. But as Moody points out, Pound not just selected random elements, but

[44] Laughlin, James, Pound as Wuz, 8, 106.
[45] Surette, Leon, A Light from Eleusis, 163f.

sought to create an inner coherence.[46] In portraying, for instance, Adams shortly before the presidency, Pound employed the strategy to extract from the politician's writings and diaries certain elements not explicitly stated in the sources, yet brought to light in the Cantos, an aspect not acknowledged by Surette.

Miscellaneous Examples

The strongly documentary style of the Siena Cantos (C42 to C44) does not prevail throughout the poem. Although the *Cantos* start with a bibliographical reference to Andreas Divus's translation of Homer (C1.5), we have to wait until C8, the beginning of the Malatesta Cantos, for a first systematic use of historical sources with extensive quotations from original documents. It was through his reading of Charles Yriarte's biography of Sigismundo Malatesta in 1922 that Pound came into touch with archival sources. The appendix of Yriarte's book provided transcriptions of historical documents that would serve as a model for Pound's own incorporation of sources into his poem.[47] What Peter Makin stated about Yriarte's transcriptions equally applies to Pound's own use of documents, especially the Sienese papers: "Bibliographical references are given; manuscript lacunae are noted; scribal idioms are kept, suggested or heightened; there is no attempt to rework into homogeneous prose. Indeed, the scraps are merely placed together."[48] It was during his work with the Malatesta documents that Pound discovered a method of quoting that tended to dissolve the boundaries between poetry and historiography.[49] Compare one of the excerpts in the second Malatesta Canto:

> "Magnificent and Exalted Lord and Father in especial my
> "lord with due recommendation: your letter has been pre-
> "sented to me by Gentilino da Gradara and with it the bay
> "pony (ronzino baiectino) the which you have sent me, […]
> "we are all in good health, as I hope and desire your Ex^{ct}
> "Lordship is also: with continued remembrance I remain
> "Your son and servant
> **Malatesta de Malatestis.**
> *Given in Rimini, this the 22nd day of December*
> *anno domini 1454"*
>
> (C9.39)

[46] Moody, A. D., "Composition in the Adams Cantos," 79, 85.
[47] Rainey, Lawrence S., Ezra Pound and the Monument of Culture, 65f.
[48] Makin, Peter, Pound's Cantos, 102.
[49] Comp. Hesse, Eva, Die Achse Avantgarde – Faschismus, 254.

Pound is not suddenly writing a novel in letters, but begins to interrupt the poetic-epic narrative of the *Cantos*, disruptive as it has been even before, and to confront readers with a new historical paradigm. Pound's shift towards extensive and, as we will name it, *transcriptional quoting* from sources marks an important change of style in the poem, towards a fiction of authenticity. This affects textuality and historicity. The transcriptional form of a quotation not only establishes a network of historical references, which is something any hidden quotation from a historical document may achieve. It also creates a system of biblio-textual references, whose details of style and format bring to life an additional paradigm between the historical event and the poem. A poet who seamlessly inserts a quotation from a letter into a poem (we call this an *integrational quotation*) separates the quotation from its specific background. A poet who does exact transcriptions of documents, however, introduces the fictional persona of an archivist who aims to preserve whole documents. Transcriptions introduce a new paradigm into the poem, whereas conventional quotations adapt the quotation to fit the poem, e.g. by versification. This is a substantial difference, dividing the integrational from the transcriptional quotation. The transcriptional tendency continues in C25 with its passages of historical documents. With their official character, they anticipate the Siena Cantos. Like them, they include legal formulations like "1255 be it enacted" (C25.115) and signatures by notaries and officials like "Ser Leonardus Emo, Sapiens Consilij" (C25.119).

Canto 45

C45 provides us with other types of quotations. First, allusions hidden in its language: C45 has sometimes been perceived as Mosaic in tone for its use of the language of the *King James Bible*.[50] As Hesse has suggested, it may have been influenced by Mandeville's economic parable, *The Fable of the Bees*.[51] Mandeville's poem *The Grumbling Hive: or, Knaves Turn'd Honest*, the core text of his fable, describes the consequences of not spending money on arts, similarly to Pound's desription of the consequences of usury (Mandeville ll. 351-354):

---

[50] Twitchell, Jeffrey, "Art and the Spirit of Capitalism," 24.

[51] Hesse suggests a connection between the writing of C45 and J. M. Keynes's *The General Theory of Employment, Interest and Money* (published in February 1936). She speculates that Pound may have received a reviewer's copy of the book in December 1935. Keynes quotes from Bernard de Mandeville's *The Fable of the Bees* (1714), which employs similar motifs and language as C45; see Hesse, Eva (ed.), Ezra Pound: Usura-Cantos XLV und LI, 73.

The Building Trace is quite destroy'd,
Artificers are not employ'd;
No Limner for his Art is famed;
Stone-cutters, Garvers are not named.

As should be kept in mind, however, Mandeville's text is a satire, while Pound's C45 is a sermon against evil. In C45 we also find verbal repercussions of Francis Bacon's arguments against usury in his *Of Usurie*. In addition, the Canto gains a highly allusive character by its references to paintings.

C45 also contains an important quotation from a non-literary source. With usury, Pound warns us, "Came no church of cut stone signed: *Adamo me fecit.*" (C45.230). The text refers to a signed column in the church of St Zeno in Verona: "ADAMINUS / DESCO / GEORG / IO. ME / FECI / T."[52] Pound discovered the column in 1911, when he visited the place together with W. C. Williams's brother, an architect. He counted San Zeno among the "Perfect gifts" from the 12th century.[53] In fact, Pound was not the first traveller to notice the column. From passages in Ruskin's *Stones of Venice* and others, Witemeyer draws the conclusion that it was "a well known cultural landmark."[54] Pound exlained his fascination with the inscription in a later comment of 1942: "I was interested in LATIN order. Order in stone work, in paintin', *Adamo me fecit*. S. Zeno Verona, architect had cut that column by HAND, by his own hand, want INTEGRAL, totalitarian interest in the job of buildin' S. Zeno."[55] From a genetic point of view, the passage in C45 is less interesting, as Pound made few adjustments to his original draft version "Came no church of cut stone. [/] Adamo me Fecit" (item 53). Textually more interesting is the transformation of the long inscription into a brief paraphrase: Pound gives up authenticity for the sake of brevity and versification. The passage provides an instance of a condensed poem in which literary form is granted priority over documentation. The Latin text is the only hint at the historical paradigm in which the column was created. The main attraction of the quotation lies in its origin in a non-literary source.

Rudolf Hess and Canto 51

A quotation in C51 is noteworthy for its textual history. A passage in the Canto reads: "Grass; nowhere out of place. Thus speaking in Königsberg [/]

52 Kenner, Hugh, The Pound Era, 323ff.

53 Pound, Ezra, The Spirit of Romance, 22.

54 Witemeyer, Hugh, "Ruskin and the Signed Capital in Canto 45," 87. Comp. Ruskin, John, The Stones of Venice, vol. I, ch. 7, § 27, 29.

55 Pound on 18 May 1942, see Pound, Ezra, "Ezra Pound Speaking," 137f.

Zwischen die Volkern erzielt wird [/] a modus vivendi." (C51.251). Pound does not mention the source of the German and Latin words. In their published form, they merley advocate the humanitarian ideal of a peaceful coexistence of countries. A typescipt draft of C51 gives the quotation and a hint at the source, mentioning a person called Hess and the year 1934 (item 236). In addition, it contains an emphatic exclamation of assent, of which it is not certain whether it is still part of the quotation or has been added by Pound. For more information, it is necessary to go back one step further. An early note contains the quotation and additional details about the source, mentioning Rudolf Hess, Königsberg and July 8 of 1934 (item 242). The emphatic exclamation can now be identified as genuinely Poundian, because it was added to the same, typewritten item in his handwriting.

Originally, the passage derives from a speech by Hitler's deputy Rudolf Hess of 8 July 1934, after the Roehm massacres[56]: "Es ist höchste Zeit, daß endlich eine wirkliche Verständigung zwischen den Völkern erzielt wird."[57] In 1938 Pound commented: "Some years ago Rudolf Hess said it should not be beyond European intelligence to work out a system of living together, meaning between European peoples." Strongly interested in Hess and the political events in Germany,[58] Pound tries to make Hess an advocate of peaceful coexistence and civilization.[59] Textually, Pound deleted all traces of the fascist origins of the words. The remaining clue, "Königsberg," is not suspicious and has appeared to some scholars as a reference to philosopher Immanuel Kant. In revising the quotation, Pound removed both the original speaker's name and his own enthusiastic reaction to fascist propaganda, leaving only the idealistic message. By de-contextualizing the quotation, Pound denies its original propagandistic reference system and discards its specific historicity in favor of a new, authorially governed context.

Siena

I will now discuss some quotational clusters, i.e. groups of quotations in *The Fifth Decad*. Siena Cantos C42 to C44 constitute one of those clusters and the largest in terms of quantity. Like the Malatesta Cantos, the Siena Cantos

[56] Hitler had Ernst Roehm, leader of the SA stormtroops, killed, because he considered Roehm and the SA men increasingly dangerous rivals.

[57] Transl. "It is high time that a real understanding is achieved between the peoples [i.e. nations]." The speech was printed on the first two pages of the Berlin edition of the *Völkischer Beobachter* of 10 July 1934.

[58] As discernible in P&P VII.310.

[59] P&P VII.393.

represent Pound's transcriptional approach to his sources.[60] Pound's close reproduction of his sources might be one of the reasons why, for all three Siena Cantos, genetic stages are few. While this chapter is not attempting to achieve a detailed reconstruction of their genesis, it will nevertheless consider some of the strategies of borrowing that Pound employed during writing.

Pound did not create a poetic fiction in which quotation and poem are identical. Rather, he included authorial signifiers to remind the readers of his own authorial presence, as in the following lines:

> FIXED in the soul, nell' anima, of the Illustrious College
> They had been ten years proposing such a Monte,
> That is a species of bank---damn good bank, in Siena
>
> (C42.209)

Pound not only creates philosophical overtones by the double reference to "soul" and "anima," but also disrupts the quotation to remind us of the epic narrator, who has an opinion of his own on the importance of the bank. Pound used this device systematically, for three purposes. First, to emphasize certain facts he regarded as crucial. Hence, Pound inserted remarks like "All of this is important" (C42.209; addition not recorded in the notebooks, but in later drafts). Second, he interrupted quotations for explanations, like in C42, where Pound explains the Italian abbreviation "AA. VV." His Sienese notebooks already include this explanation (item 305, [40]), as do later drafts and of course the final version: "& being sent to YY. HHighnesses (AA. VV. = YY HH)" (C42.211).

Third, Pound inserted authorial remarks into quotations, references to his own work with archival sources and the problem of deciphering them. The impact of that problem on Pound should not be underestimated. Pound even mentions "Livio Pasquini's hand-writing" in an essay,[61] and he refers to his struggle with the script both in his Siena notebooks and in the finished texts. The passage "in what wd. seem to have been 1622" (C42.211) derives from an almost identical formulation in a notebook (item 305, [41]). Sometimes Pound was simply ignorant or uncertain of a fact and therefore added a question mark. In C42 he expresses his uncertainty about the exact value of the *scudo*: "? one scudo worth 7 lire" (C42.214; also item 305, [71v]).

Pound's use of transcriptional quotations becomes apparant in his adaptation of official documents in the Siena Cantos. We will concentrate on

---

[60] Glimpses of the original documents can be caught from their transcriptions in Centenario 167-184 and Monte III.261-268.

[61] "Built for Stability" (1936), in: P&P VII.84. Similarly "L'Economia Ortologica" (1937), in: P&P VII.220.

a brief passage[62] shaped by Pound to take the form of a legal instrument. Pound recorded the text in his notebooks (especially item 302, [26-33]; item 305, [48-52]; item 301, [28-32]). They contain the transcription of the document in a very rough form, with short lines (due to the small size of the notebooks) and changing indentations. The passage later assumed the following form:

> TTheir HHighnesses gratified
> the city of this demand to
> erect a New Monte
> for good public and private and to facilitate ...
> ..agreed to accommodate
> ......and to lend the fund against the Gd Duke's
> public entries to the sum of
> 200,000 scudi
> capital for fruit at 5% annual
> which is 10,000 a year
> assigned on the office of grazing
> on caution of said security offered
> leaving ground for other towns that
> wish to participate
> with TTheir HHighnesses
> approbations as follows:
> Maria Maddalena Tutrice
> Hor° della Rena   30 Xembre   1622
>
> (C42.212[63])

The quotation shows some deviations from the original. First, in terms of layout. The main part of the source document consists of continuous text without the line formatting Pound applied to it. The "approbations" are part of the text block and the signatures are indented differently than in the Canto.[64] The final version bears more likeness to the short lines of the first notebook version (item 302, [26-33]) than to the documents as printed in Monte and Centenario. Only that the notebook version comes closer to the original, as can be seen from the Italian words which still permeate the notes. The second notebook draft (item 305, [48-52]) approximates the wording of the drafted and published version. Several shorter passages have been condensed.

If Pound's intention for his extensive use of source documents in the Siena Cantos was to illuminate the long and difficult process through which

[62] Reproduced in Monte III.262f.; Centenario 181f.
[63] Draft items 7f. are basically identical.
[64] Monte III.262; Centenario 182.

the *Monte* was achieved,[65] then this was the undertaking of a historian. Should we therefore criticize Pound for abandoning poetry in favour of economic and administrative minutiae? Not at all – what some critics have called a lack of poetry, namely Pound's immediate approach to his sources by quoting from them extensively and in detail, is exactly what makes the Siena Cantos so thoroughly modern. They are not merely reproductive, i.e. historical excerpts without artistic shape. Of course Pound to some extent reproduced the linguistic and bibliographial codes of the original documents. However, Pound is not an editor, but a poet. And in the context of a poem, authenticity itself becomes a fiction and the historian a persona. If Pound seems to assume the role of a historian, then this role is part of an epic poem. Even his palaeographical difficulties are transformed into fiction.[66] The reproduction of authenticity is not a scholarly act, but a poetic device. What critics actually miss is a conventional form of lyricism, not "poetry" itself, as the Siena Cantos are as poetic as any other part of Pound's epic. It may even be considered a merit of the Cantos to have established a really comprehensive poetics of history which includes an archeology of economics. Pound not only writes about the traditional heroes of history, but seeks for yet undiscovered paths leading from the past to the present. The history of the *Monte dei Paschi* is one of these paths. To have included economics in poetry is what makes Pound a truly modern author. He was one of the forerunners of our present-day obsession with economics. He opened his poem for economic and administrative discourses by weaving them into the text as quotations.

China

Whereas the Siena Cantos show how closely Pound would sometimes adhere to his sources, C49 can serve to highlight the liberties he took in transforming quotations and translations. C49 has its roots in some traditions of Chinese poetry which range from political advice to landscape descriptions. Pound was well-acquainted with the background of Chinese writing. In *Lustra* we find some pieces in a Chinese style.[67] But they are exercises in exotic impressionism and imagist compression, rather than full explorations of a complex tradition. With their glades, maidens, fans and falling petals, they continue the delicate elegance of Pound's earlier texts. Pound's subsequent translations of Chinese poetry were steps towards a more comprehensive and original understanding of Asian literature.

---

[65] Kearns, George, Guide to Ezra Pound's *Selected Cantos*, 104.
[66] Makin, Peter, Pound's Cantos, 103.
[67] Pound, Ezra, The Collected Shorter Poems, 118f.

The traditional subjects of Asian poems do not diverge too much from European ones. They include warfare, the separation of wives from husbands, agriculture, hunting, marriage, feasting or complaints against officials.[68] Old Asian poems are sometimes political in their content, praising kings for their virtues and condemning them for their vices, just like European poets did.[69] Asian and European poetry both include typical political modes of poetic perspective – e.g. the point of view of the ordinary citizen, who does not consider himself worthy of the ruler's attention, or that of the experienced counsellor, who expects the ruler to listen to his voice. The latter tradition informs Confucius's texts, the former governs C49, in which the harmonious regularity of the ideal state is expressed through the every-day routine of ordinary peasants. Like C49, Chinese poems often celebrate the beauty of rural landscapes. In this respect, Pound's Canto resembles classical poems like "Autumn Evening in the Mountains" with its rainy landscape of moon, pines, bamboos, fishermen, boats and lotus leaves.[70]

Pound drew his inspiration for C49 from a book of Chinese and Japanese poems he received from his parents.[71] The poems accompanied a traditional set of eight landscape scenes that depicted spots located in the Hsiao-Hsiang region in Hunan, an area with many lakes called Seven Lakes region. What Pound obtained in 1928 was a manuscript book with ricepaper pages[72] and gilded edges, the pages "hinged together to stand up like a zigzag screen."[73] In 1928 the Chinese school teacher Miss Tseng visited Rapallo and spent an afternoon at the Pounds' home, where she translated, on Pound's request, the Chinese poems, while the poet recorded some notes.[74]

The manuscript book includes eight scenes "along the Sho (Hsiao), the upper part, and the Sho (Hsiang), the lower part, of the river which pours into

[68] Giles, Herbert A., A History of Chinese Literature, 16.

[69] For criticism of political rulers in Chinese poetry see Hawkes, David, A Little Primer of Tu Fu, 17.

[70] Wang Wei / Li Po / Tu Fu / Li Ho, Four T'ang Poets, 30f. For more T'ang poems see Erwin von Zach, Tu Fu's Gedichte; David Hawkes, A Little Primer of Tu Fu.

[71] The original source document is reproduced in appendix B of Pearlman, Daniel D., The Barb of Time.

[72] Makin, Peter, Pound's Cantos, 207. According to Kenner, the book came to Rapallo when Pound's parents moved there in the 1930s; see Kenner, Hugh, The Pound Era, 265.

[73] Kenner, Hugh, The Pound Era, 265; also comp. Kodama, Sanehide, "The Eight Scenes of Sho-Sho," 133.

[74] Kodama, Sanehide, "The Eight Scenes of Sho-Sho," 132; Stock, Noel, The Life of Ezra Pound, 328; Taylor, Richard, "Canto XLIX, Futurism, and the Fourth Dimension," 337ff. BL 43 / 61 / 2696 contains a letter to Homer Pound of 30 July 1928 which includes a translation of eight of the poems. Some scholars assume that Pound had the poems translated as late as 1934; Palandri, however, dates Miss Tseng's visit to 1928 (comp. chapter IV.3 of this study), see Palandri, Angela J., "The 'Seven Lakes Canto' Revisited," 53.

Lake Dotei in Central China."[75] Among the paintings, we find the same rural landscape sceneries we mentioned above and which Laurence Binyon describes in his classic *The Flight of the Dragon*, a book Pound knew: "the painter of the Vesper Bell from a Distant Temple would evoke the mellow sound of the evening bell coming over the plain to the traveller's ears, and in the Descent of the Wild Geese would bring to memory the familiar cry of the geese as they flew overhead in the mists."[76] The poems present a sequence of typical elements of Chinese poetry, like temples, bells, lakes, clouds, autumn skies and evening rain.[77] We find the same elements in other traditional poems like "An Evening View of the City of Yo-Chou after Coming from Han-Kou to Parrot Island":

> No ripples in the river, no mist on the islands,
> Yet the landscape is blurred toward my friend in Ch'u...
> Birds in the slanting sun cross Han-kou,
> And the autumn sky mingles with Lake Tung-t'ing.[78]

An idyll similar to C49, although more melancholy, is "An Autumn Cottage at Pa-Shang":

> After the shower at Pa-shang,
> I see an evening line of wild geese,
> The limp-hanging leaves of a foreign tree,
> A lantern's cold gleam, lonely in the night,
> An empty garden, white with dew,
> The ruined wall of a neighbouring monastery.
> ... I have taken my ease here long enough.
> What I am waiting for, I wonder.[79]

Representing a long and mainly anonymous tradition, none of the poems can be attributed to a clearly identifiable author, hence the "no man" at the beginning of C49.[80]

When analyzing the referential aspects of C49, we must first emphasize the strongly quotational structure of the poem – although C49 seems to many readers the most coherent part of *The Fifth Decad*, it does in fact almost fully consist of quotations from several sources. As its elements, Kenner discovered "(1) the anonymous poems [from the book] much rearranged; (2) the Emperor's poem; (3) a folk song; (4) a terminal Poundian distich and four

[75] Kodama, Sanehide, "The Eight Scenes of Sho-Sho," 133.
[76] Binyon, Laurence, The Flight of the Dragon, 80.
[77] Comp. e.g. The Jade Mountain, 7, 64f., 95, 207.
[78] The Jade Mountain, 93.
[79] The Jade Mountain, 106.
[80] Kodama, Sanehide, "The Eight Scenes of Sho-Sho," 138.

interpolated Poundian lines."[81] First, the anonymous poems. The sequence of the poems in the original book has no recognizable order, whether chronological or other. The sequence, as established by Kodama, is:[82]

1: "Wild Geese Plummeting to the Flat Sands"
2: "Sailboat Returning to Far-Off Shore"
3: "Mist over a Mountain Town"
4: "Evening Snowfall over the River"
5: "Autumn Moon on Lake Dotei"
6: "Night Rain in Sho-Sho"
7: "Evening Bell of a Misty Temple"
8: "Sunset Glow over a Fishing Village"

Pound changed the sequence to 6, 5, 7, 2, 3, 4, 1, 8 in C49. As a letter to Homer Pound shows, he executed this change as early as 1928.[83] It would be a far-fetched interpretation, and possibly an error, to clearly attribute the change in sequence to deliberate decisions by Pound. The sequence he used may be exactly the sequence in which the Chinese teacher translated the poems for Pound. As mentioned in a previous paragraph, Pound would sometimes adhere to the sequence of source materials (like in the Adams edition) without introducing a new, genuinely authorial order. As Pound had to rely on Miss Tseng for understanding the poetry, it is possible that he maintained the sequence in which she had dictated the text to him.

Pound extensively changed the wording of the quoted passages, turning them from translations into paraphrases and finally into a text of his own. The 1928 letter already introduced some cuts of the original material. For instance, the second stanzas of parts two and eight of the original sequence are missing, both of which include rather impressionistic descriptions of natural phenomena and fisherman's life.[84] In addition to shortening the original poems, Pound also inserts some authorial remarks, e.g. explanatory additions in brackets. In the early drafts of C49 Pound moved towards integrational quotations, i.e. quotations fully integrated into the final authorial text as embedded units, without distinguishing marks to allow their identification as formerly individual parts. This becomes apparent in Pound's transformations of the poems' titles. In the 1928 letter they are separated from the poems and partly typed in capital letters. In the drafts and published version of C49, the titles are integrated into the poetic text. E.g. the "Autumn Moon on Ton-Ting

[81] Kenner, Hugh, "More on the Seven Lakes Canto," 46.
[82] Kodama, Sanehide, "The Eight Scenes of Sho-Sho," 134-138.
[83] BL 43 / 61 / 2696, letter to Homer Pound of 30 July 1928. Includes the text of the eight poems.
[84] See scenes 2 and 8 in Kodama, Sanehide, "The Eight Scenes of Sho-Sho," 135 and 138.

Lake" becomes part of a sentence, "Autumn moon; hills rise about lakes" (C49.244, item 143).

Pound also integrated some additional "luminous details" into C49. One of them, "hills rise about lake [/] against sunset," is derived from one of the paintings in the Chinese source book,[85] another case of a Poundian reference to a non-literary source. The reference is to scene 5,[86] a drawing with a building and a tree in the foreground, complemented by hills and a river behind them. A vanishing sun is painted in the background. By absorbing the imagery of landscape painting, Pound's reference stresses the idyllic tone of C49, a tendency already present in the 1928 letter . By refraining from the insertion of adjectives, Pound maintains the plain composition of the picture. He only depicts hills, lake and sunset, without any more specific properties.

Besides non-authorial quotations, C49 also sheds light on Pound's use of units written by himself, which he transferred from early drafts to the finished poetry. In one draft (item 153), Pound condemns the credit policies of bankers and calls it infamy that the state should owe money to private financiers like "Johnson" and "Bernstein." He also mentions Geryon, as in the final C49: "State by creating riches shd. thereby get into debt? [/] This is infamy; this is Geryon." (C49.245). The bankers' names are not featured in the finished poem, probably because they would have disturbed the timeless surface of C49 by introducing modern persons. Instead, Pound only keeps the classical figure of Geryon.

Towards the end, C49 confronts the readers with a Japanese passage, the "Auspicious Cloud Song." It was allegedly written by the Emperor Shun on passing his power to Yu and has the following Japanese wording:[87]

Kei men ran kei
Kiu man man kei
jitsu getsu ko kwa
tan fuku tan kei

The full translation reads:

Gate, gate of gleaming
The auspicious clouds bright and colourful
Knotting, dispersing
Twist and spread
flower of sun, flower of moon

[85] Kodama, Sanehide, "The Eight Scenes of Sho-Sho," 139.
[86] See the reproduction in appendix B of Pearlman, Daniel D., The Barb of Time.
[87] Kenner, Hugh, "More on the Seven Lakes Canto," 45f.

The sun and the moon shed their rays
day's dawn after day's dawn new fire
Morning after morning.

What is noteworthy about the Japanese quotation in C49 is its typographical ambiguity. We read the Latin transliteration of a Japanese poem, which at the same time strictly adheres to the column-like order of Japanese ideograms. The quotation was designed to be legible for the average reader and to preserve some of the typographical authenticity of the original. In C49 Pound also included fragments from notes by Fenollosa (May/June 1901), like the "Beating Soil Song." It is quoted by Kenner as follows[88]:

sun	go out	and	drink
sun	enter	and	eat
dig	well	and	works
till	field	and	rest
Emperor's	might	for me	what is ?

Hesse assumes that Pound used a later version of Fenollosa's notes and reproduces the "Beating Sod Song" differently[89]:

sun	go out	and work
sun	enter	and rest
dig	well	and drink
till	field	and eat
	might	
Emperor's	power	for me what is?

In an early draft (item 155) Pound provided the quotation with a minimal background, suggesting that it was sung by "old folk." He later discarded the introductional lines in favour of a plain reproduction of the song (item 152). Pound's rendering of the question about imperial power is a close translation of the Chinese original. Hawkes translates two lines in Tu Fu's "Ballad of the Army Carts" with a similar word-order: "District-officers urgently seek land-tax / Land-taxes from-what proceed?"[90] Only that Pound gives the question a more abstract character by not simply asking what imperial power is "to us" (C45.245), but "Imperial power is?," calling for a

[88] Kenner, Hugh, "More on the Seven Lakes Canto," 45.
[89] See Hesse's note in *Paideuma* 3.1 (1974), 143. Note that Hesse gives no source for Fenollosa's text!
[90] Hawkes, David, A Little Primer of Tu Fu, 16. It is one of the merits of Hawkes's book that it not only offers exact prose translations, but also line-by-line readings of Tu Fu's poems.

general definition of it (which is implicitly given in the preceding parts of the Canto: peace, absence of debt etc.). By opening an abstract space, Pound prepares the stage for the final arcanum of the "fourth dimension."

Money

We have so far analyzed Pound's references to texts written by other authors. The following considerations will stress another strategy of borrowing: self-quotation. As Pound was strongly obsessed with economic issues when he wrote *The Fifth Decad*, it seems appropriate to select an example from the vast array of Poundian statements about credit and state debt. In 1933 Pound formulated an, as he believed, essential insight of far-reaching consequences for economics: If a state borrowed money from a bank, it was obliged to pay interest, which entailed an indirect burden on tax payers, from whose taxes the state would have to redeem the interest payments. This seemed unjust, because it would especially burden people with little money. It was exactly this bleak situation that Pound saw the U.S. in and that he would not accept. If the state "rented" money, Pound insisted, the interest-bearing debt should not be laid on the poor, but rather on citizens who had enough wealth to spend. The self-taught economist did not hesitate to distribute his arguments in written form. In fact, as he supported himself by writing essays with increasing missionary zeal, he published the above idea several times over the next few years. Shaped by varying degrees of urgency and rhetorics, it underwent transformations from one intermediary form to the next. Pound first made his idea public in the form of a Q&A game in 1933:

> Q. Why should a "country" or a "government" rent and pay rent for MONEY?
> A. It shouldn't. No intelligent government wd. pay rent for its own money. No more than I pay rent for the language I am now writing.
> The cost of money TO a government shd. be the cost of the paper and the engraving and not one damn cent more.
> Kublai Khan didn't pay rent for the legal tender receipts he gave foreign merchants for pearls (vide Canto XVIII). They worked. Those receipts functioned as money.
> Q. Any thing newer?
> A. The Woergl plan worked. Not only did the town have no need to pay rent for its money (or as they say, "issue bonds") but the people who got the money, and who therefore HAD THE MONEY and cd.

afford to pay rent, did pay a little, a very little rent for the money, AND IT WORKED.[91]

Soon the question became a standard formula which Pound repeated in more or less the same words and with slightly differing emphasis from 1933 to 1934:

> IF money is to be rented who ought to pay the rent? The people who get the money (as under the Unterguggenberger system) OR the peepul who don't?[92]

> SHOULD THE RENT ON MONEY BE PAID BY THE PEOPLE WHO HAVE THE MONEY WHEN THE RENT FALLS DUE, OR BY THOSE WHO HAVEN'T IT?[93]

> If money is rented, WHO ought to pay the rent: the man who has the money when the rent falls due, or someone who hasn't it?[94]

> When money is rented, who ought to pay the rent, the man who has it when the rent falls due, or someone who hasn't it?[95]

> When money is rented who ought to pay the rent on that money, someone who *has it* at the date when the rent falls due, or someone who has *not*?[96]

Pound became more urgent and aggressive in 1935, when he finally included his then most important opponents in the question – the "usurers," i.e. bankers:

> Should a State rent its own credit from private bloodsuckers, and guileless individuals and PAY USURY FOR IT?[97]

---

[91] "Questions" (1933), in: P&P VI.84. Refers to Wörgl, a small town in the Austrian part of Tyrol. During the economic depresssion of the early thirties, the mayor of the town issued notes based on Gesell's concept of stamp scrip money. The town went through a phase of prosperity, but when the national authorities learned about the experiment, Woergl was forced to return to standard money. Pound probably learned about the Woergl experiment from Irving Fisher's book "Stamp Scrip" which he reviewed for the NEW of 26 Oct 1933. Redman thinks that Pound read about Woergl in Gesell (Redman, Tim, Ezra Pound and Italian Fascism, 127, where you can also find a description of the Woergl experiment).
[92] "Hel ... up !!!" (1933), in: P&P VI.111.
[93] "Judas Had It" (1933), in: P&P VI.119.
[94] "From Mr. Ezra Pound" (1934), in: P&P VI.131.
[95] "E. P.'s Suspicions" (1934), in: P&P VI.148.
[96] "A Poet's Questions for Economists" (1934), in: P&P VI.196.
[97] "Again the Rev. Coughlin" (1935), in: P&P VI.332.

Pound's obsessive use of this rhetorical question proves the significance he attributed to it. It underwent a process of concentration, from a context of arguments to verbal aggressiveness, but remained similar in its formulation. In a versified form, it was integrated into C48 and now marks the beginning of one of the section's most polemical poems:

> AND if the money be rented
> Who should pay rent on that money?
> Some fellow who has it on rent day, or some bloke who has not?
>
> (C48.240)

As Pound's pre-publication documents reveal, the transformation from prose to poetry was easily achieved. By means of versification, Pound adjusted the phrase to the standard paradigm of poetry, which involves rhythm and stress.[98] Apart from the slight modification of "shd." to "should," the genetic stages between the final version and the earlier prose renderings offer few surprises. We only note a change in emphasis – the formulation "bloke who has not" occurs relatively late in the genetic process (item 129) and is soon transformed into the final version (item 93). Nevertheless, the rhetorical question has undergone a clear process of revision. The history of the self-quotation highlights how far a genetic sub-process (referring to one textual unit) may extend beyond the actual pre-publication documents of a poem.

The case of Proust shows very clearly that prose reflections can be transformed successfully into literary art. Proust started with an essay against Sainte-Beuve, but finally wrote the *Recherche*.[99] There remains, however, a crucial difference between Proust and Pound. Whereas the former allowed his essay to develop certain ramifications which were then transformed into a narrative structure that became finally independent of the original essay, Pound used his poetry to convey the same message he had expressed in his prose writings. Proust started with a seed and ended with a tree, whereas Pound worked on two complementary levels that intertwined increasingly. Self-quotation served to synchronize two different media, both of which Pound used to convey the same messages.

A Conclusion

Attempting a typology of references in Pound, we can distinguish references to *literary* and *non-literary sources*, as well as *authorial* and *non-authorial*

---

[98] The lines now almost fit the melody of "For he's a jolly good fellow."
[99] Pugh, Anthony R., "Proust's working methods: The importance of structure," 115.

quotations. Another substantial distinction is that between *integrational* and *transcriptional* quotations – the former dominate in C49 with its closely interwoven, smooth sequence of renderings of source poems. The latter are typical of the Siena Cantos and their use of official documents. If Pound re-formulated a quotation, it was mainly to condense (e.g. for versification) or emphasize. In some cases, concentration and re-formulation of a text were used for a *de-contextualization*.[100]

Pound's use of quotations was ambiguous and moved in a circle between, on the one hand, his urge to overcome the limits of traditional scholarship and philology in order to reach a "higher accuracy of the spirit," and, on the other hand, the necessity to use philology to establish the authority of historical facts.[101] But philological exactness was not Pound's major objective. According to Preda, Pound usually "slightly modifies or polishes a quotation to fit it better into the texture of his discursive field."[102] We tend to formulate our opinion less euphemistic – Pound did not hesitate to instrumentalize quotations for his purposes. Although he often sought to preserve their historical specificity (e.g. in trancriptional quotations from Sienese documents), he was also prone to de-contextualization. In other words, Pound's policies of borrowing are sometimes highly secretive.

As Rainey has shown, it is possible in some cases to establish a history of quotations, starting with an original historical source, which is then quoted in another historical text – to which Pound finally refers.[103] In the case examined by Rainey, Pound includes what looks like scraps from the *Commentarii* by Pius II into the Cantos. A close analysis reveals, however, that Pound derived the details from a work of popular history published in 1912. Research on the *Fifth Decad* enables us to confirm the results of Rainey's analysis. Pound clearly had a marked tendency not to mention intermediary sources, but to present the information he derived from them as a historical fact, like in the case of the alleged Rothschild letter in C46. This tendency is rendered problematic by Pound's extensive use of the apocryphals of history – of pamphlets, populist tracts and journalese books.

At the beginning of *The Fifth Decad*, things are still what they seem to be. The original Sienese documents used in C42-44 are always present in those Cantos. They serve to create a historical narrative that is continually interrupted by Pound's interferences, for instance when he is unable to decipher a word. Pound's remarks undermine any simple illusion of authenticity. In the other cases mentioned, however, Pound does not hint at his sources, but announces his findings like proofs in a trial, like

[100] Comp. the Hess speech in C51.
[101] Rainey, Lawrence S., Ezra Pound and the Monument of Culture, 69.
[102] Preda, Roxana, Ezra Pound's (Post)Modern Poetics and Politics, 250.
[103] Rainey, Lawrence S., Ezra Pound and the Monument of Culture, 30f.

unquestionable pieces of evidence. In C46, for example, Pound assumes the persona of a prosecutor who presents his "evidence" – a collection of quotations and references – to the public. The same applies to de-contextualized passages like the excerpt from Hess's speech in C51. These references are granted a seal of authenticity that is hardly legitimate.

In creating a quotational field of far-fetched evidence, Pound sought to establish a set of reference points based on alternative historical traditions, creating a simultanous presence of several historical periods. The quotation functions as a signifier denoting either positive examples (like the *Monte dei Paschi*) or negative forces in history (like the usurers). It reaffirms the writer's sense of historical continuity, as it establishes a connection between the past, for whose authority it serves as a proof, and the present, which seeks its roots and affirmation in history.

II.2 The Genesis of Cantos 42 to 51

This chapter proposes a set of hypotheses about the genesis of *The Fifth Decad*, a genesis that not only included the modification of Canto texts, but also of the structure of the decad as a whole. As Pound changed the numbers of individual Cantos during writing, we will subsequently use Canto names that are to some extent independent from the numbers and are rather related to the basic contents of the individual poems: C42, C43 and C44 will be called Siena/History Cantos 1 to 3, C45 the Usura Canto, C46 Evidence Canto 1 (Pound presents his "evidence" against the usurers in this Canto), C47 the Adonis Canto (the poem is a hymn to Adonis), C48 Evidence Canto 2, C49 the Seven Lakes Canto, C50 the Tuscan Canto and C51 the Conclusion.

In my remarks on the genesis of the decad, I will not only follow the development of individual Cantos as such, but also of major textual units incorporated into Cantos 42 to 51. These units consist of textual elements that range from single phrases to whole passages. Besides their being a substantial part of the poems themselves, their development is an important clue to the development of genetic paths, on which the units allow us to navigate. Typical units are the short phrase "Grass; nowhere out of place" (C51.251), the Pleiades passage in the Adonis Canto (C47.237) and long paraphrases like the "Viva Ferdinando" passage in Siena Canto 3 (C44.223). These units constitute the *textual* level on which a genetic analysis of the *Cantos* can take place, in addition to the *physical* level explained earlier. Only by the inclusion of both levels can a genetic analysis be forged.

Pound's writing methods did not change substantially over the years, and the use and transformation of discrete textual units was a constant feature of his work from early on. Froula has provided us with a general idea of how Pound shaped an early Canto, C4.[1] It first started in 1918 with a "rapid handwriting on random scraps of paper,"[2] followed by a fragment that sketched one scene, then typescripts. Pound developed the poem by adding fragments and lines from several other drafts, thus turning the poem into a cluster of borrowed individual units. The composition of the poem was a process of transformation during which an original textual cluster was supplemented with additional units that influenced the further, processual dynamics of the poem.

This very much describes Pound's standard method of writing a Canto. With the continuous re-shaping of his texts, Pound represents the so-called tower concept of authorship, as defined by Mendelson: He mentions two

---

[1] See Froula, To Write Paradise, 55-69, for Pound's work on Canto 4.

[2] Froula, To Write Paradise, 56.

models of authorship, the "fading coal" and the "gothic tower."[3] According to Shelley's fading coal model, the writer's original inspiration is bright, but inconstant, and is reduced in the course of writing. According to the tower concept, any early state of composition is merely a sketch, while perfection is acquired only through melting the text into a final form. This procedure is genetically typical of the Pound papers. Their complex sequences of sketches, notes and drafts reveal a constantly revising author. Only rarely do Pound's early sketches closely resemble the setting copies, as in the case of the Usura Canto.

Apart from the individual Cantos, Pound's typical writing-as-composition also applies to his structuring of the whole decad. The genesis of the Canto sequence is by no means a more stable process than the shaping of the included poems, as we can learn from Pound's sketches and draft numberings. They show how he progressed from first structural notes to a final order, revising sub-groups of Cantos as much as the decad as a whole. When Surette attempted a classification of the material preserved in the Beinecke folders, he mentioned "a few handwritten notations on the arrangement of groups of cantos. [...] The notes in question are no more than a column of canto numbers with a matching column of theme or subject labels.".[4] Some of the structural notes Surette refers to are relevant for the genesis of the *Fifth Decad.* They show how Pound modified his plan of the decad during writing.[5] Together with the numbers assigned to Cantos on draft sheets, the sketches allow us to reconstruct the genesis of the overall section.

Originally, the Adonis Canto was number 42 (now C47), C48 was probably 43 and the Seven Lakes Canto was 44 (now C49). Cantos 45 and 46 were in the same position as they are in the published decad, while the Conclusion was C47 (now C51). The Siena Cantos (C42-44) and the Tuscan Canto (C50) only became part of the decad at a late stage of composition. The Pound papers offer some evidence to support our case. An early note with a plan for Cantos 31-41 also contains three lines on *The Fifth Decad.* According to this note, the Adonis Canto was C42, Evidence Canto 2 was C43 and the Seven Lakes Canto C44.[6] Item 1 is even more clear about the early plan of the decad. Under the heading 42 we find Adonis, under number 43 the first lines of Evidence Canto 2. Early drafts of individual Cantos show the same numbering, although with some variations. Like item 1, item 15 has the Adonis passage as number 42.

---

[3] Mendelson, Edward, "The Two Audens and the Claims of History," in: George Bornstein (ed.), Representing Modernist Texts, 158f.

[4] Surette, Leon, A Light from Eleusis, ix.

[5] Such sketches were used by Pound more than once. Notes for other parts of the poem include, for instance, Attis and C25; see Pound, Ezra, BL 43 / 73 / 3253.

[6] Pound, Ezra, BL 43 / 72 / 3243.

The position of the Seven Lakes Canto underwent several changes. On one draft (item 143), the poem is assigned two different numbers, which were written down and erased several times: once as number 43, then as 44. On item 290, the Digenes passage from Evidence Canto 2 carries the number 44, although the earlier sketch mentioned above has the Seven Lakes Canto as C44. In this respect, item 293 is less ambiguous. It contains drafts versions of the final passages of Evidence Canto 2 and the Seven Lakes Canto, numbered 43 and 44 respectively, which allows us to identify number 3 in the mentioned sketch[7] as C48. Item 158, which is part of the Seven Lakes Canto, provides further evidence; it carries a Roman 44 in Pound's hand. That Evidence Canto 2 once was C43 is also shown by other items (93, 99, 106). Even late genetic stages of the Canto adhere to this numbering.

For the Usura Canto and Evidence Canto 1 we have no such signs of changes of position. On item 64 the Usura Canto is unequivocally called V and 45, while another draft (item 69) assigns number 46 to Evidence Canto 1. The exact positions of the Usura Canto and Evidence Canto 1 were obviously clear from the beginning. Pound published the Usura Canto in February 1936, still without a number. But when he published Evidence Canto 1 in March 1936, he called it "Canto XLVI." Therefore, it was possible he still worked with the original sequence in mind, i.e. with the present Cantos 47 to 49 as Cantos 42 to 44, and the Usura Canto as C45.

The Conclusion (now C51) was at one time number 45 (items 204, 205, 231, 232, 235, 236), then number 47, as item 211 shows. Pound possibly started to work on the Conclusion Canto before he began the Usura Canto. According to the original plan, the Canto would have had the same function as a conclusion that it has now, but with a lower number. It is difficult to state at what point exactly Pound changed the old sequence. The most substantial alteration was the insertion of the Sienese History Cantos as numbers 42 to 44. However, they were not numbered from the beginning. The early typescript drafts of the three Cantos show letters that designate them as A, B, C. It is possible that Pound added the letters when he was not yet certain about the position of the Cantos in the overall sequence, only about the relative sequence of the three Cantos. This would imply that he added the final numbers in red pencil on items 4, 44 and 84 later, i.e. after he had decided on where to place the History Cantos.

With the publication of the Siena Cantos as Cantos 42-44 in April 1937, and the insertion of the Tuscan Canto (C50), the final sequence of *The Fifth Decad* was complete. Throughout the changes Pound made with respect to the whole section, two groups of Cantos persisted in their sequences, although their general position was altered. First, a group consisting of the Adonis Canto, Evidence Canto 1 and the Seven Lakes Canto. Second, a group

---

[7] Pound, Ezra, BL 43 / 72 / 3243.

including the Usura Canto and Evidence Canto 2. In total, the following changes occurred during the genesis of *The Fifth Decad*:

Canto	Old Structure	Final Structure
42	Adonis Canto	History Canto 1
43	Evidence Canto 2	History Canto 2
44	Seven Lakes Canto	History Canto 3
45	Usura Canto (before: Conclusion)	Usura Canto
46	Evidence Canto 1	Evidence Canto 1
47	Conclusion	Adonis Canto
48		Evidence Canto 2
49		Seven Lakes Canto
50		Tuscan Canto
51		Conclusion

Cantos 42-44

The Siena Cantos and the Tuscan Canto (C50) are distinguished in their genesis from the other Cantos in the section, because they are mainly based on Pound's Siena notebooks (items 301-305). The notebooks are the result of Pound's research in the *Archivio di Stato* in Siena, where he read books and documents related to Sienese and Tuscan history. Pound's use of the Sienese sources has been analyzed scrupulously by Kimpel and Eaves.[8] In their essays they address several issues in detail, especially the question which sources Pound used and how he modified them textually for the Sienese Cantos. The essays are helpful for everybody who wants to analyze the textual relation of sources and poems. We have already provided additional comments on Pound's use of quotations from the Sienese sources in the preceding chapter

[8] See the research of Kimpel and Eaves in their three essays "The Sources of Cantos XLII and XLIII," "The Sources of the Leopoldine Cantos," "Pound's Use of Sienese Manuscripts for Cantos XLII and XLIII."

of this study. In the present part, we will therefore place a slight emphasis on units that are not related to the Sienese sources.

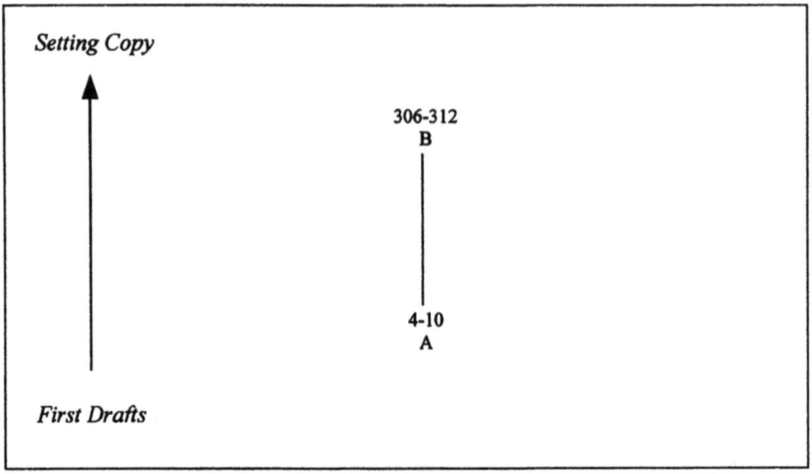

Fig. 1: The stemma of Canto 42.

Pound wrote Siena Canto 1 after C46, in which he had already developed the Antoninus passage (item 284) which is not included in the notebook, but in the typed versions of Siena Canto 1. After Pound had finished C46 by February 1936, he began working on the Siena Cantos in July 1936.[9] Genetically, Siena Canto 1 is mainly derived from pages [6]-[71] of notebook 5 (item 305). On page [6] Pound recorded the initial quotation of the Canto (Palmerston to Russel) in black ink, while the major part of the notebook is written in pencil. Throughout the notebooks Pound used pencil mainly for excerpts from the sources he read in Siena, and black ink for other textual elements, i.e. either for his own inventions or references to sources not related to Siena, like the Palmerston quotation. The same applies to pages [9] to [12], which contain the H. G. Wells quotation and the *lex salica* passage. The formulations differ from the final version, in which Wells is named, while the notebook draft only mentions him as a liberal former supporter of Cobden, but without Wells's name (p. [10]). Another modification: In the notebook, he sees several Italian cities joined in the imaginary figure of a woman (p. [57]), but "in one figure" in the finished Canto (C42.213). In addition, he later cancelled a passage on the fall of Troy (p. [58]).

---

[9] For detailed chronological references see the genetic chronology in part IV.3 of this study.

The notebook stage of C42 is then transformed into typescripts A (items 4-10) and B (items 306-312), as shown in fig. 1.[10] They are top and carbon copies of the same typescripts, but with different revisions. Typescript A is marked with a XLII in red pencil, respectively a pencilled A. The same formula applies to typescript B. A and B represent completed versions and setting copies of the poem, similar to stages A and B of the other two Siena Cantos.

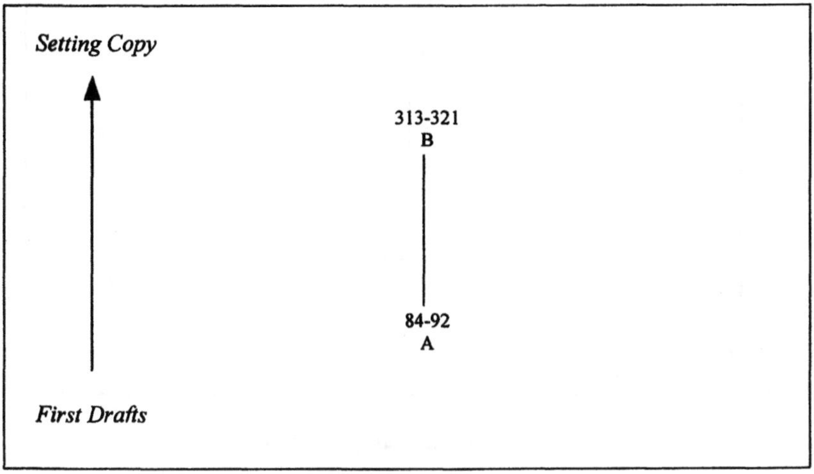

Fig. 2: The stemma of Canto 43.

The genetic roots of Siena Canto 2 (fig. 2) can be found in miscellaneous passages from notebook 1 (item 301), in pages [1] to [43] of notebook 2 (item 302) and in pages [31] to [38] of notebook 4 (item 304). The latter passage is of particular interest, because it is one of the few longer, genuinely Poundian creations in the Siena Cantos – the description of the *palio* race. Pound applied few changes to the text when he transferred it to subsequent stages. He mainly introduced some typographical intricacies, like the "Mn-YAWWH!!!," "pnAWH!" and "Nicch-iO-né!!".[11] Obviously Pound wrote the excerpts into the notebooks with his audience already in mind. In the published Canto, he addresses the readers with "if you follow me," when he explains Pietro de Medici's family relations (C43.220). The same address is already found in the notebook (item 301, [77]). This shows that Pound did not strictly separate his excerpts from the actual poems. In the notebooks, as

[10] The stemmata used here define genetic stages (A, B, etc.) and sub-stages (AA, AB) by listing the item numbers associated with them. See the remarks in chapter IV.1.d.
[11] C43.216f.; originally small letters.

in the actual Cantos, historical events and poetical invention interact. The subsequent genetic stages of Siena Canto 2 are typologically identical with those of Siena Canto 1, i.e. they include a typescript top copy A (here: items 84-92) and carbon copies collected as B (items 313-321). The text is numbered XLIII, III and B in version A and simply B in version B.

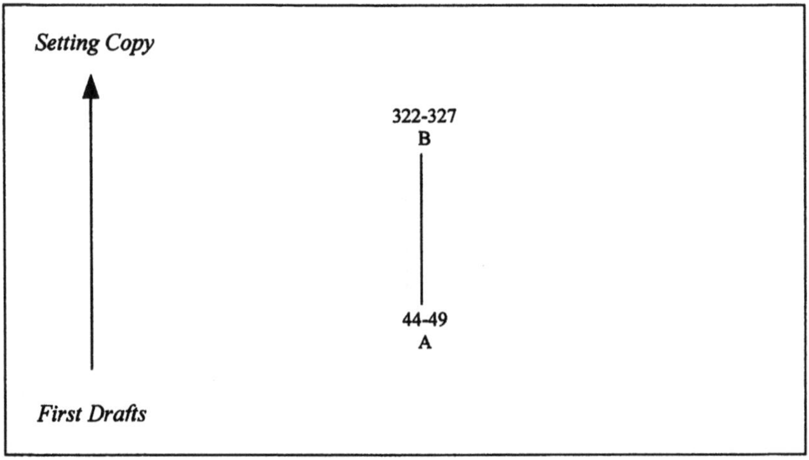

Fig. 3: The stemma of Canto 44.

Siena Canto 3 is derived from pages [44]-[57] of notebook 2 (item 302) and pages [1]-[78r] of notebook 3 (item 303). Again Pound combined his own lines with source transcriptions and paraphrases. A major part of them describes the parade in honor of Ferdinando III, which Pound adapted from the notebook without substantial changes (C44.223ff.; item 303, [1]-[22]). Both the notes and the finished Canto share an elliptical style that omits syntactical elements, as in dense sequences of partial sentences like "declared against exportation [/] thought grain was to eat" (C44.223). Hence, Pound did not change the verbal and factual substance of his notes in subsequent stages of the text, as opposed to other Cantos, where he changed the wording of whole passages in the course of writing. Like the other Siena Cantos, Siena Canto 3 continues its development after the notebook stage with a top copy version A (items 44-49) and carbon copy version B (items 322-327), except for items 47 / 325 and items 49 / 327 (fig. 3). In the latter two cases, top copies and carbon copies were interchanged between stages A and B: Version A (BL) contains the carbon copies of pages 4 and 6; version B (HRC) the respective top copies. In accordance with the numbers on the other two Cantos, A is marked XLIV and C, while version B simply shows a capital C.

For all three Siena Cantos, the revisions in genetic stages A and B are mostly limited to minor corrections and layout specifications. In addition, Pound also added drawings of a cross (items 5, 307) and the symbol of the *Monte* (items 10, 312), both of which are also in the notebooks (item 305, [27], [68]). As should be noted, revisions in A and B are not fully identical, but differ in small details. The same applies to many revisions made in the final versions of other Cantos. Pound would e.g. add or delete definite articles or execute other minor changes. As to the final genetic stages (B for all three Cantos), it is noteworthy that none of the drafts carries a Canto number, but is only distinguished by letters from A to C. Hence, the drafts must have been written at a point when Pound was not yet certain about their final position. This hypothesis is also supported by a note on item 322, which refers to a line originally intended for Evidence Canto 2 (C48), but finally discarded. Pound finished the Siena Cantos in September 1936; hence he must have brought Evidence Canto 2 into its final form and position at a later date.

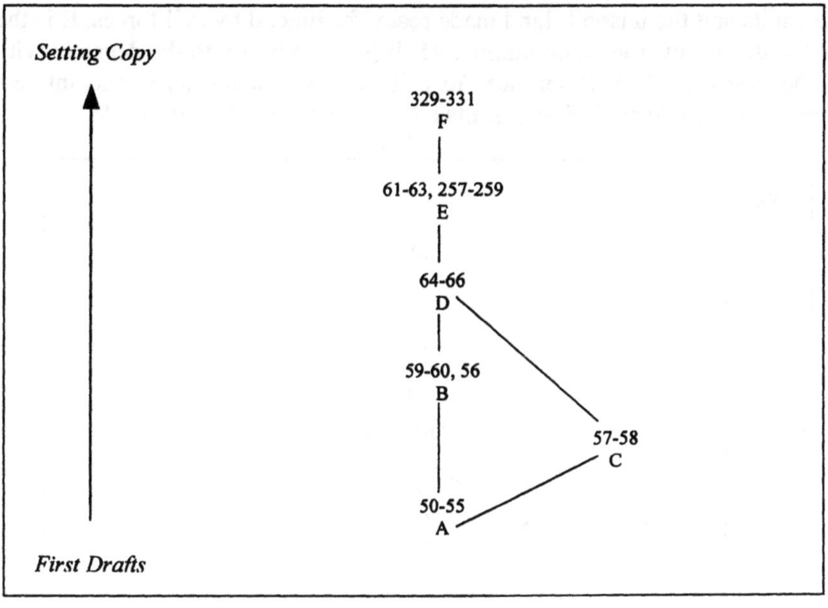

Fig. 4: The stemma of Canto 45.

Canto 45

The genesis of the Usura Canto begins with an ink draft (genetic stage A) that contains an almost complete version of the text (fig. 4). Only the Villon quotation is longer and the final passage more detailed than in later drafts, including vaults, cellars and a reference to unspoilt land, which symbolizes fertility and complements the young couple (bride and groom). The draft shows that Pound was certain about the language and images of the Canto from the beginning. This stage is followed by a comprehensive typescript draft (B), which treats every allusion already contained in A in even more detail and includes an additional reference to interest rates (item 60). It also emphasizes the sacrilege aspect at the end of the Canto by introducing a – later discarded – cannibalism motif, with ghoulish corpses gnawing living meat (item 56). The draft represents an attempt to develop the more elliptical first draft into a text with a fully-fledged system of references. The allusion to interest rates, for instance, placed among cultural aspects of usury, stresses the economic side of the poem. Stage C is an alternative version of the beginning of the poem. The draft still has a reference to taxes in connection with sheep and wool, which will subsequently disappear. Stage D approximates the final form of the text. The number of the Canto has been added and some details from B have been cut, like the mentioned taxes. Yet this version still includes the vaults and the unspoilt land made ready for funeral by evil forces. E is the first draft to show the typed number 45. It is also a return to the dense brevity of the first draft (A): References to cellars, cannibalism, taxes and interest rates have been deleted. F represents a final or near-final draft of C45.

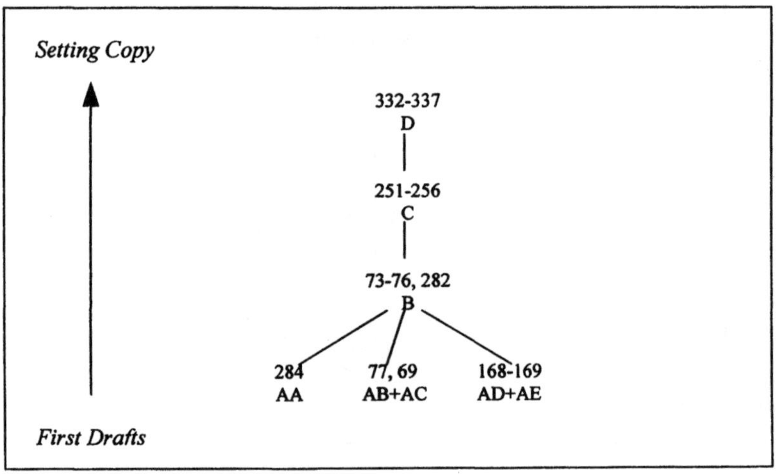

Fig. 5: The stemma of Canto 46.

Canto 46

Pound knew early where to place Evidence Canto 1, because he published it with its final designation as C46 in 1936, i.e. one year before the publication of the actual decad.[12] The text emerged from several units on items now collected in genetic stage A (fig. 5). First, the Antoninus passage (AA), here embedded in a number of additional references to hell and excessive lending. In 1935 Pound read a book on usury by Salmasius, in which Antoninus is mentioned. The fragment can be identified as a part of Evidence Canto 1 by a line that refers to Rhodus, which appears in a slightly modified form in C46 (C46.234), but not in C42, in which we find another reference to Antoninus (C42.209).

Stage A also includes a draft version of the poem's first lines up to the falling snow (AB/AC). Ideally, this could have been the first page of B, but the page numbers of draft B begin with a Roman I in Pound's hand, which excludes the A draft from B, although my hypothesis is that AB was originally part of the same draft as B, which is supported by Pound's use of the yellow lily paper for the draft. Third, stage A contains a fragment with verbal attacks on some of Pound's typical targets, like Rothschild and Morgenthau. The genetic stage establishes a context that is still present in the final C46 with its condemnation of "hyper-usura" (C46.234).

B represents an incomplete draft version of the poem. It begins with the *leitmotif* of the Canto ("Seventeen years on this case"), while the introductory landscape scene of the final C46 is missing. The draft continues to "this case is the first case" on page 4 (i.e. C46.234). The lack of additional pages allows no conclusion as to whether the draft was ever finished. Page 3 is also missing; it probably contained the rest of the camel driver story. Stages C and D are complete versions of the Canto, including minor revisions and setting instructions.

Canto 47

The genesis of what became C47 begins with an Adonis hymn recorded in items 31-37 (stage AA, see fig. 6). It is a free-verse text with a much broader scope than the condensed piece that finally found its way into C48. AA already includes the key elements of the Adonis Canto, plus the Digenes passage later moved to C48. The language of the draft is sexually more explicit than that of later versions. The mythological references to Odysseus are fewer than in the actual Canto; he is chiefly evoked by the mentioning of Moly (item 34).

[12] It was published as: "Canto XLVI," in: *New Democracy* VI.1 (March 1936), 14-16 (P&P VII.28-31), but without a date at the end of the Canto.

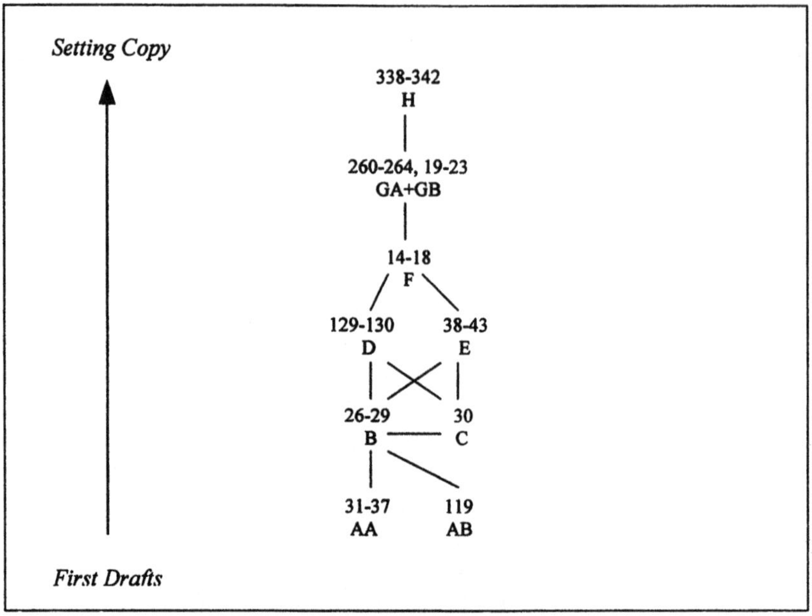

Fig. 6: The stemma of Canto 47.

AB contains an element not found in AA, the complete Pleiades passage from Hesiod in a heavily revised draft form. Pound was then still working on individual formulations in the quotation from the *Works and Days*. B is a combination of the preceding drafts, with elements from the Adonis hymn, the Digenes motif (now C48) and the Pleiades passage. C is an alternative version of the Pleiades passage. This version is more detailed, as it includes the cranes that appear in the final version (C47.237). They are missing in B. Considered as a specific referential unit, C is more advanced than B, although B is the more comprehensive draft of the two in terms of content.

By their combining of the Adonis Canto with elements from Evidence Canto 2, D and E signify a new step in the development of the poem. D is a draft version of the beginning of Evidence Canto 2, up to the puppy letter, with the Pleiades passage inserted before the reference to the ex-sultan. E, carrying the Canto number 42, mixes the Adonis Canto and Evidence Canto 2 on six pages and thus constitutes the most comprehensive version of the original Evidence/Adonis Canto. It starts with the Van Buren / cellarage unit from C48.240, but in an extended form that was later cut, including anti-Semitic attacks on Einstein and other Jews. After returning to a sexually explicit passage from AA, Pound inserted lines on Digenes and the twice-born, followed by the main body of the finished Adonis Canto, from the lamps in the bay to the reference to Diona. F is a pure Adonis draft, still numbered XLII, yet without elements from C48. Together with item 14, items 15 to 18 form a complete version of C47 up to the final Diona reference. The draft is numbered, starting with item 15 as page 1, but item 14 contains the exact passage actually preceding that part. In other words: Although they may have been written at different times, item 14 and items 15 to 18 form a textual unit. Draft F is coherent and complete, but still lacks the two final lines on the power over wild beasts. They are introduced in the subsequent stages: GA, GB and H represent the Canto's final versions and setting copies, which exist in similar form for most of the ten Cantos. They also introduce the Greek letters to accompany the Greek quotations.

Canto 48

While the Adonis Canto underwent a relatively small number of tansformations, the genesis of Evidence Canto 2 is far more intricate (fig. 7). One remark with regard to the stemma: The letters denoting the genetic stages do not constitute an absolute chronology, but should be regarded as an aid intended to achieve groupings of separate textual clusters. We cannot state with absolute certainty whether stage AA was written before GA, as both are very basic units that represent genetically early drafts. That the letter G follows A is a habit forced upon us by a century-long tradition. But what is more important than such sequences are the clusters of elements created by the graphical arrangement of the stages. And even this arrangement cannot convey the full implications of a genetic process.

The AA-AB-AC thread is based on two units, the Digenes-"twice-born" unit and a reference to Frobenius, both included in all three stages. AA has an indirect reference to the Baluba story about Frobenius. AB and B mention Frobenius's setting out for his travels. B also includes additional units that establish a link to another genetic thread. Together with references to a Helen and to Kharkov wheat, B further mentions the Woergl experiment, which reappears in CA/CB. The latter draft also includes the Galileo quotation as a marginal note, plus a general, concluding passage on the *Monte dei Paschi*. AD mentions the "divine honours" that also appear in AE, a draft which combines this unit with the Digenes unit. Both the A thread and the B-CA/CB path are joined in genetic stage JC. This comprehensive draft includes the Diona element from the Adonis Canto (item 13), as well as the "irritable and unstable" unit from C37 (C37.185). This does not necessarily imply that the draft was written earlier than C37: Pound sometimes quoted from his own, already finished poems. In addition, JC contains units from the preceding stages: Galileo, twice-born (Digenes), Helen, Kharkov wheat, the "divine honours."

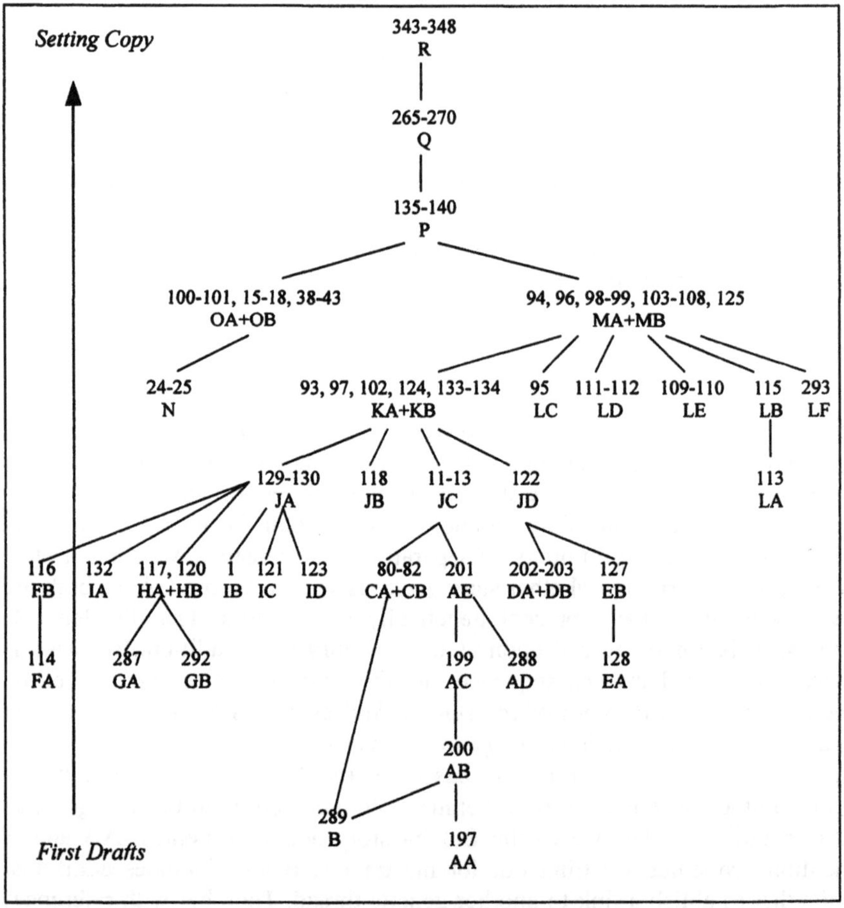

Fig. 7: The stemma of Canto 48.

Another genetic thread is constituted by the puppy unit, which begins with an original document, a letter by a Mr Evans (FA). The source is then transformed into a first Poundian variation of the unit in FB. The same stage also contains a newspaper clipping about a young Dutchman. IA introduces a new unit, the death of the former sultan in San Remo, together with a manuscript addition of the already mentioned "divine honours" unit. Hence, IA is indirectly related to AD and AE. With GA (sea-fowl unit) and GB (interest rates in Trajan's time), more new units enter the genetic process.

Both units are then continued in two very different stages, HA and HB, which are not directly interrelated, but refer to identical units. Manuscript note HA has the sea-fowl, Trajan, Harriet Martineau and a young Dutchman. Typescript HB includes the same units, except for the Dutchman, and several other elements from Cantos preceding the *Fifth Decad*. HB also contains subsequently discarded units, like a reference to camphor trade. Given the outline for Cantos 31 to 38 in HB, it is likely that Pound wrote the item before he published *Eleven New Cantos* (1934), which would imply that the GA and GB units are even older. The puppy letter by A. E. Evans (FA) may help. It carries the date 1933. FB then refers to the letter and the Dutchman in year XI, i.e. 1933. As HA includes a reference to the Dutchman, it cannot have been written before 1933. Unfortunately, we cannot establish a similar timeframe for HB.

IB is one of the structural outlines we have already commented on in the introductory paragraphs of this chapter. It lists the Adonis Canto as number 42 and Evidence Canto 2 as 43. As it refers to the puppy in the 1933 letter by Evans, it was probably written after 1933. IC introduces the trustees of the Salem Museum, ID contains quotations about London conversation and Browning. The genetic clusters from F to I are combined in stage JA. It begins with the "money be rented" unit also used in the final version of C48. Apart from the mentioned elements, it is noteworthy for its inclusion of the Pleiades passage that later became a part of the Adonis Canto. JB is mostly a collection of Poundian remarks on Harriet Martineau (not a reference to Adams's recollection of the journalist) based on Pound's own reading of Martineau, as can be seen from the notes on the item (118).

While we already mentioned JA to JC, we still have to deal with JD and its preceding stages. EA introduces the Marchesa and her rather melodramatic confession, which continues into EB, where the Marchesa unit is combined with references to the Viennese coffee-houses and Mary de Rachewiltz's experiences on a shopping trip and at a procession (later C48.242). In a parallel development, genetic stage DA/DB introduces an allusion to the philosopher Leibniz's refusal of the holy wafer. JD combines units from the D and E threads in a single draft fragment. Its function was probably to develop a specific passage, yet not within the full environment of the Canto, but in a limited local context. In addition to a passage from Crevel, the draft introduces writer von Unruh at Verdun and continues with the Viennese coffee-houses, Leibniz and the Marchesa. As can be seen from the stemma, KA and its carbon copy KB comprise several of the genetic clusters we have just described: KA is a draft version of the first part of C48 up to the passage about stock-printing. While some units are still missing in KA (like the Rothschild passage), others are present that were later discarded, like the Kharkov wheat (item 102), camphor, a passage about Geryon, Martineau,

Helen, a reference to Marcel Schwob and the Pleiades. The draft lacks the Digenes unit, which was present in a whole thread preceding KA/KB.

KA/KB serves as a basis for MA/MB, together with some additional units: LC introduces Athelstan and his theigns, together with the trustees of the Salem Museum also present in IB, IC, JA and KA/KB. LC is a preparation for the final version of the Canto and must be read as a parallel to KA/KB. LD is a draft of the final passages of the Canto, from the orchis to falling Mars (C48.243), except for the lines on the old man with the stones, who is introduced in LF. The draft mentions him in connection with pieces from the Seven Lakes Canto and references to the supreme power of the *nous* and the fourth dimension. LE is a manuscript note with the procession passage of C48.242, a brief reference to which we already encountered in EB. LE is either the original note from which EB originated, or a parallel draft for the more comprehensive rendering in MA/MB. In LA Pound introduces secretary of state Rhumby, here in the form of an autobiographical memoir. The detailed account of the appointment in LA is voiced more concisely in LB, in which Pound concentrates on the essence of the unit, the dubious decision made by drunken senators. LA and LB parallel KA/KB and MA/MB, as the appointment scene is contained in both drafts.

From the K and L threads, MA/MB emerges as another extended version of Evidence Canto 2 (still numbered XLIII in the typescript). While MA still includes some finally discarded units – like the Pleiades, Helen, Martineau and the Marchesa –, some other units are nevertheless still missing in the M drafts: Van Buren, the Digenes unit, the major part of the puppy letter and the Rothschilds. Van Buren, Digenes and the Rothschilds enter the genesis of the poem with stages N and OA/OB. They correspond to stages D and E of the Adonis Canto, on which we already commented. The drafts link the cellarage/Van Buren unit to a draft version of the Adonis Canto. Genetic stage OA (still numbered XLII) provides allusions to the Rothschilds, Zaharoff, the Rothschild-Waterloo legend and the "Elders of Zion." It introduces the cluster ranging from the cellarage to the Rothschild allusion, although the latter is not present in the draft in its final wording, but rather as a general reference. The anti-banking and anti-Semitic units are followed by parts of the Adonis Canto. With P we then enter the final genetic part with the complete versions and setting copies, up to Q and R, which were subject to minor corrections only.

The genesis of Evidence Canto 2 has its roots in the early 1930s, as we can conclude from the connections to *Eleven New Cantos*. They become obvious from stage HB and other evidence. Another note, for instance, contains a plan intended for C34, but also includes the secretary of state and the 80 loudspeakers from Evidence Canto 2.[13] The stemma of C48 not only

[13] Pound, Ezra, BL 43 / 73 / 3258.

ramifies within the *Fifth Decad*, covering other Cantos like the Adonis Canto, but also reaches beyond the limits of the 1937 section as a whole.

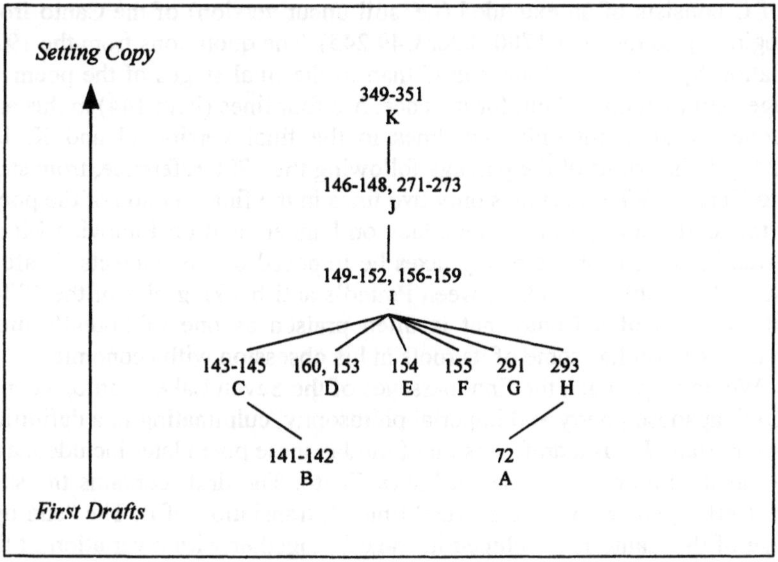

Fig. 8: The stemma of Canto 49.

Canto 49

The central source of the Seven Lakes Canto is Miss Tseng's translation of the Chinese and Japanese poems from the Pounds' ricepaper book, which we analyzed in an earlier chapter. Only the early genetic stage A (fig. 8) does not contain units from the translation. A is a draft with an element from the Tuscan Canto (Bowring) and two added lines on the fourth dimension, here denoted as the dimension of fixed relations. This is a key definition we can also find in another note.[14] B (items 141f.) is a fragment consisting of several elements from the translation by Miss Tseng, together with additional pieces of text in an imitated Asian style.[15] I propose to classify fragment B as an alternative, early version, in which no clear structure is developed yet. Rather, it represents a loose sequence of pieces from the translation and reads like an exercise in style.

[14] Pound, Ezra, BL 43 / 73 / 3258.

[15] There is currently no evidence as to whether those pieces are borrowings or Poundian inventions.

Stages C to H are partial drafts subsequently joined in draft I. C contains an introductory passage on Henry James, Byron and Swinburne with no obvious connection to the later introduced Asian elements of the draft. The rest of C consists of an extended (i.e. still uncut version) of the Canto from the beginning to the year 1700 (later C49.245). The quotations from the 1928 translation by Tseng are longer in C than in the final stages of the poem. A passage about a monk's bell, for instance, has four lines (item 144) in this and subsequent drafts, but only two lines in the final version (J and K, i.e. C49.244). D is a draft of the passage following the 1700 reference, from state debt to Geryon. What occupies only two lines in the final version of the poem is, at this early point, a one-page attack on bankers and on Ludovico Moro, who was infamous for the heavy taxes he imposed on his subjects. Draft D allows us to establish a link between Pound's anti-banking bias of the 1930s and the origins of a Canto that is often praised as one of Pound's most "lyrical" texts, yet has some of its roots in his obsession with economics.

We now approach the final passages of the Seven Lakes Canto, a dense blend of Japanese poetry and imperial philosophy, culminating in a definition of power. Stage E has a draft version of the Japanese poem later included, as a Latin transliteration, in the Seven Lakes Canto. The draft contains the sub-poem itself together with a discarded English translation of it. The "sun up" passage of the Canto is developed in stage F, together with a variation of the grass motif later incorporated into the Conclusion (C51.251). Still missing is the canal built by the benevolent king, which appears in stage G, together with several other references to events in Chinese history, e.g. to a writer named Yodai, who killed another writer because Yodai envied his writings. H contains the key elements of the final passage of the poem: the fourth dimension, the "power over beasts and a later discarded reference to the Canale della Giudecca in Venice. Regarding the component parts assembled in stages C to H, the question arises whether C to H might be parts of one long draft. But the included items do not carry page numbers or show other signs of coherence.

I is a combination of the previous stages. This draft still includes passages that were finally deleted: an introductory passage with H. James and Byron, the Venetian canal, Moro, the names of bankers and the Yodai passage from stage G. J and K are the final draft versions of C49 and contain only minor revisions of mistyped words and punctuation. As we should emphasize, Pound's revisions eliminated, to a major part, specific historical references, either to literary figures (James, Byron), Chinese history, places (the Venetian canal) or other persons, like the bankers in stage D. Pound aimed at an atmosphere of modest timelessness.

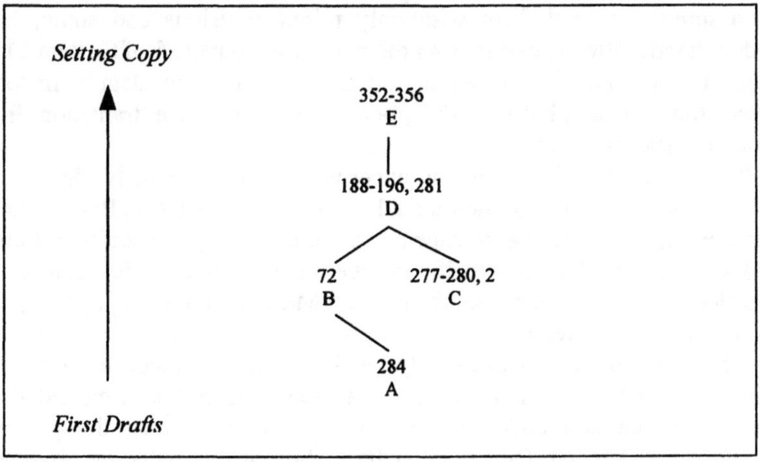

Fig. 9: The stemma of Canto 50.

Canto 50

The Tuscan Canto has its origins in Antonio Zobi's *Storia Civile della Toscana*, a five-volume work from the 1850s.[16] Pound read it in 1936 and recorded excerpts in a notebook. The major part of the Canto is based on pages [3] to [68] of Siena notebook 4 (item 304), except for the initial lines on Adams and the final lines on Lalage and Dirce. The Adams quotation is an old unit Pound had already inserted in C33, where he also used a quotation mentioning the Grand Duke of Tuscany.[17] The Orso unit is from the documents in the Sienese *Archivio di Stato* which Pound also used as sources for the Siena Cantos. He recorded the passage on page [3] of Siena notebook 4. Pound's lines refer to Tuscany under the Medici, while the rest of C50 describes the events under the ruling house of Habsburg-Lorraine.

The genesis of the Tuscan Canto after the notebook stage lacks the genetic complexity of other Cantos, a feature it has in common with the other notebook-based Cantos (42-44). Item 72 is interesting for its combination of diverse elements later incorporated into different Cantos, i.e. the fourth dimension of C49 plus Bowring and Tuscany from C50 (fig. 9). The fragment may have been intended as a beginning either of the Tuscan Canto or Canto 52, as noted in the heading of the item. From stage C onward, the Tuscan

[16] For a detailed analysis of Pound's use of Zobi's book see Kimpel, Ben / Eaves, T. C. Duncan, "The Source of Canto L."
[17] Both C33.161; for drafts of C33 with Adams's statement on the revolution in the minds of the people see Pound, Ezra, BL 43 / 73 / 3252.

Canto assumes its final form with only minor revisions and some, later discarded, handwritten excerpts from the notebook on page 5 of C (item 2), as if Pound at one point thought about adding more historical details. In total, however, the crucial phase of the poem's genesis is the transition from notebook to typescript drafts.

Pound closely adhered to his excerpts. He would mostly change the wording of passages, but not their actual contents. For instance, Pound would change the register or give a passage a less rude wording. In addition, Pound discarded many details, e.g. specific numbers and bibliographical references he recorded in the notebook (like the note on Mazzei's book on page [7]). On the other hand, he extended brief notes to complete sentences. Some very characteristic expressions can already be found in the notebooks and were also used in the finished Canto. At the same time, though, Pound extended the notebook passage and added some fierce polemics against the political establishment of Vienna. On the other hand, he polished what he obviously regarded as rude language. While the notebook describes Pius VI in very obscene terms (p. [24]), the final version "vicar of foolishness" (C50.247) is much more moderate. That Pound conceived of the Canto as a specifically historiographical one becomes clear from his discarding of contemporary references. In the notebook, he mentions Zaharoff (p. [46]) and Geneva (p. [49]), but removed them in the finished Canto.

Canto 51

Like Evidence Canto 2, the conclusion of the decad is noteworthy for its complex genesis (fig. 10), which can be resolved, however, by a clear distinction of texual units and their development.

One major unit is the fly-fishing sequence, which starts with Pound's handwritten excerpts from the source book (A). The sequence is developed in two branches of the stemma. First, PA/PB, a heavily cut and revised one-page extract, which is even more reduced in TA/TB, the draft to most closely approximate the final version of the passage, as included in C51. Second, CA/CB, with other excerpts, leading to the more comprehensive stage EA/EB. One line on fishing is also found in fragments FA/FB, which occupy an alternative position not clearly located within the fishing thread, as the fragment emphasizes other aspects: the ignorance of bankers, Marx's alleged ignorance of money and Carleton's service to mankind. The grass motif (later to become "Grass; nowhere out of place") appears in a cluster consisting of BA, BB and BC. BA and BB share the same formulation of the motif in different contexts, while BC is distinguished from them in both formulation and context. It develops into a draft (DA/DB) that also includes the Hess quotation about the "modus vivendi" (C51.251) we find in a parallel draft

(LA), plus a reference to the divine intellect, as developed in a parallel thread (GA/GB, LB, LC). The latter ranges from the handwritten free-form variations in GA, over the typed and more concise version in LC (introducing the final "light of the doer" phrase) to an alternative trial version in LB.

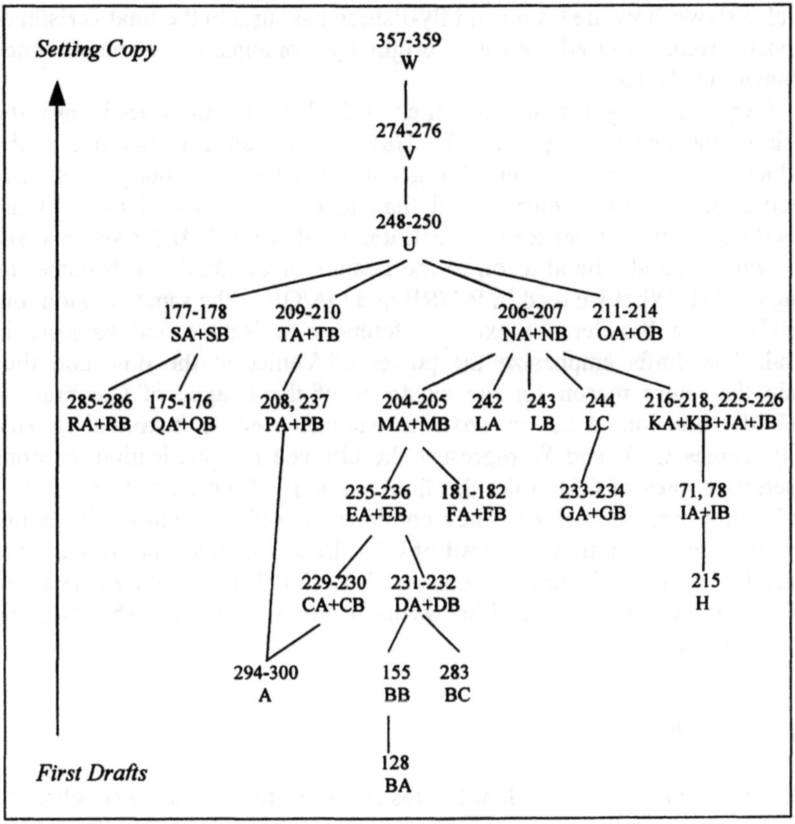

Fig. 10: The stemma of Canto 51.

EA/EB combines the mentioned elements (fishing, Hess, grass, intellect) and continues them, together with FA/FB, into MA/MB. The latter includes an additional element, the "mind of heaven" passage from Guinizelli's poem *Al Cor Gentil*. The Guinizelli thread begins with H, a translation of the source poem, which is then revised and cut in IA/IB. KA/KB combines the Guinizelli unit with a Napoleon quotation ("mud") that also appears in JA/KB, where it is combined with the "divine intellect" motif. The mentioned units are then joined in a draft of the poem's beginning,

NA/NB with its several units: Guinizelli, the "divine intellect," grass, Hess; only the fishing sequence is missing. This stage is noteworthy for its emphasis on philosophical ideas Pound regarded as related to each other: the "mind of heaven," the "divine intellect" and the good politician. As we will explain in a later chapter, these elements outline Pound's metaphysics of politics. The draft also shows how the Usura and fly-fishing passages in the final verison of the poem were inserted between originally homogenous elements once combined in NA/NB.

Geryon's song ("sang Geryone," C51.251) is introduced into the genesis of the text in stage OA/OB. This draft includes a reference to the introduction of Evidence Canto 1 ("get through hell in a hurry") and has Geryon expose itself in more detail than in the concentrated form of the finished C51. Another cluster is constituted by RA/RB, QA/QB and SA/SB, all of which include the allusion to the League of Cambrai that became the ending of C51. What we read in RA/RB and QA/QB is the same allusion, but embedded in a broader context of references to Venice and banking in general. The drafts emphasize the power of Venice at the time and thus explain the major reason for the existence of the League of Cambrai. In SA/SB the allusion is cut in order to exclude specific historical details. Finally, stages U, V and W represent the ultimate pre-publication versions and setting copies of C51. Like the final versions of the other Cantos, they include only minor revisions. They combine the units developed in earlier stages, with one exception: No draft of C51 already includes the passage that repeats lines from the Usura Canto (now C51.250). This unit only appears in the final versions, i.e. Pound either wrote it without further drafts, or some drafts are missing.

Concluding Remarks

The genetic analysis of individual Cantos allows us to draw some conclusions about Pound's overall objectives in writing the poems. He would often draft a Canto as a poetic combination of the timeless and the historical, but, as a general tendency, would then separate those two levels in the process of writing. He did so in the case of the Adonis Canto and Evidence Canto 2 – initially begun as joint drafts that included both mythological and historical references, they were subsequently split into separate poems. One Canto now deals with myth and ritual, another with Jewish bankers and conspiracies. The same phenomenon occurs during the genesis of the Seven Lakes Canto. Its early stages included the writers H. James, Lord Byron and A. C. Swinburne, but the text was then revised as to exclude all reminders of the modern world. As we should remember for later, Pound, out of structural considerations, obviously wanted to create some Cantos which were more "lyrical," in the traditional sense, and others with a clear historiographical emphasis.

The micro-structure of the Cantos is largely determined by the textual units used in them.[18] In the case of the Siena Cantos, large units are constituted by whole passages from source books and documents. C48, on the other hand, consists of a myriad of atomic units, sometimes only one or two lines in length. Although Pound modified the units themselves (mostly by condensing them) and the sequence in which they appear, it is the same units that allow us to identify the genetic roots and branches of the texts. Reconstructing the genesis of the Cantos entails, to a large extent, reconstructing the genesis of inidividual units. Although subject to textual dynamics, they are at the same time the only really constant elements within the genetic process. As the present chapter wants to underline, we have to think in textual units to understand the development of Pound's poems.

The changing positions of the textual units are the realization of the dynamics of Pound's writing, a process of constant re-shaping and re-arranging. Even in the Siena Cantos, which closely follow the notebooks, we find shifts and changes of units, as can be seen from the genesis of C43. The stability achieved by textual units in the notes and drafts is always relative. Hence, Pound not only represents the tower concept of writing, as we explained above. He is also a representative of procedural writing, as opposed to programmatic writing. The programmatic type follows a logical, if not hierarchical, plan which outlines the steps necessary to achieve the text. In procedural writing, the text is generated *through writing* and developed during work: a text in progress.[19]

Genetic analysis reveals multiple links between textual units used in Cantos 42 to 51 and those found in other, earlier Cantos. A draft of the Adonis Canto (item 30) includes stars falling from an olive tree, an element from C35, which reads: "When the stars fall from the olive [/] Or with four points or with five [/] Toward St John's eve."[20] A note for C39 also includes a motif we encounter again in Cantos 47 and 49, the power over "beasts" and the power of healing.[21] Drafts in the context of Evidence Canto 2 (items 117, 118, 120) contain an excerpt on Harriet Martineau, quoted from the diary of John Quincy Adams, which Pound used in C34:

---

[18] Those key units are not to be confused with what Lebrave calls proto-expressions, i.e. formulations written in a first version, but replaced by other, semantically more exact expressions in later versions; see Viollet, Catherine, "Schriftlichkeit und Literatur," 665.

[19] On the two types of writing see the remarks in: Viollet, Catherine, "Schriftlichkeit und Literatur," 668.

[20] C35.175. The "stars" are the small flowers of the olive tree, which blooms in late spring and loses its petals in midsummer, see Companion I.141. The lines are also part of a note in the Pound papers; see Pound, Ezra, BL 43 / 73 / 3259.

[21] Pound, Ezra, BL 43 / 73 / 3274.

"Miss Martineau....author of *Conversations upon Political Economy*
..a young woman...deaf...and hearing only through an ear-trumpet
Her conversation is lively and easy....

(C34.170)

The mentioned item 120, besides the passages on London conversation and Trajan, also contains a reference to oil-drilling in Persia that appeared in two earlier Cantos, C38 and C40.[22] The same item contains a part of C39:

DESOLATE is the roof where the cat sat,
Desolate is the iron rail that he walked
And the corner post whence he greeted the sunrise.

(C39.193)

Two items from the context of the Conclusion (items 71, 78) include lines from C36, stating that "Authority comes from right reason, [/] never the other way on" (C36.179). In connection with Evidence Canto 2 (item 11), we come across a reference to the "Irritable and unstable" from C37 (C37.185). And the initial, hymnic draft of the Adonis Canto refers to the "nec ivi in harum [/] Nec in harum ingressus sum" we find in C39.[23] The Hume quotation about interest rates in Trajan's time appears in a draft with elements from Cantos 38 to 40, but finally came to rest in Evidence Canto 2. The textual voyage of the quotation testifies to Pound continuing interest in economic history. It also shows how certain motifs, and sometimes even individual expressions, kept fascinating him over several years, until he found the right place, and the right poem, for them.

Those frequent links between two sections of Cantos, *Eleven New Cantos* and the *Fifth Decad*, show to what large extent Pound used the textual unit as a structuring element that could be placed in any appropriate setting and context, sometimes moving from one Canto to another. Many key phrases found their actual place and meaning only some time after their writing, when they were finally inserted into a context that allowed them to develop their full range of historical, mythological, and other references. The composition of the decad, therefore, was not only achieved in time, but also in textual

[22] Comp. C38.188, C40.197, see Companion I.155.

[23] C39.194, see Companion I.161. The passage is an excerpt from the Latin *Odyssee* X.255ff. of Clark and Ernestus (1804), meaning "Nor went I to the pigsty / Nor into the pigsty did enter."

space, in a system of coordinates constituted by units that moved from one location to another to form new constellations recorded in Pound's dynamic maps of paper.

space, in a system of coordinates is not rotated by itself, then [illegible]

[illegible]

III. Mnemosyne 3 – The Historical Condition

Western civilization is at the mercy of an international conspiracy of bankers, or, as [Pound] calls them, usurers.
Wars are caused by this "usurocracy" in order to run nations into debt and create opportunities for manipulating the currency.
The worst of the usurers are Jews, especially a few big Jews conducting a "vendetta on the goyim."
Usury cheapens art, falsifies history, and reduces literature to lying journalism.
The usurocracy could be abolished by a simple reform of currency, namely, the issuance of stamped and dated script based on the goods available for consumption.
Such a reform would have to be instituted by a benevolent despot on the order of Mussolini or the best Chinese emperors.

(Malcolm Cowley, *Pound Reweighed*)

III.1 Pound in Fascist Italy

The popular image of Pound the "rebel poet" is dominated by some rather limited periods of his life. Many people remember the Paris years, where he met the writing celebrities of his day, also recall his fierce propaganda broadcasts of the final years of World War II and Pound's subsequent confinement in an asylum. But we should also remember the years between the great ruptures, fruitful years lived at the Italian seaside. It was in Rapallo that Pound spent an important period of his life, and not merely a quiet life in an isolated small town, but one of many cultural encounters and acitivities in a time of growing political tensions. On the one hand, he surrounded himself with relatives and friends, such as Dorothy Pound, Olga Rudge, his parents and W. B. Yeats. At the same time, though, it was during exactly the same period that he developed into an ardent amateur economist and a devoted fascist.[1] Hence, speaking of Pound's Italian years, we have to speak of his radicalization.

Although we will later treat Pound's obsessions in more detail, it is necessary to outline his intellectual development in order to grasp the contradictions he embraced. Pound's Italian odyssee began in a harmonic year, 1922, when he was still living in Paris. That year he met Olga Rudge and spent the December month in Italy where he conducted research on Malatesta and attempted to meet Mussolini, but without success.[2] Although he was not granted an audience, the country appealed to him as a positive alternative to Paris. Two years later Pound left the metropolis and moved to the coastal town of Rapallo, where he immersed himself in activities among which the *Cantos* played only a small part. Apart from organizing a series of concerts, Pound started the magazine *Exile* in 1927. After a decline of his reputation in the preceding years, he was now finding his way back to the top: he was awarded the *Dial* award in 1928 and *A Draft of XXX Cantos* was published in 1930. But those achievements represented only one facet of Pound's work. The award-winning poet was at the same time an amateur economist of missionary spirit, who felt the urge to publish his views on economics in any available journal. Pound's publications of the mid-1930s were not all published in renowned periodicals like Orage's *New English Weekly*, but also in more remote, if not obscure, journals – *Prosperity* or *The Way Out*, to name but a few.

[1] For definitions of fascism see Payne, Stanley G., A History of Fascism, 5-14.
[2] Tytell, John, Ezra Pound: The Solitary Volcano, 182.

Pound's move away from Paris was more than merely a geographical change. It was symptomatic of an intellectual shift away from the artistic world of the French capital. In political terms, it announced a change of attitude that would create a widening gap between Pound and all those former friends and allies who were, like W. C. Williams, more liberal or, like Joyce, more leftist than Pound.[3] After World War I he had developed increasing sympathies for the idea of political order as a means of maintaining peace.[4] The death of Gaudier-Breszka in the trenches of the Great War might have contributed to this notion. Pound's interest moved from the bohemian worlds of London and Paris to what Bush calls a "fixation with strong and patriarchal cultural forms."[5] During the 1930s, Pound became even more obsessed with ideas of hierarchy and natural order, whereas only in the later Cantos, especially the *Pisan Cantos*, he would re-discover his sympathy for outsiders.

Pound's shift towards authoritarian ideas, however, did not result in some form of classicist purity. He was not the conservative Tory so perfectly impersonated by T. S. Eliot. Rather, Pound's rhetorical aggressiveness progressed in equal pace with his political radicalization. It would be too much psychologizing to claim that "his state of mind progressively declined during the 1930s and 1940s."[6] Reality was more complicated. The Pound of the late 1930s was still fairly clear on literary matters, but as regards his economic and political ideas, the polemic attack increasingly replaced the balanced argument. After 1930 Pound became more fierce than ever. He conducted ferocious verbal attacks on the U.S. and its political and legal system, and even wrote disparaging remarks about Eliot. At the same time, though, he managed to create images of idealized serenity in C49. Obviously, the more contradictions in Pound's utterances increased, and the more tensions mounted, the more he looked for the "unwobbling pivot," as the Chinese called it. He found it in an Italian leader – after all the historical figures he had revered, such as Malatesta, Pound finally discovered a real-life hero who seemed a strong alternative to that "nebulous figure" Roosevelt: "Mussolini a male of the species, and the author of this year's *consegna*."[7]

---

[3] On the political attitudes of Williams and Joyce see David Frail, The Early Politics and Poetics of William Carlos Williams, Ann Arbor 1987; John Beck, Writing the Radical Center: William Carlos Williams, John Dewey, and American Cultural Politics, Albany 2001; Dominic Manganiello, Joyce's Politics, London 1980; Ian White, Going with Fergus: James Joyce and the Politics of Irish Nationalism 1891-1916, PhD thesis, University of York 1993.

[4] Bush, Ronald, The Genesis of Ezra Pound's Cantos, 247.

[5] Bush, Ronald, "Excavating the Ideological Faultlines of Modernism," 76; also see Bush, Ronald, "Late Cantos LXXII – CXVII," 111.

[6] Flory, Wendy S., The American Ezra Pound, 85.

[7] "Date Line" (1934), in: LE, 83.

Italy – The Economic Situation

Before we take a closer look at Pound's affection for Mussolini, we must look at the country whose condition obviously contributed to the poet's positive image of the dictator. Reading Pound's hymns on the supposed qualities of Mussolini, we might be tempted to condemn them as misguided expressions of a politcally naïve mind. But before we pass such a severe judgement, we should at least look for reasons which might have caused Pound to imagine that he was living in a culturally and economically prosperous Italy.

After the 1923 reform of the Italian electoral system, 1924 brought new elections with an electoral campaign accompanied by political violence. The outcome of the elections was a clear Fascist majority. After the murder of a Socialist leader, Mussolini declared himself responsible and threatened to silence his critics by force. With the increasing use of censorship and imprisonments, the former movement became a fully-fledged regime in 1925.[8] Control over the press and over academic institutions increased, and several non-fascist organizations were banned. In 1926 Mussolini finally gained full control over parliament by severly restricting its legislative powers.[9]

Economic policy was first marked by a liberal phase under chief economist De' Stefani, who, in order to encourage investments, reformed the tax system and granted private enterprises more freedom beyond state regulations. He was also responsible for privatizations and serious cuts in public spending. In general, Italy recovered from the depression and saw a rise in incomes, savings and employment. But the lira was weak and despite the economic reforms, the shadow of inflation still hovered over the country. Rising prices led to increased stockmarket speculations, which De' Stefani countered with strict controls of stockbrokers. His measures, however, touched the interests of some industrialists who talked Mussolini into sacking his chief economist in 1925. He was succeeded by Giuseppe Volpi, who managed to reduce state debt, supported, among others, by the J. P. Morgan bank that Pound detested so much. Facing a still weak lira, Mussolini swore in 1926 to do his utmost to prevent the currency from collapsing. He ordered his ministers to stabilize the lira at any cost. But when the currency had gained some stability in 1927, the goverment's deflationary policy led to an economic crisis. With a slump in imports and exports, and with unemployment figures rising, it became obvious that the Fascist system had not yet adopted an adequate policy to affect the recovery of Italy's trembling economy. The late twenties saw decreasing wages in some branches of the

[8] Clough, Shepard B., The Economic History of Modern Italy, 220.

[9] The following remarks represent the essence of Clough, Shepard B., The Economic History of Modern Italy, 222-258.

economy. At the same time, the Fascists established measures to cut taxes, keep prices stable and prevent rents from rising.

But all those attempts were too weak to take the pressure off the workers. A number of strikes were organized, particularly in 1925. Because the Italian government was not willing to tolerate social unrest, it re-organized the labor unions in 1926. Strikes became illegal. The Fascist trade unions soon gained a clear hegemony over the labor market, because jobs were increasingly distributed among members of the Fascist party or a Fascist trade union. The result was a corporative state. It underwent another change in February 1934, when – in addition to the existing confederations – 22 Corporations were created. They provided a means to transmit new rules or labor plans to the workers. As a result, the state achieved even stronger control over the economic sector. But that dictatorial power was used to pursue military and imperialistic goals, not to improve the economic condition of the population. In total, the Fascist state still clung to the ideal of private economic initiative, but, in reality, came closer and closer to an interventionist economy. This became evident in Mussolini's movement towards autarchy during the 1930s. Grain exports decreased, as the production of grain in Italy rose to new heights. The "bonifica integrale" was an additional program created in order to improve and cultivate land, reforest mountains and drain marshes, a measure applauded by Pound. Loans to farmers were issued to strengthen small landowners. Apart from that, the government spend large sums on building and construction.

Despite some currency problems, public finances were in a fairly healthy condition. But the U.S. stock market crash of 1929 seriously affected the Italian economy. Net and foreign trade deficit increased, and so did public debt. To counterbalance the effects of the crisis, the state established several public "institutes" to support the private sector by issuing loans and other measures. But unemployment still loomed large. It was one of the problems of Mussolini's policy that it never adopted a rational or sophisticated policy of economic growth. According to Clough, "it never attempted a program of investment on a large scale to create productive plant for the benefit of the collectivity," nor did it strengthen economic ties to other nations.[10] After Italy's invasion of Ethiopia in 1935, the League of Nations imposed sanctions on the Fascist state, sanctions that heavily damaged the Italian economy. For instance, the government was now denied any credit from abroad. But as the sanctions were not carried out seriously, Italy continued to acquire all sorts of goods from abroad. The League's policies even strengthened German-Italian ties, resulting in the Anti-Comintern Pact of November 1937. In 1936, the Bank of Italy became a public institution, other banks were now called "banks of national interest" and were confronted with new regulations that expressed

[10] Clough, Shepard B., The Economic History of Modern Italy, 250.

a new level of state control over banking. A new "credit committee," presided over by Mussolini, functioned as a central institution to control the banks.[11]

Payne offers a critical overall account of Mussolini's economic policy.[12] The fascist economy rested on national syndicalism and productionism as its main pillars. Italy was subject to economic expansion during the twenties, but at the same suffered from inflation. The depression led to an increase in state interventionism, i.e. the creation of state-controlled agencies to support enterprises affected by the crisis. Recovery from the depression was mainly due to expanded arms production. The banking sector was put under state control, in 1936 the Bank of Italy was nationalized and the gold standard abandoned, whereas taxes increased and prices were controlled by the state. The fascists did not achieve thorough structural reforms. They neglected the countryside; many people moved to the cities and few laborers became landowners. When Mussolini addressed the issue of the distribution of wealth in October 1934, by announcing a fight against "want in the midst of plenty,"[13] he stressed a point that many monetary reformers, who were supported by Pound, had also emphasized. But despite his reform claims, Mussolini used conventional means – i.e. debt – to finance public spending, which suggests a good deal of naivité on Pound's side about what Mussolini promised and what he actually did.

Hamilton stresses Mussolini's talent to accomplish short-term reforms with an immediate appeal and a large potential of publicity. As to large-scale reforms, however, Mussolini, to the disappointment of many fascists, sought compromises in order to co-operate with the large landowners and employers. He failed to create a new class of officials, but instead employed many members of the old bureaucracy.[14] Psychologically, however, Mussolini managed to create the image of a moderate dictatorship and succeeded in giving Italy a confidence it had formerly lacked.

Italy – Pound's Perception

Maybe economic facts about Mussolini's Italy would not have convinced Pound, whose attitude towards fascism had a strongly subjective component. When a local fascist commander helped Pound to gain access to a library in

[11] Clough, Shepard B., The Economic History of Modern Italy, 258. For further details on fascist economy see S. La Francesca, La politica economica del fascismo, Bari 1972; Alexander DeGrand, Italian Fascism, Lincoln 1982, 82-88, 105-113; A. James Gregor, Italian Fascism and Developmental Dictatorship, Princeton 1979; for a Pound scholar's view on fascist Italy see Davis, Earle, Vision Fugitive, 163-167.

[12] See Payne, Stanley G., A History of Fascism, 224ff.

[13] Quot. in Davis, Earle, Vision Fugitive, 152.

[14] Hamilton, Alastair, The Appeal of Fascism, 70.

Rimini, where the poet wanted to study some documents on Malatesta, he received a positive impression of fascist activism that would govern his future views.[15] Pound mistook the universal presence of fascist ideology for a real closeness to the people. In 1935, Pound saw only the Italian government as showing a proper interest in the well-being of the people, whereas Germany and France seemed to him enslaved and intoxicated by their own propaganda.[16] Together with the "Italian awakening" of the early 1930s[17] Pound praised the new, state-supervised Italian economy.[18] He even claimed that fascist Italy lived the heritage of Jefferson, Jackson, Van Buren, John and Quincy Adams.[19] The quality of the government left nothing to criticize and Mussolini's "virile" style was what Europe needed in order to maintain its political balance and what Italy required to regain cultural pre-eminence. On the cultural level, Pound dreamed of a new Italian epoch that would approximate the 14th century, when "the very apex of power coincided with the apex of culture."[20] A Confucian ideal and, for Pound, almost reality. On the political level, Pound hoped a strong Italy would prevent Germany from gaining too much hegemony, while a powerful Germany was nevertheless necessary to oppose Russian socialism.[21]

Given Pound's inclination to idealize Italy, it was only logical for him to condemn other political powers that were less impressed by Mussolini's policies. From Italy, he came to regard those states that opposed fascism as mere conspirators who used illegitimate propaganda to attack a peaceful country verbally and suppress its positive achievements.[22] In "Tigullian Studies" (1936) Pound attacked the League of Nations, when he spoke of "Geneva's sanctions and plotting."[23] Whereas the international opponents of Italy were no less than powers of evil to Pound, he perceived Italy as a peaceful and beneficient welfare state. In a 1936 text Pound summarized some model measures that had impressed him:

---

[15] Rainey, Lawrence S., " 'All I Want You to Do Is to Follow the Orders': History, Faith, and Fascism in the Early Cantos," 96f., 104f.

[16] "The Individual in his Milieu" (1935), in: SP, 249.

[17] "Terra Italica" (1931-32), in: SP, 54.

[18] J/M, 44f.

[19] J/M, 12.

[20] "Marches Civilization.." (1934), in: P&P VI.121.

[21] This geopolitical point was at least by made Pound in 1957. He may have idealized his own perspective of the 1930s. See Gordon, David M. (ed.), Ezra Pound and James Laughlin: Selected Letters, 254f., a letter of 3 Dec 1957.

[22] Pound: "I wonder if the press will notice M[ussolini]'s freein the slaves. Or whether THAT will be kept out of the papers [...]," in: Gordon, David M. (ed.), Ezra Pound and James Laughlin, 45, a letter of 21 Oct 1935.

[23] Pound, Ezra, Ezra Pound and Music, 384.

> Work-valids, food-valids, family cheques, the nature of the bank reform, the war on tuberculosis, the distribution of national dividend in rice and maccaroni, the virtual dividend given the small man in the repeated 10 per cent. reduction of RENT, the effect of FIXING the PRICES of food-stuff.[24]

Pound regarded national credit as a fact, just like it supposedly had been in Jefferson's time.[25] But could he ignore that even the well-governed welfare state would sometimes show its military teeth? Flory has pointed out the crucial importance of the year 1935, when Italy invaded Abyssinia, although Mussolini had earlier denounced military adventures.[26] At that time Pound made his fatal decision to ignore the implications of Mussolini's new policy. After the invasion of Abyssinia, Pound accepted fascist propaganda and repeated its hardly justified arguments – that it was necessary to obtain raw materials for Italy, to create a market for the Italian economy, to have a place for the emigration of Italians, and to civilize the natives.[27] He concluded: "The mass of humanity in most of Abyssinia will be better under the Duce's rule, than under that of the Negus."[28] Pound went even so far as to turn the invasion into a philosophical and economic revolution.[29] The invasion of Abyssinia in 1935 constituted for Pound a new "forma mentis," because it created new facts and was part of an active pattern illuminated by the "light of the doer" he praised in C51.[30] Thus the invasion received an almost metaphysical halo and represented no less than a "sacrifice." What, in reality, was an act of violent imperialism, was interpreted by Pound as a political-economic statement designed to fight prevalent lies about credit, money, profits and international usury.[31]

Pound confused his own reformist intentions with the much more pragmatic objectives of Mussolini. By imputing his own intentions to Mussolini, Pound performed an important step from observer to propagandist. This becomes obvious from remarks made by Pound in 1936, which show his increasing tendency to identify his motives with those of fascism and integrate the movement into a context of economic reformism. What he found realized in fascist Italy was "1. Bank reform. (money controlled by the nation

---

[24] "British Labour's Great Blunder" (1936), in: P&P VII.57.
[25] Pound, Ezra, "Borah" [1936], BL 43 / 69 / 3063.
[26] Flory, Wendy S., The American Ezra Pound, 82f.
[27] Wilhelm, James J., Ezra Pound: The Tragic Years, 109.
[28] ("Twelve Years and Twelve Years" (1935), in: P&P VI.349.
[29] For Pound's justification of (supposedly heroic) colonization and conquest, which can be read as a defense of Mussolini's African campaigns, see Pearlman, Daniel D., The Barb of Time, 166.
[30] Hesse, Eva (ed.), Ezra Pound: Usura-Cantos XLV und LI, 95f.
[31] Pound, Ezra, "Italy: The Second Decennio," BL 43 / 108 / 4554, 12.

not by financial bandits.) 2. Wheat law. (just price of wheat.) 3. This week the raise in wages for several million workers."[32] As we will see later, the issue of bank reform and the ideal of the "just price" were exactly the subjects Pound himself so ardently embraced.

Pound's Image of Mussolini as Leader

Although Pound praised the general Italian spirit of the period, he mainly focused his attention on Mussolini. We will later analyze Pound's concept of political leadership, but some remarks on his image of Mussolini are appropriate here. Impressed by the simplicity of the politician and his rhetoric straightforwardness,[33] the poet came to view Mussolini as an alternative to democratic politicians. Pound was not alone in his admiration for the Italian dictator. Mussolini was well-liked among many politicians and intellectuals. European statesmen were on friendly terms with him and he used the years up to 1935 to establish himself as a champion of peace. With the invasion of Ethiopia, Mussolini confirmed the imperial pretensions of his state and damaged Italy's foreign relations. But although he was now no longer Europe's political friend and ally, he nevertheless became a hero in Italy and received wide-spread support from Italians at home and abroad. The sanctions imposed on Italy by the League of Nations (the same sanctions attacked by Pound) aroused a wave of solidarity throughout the country.[34]
For Pound it was Mussolini's well-known Milan speech that cemented his image of Mussolini as an economic genius. On 6 October 1934, the poet claims, Mussolini announced the end of scarcity economics. Pound's enthusiasm reveals more than just a hint of political aestheticism, as the speech reminds him of the sculptor "Brancusi, the stone blocks from which no error emerges, from whatever angle one look at them."[35] Whereas, in C45, Pound diagnoses the loss of demarcations and the decline of stonecutting under usury (C45.229f.), stating that "with usura is no clear demarcation," Mussolini stands as a rhetorical and political monument against the usurers' power. Pound obviously regarded Mussolini as a classicist sculpture, not a real-life politician who was supported by the administration of Sinclair Oil and Jewish financiers like Otto Kahn, Kuehn & Loeb and William Wiseman, some of Pound's favorite scapegoats.[36] Pound's statuesque image of

[32] Pound, Ezra, Ezra Pound and Japan, 31f., a letter of 13 Aug 1936, written from Siena, where Pound was doing research for Cantos 42, 43, 44 and 50.
[33] Pound in 1939: "Duce Mussolini signified among other things a great drive for direct utterance, for clear and simple speaking," see Pound, Ezra, Ezra Pound and Japan, 151.
[34] Hamilton, Alastair, The Appeal of Fascism, 67ff.
[35] J/M, ix.
[36] Wilhelm, James J., Ezra Pound: The Tragic Years (1925-1972), 75.

Mussolini served to counterbalance his more ambiguous image of Europe's other fascist ruler, Hitler, whom he called pathetic and hysteric.[37]

For Pound, Italy's fate rested solely on Mussolini. The Italian system was not actually state-centered, as the state merely had a controlling function to prevent abuse and arbitrate in conflicts.[38] Rather, it was Mussolini, as the central political actor, who sought to create a more human and more representative system.[39] This image of Mussolini as a mediator was influenced by Odon Por, who had attributed the following objectives to the politician: the achievement of social peace by a co-operation of capital and labor; autarchy and business regulations; the introduction of farmers' cooperatives; the cultivation of new land; the establishing of social security measures, adjustment of wages and the control of prices.[40] As Pound emphasized, Mussolini worked towards high standards in both administration and national production, thus becoming "the first man in power to publish any such recognition [of quality] *since*, since whom?- since Sigismond Malatesta, since Cosimo, since what's-his-name, the Elector of Hanover"[41] – a pantheon of Poundian heroes.

Pound's worship of Mussolini continued the poet's cult of strong leaders like Malatesta, John Adams and Jefferson. When Pound claimed to write about Italy as a "Jeffersonian Democrat,"[42] he showed to what large extent Mussolini embodied a larger-than-life image of the American model of dictatorial presidency. But whereas the American ideal has always rested on liberty, Pound conceded that the responsibility of the fascist leader was "vastly higher than the ideal of liberty."[43] It was an ideal concept of responsibility which embraced both the economic "REE- [/] sponsibility" in C43 (C43.218), i.e. responsibility for the capital entrusted to administrators, and the cultural responsibility of a sponsor of the arts. It affected economic well-being and cultural life, both of which reigned supreme in Pound's hierarchy of values, among which liberty played a minor role.

Pound found liberty not even substantially damaged by Mussolini's regime, for he never called it a dictatorship, which would imply severe restrictions on the civil liberties of the citizens. Pound expressed himself very clearly on this point: "Dictatorship is not in our time a word current in Italy.

---

[37] Pound, Ezra, "Italy 1934," BL 43 / 108 / 4551, 2.
[38] "The Revolution Betrayed" (1938), in: P&P VII.285.
[39] "In the Wounds (Memoriam A. R. Orage)" (1935), in: SP, 412.
[40] For Mussolini's economic achievements according to Por see Davis, Earle, Vision Fugitive, 157f.
[41] "Murder by Capital" (1933), in: SP, 200.
[42] "Letters to the Editor" (1934), in: P&P VI.178. A democrat with Republican allegiances, however.
[43] "The Fascist Ideal" (1936), in: P&P VII.47.

The idea here is leadership."[44] Pound avoided strict political terms like dictatorship in connection with his favorite leaders – such terms were not part of his political, but of his polemical vocabulary, and he applied them only to his antagonists. Rather, Pound etsablished links from fascism to Jefferson and Confucius, two persons one would hardly call tyrants. Embedding fascism in a continuity of great political concepts led to, from today's perspective, grotesque results, as when Pound claimed: "You find Hitler almost quoting Confucius; you find Mussolini almost citing Jefferson. The answers to the statal problem are known."[45] Increasingly, Pound glorified both Mussolini and Confucius and began to acknowledge the authoritarian state as an eternal and natural phenomenon.[46] As Redman points out, Pound followed the fascist propaganda in identifying fascism with Mussolini.[47] One could even say that it was quite natural for Pound to believe in this kind of personality cult. After all, it was Pound who had, in the Cantos, praised the outstanding individual and had pursued the ideal of the omniscient, wise ruler who united power and culture. This "monumentalic" strain, as Nietzsche would have called it,[48] led Pound to the assumption that Mussolini embodied the same qualities he had found in Malatesta and Jefferson. He saw both Malatesta and Mussolini as politicians with a strong interest in the integration of cultural elements into politics. Pound hoped that Mussolini would reconcile power and art, thus repeating the achievement of Malatesta.[49] As Pound's quoted comparison of Mussolini's speech and sculpturing proves, the poet saw Mussolini as a creative artist and artifex of many talents.[50] The fact that Pound found an artistic dimension in fascism should not be underestimated. How could the poet have preferred Rapallo to Paris, if he had not discovered a cultural potential in the Italian system?

We will never know what Pound really thought about Mussolini's now obvious mistakes, that is, whether he recognized them, but remained silent, or fully believed in the Italian propaganda. Only from the perspective of later years, Pound attempted a justification of the politician by attributing Mussolini's failure to misinformation – Mussolini had been surrounded by

[44] Pound, Ezra, Polite Essays, 52.

[45] Pound, Ezra, Ezra Pound and Japan, 179; also comp. Redman, Tim, Ezra Pound and Italian Fascism, 76f.

[46] As Bush emphasizes, this tendency became prevalent in about 1940; see Bush, Ronald, "Excavating the Ideological Faultlines of Modernism: Editing Ezra Pound's *Cantos*," 77.

[47] Redman, Tim, Ezra Pound and Italian Fascism, 104.

[48] In his Unzeitgemäße Betrachtungen II: Vom Nutzen und Nachtheil der Historie für das Leben (1874).

[49] Dasenbrock, Reed W., "Pound and the Visual Arts," 233.

[50] Pearlman, Daniel D., The Barb of Time, 141f.

incompetent people who had counseled him insufficiently.[51] This defense of Mussolini once more shows Pound's tendency to maintain a pure image of the fascist leader. He worshipped Mussolini despite the flaws in the latter's character and with an unirritable hope for economic reform. After all, Pound's backing of Italian fascism was consistent with his ideas about social and economic reform.[52]

In terms of politial typology, Pound represents a generic type of fascism, because, although he denied being "fascist," he adhered to its ideological principles.[53] Yet Pound always claimed to be an American patriot and democrat. On the surface, Pound's attitude must appear paradoxical. How could an American intellectual with a deep reverence for politicians like Jefferson and John Adams deliberately champion an ideology for which most Americans felt nothing but hostility? Which of Pound's American roots made it possible for him to embrace, at the same time, sober democracy and Mussolini's opera-like fascism? After all, Pound's American heritage may not have been that harmless.

---

[51] Pound: "There aren't yet twenty americans who can understand Pellizzi's saying (to me) 'IF ONLY he would see you or someone like you. He (Mus) sees all the wrong people. Our job is to reeducate Mussolini.' end quote You can't run forever on misinformation." In: Gordon, David M. (ed.), Ezra Pound and James Laughlin: Selected Letters, 254f., letter of 3 Dec 1957. Camillo Pellizzi was a member of the Institute of Fascist Culture.

[52] Comp. Redman, Tim, Ezra Pound and Italian Fascism, 7.

[53] Casillo, Robert, The Genealogy of Demons, 15.

III.2 Populist Heritage: Conspiracy Theory and the *Cantos*

From Thaddeus Stevens and Coin Harvey to Father Coughlin, and from Brooks and Henry Adams to Ezra Pound, there has been a curiously persistent linkage between anti-Semitism and money and credit obsesssions.

(Richard Hofstadter, *The Age of Reform from Bryan to F.D.R.*).

Introduction

Popular writing is sometimes flawed by sensationalism, which has its traditional place in the headlines of the tabloids and sometimes even in the backlists of serious publishers, but more frequently in the shadowy zone of pamphlet literature. The world of pamphlet literature constantly hovers between fact-finding and polemics, serious investigation and boundless paranoia. Sensationalism promises to unveil important secrets by presenting unseen evidence. It announces shocking revelations about the powerful and the wealthy, and claims to have discovered relations between the elite and some suspicious activity, like armament traffic or financial fraud. When sensationalism is extended into a system, it becomes conspiracy theory. Its fervent forging of legends is supported by the public imagination, as popular culture serves to circulate many smaller narratives that can become part of conspiracy theories.[1]

Pound was not immune to sensationalism and conspiracy theories. Despite the complex arguments discernible in many of his essays, he had a talent for simplification, especially in the field of politics. We all know the typical communist who rages against "the system" – just like Pound did: "The system is unending betrayal. restriction, leading to war."[2] Pound's explicit anti-establishment attitude was nourished by his reading of sensationalist books, some of which I will highlight in the course of this chapter. As Pound's obsessions show links to general cultural tendencies, I will also insert remarks on traditional movements like populism and anti-Semitism. I will

[1] Fenster, Mark, Conspiracy Theories: Secrecy and Power in American Culture, 61.
[2] Gordon, David M. (ed.), Ezra Pound and James Laughlin: Selected Letters, 48, letter of 5 Dec 1935.

argue that parts of Pound's controversial poems are written in a sensationalist style, as he had learned it from some of the works he read – like Brockway's *Bloody Traffic* or Lewinsohn's *Zaharoff*.

It is sometimes assumed that we live in a genuine age of conspiracy theories. Pound's time, however, seems to have welcomed the lure of irrationality no less than present-day readers. During the last years of the 19th century, many pamphlets were published in the U.S., forerunners of later anti-banking and anti-Semitic texts.[3] From the beginning, those pamphlets shared a set of common features by which conspiracy theories can still be distinguished. As leftist critics like Noam Chomsky stress, conspiracy theories often base their assumptions on wrong or incomplete information from doubtful sources, which are often uncredited, anecdotal or apocryphal. They lack documentation and draw illogical or purely speculative conclusions.[4] Conspiracy theorists often target the "internationalism" of bankers, as opposed to national virtues.[5] Conspiracy theorists share the notion of a secret knowledge on which the power of the international bankers is founded.[6] Given to simplifications, conspiracy theories often link polar opposites, especially when dealing with groups defined as enemies. Then we find binary opposites like "the people" versus "the Jew."[7]

Conspiracy theories are part of what Richard Hofstadter has called the "paranoid style." In 1963 Hofstadter delivered his influential lecture on "The Paranoid Style in American Politics," in which he defined the intellectual, mental and rhetorical framework that defines most conspiracy theories. The paranoid style is marked by "heated exaggeration, suspiciousness, and conspirational fantasy."[8] It is usually based on an intense feeling of persecution. A hostile and conspiring group is considered a threat, not only to the individual, but to society, nation or culture as a whole. The political paranoid always imagines the existence of a vast, international conspirational network. But whereas 18th century paranoids imagined conspiracies enacted

[3] Examples of contemporary conspiracy literature include S. E. V. Emery, Seven Financial Conspiracies Which Have Enslaved the American People, Lansing 1887; William H. Harvey, A Tale of Two Nations, Chicago 1894; Gordon Clark, Shylock as Banker, Bondholder, Corruptionist and Conspirator, Washington 1894; Ebenezer Wakely, The Gentile Ass and the Judean Monetary Establishment, Chicago 1895; Mary E. Hobart, The Secret of the Rothschilds, Chicago 1898.

[4] Fenster, Mark, Conspiracy Theories: Secrecy and Power in American Culture, 58.

[5] Johnson, George, Architects of Fear, 24.

[6] For a grotesque survey chart of the alleged connections between medieval usurers, the Rothschilds, the League of Nations and several secret societies see Johnson, George, Architects of Fear, 82. Note the similarities between this pattern and Pound's favorite targets, as outlined in this chapter.

[7] Fenster, Mark, Conspiracy Theories: Secrecy and Power in American Culture, 63f.

[8] Hofstadter, Richard, The Paranoid Style in American Politics and Other Essays, 3.

by obscure sects like the Illuminati, 19th century pamphleteers targetted Catholicism or a wholly secular power: finance. Hofstadter quotes from a Populist party manifesto of 1895, which accuses "the secret cabals of the international gold ring" of undermining the prosperity of the American citizens and the financial independence of the U.S.[9] Hofstadter discovers the paranoid style in the writings of populists who aimed at revealing an alleged conspiracy of bankers, and in the texts of self-appointed "investigators" who thought they had discovered an armament makers' conspiracy in World War I. In Europe, fascism was the genuinely paranoid political movement.[10]

The exponents of the paranoid style not only believe in individual conspiracies, but sometimes see one gigantic conspiracy as the driving force behind history. For them, history itself becomes a conspiracy. Warnings are issued with utmost urgency, as if time could run out any minute, which marks the apocalyptic aspect of the paranoid style. The "enemy" is characterized by some typical, recurring features, which the reader of Pound's texts is likely to associate with the poet's image of armament mogul Basil Zaharoff:

> he is a perfect model of malice, a kind of amoral superman: sinister, ubiquitous, powerful, cruel [...] a free, active, demonic agent. [...] He makes crises, starts runs on banks, causes depressions, manufactures disasters, and then enjoys and profits from the misery he has produced [...] he controls the press; [...] he has unlimited funds [11]

The paranoid style usually has a pseudo-scholarly tendency, as its proponents are always eager to collect "facts" and "proofs" of what they deem the "truth" about the vast conspiracies they suppose to exist. As Hofstadter points out, the paranoid style is not necessarily based on unverifiable facts, but always at some point performs a leap in imagination which leads to sudden, mono-causal conclusions not inherent in the facts themselves. Conspiracy theories are fostered when the representatives of a particular political interest – "perhaps because of the very unrealistic and unrealizable nature of their demands" – find themselves exluded from political bargaining or decision-making processes. Hence, they feel confirmed in their suspicion of hostile, omnipotent powers. This passage in Hofstadter is a brilliant analysis of what actually happened to Pound when he came to realize the ultimate futility of his reformist lobbying in the U.S. during the 1930s.

Pound was no doubt prone to the paranoid style. At an early stage of his career, he imagined a conspiracy of mediocre publishers who used their

---

[9] Hofstadter, Richard, The Paranoid Style in American Politics and Other Essays, 8.

[10] Hofstadter, Richard, The Paranoid Style in American Politics and Other Essays, 7; a thesis which Hofstadter, unfortunately, does not treat in detail.

[11] Hofstadter, Richard, The Paranoid Style in American Politics and Other Essays, 31f.

publishing monopoly to spoil the public through inferior texts.[12] He was interested in conspiracy theories and books like the *Protocols of the Learned Elders of Zion*. As Pound's correspondence with Kitson suggests, the poet was not yet convinced of a Jewish world conspiracy in 1933 to 1935, when he showed no signs of sharing Kitson's views.[13] Yet he surrounded himself with acquaintances of anti-Semitic bias. In a 1935 letter, the economist Hugo Fack claimed history could not be understood without knowing the activities of the Jews. He saw Roosevelt, whom he took to be Jewish, surrounded by malicious Jews. It is difficult to assess the exact influence of such opinions on Pound, because many anti-Semitic remarks represented views common at the time. A very clear influence on Pound, however, were the pamphlets he devoured.

From Pound's remarks in letters and essays, it is possible to establish a Poundian canon of populist-sensationalist literature. One group of works deals with armament firms or dealers. It includes pamphlets like Maurice Rostand, *Les marchands de canons*; Paolo Zappa, *Mercanti di Cannoni*; The Union of Democratic Control, *The Secret International: Armament Firms at Work*; Richard Lewinsohn, *Zaharoff. L'Européen Mystérieux*; Fenner Brockway, *Bloody Traffic*. A second group includes books on economic and political issues: Jeffrey Mark, *The Modern Idolatry, being an Analysis of Usury and the Pathology of Debt*; Arthur Kitson, *The Bankers' Conspiracy! Which Started the World Crisis*; J. R. Jarvie, *The Old Lady Unveiled: A Criticism and an Explanation of the Bank of England*; A. Raffalovitch, *L'Abominable vénalité de la presse: d'après les documents des archives russes 1897-1917*.[14] Most of the mentioned pamphlets were published during the 1930s, a formative period in Pound's life, in which they contributed to his radicalization. As late as 1943, Pound quotes a newspaper article of 1934 which provides details on the allegedly close relations between Morgenthau, Herbert Lehman and the bankers Lewisohn and Warburg.[15]

One of the pamphlets, Brockway's *Bloody Traffic*, may serve to illustrate my point. As is obvious from the beginning, Brockway's book is about (and against) war and profit, about the business of selling arms to both one's own nation and its enemies. It makes statements such as "Mankind must either destroy the Bloody Traffic or be destroyed by it".[16] As Brockway claims, armament firms sell weapons to the enemies of their home country,

---

[12] Chace, William M., The Political Identities of Ezra Pound and T. S. Eliot, 7f.

[13] Surette, Leon, Pound in Purgatory, 216, plus 219 for a brief biography of Kitson.

[14] Some of the passages in which Pound mentions his favorite pamphlets are found in: Stock, Noel, The Life of Ezra Pound, 305 and 313; Pound, Ezra, The Selected Letters of Ezra Pound, 246 and 249.

[15] Pound in a broadcast of 19 March 1943, Pound, Ezra, "Ezra Pound Speaking," 252.

[16] Brockway, Fenner, Bloody Traffic, 19.

they maintain close and profitable ties to banks and influence the press.[17] Armament firms are alleged to have "armed both sides in the wars between Bolivia and Paraguay and Peru and Columbia."[18] Basil Zaharoff serves as the typical example of the perfect arms merchant. He is attributed an amount of influence even larger than that of many politicians: "Zaharoff developed from a mere armament producer and salesman to the status of a great political power."[19]

The pamphlets enhanced Pound's tendency to think in certain typical patterns. What is common to many pamphlets is their attempt to establish links between banking, armament firms and politics. Also, they accuse individual figures of being too wealthy and influential. It is always the same names that occur in this context: Zaharoff, Creusot, Schneider, de Wendel, the Rothschilds. For instance, Lesley Fry, a conspiracy theorist who believed in the *Protocols*, argued that a group of Jewish financiers and politicians ruled the world. Among them he named the Rothschilds, Warburgs, Sassoon, Bernard Baruch and Kuhn, Loeb & Co.[20] Lewinsohn, Zaharoff's unauthorized biographer, mentions Skoda, Schneider and Creusot and close connections between British Prime Minister Balfour and the armament firm Vickers.[21] Paolo Zappa attacks Creusot, Sassoon, Schiff and the Rothschilds; in addition, he calls Talleyrand an ally of international finance, an opinion shared by Pound.[22] Pound attacked the same group of people, and did so with a strong consistency. In 1934 he mentioned the "power of De Wendel, Deterding, Rothermere, Herb. Lawrence, the Schneider family" to influence the press.[23] Almost ten years later, he was still making similar accusations, this time against Dupont, Vickers, Morgenthau, Lehman, Warburg,[24] Sassoon and Sieff.[25]

As the above examples show, Pound readily adopted a mode of thinking that was more common to polemicists than to modernist writers. Hence the question arises how Pound could accept such litanies of hatred.

---

17 Brockway, Fenner, Bloody Traffic, 22, 23, 26, 30f.

18 Brockway, Fenner, Bloody Traffic, 89. Similarly, Pound in item 100, mentioning Argentina, Brazil and Chile.

19 Brockway, Fenner, Bloody Traffic, 47f.

20 Casillo, Robert, The Genealogy of Demons, 355, n. 40. The pamphlet is: Lesley Fry, Waters Flowing Eastward, Chatou: British American Press 1934. For background information on the mentioned bankers see Chace, William M., The Political Identities of Ezra Pound and T. S. Eliot, 231, n. 18.

21 Lewinsohn, Richard, Zaharoff, 83, 90.

22 On Creusot see Zappa, Paolo, Oro Cannoni Democrazie, 32; on the Sassoons, Schiff, Rothschilds see ibid., 58f. For Talleyrand see ibid., 60.

23 "Letters to the Editor" (1934), in: P&P VI.178.

24 Radio broadcast of 7 December 1941, Pound, Ezra, "Ezra Pound Speaking," 21.

25 Radio Broadcast of 30 March 1942, Pound, Ezra, "Ezra Pound Speaking," 79.

Was he not born in a country that has always championed tolerance and liberty? It was precisely his American background, however, that was partly responsible for Pound's submission to the paranoid style.

American Roots: Populism and Agrarianism

Pound grew up in an environment in which the predjudices of populism were not an exception, but common. He spent his childhood in a mining outpost in Idaho, a rough place in an environment where tolerance was not among the prime virtues: "When Ezra was ten, a popular Wyncote hotel announced that it was discontinuing boarding Jews."[26] Chace provides a complex account of Pound's family roots as formative for his later attitudes. The son of a mother with upper-class family ties and pretensions, his father's humble status as a civil servant did not exactly continue the prosperous family tradition. Rather, the Pounds are to be classified among those established families who slowly became displaced in social rank and status by groups of zealous immigrants. The latter possessed a social mobility which the former lacked. Perhaps as important as the real transformations occuring within society was the emotional response of many Americans to the challenges of a changing social order. Chace interprets the rise of populists like Coughlin and Long as a reaction to the inflow of immigrants and the subsequent competition for wealth and status.[27]

Generally speaking, economic problems were one reason for the rise of the populists.[28] The 1890s brought a surge in unemployment and private debt, a situation readily exploited by populists who detected fraud everywhere and did not hesitate to lay the blame for the desolate state of the American economy on "the manufacturers, the railroads, the money-lenders, the middlemen – plutocrats all," as John Hicks remarked in 1931.[29] This antipathy had its roots in some essential beliefs of agrarianism, the once liberal movement of many Jeffersonians. Agrarianism was in every respect a rural movement with a distinct hostility towards certain, typically urban, businesses. Many agrarians disliked banks, just as Andrew Jackson had.[30] They accused the

---

[26] Tytell, John, Ezra Pound: The Solitary Volcano, 16.

[27] Chace, William M., The Political Identities of Ezra Pound and T. S. Eliot, 18f. Chave speculates (!) that Pound's family "would presumably have been quite vulnerable to some of the appeals first of the Populists and later of their more demagogic followers," see Chace, William M., The Political Identities of Ezra Pound and T. S. Eliot, 20.

[28] A perspective adopted, for instance, in: Alan Brinkley, Voices of Protest: Huey Long, Father Coughlin, and the Great Depression, New York 1982.

[29] See Douglas, Louis H. (ed.), Agrarianism in American History, 103.

[30] Even Jackson, held in high esteem by Pound, is now sometimes regarded as a populist, e.g. in McKenna, George (ed.), American Populism, 73f.

banks of artificially creating a demand for credits. Agrarians mistrusted the world of finance; what they believed in was land. In 1852 a member of the House of Representatives, W. Cobb, claimed that land was "the true basis of all individual and national prosperity."[31] One is reminded of the Poundian "abundance of nature," as embodied by the Sienese pastures in Cantos 42 to 44. The same tendency was already discernible in one of the founding fathers of American agrarianism, John Taylor (1753-1824), a farmer, Jeffersonian Democrat, U.S. Senator and one of the early opponents of an American central government. He defended his views in *An Inquiry into the Principles and Policy of the Government of the United States* (1814). For Taylor the banking system was an elite aristocacy, worse (and affecting more damage) than national debt. He accused the founders of the first Bank of the United States of a conspiracy. They had founded the bank, Taylor claimed, solely in order to turn their stocks into money. In general, bankers had too much influence on decisions of the government while at the same time showing no sense of public responsibility.[32] We will encounter this notion again later.

The more "reasonable" side of populist agrarianism was its call for economic reforms. A paper published by the People's Party Platform in 1896 reveals some striking similarities to Pound's reformism:

> We demand that the volume of circulating medium be speedily increased to an amount sufficient to meet the demand of the business and population, and to restore the just level of prices of labor and production. [...] We denounce the sale of bonds and the increase of the public interest-bearing debt made by the present Administration [...] We demand such legislation as will prevent the demonetization of the lawful money of the United States by private contract.[33]

This pamphlet contains three demands that Pound would repeat in the 1930s. First, the establishing of a "just price;" second, the abolition of public debt; third, the exclusion of private interests from American monetary policy.

The populists' call for an improvement of the economic situation of the "common people" had always included an anti-banking bias. At the beginning of the 20th century, American populists frequently used epithets like "Rothschild," but less as a degradation of Jews than to denote Wall Street and English bankers, which were then presented as the farmers' enemies. One populist who addressed the issue was an early hero of eleven-year-old Pound, W. J. Bryan. He attacked both the banking establishment and the gold

[31] Quot. in: Douglas, Louis H. (ed.), Agrarianism in American History, 48.

[32] Hill, C. William, The Political Theory of John Taylor of Caroline, 111-115. For Taylor's views on banking and finance see Shalhope, Robert E., John Taylor of Caroline: Pastoral Republican, 76-81.

[33] Quot. in: Douglas, Louis H. (ed.), Agrarianism in American History, 100f.

standard.[34] Scholnick quotes Bryan as saying: "Our opponents have somtetimes tried to make it appear that we were attacking a race when we denounced the financial policy of the Rothschilds. But we are not ... attacking a race; we are attacking greed and avarice, which know neither race nor religion."[35] Yet what began as commitment to economic improvements finally turned into anti-Semitic predjudice. Although it possessed liberal and progressive roots and desired economic reforms, populism was both Manichean and xenophobic, dividing the world into "us" and "them," into good producers or businessmen on the one hand, and evil financiers and parasitic monopolists on the other.

The predjudices of American populism were the open expression of veiled resentments also shared by members of the elite: "While the silverites were raging openly and earnestly against the bankers and the Jews, Brooks and Henry Adams were expressing in their sardonic and morosely cynical private correspondence the same feelings," as Hofstadter concludes.[36] Hofstadter interprets the resentments of populists and elite as a reaction against the prevailing power of industrialism and a new financial aristocracy. The "gentlemen" longed for the vanished splendour of their class, while the populists dreamed of an agrarian democracy. What united them was their opponent, the *nouveau riche* capitalist. Populism embraced a shared set of assumptions: "the idea of a golden age; the concept of natural harmonies; the dualistic version of social struggles; the conspiracy theory of history; and the doctrine of the primacy of money," notions that were strongly derived from the agrarian tradition.[37] They adhered to Jacksonian principles and opposed special privileges. They regarded land as America's wealth and assumed a natural order which was disturbed only by human influence. Their concept of society was manichean: here the honest producers of real wealth, there the

---

[34] Tytell, John, Ezra Pound: The Solitary Volcano, 17f.

[35] Quot. in Scholnick, Myron I., The New Deal and Anti-Semitism in America, 45. William J. Bryan (1860-1925) was one of the most impressive populists of his age and is now well-remembered as a political orator of outstanding vigor. As a Democratic leader he ran for the U.S. presidency in 1896, 1900 and 1908, but always failed to achieve his goal. His influence showed in the adoption of several political reforms. Because of his Midwestern roots he identified himself with agrarian interests. See Louis W. Koenig, Bryan: A Political Biography, New York 1971; Paolo E. Coletta, William Jennings Bryan, 3 vols., Lincoln 1964-1969. For W. J. Bryan as an enemy of usury see Hollis, Christopher, The Two Nations, 214.

[36] Hofstadter, Richard, The Age of Reform from Bryan to F.D.R., 91.

[37] Hofstadter, Richard, The Age of Reform from Bryan to F.D.R., 62. Hofstadter: "The populists looked backward with longing to the lost agrarian Eden, to the republican America of the earl years of the nineteenth century in which there were few millionaires and, as they saw it, no beggars, when the laborer had excellent prospects and the farmer had abundance, when statesmen still responded to the mood of the people and there was no such thing as the money power," ibid.

monopolists of money. For all their radicality, they were more than just a marginal group. They even had representatives in the U.S. Senate. In 1891 Senator Pfeffer called for "the destruction of the money power." And a later manifesto by Ray A. Billington declared war on "the allied hosts of monopolies, the money power, great trusts and railroad corporation."[38] In total, many populists held the conviction that American history since the Civil War was secretly dominated by a conspiracy of the international aristocrats of money.

Performing the step from reformism to fanatism, we now come to one of the most eminent populists, and one of the most radical. Scholars have identified Huey Long and Father Coughlin as American populists with fascist tendencies.[39] Unfortunately, the latter found an ardent admirer in Ezra Pound.

Father Coughlin

Charles E. Coughlin (1891-1979), called the "Radio Preacher," was one of the most crucial populist influences on Pound.[40] Pound was aware of the fact that Coughlin's used "polemics," not reasonable arguments, but nevertheless regarded him as important.[41]

Pound was only one among many who appreciated the preacher. Known as the "radio priest," Coughlin made use of the medium to reach an audience of thousands of people after 1930. Originally a supporter of Roosevelt, he soon opposed the New Deal, as well as communism, finance and the Jews. Because of the radicality of his views, his superiors would finally prohibit him from broadcasting.[42] Coughlin was more of a Savonarola than a civic pastor. Apart from basic links between Coughlin and right-wing conspiracy theorists,[43] he is now considered by some scholars as a proto-

[38] Both quot. in Hofstadter, Richard, The Age of Reform from Bryan to F.D.R., 64f.
[39] Lipset, Seymour M. / Raab, Earl, The Politics of Unreason, 152.
[40] As should be noted, Coughlin was a Catholic. Surette claims that both Pound and the populists were anti-Semitic, right wing, anti-socialist and anti-Catholic (Surette, Leon, Pound in Purgatory, 67ff.). We regard this as an over-simplification. Pound's support for the Catholic Coughlin was free from anti-Catholic sentiments on Pound's side. As we will emphasize in chapter III.5, Pound's antipathy was mainly directed against Catholicism as an institution, not against every member of the Catholic community. Despite the simplifications, Surette gives a fairly balanced account of Coughlin and his influence on Pound in: Surette, Leon, Pound in Purgatory, 261f.
[41] Pound, Ezra, "Italy: The Second Decennio," BL 43 / 108 / 4554, 9.
[42] On Coughlin see, for instance, Scholnick, Myron I., The New Deal and Anti-Semitism in America, 73-77; Johnson, George, Architects of Fear, 99f. For a general account of Roosevelt's New Deal policy see Bernstein, Michael Alan, The Great Depression, 184-206.
[43] Bieberstein, Johannes Rogala von, Die These von der Verschwörung 1776-1945, 144.

fascist. Ferkiss calls Coughlin one of the founding fathers of American fascism, whose beginning he dates to 1930. Its economic program championed strong governmenal controls in key areas as well as "control of the monetary supply so as to stabilize the ratio between goods and prices and to destroy the usury of private banking."[44] The pledge for monetary reform was common among American populists of the 1930s. Huey Long championed the redistribution of wealth. The anti-Semitic journalist William D. Pelley wrote a whole book about the subject.[45] According to Ferkiss, Coughlin wanted to organize a corporate state, an idea also embraced by Pound.[46] In brief, Coughlin's favorite subjects included the necessity of government control and ownership of banks, the virtues of state capitalism, anti-Semitism, anti-communism, plus aversions against Roosevelt, the New Deal, international financial conspiracies and other forms of monopoly.

Before 1936, Coughlin avoided direct verbal attacks on Jews. Instead, he directed his verbal assaults at international bankers, which were of course only too often identified with Jews. To him, Morgenthau was a particularly close ally of those bankers.[47] In a panic reaction against war and economic collapse, Coughlin's anti-Semitism increased after 1934, as did his violent verbal attacks on the Rothschilds, the Lazars, Warburgs, Kuehn-Loebs and Morgans. Coughlin suspected the Jews of controlling the media and of giving financial support to Communists. He regarded them as a minority, but a particularly aggressive one.[48] In many speeches from 1930 to 1936, Coughlin often referred to the usual, mostly Jewish, bankers, i.e. those also mentioned by Pound: the Rothschilds, Morgans, Kuhns and Loebs.[49] In the *New York Times* of 12 March 1935 Coughlin named some of the people Pound, too, never ceased to mention: Baruch, "the Rothschilds in Europe ... the Warburgs, the Kuhn-Loebs, the Morgans and the rest of that wrecking crew of internationalists whose God is gold and whose emblem is the red shield of exploitation."[50] In addition, Coughlin, like Pound, would quote from the anti-Semitic *Protocols of the Elders of Zion* after 1937.

Coughlin treated financial issues in the book *The New Deal in Money*, in which he strongly argued against international bankers. In a populist

---

[44] Ferkiss, Victor C., "Populist Influences on American Fascism," 311.
[45] Pelley, No More Hunger, Asheville 1936.
[46] Ferkiss, Victor C., "Populist Influences on American Fascism," 313.
[47] Scholnick, Myron I., The New Deal and Anti-Semitism in America, 74f.
[48] Athans, Mary C., The Coughlin-Fahey Connection, 171. See ibid., chapter V, 153-207 for a general treatment of Coughlin's anti-Semitism. See 138f. for a religious version of classic conspiracy theories about alleged Jewish internationalism and manipulations of the money market.
[49] Lipset, Seymour M. / Raab, Earl, The Politics of Unreason, 182.
[50] Quot. in Scholnick, Myron I., The New Deal and Anti-Semitism in America, 75f. Germ. "Rothschild" means "red shield."

manner, he warned his readers of unsound money and bankers who wanted "your farm, your business and your job, your cheap wheat and your high debts."[51] He attacked the financial power of the "international" Rothschilds after 1816 and the "powers of the Morgans, the Kuhn-Loebs, the Rothschilds, the Wall Street international tyrants."[52] He spoke of "the two modern Shylocks, the United States bankers and the Bank of France," and called the right of the Federal Reserve Bank to print money an "unconstitutional privilege."[53] In *Father Coughlin's Radio Discourses*, Coughlin devoted a whole chapter, "The Next War," to loans and the malpractices of financiers. Sharing a Rothschild legend always well-liked among conspiracy theorists, Coughlin explains in his book how a "little money changer" rose to power after the battle of Waterloo.[54] Since then, mankind has been enslaved by international finance, the preacher claims.

Coughlin's radicalism left its traces in the *Cantos*. Pound read Coughlin's *Money!* in October 1936, discovering a master of the paranoid style. C46 uses Coughlin as a source.

> Said Mr RothSchild, hell knows which Roth-schild
> 1861, '64 or there sometime, " Very few people
> " will understand this. Those who do will be occupied
> " getting profits. The general public will probably not
> " see it's against their interest."
>
> (C46.233)

The passage derives from Coughlin's *Money!* Coughlin quotes from a letter of 25 June 1863, allegedly written by the "Rothschild Brothers" to "Messrs. Ikleheimer, Morton and Vandergould," New York, concerning the establishment of a National Bank for New York. The Rothschilds quote from a letter by a "John Sherman," who advises them to found a National Bank, as follows:

> The few who can understand the system [...] will either be so interested in its profits, or so dependent on its favors, that there will be no opposition from that class, while on the other hand, the great body of the people, mentally incapable of comprehending the tremendous advantages what capital derives from the system, will

---

[51] Coughlin, Charles E., The New Deal in Money, 17.

[52] Coughlin, Charles E., The New Deal in Money, 43. For Coughlin's attacks on the Morgans, Kuhn-Loebs, Warburgs, and Kreuger see Coughlin, Charles E., The New Deal in Money, 91, on Lazere see 109, on Bernard Baruch see 92f.

[53] Coughlin, Charles E., The New Deal in Money, 20, 30.

[54] Coughlin, Charles, Father Coughlin's Radio Discourses, 163. Comp. items 100f. and the paragraph on "The Rothschilds" in the present chapter.

> bear its burdens without complaint and perhaps without even suspecting that the system is inimical to their interests.[55]

In addition to deleting the exact date of the letter (1863), Pound also changed the register, making the quotation less formal. In Pound's text, the system is not "inimical to," but simply "against" their interest. Hence, the populist source (which is doubtful from the beginning) is simplified even more in order to make the message as clear as possible: a warning against Jewish bankers.

Anti-Semitism

After encountering the radicality of Coughlin, it is time for some words about Pound's anti-Semitic predjudices, a subject that has gained increasing attention during recent decades. Scholars have identified influences and contexts that made Pound's anti-Semitism possible, and their contextual approach has replaced the evasiveness of New Criticism, which was the origin of apologetic Pound criticism that remained silent about the subject.[56] Psychologizing is another problem to be avoided – Flory, for instance, claims that Pound's anti-Semitism derived fully from a psychosis. After Mussolini's invasion of Abyssinia in October 1935, Pound's state of mind detoriated, because the poet had to rationalize the dictator's aggressive policies by turning him and Hitler into economic reformers threatened by an international conspiracy of Jewish usurers and arms dealers.[57] Although Flory acknowledges the existence of a "common" anti-Semitism in the U.S., she does not explore the American roots of Pound's radical notions.[58] Exploring Pound's populist roots, however, allows us to challenge Chace's claim that Pound was "a most unusual kind of anti-Semite"[59] and to ask whether his anti-Semitism was not in fact rather ordinary.

Anti-Semitism became a minor, yet recognizable force among American extremists during the latter half of the 19th century.[60] At that time, anti-Semitism was not despised in society, but represented a common social

---

[55] Coughlin, Charles, Money!, 170f., also in Coughlin, Charles E., The New Deal in Money, 88. Pound cites the letter in several published and unpublished texts, such as "Nesckek Rothschild Arrested" [1938], BL 43 / 113 / 4850; "The American System: Why not revive it?" [1939/40?], BL 43 / 67 / 2913, 3f.; SP, 281.

[56] I follow Casillo, Robert, The Genealogy of Demons, 9.

[57] Flory, Wendy S., "Pound and Anisemitism," 287-290.

[58] For other common positions on Pound's anti-Semitism see Casillo, Robert, The Genealogy of Demons, 8-16.

[59] Chace, William M., The Political Identities of Ezra Pound and T. S. Eliot, 3.

[60] Lipset, Seymour M. / Raab, Earl, The Politics of Unreason, 92-95.

predjudice even used by political groups, particularly the populists.[61] The obvious presence of Jewish communities in the cities increased with new waves of immigration from Eastern Europe, a tendency not welcomed by everybody. Many agrarian groups added xenophobia to populism and nationalism, and attacked what finally became the cliché of "the Jewish banker." In an attempt to benefit from the unease of many farmers, who saw banking institutions as the primary source of their financial troubles, agrarian populists created the image of the non-producing, capitalist usurer.

In the cities, Jews experienced the hostility of other immigrant groups, with whom they competed for status and wealth. In addition to that, many upper-class groups were not free from anti-Semitism, too, which resulted in the exclusion of Jews from clubs. Henry Ford was another member of the upper-class who, in his *Dearborn Independent*, warned the common people against the far-reaching influence of Jewish financiers.[62] The so-called intellectual elite also participated in anti-Jewish predjudice. Henry and Brooks Adams, for instance, used their private correspondence for many an attack on what they deemed a Jewish syndicate which, as they believed, controlled the world from London. In total, the assumption of an "international conspiracy of finance" was much more than merely a *suburban* predjudice – it was a commonplace among populists and paranoids alike.

Significantly enough, American anti-Semitism before 1890 centered on financial issues and portrayed Jews as sinister Shylocks of usurious character. In the years around the panic of 1837, populists attacked the Rothschilds for their alleged influence on the American economy.[63] Some politicians were denounced as agents of Jewish bankers. As early as 1890, the Jews were considered a subversive race, which sought to control the international money markets and was able to create economic depressions. The 1920s saw a rise in biological anti-Semitism. Jews were now portrayed as "part-banker controlling the world economy, part-Bolshevist subverting the nation, and a racial pariah destroying Anglo-Saxon America."[64] During the 1930s, anti-Semitism would become an integral notion of populist/facist groups, among them Pelley's Silver Shirts and Coughlin's followers.

---

[61] For historical surveys see Leonard Dinnerstein, Antisemitism in America, New York 1994; Louise A. Mayo, The Ambivalent Image: Nineteenth-Century America's Perception of the Jew, London 1988. Mayo remarks: "There is no doubt that in their intense hatred for the 'money power,' some Populists accepted anti-Semitic stereotypes and identified Jews with the evils of society. [...] There is doubt, however, that the Populists did this any more frequently than other groups in society." Thus Mayo, Louise A., The Ambivalent Image, 131.

[62] On Henry Ford's anti-Semitism see Lipset, Seymour M. / Raab, Earl, The Politics of Unreason, 135-138.

[63] Hofstadter, Richard, The Age of Reform from Bryan to F.D.R., 77f.

[64] Bayor, Ronald H., "Klans, Coughlinites and Aryan Nations," 580.

During the 1920s Henry Ford's newspaper, the *Dearborn Independent*, published a series called "The International Jew." It contained many theories and suspicions typical of what Pound later called "suburban" anti-Semitism. Without condemning Jews on racial grounds, as biologically oriented anti-Semitism did, the series nevertheless showed marked signs of racist paranoia: Jewish bankers, it claimed, manipulated American presidents, corrupted American culture, dominated many branches of industry and had assumed control over America's financial markets. The names occuring in "The International Jew" were largely identical with those Pound and Coughlin attacked – the Rothschilds, Jacob Schiff, Bernard M. Baruch, Paul Warburg. Of course, the authenticity of the *Protocols* was simply taken for granted.[65]

After 1933, many right-wing anti-Semites and members of the "Upper Class" grew increasingly hostile towards the New Deal policies of the Roosevelt government, policies they believed were initiated by Jews whom they alleged to have infiltrated the administration. Like Pound, they saw Roosevelt surrounded by Jewish advisers. In their excessive hatred, some even went so far as to believe Roosevelt himself had Jewish ancestors.[66] The extremist Winrod, for instance, denounced the Roosevelt administration as controlled by Jews.[67] Others regarded all Jews as agents of Communism and warned of their revolutionary potential.[68]

Anti-Semitism was also common in the circles in which Pound moved. Arthur Kitson, with whom Pound exchanged letters, attacked "Jew moneylenders" whom he supposed to rule the great banking houses of the Western world. And a figure like *New Age* contributor J. Finn uttered a thought later adopted by Pound: The rich Jews were above anti-Semitism, while the poor Jews had to suffer.[69] C. H. Douglas eventually not only blamed the Freemasons, but also the Jews for the lack of success of his Social Credit theory.[70] Surette diagnoses a prevalence of anti-Semitism among underconsumptionists like Douglas, Kitson, Chesterton, Belloc and Orage.[71] Pound's friend Wyndham Lewis made disparaging remarks on "the extremely bad manners and barbaric aggressiveness of the eastern slum-Jew immigrant, dumped into America yearly in such great numbers."[72] He demanded that one should find a "*modus vivendi*" to live with Jews, but mostly stressed their

65 See Ribuffo, Leo P., "Henry Ford and *The International Jew*," in: Jeffrey S. Gurock (ed.), Anti-Semitism in America 1 (= American Jewish History 6), 2 vols., New York / London 1998, 413-453.
66 Scholnick, Myron I., The New Deal and Anti-Semitism in America, 62 passim.
67 Lipset, Seymour M. / Raab, Earl, The Politics of Unreason, 160.
68 Scholnick, Myron I., The New Deal and Anti-Semitism in America, 80.
69 Redman, Tim, Ezra Pound and Italian Fascism, 39.
70 Wilhelm, James J., Ezra Pound: The Tragic Years (1925-1972), 61.
71 Surette, Leon, Pound in Purgatory, 61.
72 Lewis, Wyndham, Hitler, 36.

negative sides. Lewis expected that Hitler, once in power, would behave moderately towards the ordinary Jews and would tolerate Jews like Einstein, but fight the Jewish bankers. Christopher Hollis, whose *The Two Nations* Pound read with great interest, said: "Jews have been the world's usurers."[73]

We could finally mention another influence on Pound, William Hope Harvey (1851-1936), an American writer on economics, sometimes called "Coin Harvey." He was a vigorous advocate of bimetallism[74] when the argument over the coinage of silver was at its height. Through his pamphlets Harvey wielded great influence on the populists. His novel *A Tale of Two Nations* tells the story of London banker called "Baron Rothe" who develops a plot in order to prevent the U.S. from using a silver currency. Pound mentions Harvey in a fragment (item 223) and calls his heritage a worthy tradition – the confession of an American poet in search for intellectual roots.

Like American anti-Semitism in general, Pound's anti-Semitism, too, underwent a development from predjudice to biologism. According to Casillo, Pound's anti-Semitism can be divided into four groups: suburban predjudice (1885-1910), overtly anti-Semitic remarks (1910-20, after his brief return to the U.S., when he learned about Jewish immigration), a virulent stage from 1920 to the late 1930s, followed by a final phase of biological racism after 1940.[75] As early as 1912, when he wrote "Patria Mia," Pound showed clear traces of anti-Semitism. At that point he placed the Jews among those "alien forces" he believed to have infiltrated the older, Anglo-Saxon population of the U.S. As Chace suspects, this early anti-Semitism may have been "a direct legacy of his family background and social class, Protestant professional and upper-middle class."[76] Pound's anti-Semitism increased towards the end of the 1930s. In his essays, the identification of Jewry and financial practice became more dogmatic and fierce. Pound's anti-Semitism began as a mere "sneering" at the Jews, but during the 1930s, it developed into a set of conspiracy theories.[77] In the years around 1937, Pound's anti-Semitism grew stronger and in 1939 he even advocated the idea of racial purity as opposed to any melting-pot concept of racial integration.[78] Thus, he came dangerously close to ideas that right-wing nationalists were promoting in certain parts of Europe, most fervently in Nazi Germany.

---

[73] Hollis, Christopher, The Two Nations, 140.

[74] I.e. the use of a silver and gold currency, as opposed to the use of a mere gold currency.

[75] Casillo, Robert, The Genealogy of Demons, 4ff. Surette has the final stage begin after 1934.

[76] Chace, William M., The Political Identities of Ezra Pound and T. S. Eliot, 7.

[77] Goldensohn, Barry, "Pound and Antisemitism," 401.

[78] Redman, Tim, Ezra Pound and Italian Fascism, 176ff., 196.

Although the young poet had had positive experiences with Jews,[79] he later left no doubt about his antipathy to them. To him they represented an amorphous mass whose prevalence would throw society into decadence. In his family memoir *Indiscretions* Pound provides a good example of this notion, when he talks about cultural decadence of the U.S.:

> Old man Bohun was not only a gentleman but the fine old type. And his son is a stockbroker, roaring himself hoarse every day in the Wheat Pit [...]; and *his* son will look like a Jew, and his grandson, old Bohun's great-grandson, will talk Yiddish. Aud [sic!] this dissolution is taking place in hundreds of American families who have not thought of it as a decadence and may, reasonably, be mirrored in the national modus and institutions [80]

Whereas Pound praised Mussolini and his speeches as the expression of a statuesque personality with clear thoughts, the Jews represented a confused mode of thinking without the "unwavering middle" Pound had discovered in the teachings of Confucius: "The Semitic poison is in the Semite tempered by Semitic instability, by the Semite's wobble from one excess to another."[81] This alleged "poison" had been injected into European culture. It was a European error to treat Jewish culture seriously, Pound emphasized, and for that error Europe had paid.[82] Pound saw European tolerance towards Jews as a sign of decadence. As Pound believed, even the Christian Church had originally been anti-Semitic and had opposed "near-eastern superstition." Its decay began with "banker popes and the revival of semitic texts" as mythology.[83] As opposed to both the Roman concept of empire and the medieval sense of form, Pound accused the Jews of never having gained cultural or artistic importance. Hence, Pound claimed the cathedrals were "built in open defiance of the Jew slime, and of the Talmud. They are an offense in the eye of the Jew; they are what his oily race has NOT accomplished."[84] Pound's 1942 words take his predjudice to a new, biological level – Jews are not only used as scape-goats of economic shortcomings, but, in *Guide to Kulchur*, are criticized on a broader level, as a threat to mental clarity.

---

[79] Tytell: "Disembarking in Gibraltar in April, he met a Jewish man who helped him find accommodations and work as a guide, and who took him to a synagogue, where Pound watched a rabbi pass around a snuffbox after a ceremony. The snuff was passed to Pound." See Tytell, John, Ezra Pound: The Solitary Volcano, 35.

[80] Pound, Ezra, Indiscretions, 58.

[81] "The Revolution Betrayed" (1938), in: P&P VII.279.

[82] Pound, Ezra, "Jewish Legacy" [1940], BL 43 / 109 / 4586.

[83] "Ecclesia" (1939), in: P&P VII.470.

[84] Pound on 26 July 1942, Pound, Ezra, "Ezra Pound Speaking," 219.

This contradicts Pound's claims that he was not attacking the Jews as a race, but only as individuals. On the one hand, he regarded the Jewish people as a "sacrificial goat for the usurer," who would always try to hide and leave "the plain man Jew to take the bullets and beatings."[85] Pound saw the common Jews "endangered by the activities of high finance and monopoly."[86] On the other hand, Pound transferred the negative properties of individuals to Jewry in general: "A race may possibly be held responsible for its worst individuals. The Jewish race has not for ages taken the responsibility for the enforcement of its own law," as in the case of Jesus, whose crucifixion was executed by the Romans, not the Jews. Cynically, Pound accused the Jews of having contributed to the contempt they encountered: "The Jew has brought anti-Semitism on himself by LACK OF ORGANISATION, by refusal to undertake responsibility."[87] This was not written during the 1940s, but in 1938, only one year after the publication of *The Fifth Decad*.

Another target of Pound were what he denoted by the curious term "aryo-kikes," which calls up associations with mob anti-Semitism (the colloquial, contemptuous word "kike") and bio-racism (the division of races into aryans and Jews). This group includes such bankers as Morgan and Baruch, and politicians like Morgenthau. Given to "false morals" and envy, they are, in Pound's eyes, worse than Jews.[88] In 1938 Pound was very clear about his opinion: "The aryio-kike is filthiness of whatever racial compost; he has all vices which the anti-semite attributes to the Jew. [...] The monopolists of money are the lowest and largest variety of louse known to man, and no mercy is due to them."[89] Pound's introduction of a category like "aryo-kike" to denote the most negative representatives of finance does not imply a more moderate view on "proper" Jews. After all, the poet did not hesitate to refer to statements by Hitler when denouncing Jews and bankers.[90] Although Pound acknowledged Jewish achievements,[91] he would not accept a zionist like Israel Sieff.[92]

[85] "American Notes" (1935), in: P&P VI.343.
[86] Gordon, David M. (ed.), Ezra Pound and James Laughlin: Selected Letters, 113, 18 Jan 1940.
[87] "The Revolution Betrayed" (1938), in: P&P VII.280. Also comp. Gordon, David M. (ed.), Ezra Pound and James Laughlin, 114f., letter of 24 Feb 1940.
[88] "The Revolution Betrayed" (1938), in: P&P VII.279ff.; also Pound, Ezra, "Is Antisemitism a Dangerous Subject?," BL 43 / 108 / 4546, 2.
[89] "Symposium - I. Consegna" (1938), in: P&P VII.337f.
[90] Pound, Ezra, BL 43 / 66 / 2899.
[91] Pound, Ezra, "Is Antisemitism a Dangerous Subject?," BL 43 / 108 / 4546, 1.
[92] Israel Sieff (1889-1972) was a British industrialist and Zionist. He collaborated with Weizmann in Zionist affairs and was associated with a number of Zionist and educational organizations in England (EB).

In the end, aggression and ridicule prevailed in Pound. For him, "These pimps for Lazard, Rothschild, Beir, Sieff etc/ are all part of a pox," as he wrote in a letter to Senator Burton K. Wheeler of 18 June 1940.[93] As to the ridicule – it can be felt, for instance, in a poem on Bernard Baruch as the typical Jewish usurer: "When grandma's stock went down, [/] They *said* he'd been in town."[94] This was not the later Pound of the 1940s, when, as some scholars suppose, he conducted the fiercest attacks on Jews. Just months before the publication of *The Fifth Decad*, he wrote in a letter to Lina Caico of 15 or 16 March 1937: "I know ALL about jews/ [...] They are the GREAT destroyers of value/ the obliterators of all demarcations/ the shifters of boundary stones. // Occasionally a good one has to suffer for the sins of the race."[95] At this point, Pound revealed how little he believed in his own words about the merits of the race, as opposed to some negative individuals. He now talked about races, not persons, and fully adopted the paranoid style.

Among the Pound papers, we find traces of polemics and myths well-used in populist conspiracy theories. Item 24 includes a reference to Freemasons and the so-called Elders of Zion. This represents a remarkable combination of two typical scapegoats of populism. Freemasons have always been accused of plotting diabolically against mankind. In the *Protocols of the Learned Elders of Zion*, Jews and Freemasons are claimed to have developed plans for the destruction of Christian civilization and the erection of a world state under their rule. Although identified as a forgery as early as 1921, the *Protocols* had a lasting influence on anti-Semites around the globe.[96]

The Poundian lines about the Jews and the Civil War (C48.241) are a reference to the American fascist William D. Pelley (1890-1965). Scholnick calls Pelley one of the most fervent "professional Jew-baiters."[97] An admirer of Hitler, he founded the fascist Silver Shirts in 1933 and subsequently published the weekly *Liberation*. Pelley praised the *Protocols* and condemned Jews like Baruch, whom he claimed to control the U.S. government and the League of Nations.[98] For him, the Jews represented international financial manipulation and the spiritual destruction of Christian America. Pound refers to Pelley's article "The Mystery of the Civil War and Lincoln's Death" in *Liberation* 5.25 (10 Feb 1934), where Pelley writes: "According to Bismarck, the awful Civil War in America was fomented by a Jewish Conspiracy, and

[93] Quot. in Redman, Tim, Ezra Pound and Italian Fascism, 201.
[94] "Very Old Tune" (1934), in: P&P VI.128.
[95] Quot. in Redman, Tim, Ezra Pound and Italian Fascism, 177.
[96] On the *Protocols* see Bieberstein, Johannes Rogala von, Die These von der Verschwörung 1776-1945, 138 passim. Henry Ford's newspaper, the *Dearborn Independent*, often cited them as evidence of a Jewish threat.
[97] Scholnick, Myron I., The New Deal and Anti-Semitism in America, 80.
[98] Scholnick, Myron I., The New Deal and Anti-Semitism in America, 80f.; Bayor, Ronald H., "Klans, Coughlinites and Aryan Nations," 582ff.

Abraham Lincoln, the hero and national saint of the United States, was killed by the same Hidden Hand which killed six Romanov czars, ten kings, and scores of ministers only to bleed nations."[99] Pound has some irritating remarks to offer about this passage, remarks he made to his friend Zukofsky (a Jew!) on 6/7 May 1934: "Mr Pelley's dope about Bizmark sounds all right. [...] Speakin to you aza anti-semite?? If you don't want to be confused with yr/ ancestral race and progromd ... it wd/ be well to modernize."[100]

Scholars have attempted different explanations for Pound's anti-Semitism. Flory champions a political approach: As she claims, Pound felt little hatred of individual – and especially poor – Jews, but disliked them as a group that was supposedly under the control of international capitalists. Hence, Pound's was a political anti-Semitism.[101] Casillo argues in psychological terms: The Jews are essential to the Cantos, because they represent "the unrecognized double of the confusion and uncertainty which lurks at the putative center or core of Pound's writing." Assigning his own difference and "confused otherness" to the Jews in an act of violent repression, the poet can approach a clarity he would not achieve otherwise – the clear definition of terms.[102] Within a historical context, Pound represents a particularly American anti-Semitism. On the one hand, a common anti-Semitism that excluded Jews from certain social activities, but shunned the overt violence of pogroms.[103] On the other hand, it was an anti-Semitism of *verbal* pogroms, like the general condemnation of Jews for alleged crimes committed by some of them. It expressed itself in rhetorical violence and accusations based on doubtful evidence.

With verbal means, Pound sought to deconstruct the Jews and at the same time reveal the hidden Jewishness of finance. And he would play revealing games with words. A draft in the context of C48 carries a sequence of words which visualize that impulse (item 199). The name of economist John M. Keynes is transformed, in several shiftings of individual letters, from Keynes to Cohen, a common Jewish name. Pound's transformation of Keynes's name clearly signifies the paranoid style. It is quite telling that Pound selected an acknowledged economist, once more showing his contempt for the economic establishment.

---

[99] Quot. in Pound, Ezra, Pound/Zukofsky, 159.
[100] Pound, Ezra, Pound/Zukofsky, 157f.
[101] Flory, Wendy S., The American Ezra Pound, 139.
[102] Casillo, Robert, The Genealogy of Demons, 18.
[103] Redman, Tim, Ezra Pound and Italian Fascism, 176.

Wyndham Lewis once claimed that the German National Socialists were right in fighting financiers, because it was them who gained profit from wars.[104] Apart from the fact that the Nazis were less immune to financiers and their resources than Lewis believed, his assertion represents a common assumption among populists and conspiracy theorists, i.e. the belief in the negative powers of banking and finance. American politics once knew an anti-banking tradition in which even eminent figures like Thomas Jefferson, Andrew Jackson and Henry Adams participated. The renowned agrarian Taylor devoted whole chapters of his *Inquiry into the Principles and Policy of the Government of the United States* to the power of banking.[105] For a conspiracy theorist like S. E. V. Emery, the demonetization of silver (1873) was among the great crimes of American history.[106] Quite a number of American populists during the 1930s were convinced of a large-scale conspiracy of bankers and usurers, who supposedly used the gold standard as a means of manipulating the U.S. state economy.[107] As early as 1896, journalists were eager to prove a conspiracy of Wall Street, Britain and the Rothschilds.[108] And of course Ford and other American anti-Semites would always associate Jews with bankers.[109]

Even a non-paranoid writer like John Dos Passos, in "The House of Morgan," propagated the stereotype image of the banker as villain. Dos Passos treats the House of Morgan in an ironic collage including historical facts, quotations from J. P. Morgan's testament and journalese details about his private life and tastes. We learn about his Christian pretensions, his family history and his art collections, while Dos Passos is eager to raise no admiration for Morgan in the reader. This is one common feature of Dos Passos and Pound – both want to convey a moral message *ex negativo* by providing us with models of greed and immorality. In *1919*, Dos Passos leaves no doubt as to Morgan's parasitic mentality which makes him thrive in severe times of poverty: "Wars and panics on the stock exchange, machinegunfire and arson, bankruptcies, warloans, starvation, lice, cholera and typhus: good growing weather for the House of Morgan."[110] Dos Passos's

[104] Lewis, Wyndham, Hitler, 75ff.

[105] On banking see Taylor, John, An Inquiry into the Principles and Policy of the Government of the United States, 253-342.

[106] Hofstadter, Richard, The Age of Reform from Bryan to F.D.R., 75f.

[107] See G. B. Tindall (ed.), A Populist Reader, New York 1966, 25, 57f.

[108] See Pollack, Norman, "The Myth of Populist Anti-Semitism," in: American Historical Review 68 (1962), 80. Also Murray, David, "Pound-Signs: Money and Representation in Ezra Pound," 192f.

[109] See Johnson, George, Architects of Fear, 103-124.

[110] Dos Passos, John, U.S.A., 648.

portrait of a banker is an important predecessor of Pound's anti-banking Cantos.

That anti-finance tradition was not confined to American populism, but existed as an almost universal phenomenon. A well-read intellectual like Pound could find related polemics in many sources. The transfer of money from one place to a cheaper place was already known to medieval writers on economics, like Gabriele Biel.[111] David Hume detested rich stockholders for their "internationalism" and criticized them for supporting corruption.[112] The rise of finance reached its acme in the 19th century and Hollis, one of Pound's sources, believed it was "the Napoleonic wars which brought the final and complete triumph of the money-lenders."[113] Pound champions the same notion in C50. The 19th century responded to the rise of finance in populist pamphlets, but also in poetry: Byron, in *The Age of Bronze*, accused the Jews of an economic conspiracy designed to control states and monarchs.[114]

During the first half of the 20th century, Pound's acquaintance Arthur Kitson was convinced that finance ruled industry and that wealth controlled nine-tenths of society.[115] He openly attacked bankers and financiers and even cited the anti-Semitic *Protocols* to prove the alleged schemes of the "leading international Jewish bankers."[116] He also cites Lord Bryce's *Modern Democracies*, a passage which deserves to be quoted in full for its parallels to Pound's Geryon in C49:

> Democracy has no more persistent or insidious foe than the money-power, to which it may say, as Dante said when he reached in his journey through Hell the dwelling of the God of Riches, 'Here we found Wealth, the great enemy'. That enemy is formidable because he works secretly by persuasion or deceit, rather than by force, and so takes men unawares. He is a danger to good government everywhere.[117]

---

[111] Biel in 1516: "Tranfferens monetam de certo loco vbi minoris valoris eftimat/ad locum vbi magis valet/non peccat/finon alias fraudem committat"; in: Biel, Gabriele, Tractatus de potestate et utilitate monetarum, 7.

[112] Hume: "These are men who have no connections with the state, who can enjoy their revenue in any part of the globe in which they choose to reside, who will naturally bury themselves in the capital, or in great cities, and who will sink into the lethargy of a stupid and pampered luxury"; see "Of Public Credit," in: Hume, David, Essays Moral, Political and Literary, 363.

[113] Hollis, Christopher, The Two Nations, 50.

[114] See Watts, Cedric, Literature and Money, 44; Byron, Lord John, The Poetical Works of Lord Byron, London 1896, 172f.

[115] Kitson, Arthur, A Scientific Solution of the Money Question, xi f., 35.

[116] Kitson, Arthur, The Bankers' Conspiracy, 41.

[117] Quot. in Kitson, Arthur, The Bankers' Conspiracy, 41.

Kitson was strongly opposed to the gold standard and championed paper money instead of a gold currency. He argued that the gold standard would ruin most countries, as it had done after being re-established in 1925. The economic crisis of the 1930s was mainly due to the gold standard. By its introduction with the help of the League of Nations, "an irresponsible super-Government was created, composed of a group of International Bankers."[118] Here we find all the typical elements of economic conspiracy theory – bankers, internationalism, the League of Nations and a hidden conspiracy of elite interests.

In accordance with such theories, Pound considered "Credit the ultimate fulcrum of power."[119] As early as 1920, he stated "the ultimate control of industry is financial control."[120] That control implied negative consequences. For Pound, bankers and financiers were no less than destructive in cultural and political terms. He believed they perverted the press and, by founding professorships, influenced education for the worse.[121] For Pound, financiers not only failed to contribute productively to society, but were actively evil in their aim to drive states and individuals into debt.[122] Pound shared the populists' antipathy towards bankers as a historically universal phenomenon: John Taylor saw them as a suspicious force that eroded the foundations of the American state. By corrupting the government, he assumed, bankers would finally destroy the ideal of liberty.[123] Even Adams expressed contempt for banking: "The Medici rose to the despotism of Europe, ecclesiastical and political, by the machinery of banks. Hundreds of mushrooms or Jonah's gourds have sprung up in one night in America by the strength of the same rotten manure."[124] As a consequence, Pound proclaimed his solidarity with Hitler's statement in *Mein Kampf*, as paraphrased by Pound: "War on international finance and LOAN CAPITAL becomes the most weighty etc. in the struggle towards freedom."[125] To the poet, bankers became the real-life personification of usury.

---

[118] Kitson, Arthur, The Bankers' Conspiracy, 27. On the general history of the gold standard see chapter 4 of Kindleberger, Charles P., A Financial History of Western Europe.
[119] "Fungus, Twilight or Dry Rot" (1931), in: P&P V.318.
[120] "Probari Ratio" (1920), in: SP, 177f.
[121] GK, 163, citing the Regius Professorships also mentioned in C46.233.
[122] Similarly Kenner, Hugh, The Pound Era, 464.
[123] Taylor, John, An Inquiry into the Principles and Policy of the Government of the United States, 293.
[124] Adams in a letter to Jefferson, 29 Jan 1819, in: Adams, John / Jefferson, Thomas, The Adams-Jefferson Letters, 532.
[125] "Communications" (1939), in: P&P VII.439. Pound's source for Hitler's statement was probably Wyndham Lewis. In *Hitler*, Lewis quotes from a book which in turn quotes Hitler's statement about the "Leihkapital" from *Mein Kampf*; Lewis, Wyndham, Hitler, 147.

Pound's anti-banking predjudices were present in his work from early writings to later Cantos. The early poems by "Alfred Venison," a joint product of Pound and Orage, created the image of an unlearned, but witty commentator, who lives among the lower strata of society and has a first-hand knowledge of social problems. Venison's attacks are directed at some of Pound's favorite enemies, especially the bankers. They are called responsible for the misery of England. When it comes to attacking the bankers, the light ironical tone of the Venison poems is replaced by a gravity which reminds one of the Usura Canto:

> In his eye there is death,-I mean the banker's,-
> In his purse there is deceit,
> It is he who buys gold-braid for the swankers[126]

"Safe and Sound" portrays the banker as a manipulator who controls currency and exchange:

> My name is Nunty Cormorant
> And my finance is sound,
> I lend you Englishmen hot air
> At one and three the pound. [...]
> There is blokes in automobiles
> And their necks sunk into fur
> That keep on gettin' usury
> To make 'em cosier.[127]

In the *Cantos* we find several bankers and financiers. C12 mentions the avaritious Baldy who is only interested in "money business" (C12.53). At this point, the money elite is still satirized and not yet targetted as fiercely as later. In C38, between allusions to the overwhelming influence of industrialists, a memorial statue for a banker is raised (C38.192). In C41, a Jewish consortium of financiers is anxious to maintain secrecy about its resources (C41.202). Here the secretive financiers are juxtaposed with a firm and decisive Mussolini.

In a draft of which parts would later be inserted into C49 (item 153), Pound condemns the credit policies of bankers (and indirectly expresses his preference for a state-centered economy). As he claims, it is infamy that the state should be indebted to private financiers. On the same page, Pound complains that bankers pay liars, an allusion to the alleged corruption of the press. Pound concludes by cursing the powers of gold and money with a reference to Midas. Pound's hint at the ancient king opens perspectives on the

---

[126] Pound, Ezra, The Collected Shorter Poems, 280.
[127] Pound, Ezra, The Collected Shorter Poems, 287.

deep historical dimension of a criticism of wealth, stretching from tales of greed in Greek mythology to the political debates of the 20th century. We sense a broad continuity which by far exceeds 19th-century American populism. In a modified form, this continuity of wrath is preserved in the finished C49. Between idyllic images of ancient China, Pound once more makes his case against the accumulation of debt and the power of bankers embodied by Geryon (C49.245). Like Bryce, Pound was convinved that money power threatened good government.

The League of Nations

Pound's dislike of bankers and financiers had a political dimension, which manifested itself in his polemics against the League of Nations. As he remarked in 1936 in connection with the League: "England's danger is not from bullets. It is from a monster more deadly and pervasive. Dante saw it swimming in black fog in nether Inferno, with the face of a just man, and the tail of a serpent, Gerion that passeth mountains and crusheth down walls and towers."[128] On 11 March 1937, in the year of the publication of *The Fifth Decad*, Pound condemned "that sink of hypocrisy the League of Nations."[129] As we will see, his strong words can be explained in the context of his anti-banking predjudices. In general, Pound's verbal attacks on the League represent a recurring element in his political writings. As early as 1920, he had warned his readers of the dangers of the League of Nations,[130] a tendency that continued in the 1930s,[131] and not only in his published, but also in unpublished essays.[132] For Pound the League was based on arbitrary values and did not possess any uniform standards to govern its actions. Others shared this view, especially intellectuals from Axis countries, who ridiculed the behaviour of the League during the Abyssinia crisis. Even leading jurists like the German Carl Schmitt participated in this type of fundamental criticism, more rational in tone than Pound, but no less destructive.[133]

For Pound, the League represented private financial interests. He believed it was controlled by bankers and designed to carry their interests into political and legal action, similarly to the Venetian Banca San Giorgio, which

---

[128] "Italy's Frame-up" (1936), in: P&P VII.23.

[129] Pound, Ezra, Ezra Pound and Japan, 40.

[130] Pound, Ezra, Impact, 217, written in 1920.

[131] For instance, see "Swelling of the Occiput" (1932), in: P&P V.354.

[132] Comp. the typescript draft in BL 43 / 113 / 4839.

[133] See the 1936 statement in: Schmitt, Carl, Positionen und Begriffe, 210-213. For American critics of the League see Ralph Stone, The Irreconcilables: The Fight Against the League of Nations, New York 1973; Herbert F. Margulies, The Mild Reservationists and the League of Nations, Columbia 1989.

had assumed jurisdictive powers in Venice in 1793. It was Pound's firm conviction that the League, too, was created to impose the usurers' will on nations.[134] In 1942 he passed a final, devastating judgement on the League, no less severe than his earlier statements: "It stank of the Bank of Basel, the Warburgs, the Regents of the Banque de France and the ulcer of England."[135] According to Pound, the League of Nations was founded on fear, terror and tyranny, not on an understanding of the true – i.e. economic – causes of war.[136] Hence, it did not contribute to the prevention of wars. The League was a "shop-front" of international usury, "covering the hands of the Jew, Barney Baruch" and manipulated by Paris and London bankers, who used it to exert political influence on the international community.[137] Pound's negative image of the League combines his bias against banking with his anti-Semitism, because he detected the influence of mainly Jewish bankers behind the organization – "The two-standards system of Geneva cannot be blamed on the Semites, but the Semitic avoidance of their own law on usury while wishing to be accepted as neighbours is on a par with Geneva, and Geneva is at heart [...] the frontage of Basel and the international bank of that usurers' stronghold," as he stated in 1939.[138]

Armament Dealers

Wyndham Lewis, always a champion of the paranoid style, believed that when "*two nations* fall out, the armament-king and chemical-king rake in the shekels."[139] This remark could have been written by many conspiracy theorists, including Pound, because armament firms were one of the economic forces he most strongly opposed. Pound accused the Bank of England of upholding "a pernicious financial system which makes for continued wars," as armament trusts did "aggravate the situation by direct efforts to cause wars in particular."[140] In his polemics against armament companies, Pound always used the same set of firms and individuals – Zaharoff, Vickers, Schneider-Creusot, De Wendel and Skoda, all politically well-established and with connections to banks and oil firms.[141]

---

[134] "A World Liability" (1936), in: P&P VII.17f.
[135] Pound on 19 February 1942, Pound, Ezra, "Ezra Pound Speaking," 42.
[136] "Failure to Tackle Money Problems" (1935), in: P&P VI.310.
[137] "Bury the Corpse!" (1938), in: P&P VII.307.
[138] "On the Degrees of Honesty in Various Occidental Religions" (1939), in: P&P VII.464.
[139] Lewis, Wyndham, Hitler, 75.
[140] "The European in America" (1933), in: P&P VI.12.
[141] See Pound's "Academic" (1933), in: P&P VI.81; "Is It War?" (1933), in: P&P VI.80; "Italy 1934," BL 43 / 108 / 4551, 4; "Gaudier: A Postscript" (1934), in: P&P VI.191; [Zaharoff], BL 43 / 140 / 6192; J/M, 61f., 71f.; Laughlin, James, Pound as Wuz, 152.

Pound's arch-enemy was Sir Basil Zaharoff, a secretive arms dealer, called "Metevsky" in C31. During the 1920s, Pound collected newspaper clippings about him.[142] Pound's knowledge of Zaharoff was chiefly based on a biography by Richard Lewinsohn. Of rather humble origins, Zaharoff was born in Anatolia in 1849. As a young man, he supported his family by acting as a guide for tourists. Then he entered the firm of a relative. Zaharoff substantially contributed to the success of the firm and his relative promised him a good share of the earnings, but never gave the money to him. So Zaharoff decided to quit the business. Without informing his relative, he took what he regarded as his proper share and left for London, where he was charged with thievery by his former business partner and had to stand trial, but was acquitted under mysterious circumstances. He then went to Athens, where he gained the protection of an influential politician who introduced him to the owner of the Nordenfeldt arms company. In this company, Zaharoff started his long and successful business career. He eventually became a representative of Vickers, one of the most important armament companies of his time. According to his biographer, he died an immensely rich and influential man, with connections to the highest level of politics. Lewinsohn, however, is quite silent about his sources. It is therefore difficult to decide whether his book is an attempt at serious biography or plain mystification. That Zaharoff sold weapons to any war party that was ready to pay him is mentioned in several parts of the biography.[143]

The figure of Zaharoff appears in many networks constructed by Pound. For instance, Pound mentions that Krupp allegedly received money from the British government as payment for munitions used to kill Germans, and Zaharoff owned stock in both Krupp and Vickers. Complicated networks like this led Pound to demand that, instead of old dynastic intrigues, one should investigate the dealings of ammunition makers.[144] Zaharoff embodied the concentration of power in a person with no political legitimation, but excellent connections to politicians. On item 100 and in a letter of 1934, Pound mentioned the friendship of Zaharoff and British Prime Minister Arthur Balfour and concluded that the world suffered under a secret government.[145] It was not only the bankers, but also the armament firms that threatened the order of the state by promoting private interests and by exerting far-reaching influence on politics. If Mussolini was the model politician in

142 Wilhelm, James J., Ezra Pound: The Tragic Years (1925-1972), 54.

143 Lewinsohn, Richard, Zaharoff, 55f., 71. Also see Guiles Davenport, Zaharoff: High Priest of War, Boston 1934; Robert Neumann, Zaharoff: The Armaments King, [s.l.] 1935. For more recent research on Zaharoff see Anthony Allfrey, Man of Arms. The Life and Legend of Sir Basil Zaharoff, London 1989.

144 "By All Means Be Patriotic" (1932), in: P&P V.377. Similarly "Correspondence" (1930), in: P&P V.228.

145 Quot. in Stock, Noel, The Life of Ezra Pound, 318.

Pound's private pantheon, Zaharoff and his fellow armament executives represented the sinister opposite of that ideal.

The Rothschilds

Intellectuals, just like ordinary people, have always been fascinated by the wealthy. In his *Economics* Aristotle recommends the study of wealthy men, and the philosopher himself portrayed some of them. I already mentioned Dos Passos and his chapter on Morgan in *1919*. Although critical in attitude, Pound, too, was as interested in wealth as he was in power. One family embodied both and therefore became the preferred target of populists – the Rothschilds. In the course of this chapter, we have encountered the Rothschilds several times. Coughlin used a probably forged letter by them to show the malevolence of powerful financiers and Pelley accused them of causing the Civil War, which led Pound to the blunt conclusion: "You may say that Rotschild [sic!] started the American civil war (Bismark is supposed to have thought so)."[146]

The power of the family was indeed considerable. During the 19th century, it was the Rothschilds who dominated Europe's stock exchanges and who granted substantial loans to governments. Bagehot called them "foreign bill-brokers."[147] But as opposed to the charges brought forward by populists, the Rothschilds were anything but war-mongers. Their business required political stability, because any armed conflict was likely to disturb the delicate system of international finance. Defeated and ruined governments would hardly be able to pay their debts, not to mention interest. The fact that the Rothschilds owed their fortune to loans and speculations had always stirred mistrust, even from so distinguished a person as Queen Victoria. To many observers, theirs did not seem a healthy form of business. And when Pound condemned usury as being "against nature's increase," his attitude was anything but unusual. The public view of the Rothschilds has for a long time been an awkward mixture of fascination, conspiracy theories and downright anti-Semitism. As late as 1995, a former environmentalist called David Icke claimed that the Rothschilds were part of a hidden brotherhood secretly governing the world in cooperation with other bankers and financiers, such as J. P. Morgan, Loeb and the Bank of England – institutions familiar from Pound's writings. Icke accused them of a whole number of crimes, including the murder of Lincoln, the Boer War and the support of Hitler.[148] For some

[146] Pound, Ezra, "American Notes," [1935], 43 / 66 / 2893.
[147] Bagehot, Walter, Lombard Street: A Description of the Money Market, London 1873, 104.
[148] Ferguson, Niall, The World's Banker, 27f.

conspiracy experts, nothing has changed since Alfred de Vigny's 1837 exclamation: "A Jew now reigns over the Pope and Christianity. He pays monarchs and buys nations."[149]

Ferguson mentions a whole number of Rothschild myths which persisted for more than a century. There was, for instance, the well-known story about the Elector of Hesse entrusting his fortune to the Rothschilds in 1806, when he had to flee from the invading French. Another myth made Nathan Rothschild witness the battle of Waterloo and head back to London in order to reach the exchange before the official news arrived, so he could make huge profits when stocks rose again. Pound believed in this myth, while in reality, however, Napoleon's defeat was rather against the Rothschild's financial interests, as Ferguson stresses.[150] But Pound preferred the myth to reality.

Items 100 and 101 show to what large extent Pound was rooted in populist mythology. The drafts paraphrase a sentence from Coughlin's book *Money!*, which cites a remark allegedly made by Meyer A. Rothschild: "Permit me to issue and control the money of a nation, and I care not who make its laws."[151] As is typical of conspiracy theories, the source is uncredited. The Waterloo legend, too, can be found in the mentioned items and in a book by Coughlin. In Coughlin's words:

> When he [Rothschild] was certain that Napoleon was doomed, he set off post-haste to the nearest port, weighed anchor on the speediest vessel; arrived in England even before the news of victory had been heralded. First, he spread the news that Wellington had been defeated. Then he purchased thousands of English governmental bonds which were selling for almost nothing. Over night this man, Rothschild by name, became a power in the financial world.[152]

Sharing this view of events, Pound commented on Rothschild's cleverness in a 1935 article.[153] Pound also believed in a conspiracy of the Rothschilds and arms dealers. He praised pamphleteer Paolo Zappa for revealing the names of armament dealers linked to the Rothschilds.[154] In another draft (item 168) Pound mentions Rothschild's steel-protected cellar, in which the banker allegedly stored his art collection. Pound would later

---

149 Quot. in Ferguson, Niall, The World's Banker, 271.

150 Ferguson, Niall, The World's Banker, 16f., for details v. 103ff. The Waterloo story is also mentioned in: Rothschild, Victor, The Shadow of a Great Man, London 1982.

151 Coughlin, Charles, Money!, 76, 114.

152 Coughlin, Charles, Father Coughlin's Radio Discourses, 163.

153 P&P VI.245.

154 Pound, Ezra, [on Paolo Zappa], [1939], BL 43 / 140 / 6193.

develop this motif in C52, where he mentioned the "specialité of the Stinkschuld [/] bomb-proof under their house in Paris [/] where they cd/ store aht voiks" (C52.257). By locking away works of art, the Rothschilds hide a part of culture from the public, Pound suggests.

Pound brought forward three main charges against the bankers. First, the Rothschilds used secret means to gain influence on governments all over the world. Second, they benefitted from and started wars, as in the case of Napoleon's defeat at Waterloo or the American Civil War. Third, the Rothschilds bought valuable art and hid it in their private cellar, instead of making it accessible to the public. Pound based his findings on populist mythology and on the opinion of agitators like Charles Coughlin.

Writing Secret Histories

Pound's writing bears more than one mark of his contempt for the aristocracy of finance. He imitated polemicists like Coughlin to an extent which also included verbal aggression. Inserted between some drafts of *The Fifth Decad*, we find an unpublished document which combines, and can therefore serve to exemplify, several of Pound's obsessions (items 246 and 247). A fierce litany against the powers of usury, it bears witness to Pound's development from an intellectual with clearly defined enemies to a conspiracy theorist. At the same time, it offers a glimpse of how Pound associated economics and power. He sets the virtues of "fair sharing" and natural reproduction against what he deems unnatural. He creates a semantic field of negative elements to denote the things he detests – sterility, sodomy, incest. Advocating a state-controlled financial sector, the text strongly opposes the proponents of banking and finance and condemns them to hell. Pound accuses them of verbal incompetence and greed. Pound also provides the names of those he considers as the chief usurers, among which we once more find the names of Zaharoff, Rothschild and Morgenthau. And when Pound likens taxation to "sodomy," he combines homophobia with a favorite issue of modern populists, the right of the state to tax its citizens. In this unpublished, private document the balanced argument has finally given way to fierce attack. The text is unaffected by fear of libel and represents Pound's opinions without the personas he adopted in the *Cantos*. Written on Christmas 1934, the text became Pound's private "Christmas litany," a sequence of urgently repeated phrases, primal sounds and obscenities.

But whatever rhetorical fireworks Pound may have lighted – the scope of his attacks was clearly limited. He kept mentioning the same groups over and over again: Jews, financiers, banker-friendly politicians, allegedly corrupt newspapers, munitions-makers. Pound thus adhered to the populist canon of villains. To the Rothschilds and Zaharoff, one may add Metternich and

Talleyrand, the “jew’s pimp” (C50.248). Pound regarded it as his personal duty to reveal the “truth” about these persons, “truth” being defined mainly as everything likely to prove their malicious character. Pound was not interested in letting facts speak for themselves, but instrumentalized facts for political purposes. Most of the time, it is even difficult to speak of proper “facts,” as Pound was hardly scrupulous in the choice of his sources, as long as they helped him to reconstruct the secet history of usury.

Pound’s interest in secret histories converges with his general preoccupation with history. He used the sensationalist pamphlets of writers like Coughlin and Kitson to write an anti-power history. What made the pamphlets credible to Pound was not an objective representation of facts, but their attitude, which determined their choice of pseudo-facts. When Pound asks on item 24 if there is anything in his accusations that is not wholly probable, it becomes clear that his arguments are based on assumptions and probabilities, not facts. Whatever “fact” seemed to support Pound’s position against the power of certain elites would be used by the poet as a historical source and evidence of facts. This approach, however, does not imply opposition to all forms of power, only to what Pound deemed its destructive and unnatural use. In fact, Pound admired power when it manifested itself in what he acknowledged as a wise ruler, whether Chinese king or fascist dictator.

III.3 The Fourth Dimension: Good Government

Così la religione, anzi la superstizione, diventava arte di governo.

(Pietro Rota, *Storia delle banche*)

Will, Action and the Metaphysics of Power

The preceding chapter was not intended to reduce Pound to a paranoid mind of aggressive attitude. To over-emphasize this aspect of his life and work would mean to belittle a poet whose polemical strain represents only one layer within a complex network of assumptions and preconditions. Pound's populist opinions constitute the lower level of a hierarchy whose top is occupied by a political ideal: good government. In the following paragraphs, I will analyze this ideal with its implications, which range from a metaphysics of power to Pound's perception of fascist Italy. I will highlight historical references and ideological preferences that describe Pound's concept of government. Historically charged as any of Pound's theories, the roots of that concept stretch back over Early Modern Tuscany to dynastic China.

Many of Pound's political concepts are based on his notion of the superior intellect. This type of intellect is distinguished from other, contemplative types by its natural proneness for translating ideas into action. It is the intellect of a leader and political genius who does not distinguish thought from action and from whom order radiates as from a center, from an "unwobbling pivot." Pound left no doubt about his activist approach: "The idea is not well planned until it is capable of going into action"[1] was one of his dictums; another was: "Let us deny that *real* intelligence exists until it comes into action."[2] We might be tempted to apply this sentence to Mussolini, but the idea behind it is much more universal. What Pound called a genius was not merely an anthropological, but a natural phenomenon. When Pound observed a wasp dissect a spider, he assumed the wasp acted deliberately and not out of mere instinct. Similarly, human genius is subject to the same laws, moving between instinct and a metaphysical knowledge of how to act: "When a human being has an analogous completeness of knowledge, or intelligence

[1] Pound, Ezra, Impact, 74.
[2] J/M, 18.

carried into a third or fourth dimension, capable of dealing with NEW circumstances, we call it genius."[3]

A central term in this context is *directio voluntatis*, which denotes the particularly human qualities of the mind.[4] For Pound, in 1942, it meant the "basic assertion that man is OVER matter. That the human will (or spirit) is lord even over the mud of this planet."[5] The *directio voluntatis* represents the drive required to catapult intelligence into the higher dimensions mentioned above. Whereas instinct is "PERFECT and complete intelligence *with a limited scope* applied to recurrent conditions,"[6] *directio voluntatis* allows the mind to adjust itself to changing conditions. It functions as an important drive behind the great cultures of the world. Pound mentions the Roman virtue of carrying thoughts into action[7] and senses the same quality in the political order of the U.S.[8] Pound's concept had a chief predecessor in medieval thought which, like Pound, focused on the great individual that came to represent the qualities of a group. With reference to Averroes, Dante wrote in his *Monarchia* (1.3.63ff.) "that the specific potentiality of *humanitas* is a potentiality, or capacity, of the intellect" transformed into actuality by the whole multitude of humanity, but concentrated in the philosopher-monarch.[9] Both humanity and the spirit of God thus unfold through the culmination of collective intellect in the unifying ideal of the monarch.

The direction of the will makes it possible to transform the potential into the actual. This idea has left its traces in C51, where Pound praises the "light of the doer" in connection with a Latin passage ("deo similis...") derived from Albertus Magnus. The Poundian passage is best read in its full context, a partial translation of Albertus's original text:

> Possibilis speculativa recipiens cum eis lumen suscipit agentis, cui de die in diem fit similior; et quum acceperit possibilis omnia speculata seu intellecta, habet lumen agentis ut formam sibi adhaerentem... Ex possibili et agente compositus est intellectus adeptus, et divinus dicitur, et tunc homo perfectus est. Et fit per hunc intellectum homo Deo quodam modo similis [10]

---

[3] J/M, 18f.

[4] As pointed out by Stephen Sicari in "Reading Pound's Politics: Ulysses as Fascist Hero," 160.

[5] Pound on 31 May 1942, see Pound, Ezra, "Ezra Pound Speaking," 154. Note the "mud" connection to the first lines of C51.

[6] J/M, 18.

[7] Comp. GK, 40.

[8] "National Culture: A Manifesto 1938" (publ. 1960), in: SP, 135.

[9] I owe this hint to Kantorowicz, Ernst H., The King's Two Bodies: A Study in Mediaeval Theology, Princeton 1957, 472.

[10] Renan, Ernest, Averoès et l'Averroïsme, 235; from Albertus Magnus, De Apprehensione, part V. Pound mentions his source in LE, 186.

In Albertus, potential reason and speculative intellect come to resemble active reason, which Pound translated as "daily more to resemble the doer." From active reason, a divine light radiates ("lumen agentis"), in Pound's words: "the light of the doer." Replacing the more neutral "agent" by "doer," Pound personalizes Albertus's impersonal statement and evokes the figure of a human leader with god-like qualities. Davie links the "doer" to the Renaissance ideal of virtù, as embodied by Sigismundo Malatesta – a personality strong enough to give form to acts or artifacts.[11]

Pound's cult of god-like intelligence and the metaphysics of power also has some roots in periods more ancient than the European Middle Ages. Pound thought the mysteries of Eleusis still shed their light on the modern political world: "Great intelligence attains again and again to great verity. The Duce and Kung fu Tseu equally perceive that their people need poetry; that prose is NOT education but the outer courts of the same. Beyond its doors are the mysteries. Eleusis."[12] The passage testifies to Pound's belief that the "great men" participated in a knowledge of mysteries, which revealed themselves only to their superior intellect. Strange as it may seem today, this idea nevertheless was in accordance with classical philosophers like Iamblichus who held that, the higher a level of being, the purer the light shed by those beings belonging to that level – "the light of those that have the government of the world is more pure."[13]

As opposed to the twilight zone of Pound's populist strain, an imagery of light illuminates the superior world of political power. What we find in Iamblichus is also discernible in Pound's translations from Confucius: "Light to the mind from Chou / forming to all men that shall sit on thrones."[14] A passage on the decline of the state reads, in Pound's translation:

> You brawl in the middle kingdom;
> collect resentments and call it sincerity.
> There is no light in your conscience
> and your acts shed, therefore, no light
> in your inwit and you are left without ministers,
> without party.[15]

In this case, the intellect (or conscience) lacks brilliance, which damages the ruler's qualities as a leader, as only inner coherence can establish

---

[11] Davie, Donald, "The Poet as Sculptor", 204. Pound himself used the term "virtù" to denote the predominant element in one's "soul." See "I gather the limbs of Osiris" (1911-1912), in: SP, 28f.
[12] GK, 144f.
[13] Iamblichus, On the Mysteries of the Egyptians, Chaldeans, and Assyrians, 54.
[14] Pound, Ezra, The Classic Anthology Defined by Confucius, 200f.
[15] Pound, Ezra, The Classic Anthology Defined by Confucius, 174.

political power. When that coherence, that direction of the will is missing, the ruler must lose all support. The passage raises two questions, first, for Pound's definition of an ideal leader, and second, for the kind of order in which the light of the doer's intellect will manifest itself.

Doers, Leaders, Elites

In order to understand the first aspect, we must be fully aware of Pound's elitist idea of history. From the beginning, he embraced an aristocratic notion of history, which first articulated itself in relation to art: "The history of an art is the history of masterwork, not of failures, or mediocrity. The omniscient historian would display the masterpieces, their causes and their inter-relation. The study of literature is hero-worship."[16] We can hear a late-Victorian follower of Carlyle speak. Although Pound would later give up Carlyle and move to other, more remote areas, he would not change his general, elitist attitude. Rather, he extended it to encompass historical studies as a whole. Pound's historical monumentalism was fully developed in 1930, when he claimed: "THE SANE METHOD OF STUDYING HISTORY consists [...] in learning what certain great protagonists intended, and to what degree they failed in forcing their program on the mass."[17] Pound's idea of civilization is strongly biased in its endorsement of strong leadership. This applies to the whole development of a culture, as postulated by Pound – while great individuals are certainly responsible for special achievements at the acme of civilization, the same individuals may also affect cultural decay.[18] No civilization can exist without elites, but Pound hints at historical cycles that include the rise of elites, their degeneration, social revolutions against them, followed by the breeding of a new aristocracy, which finally completes a full circle.[19] In this respect, Pound argues in favor of a cyclical idea of history with elitist emphasis. He concentrates on the excellent and condemns any levelling of the great to fit a democratic average. In the healthy state, decisions are made by a few leaders, while bureaucratic power-sharing is a sign of decadence, growing like a parasitic fungus on the originally pure foundations of the state.[20]

Returning to the question of the ideal ruler's profile, we find a helpful passage in Pound's contemporary Spengler, the German philosopher of culture. Spengler defines the ideal statesman as a person capable of judging

---

[16] Pound, Ezra, The Spirit of Romance, 7, in 1910.
[17] "Correspondence" (1930), in: P&P V.228.
[18] Comp. "Terra Italica" (1931-32), in: SP, 55; similarly Pound, Ezra, [no title], BL 43 / 73 / 3252.
[19] "Definitions" (1925), in: SP, 183.
[20] "Bureaucracy the Flail of Jehovah" (1928), in: SP, 187, passim.

things and persons at a glance, according to an inborn instinct. Standing beyond the limits of program politics, he sets the logic of events over the logic of a system and does not tie himself to convictions. Spengler quotes Goethe's statement that the "doer is always conscienceless."[21] Spengler's "logic of events" and the leader's instinct correspond with Pound's concept of the divine intellect and with the activism that was virulent in his writings of the 1930s. In *Jefferson and/or Mussolini* he claimed "the best government is that which translates the best thought most speedily into action"[22] and stressed Jefferson's activism.[23] It is also expressed in Pound's use of the word "doer."

The leader's instinct mirrors the processes of nature. As Bush points out, the *Cantos* associate civilized men with natural increase.[24] Pound may have derived such notions from the Chinese tradition, which states about the ideal prince: "The bamboos grow well / under good rule." The prince is associated with growth and care for the "folk" – "a tiger with velvet paws."[25] For Mencius the relation between superiors and inferiors is "like that between the wind and grass. The grass must bend when the wind blows upon it."[26] C49 conveys the same meesage. Among scenes of rural quietness, from which political unrest seems far removed, Pound praises the qualities of imperial government:

> Imperial power is? and to us what is it?
> The fourth; the dimension of stillness.
> And the power over wild beasts.
>
> (C49.246)

Imperial power constitutes a dimension of fixed relations (item 72), i.e. fixed like the natural relations between leaders and subjects, as described by Confucius and Mencius.

When Pound places his ideal rulers in idyllic scenes, as he does in C49, we may suspect a lack of realism in the description of what are after all power relations. Goldensohn has identified elements of political *kitsch* in the Cantos, e.g. when fascist rulers are framed by decorative features such as the light of

---

[21] Quot. in Spengler, Oswald, The Decline of the West, II.442.

[22] J/M, 91.

[23] Pound represents the American version of a general tendency: Activism was an important feature of several early 20th century movements, including Italian Futurism and the Conservative Revolution in Germany.

[24] Bush, Ronald, The Genesis of Ezra Pound's Cantos, 251.

[25] Pound, Ezra, The Classic Anthology Defined by Confucius, 26f.

[26] Mencius, The Works of Mencius, 238. The Confucian Analects say: "the proper man acting according to his conscience is wind, the lesser folk acting on conscience, grass; grass with wind above it must bend," in: Confucius, The Great Digest, 247.

Dante's paradise and the *chinoiserie* of waves.[27] But Pound had a message he would not have distorted by realism. The aim of poems like C49 is to envision and conjure up an ideal order. In fact, order is another key term that serves to define the ideal ruler. The "great man" is not obsessed with power, but governed by a "will toward *order*."[28] Pound's concept is influenced by Confucius's assertion that "one man can bring the state to an orderly course."[29] What Pound desired were leaders with the highest moral standards[30] and the experience of a lifetime.[31]

State, Order, Empire and Economics

We will now move from the qualities of rulers to the order they are supposed to create and the state Pound expects them to govern. In Pound's translation of *The Classic Anthology Defined by Confucius*, we find a poem that almost seems to describe the international political situation as Pound perceived it in the 1930s under the "rule" of the League of Nations:

> Heaven has let down a drag-net of ill-doing,
> the locusts have gnawed us with word-work,
> they have hollowed our speech,
> Perverse alliances and continuing crookedness have divided us,
> evil men are set above us, in ease.[32]

As the poet diagnoses, speech has lost its essence just as the state has fallen apart. Both phenomena are connected – whereas the precise word has heavenly features,[33] the loss of preciseness conjures up evil and chaos, the fragmentation of the state. As long as words are filled with meaning, the state will prosper. This notion defines the logocentric order Pound dreams of. He imagined that the rectification of terminology would entail a complete moral order and good government: "Towards order in the state: the definition of the word."[34] Pound believed in Confucius's teachings on precise terminology:[35] The philosopher considered the definition of terminology the prime task of

[27] Goldensohn, Barry, "Pound and Antisemitism," 405.
[28] J/M, 99, 128.
[29] Confucius, The Great Digest, 61.
[30] Comp. "What is money for?" (1939), in: SP, 267.
[31] Whereas the "YOUNG aint expected to govern / only to watch, and git ready." In: Gordon, David M. (ed.), Ezra Pound and James Laughlin: Selected Letters, 40, a letter of 12 Jan 1935.
[32] Pound, Ezra, The Classic Anthology Defined by Confucius, 195.
[33] Confucius, The Great Digest, 35f.
[34] Pound, Ezra, Impact, 73.
[35] See GK, 16f.; Pound, Ezra, Impact, 72f.

every leader, because only precise instructions would be understood by subordinates. Otherwise, administrative business would not be conducted properly and, as a consequence, the religious rites would become disorderly, punishments would lose their efficiency and justice would not be enforced any longer. Hence, establishing the precise word was identical with the creation of order. Confucius defined the same idea in a passage which, for its imagery of light and emphasis on activism, comes very close to Pound's mode of thinking:

> The men of old wanting to clarify and diffuse throughout the empire that light which comes from looking straight into the heart and then acting, first set up good government in their own states; wanting good government in their states, they first established order in their own families; wanting order in the home, they first disciplined themselves; desiring self-discipline, they rectified their own hearts; and wanting to rectify their hearts, they sought precise verbal definitions of their inarticulate thoughts.[36]

Pound fully shared Confucius's conviction.[37] If terminology was well-defined, the state would be able to perform its actual functions: first, "to maintain order," second, "to provide an official means of exchange that will most facilitate just distribution of goods,"[38] i.e. enhance the circulation of everything from fuel to thought, without interfering too much in the affairs of citizens.[39] The responsibility of the government would then be to feed the people and to gain their faith.[40] What Pound called for was "the state as convenience,"[41] playing a predominant role (as opposed to private interests) in economic affairs. Davis offers a concise explanation of Pound's state-centered concept. The state has to execute leadership functions to regulate the prices and guarantee sufficient profits, support fairness in business, limit special privilege and provide money and credit without borrowing it at interest from private bankers.[42] As civilization also implies the abolition of violence,[43] the ideal state will automatically contribute to international peace and security: "You promote the peace of the world by the good *internal* government of

[36] Confucius, The Great Digest, 29, 31.

[37] For instance, in "Prolegomena" (1927), in: SP, 186; and with a more modern emphasis in "Gold and Work" (1944), in: SP, 321.

[38] "Waiting on M. Blum" (1936), in: P&P VII.60.

[39] Comp. "Definitions" (1925), in: SP, 188.

[40] "Mang Tsze (The Ethics of Mencius)" (1938), in: SP, 109.

[41] "The State" (1927), in: SP, 184, also 189.

[42] Davis, Earle, Vision Fugitive, 97.

[43] "Provincialism the Enemy" (1917), in: SP, 169.

your country."[44] The inner political system itself is nothing without a firm leader, from whom order radiates, as we explained above.

We will not repeat the conclusions of the previous chapter on populism here, but Pound's definition of political order would not be complete without mentioning its Other. As opposed to the, mostly imperial, examples of political order in the *Cantos*, like the Shang Dynasty, Jusinian's Byzantium, Napoleonic France and Mussolini's Italy,[45] Pound assures us that one group will never achieve such lofty status: The Jews have no statal order and govern by instinct, Pound claims, whereas continental Europe has a rich tradition of guilds and syndicates, i.e. order and organization.[46] As he stated in 1937, "the JEW won't take responsibility for civic order he WONT organize a state."[47] This is another point to falsify Pound's claim that he did not dislike the Jews as a group.

Although his concept of the "state as convenience" sounds modestly liberal, Pound actually preferred imperial states. Would he accept democracy in its modern form or would he support T. S. Eliots critical remark "Individualistic democracy has come to high tide: and it is more difficult today to be an individual than it ever was before"?[48] We noted Pound's preoccupation with outstanding individuals, and there is little democratic attitude in a statement like: "Damn the man in the street, once and for all, damn the man in the street who is only in the street because he hasn't intelligence enough to be let in to anywhere else."[49] Yet Pound was not completely hostile to democracy, as long as it was governed by what he called "clean men, decent men, honest men."[50] Pound called constitutions the "wisest instrument of govt. yet seen."[51] He even accepted the classical concept of liberty as "the right to do anything that doesn't hurt someone else," but complained about its decline into mere irresponsibility.[52] As he emphasized, the democratic state required a strong sense of responsibility[53] and liberty was not possible without an order created by strict political organization.[54] Despite some arguments in favor of democracy, Pound's thoughts kept circling around another, more imperial, ideal of the state.

---

[44] "The Individual in his Milieu" (1935), in: SP, 249.
[45] Comp. Stoicheff, Peter, The Hall of Mirrors, 19.
[46] Pound, Ezra, "Jewish Legacy" [1940], BL 43 / 109 / 4586.
[47] Quot. in Redman, Tim, Ezra Pound and Italian Fascism, 178.
[48] Eliot, Thomas S., Selected Essays, 398.
[49] Pound in the *Egoist*, quot. in Tytell, John, Ezra Pound: The Solitary Volcano, 103.
[50] GK, 157.
[51] Gordon, David M. (ed.), Ezra Pound and James Laughlin: Selected Letters, 68, letter of 27 Sept 1936.
[52] "The Teacher's Mission" (1934), in: LE, 59f.
[53] Comp. Pound, Ezra, "American Notes," BL 43 / 66 / 2892.
[54] "The Revolution Betrayed" (1938), in: P&P VII.282.

Among the Pound papers are some notebooks with excerpts from De Mailla's book about Chinese history. In one of them, we find the drawing of a red swastika which refers to a note by Pound on imperial laws.[55] The symbol and its association with the concept of empire grant an insight into Pound's immersion in fascism and the idea of empire. This included Mussolini's claim on the Roman heritage. Pound acknowledged a continuity from ancient Rome, over the canon law of the Middle Ages, to Mussolini's fascist state, whose "New Order" and "magnificent body" Pound admired.[56] In political terms, the secular state was less pure than Catholicism as an organization: "The papacy *as ideal* is [...] equivalent to the ideal of the empire. It is a Roman ideal of order and subordination."[57] It was only the "semitic component" in Christianity that was "irresponsible" and contradicted the idea of a secular kingdom.[58] Fascism, although secular, did not contradict the idea of empire. In this respect, Pound was less critical than T. S. Eliot, who was not generally opposed to fascism, but considered it a specifically Italian phenomenon. And the more Eliot founded his politics on Christian doctrines, the more he regarded fascism as a pagan movement and refused to identify himself with it.[59] Pound showed similar reservations about fascism only when he uttered doubts about its role in the U.S. He never wanted to establish fascism in America to the same extent as in Italy, because he thought the political system of the U.S. would function properly – at least in theory – if based on real cultural achievements and if provided with an energetic elite of intelligent men.[60] He called fascism an "organization, with the organizer at its head, to whom the power has not been GIVEN, but who has organized the power," whereas the American nation showed its decay when *calling* for a strong man.[61]

In addition to its general imperial pretensions, Pound also wanted the state to play a strong role in economic affairs. One of Pound's closest allies, A. R. Orage, was very clear on the priority of politics over economics: "The soul of economics is politics, and it is to politics that economics relegates the control of questions such as what shall be produced, by whom, and how the results shall be distributed."[62] Although Pound basically shared Orage's position, he would set different emphases and "discuss usury and money ultra

---

[55] Pound, Ezra, [Notebook], BL 43 / 115 / 4900, [21v].
[56] "Marconi's Violins" (1936), in: Pound, Ezra, Ezra Pound and Music, 393.
[57] "On the Degrees of Honesty in Various Occidental Religions" (1939), in: SP, 67. It is interesting to observe Pound's use of capital letters. While often denying them to Jews, he did not hesitate to use them in words like "Empire."
[58] "Mang Tsze (The Ethics of Mencius)" (1938), in: SP, 104.
[59] Hamilton, Alastair, The Appeal of Fascism, 275f.
[60] Redman, Tim, Ezra Pound and Italian Fascism, 106f.
[61] J/M, 108.
[62] Orage, Alfred R., Orage as Critic, 51.

any question of race or politics," as he wrote in 1940.[63] Stressing the economic competence of the state, Pound defined state sovereignty as "the right to ISSUE money (tickets) and to determine the value thereof."[64] This right was in constant danger of being usurped by non-government agents and Pound was convinced that "private individuals unfairly control public money, credit, and distribution in the world today."[65] The fascist state, which did use its economic sovereignty, was threatened by the specter of a privately controlled usury state. The latter was based on a principle of destruction that affects culture as a whole, "it attacks the health of the people, it attacks every manifestation of humanity. It attacks the arts, it destroys constructivity, it ultimately corrupts justice, thought, and the practice of cutting architectural stonework and woodwork with any fineness," it kills curiosity and creates trained officials who are unable to take real responsibility.[66] Together with repercussions of C45 (which was written at about the same time) in this statement, we notice a strong identification of economic with political well-being, and *vice versa.*

We will comment on Pound's concept of usury in the following chapter, but should at this point emphasize the close connection between his ideal, i.e. anti-usurious and interventionist, state and his sensationalist background with its antipathy to banking and finance. Where economic powers prevail, Pound claimed, the state and its citizens must suffer. Pound's position was hardly original, as the corroding power of finance was pointed out by many of his contemporaries. The pamphleteer Jeffrey Mark, in a chapter called "The League against Nations," saw Hitler fight fierce battles against the powers of finance in order to maintain Germany's sovereignty. As the writer claims, Hitler's policies aroused strong opposition from the international usurers, who now conspired against the fascist state: "France is working hand in hand with international finance, using the catspaw of the League of Nations, to tighten her stranglehold on Germany through the financial control of the surrounding nations [...] and it looks as if the powers of usury will force Great Britain to join France in an effort to crush Germany."[67] Pound used the same terminology and similar arguments.

What distinguishes the middle Cantos from the earlier parts of the poem is not only Pound's increasing awareness of the close connection between economy and culture. The middle cantos also show what Redman

---

[63] Gordon, David M. (ed.), Ezra Pound and James Laughlin: Selected Letters, 111f., 10 Jan 1940.

[64] "What is money for?" (1939), in: SP, 262; also see "Souvereignty" (1953), in: SP, 322; Gordon, David M. (ed.), Ezra Pound and James Laughlin: Selected Letters, 257, letter of 13 Oct 1957.

[65] Davis, Earle, Vision Fugitive, 79.

[66] "New Italy's Challenge" (1936), in: P&P VII.51.

[67] Mark, Jeffrey, The Modern Idolatry, 222.

calls a "statal sense", i.e. a marked admiration for rulers who assert, as Jefferson and John Adams did, that a fair economy is a "component of a well-ordered state".[68] It is just as important as culture in general. The political leader must take heed of both elements and defend the power of the state against the forces of private economy. What Wyndham Lewis wrote about the ideal modern ruler also applies to Pound's ideas: "what distinguishes the new revolutionary ruler from the commercial magnate of our own democratic society is that the former is not, first of all, a money-man, but an open political leader. His aims, however practical, are not entirely circumscribed by economy."[69]

The Chinese Ideal

A minor Chinese poet wrote in the 4th century BC: "Bad government is worse than a tiger,"[70] a statement Pound would have agreed with. Pound had a preference for pragmatic rulers who, like ancient emperor Yü, would fight the flood and "reduce the waters to order. Yü dug open *their obstructed channels*, and conducted them to the sea," as Mencius states.[71] When Pound, in a similar manner, praised Mussolini's draining of Italian marshes, he was arguing along the same lines, much like the *Sacred Edict* (ca. 1670) which advised the ideal leader to care for husbandry and the cultivation of the land, and to demand only a reasonable amount of taxes from his citizens.[72] Accordingly, when Pound praised Chinese rulers, he pointed out their practical measures. For instance, "So Shu, king of Soku, built roads,"[73] and C49 mentions an old canal still used by the people (C49.245). To Pound, the Chinese ideal of leadership represented a perfect balance of pragmatism and philosophy.

According to Jacob Burckhardt's *The Culture of the Renaissance in Italy*, the Renaissance concept of politics was marked by a strong belief in the human ability to govern a state rationally. Political thinkers like Machiavelli attempted to construct and rule political entities according to a set of unchanging principles. Pound's idea of the Chinese state is influenced by similar notions. With reference to *The Great Digest* by Confucius Pound claims: "China was tranquil when her rulers understood these few pages. When the principles here defined were neglected, dynasties waned and chaos

---

[68] Redman, Tim, Ezra Pound and Italian Fascism, 88.
[69] Lewis, Wyndham, The Art of Being Ruled, 98.
[70] Quot. in Giles, Herbert A., A History of Chinese Literature, 47.
[71] Mencius, The Works of Mencius, 279f. A reference to emperor Yü, founder of the Hsia dynasty; see Giles, Herbert A., A History of Chinese Literature, 8f.
[72] Baller, F. W., The Sacred Edict, 48ff., 150f.
[73] J/M, 100.

ensued."[74] The reference to Confucius hints at another ideal that Pound saw realized in ancient China: the function of poets and teachers as political advisers. It was a Chinese tradition to advise rulers to live in moderation and shun vice. In the *Book of History*, for instance, the good ruler is advised to avoid excessive drinking, revere the gods and constrain his lust.[75] Giving advice to rulers was also part of the European medieval tradition, as in some poems by Walther von der Vogelweide which Pound translated.[76]

Pound's positive image of the political adviser is another proof for his belief in political rationality – he thought the Chinese dynastic state was distinguished by its adherence to rational rules developed by wise men. Thus the Chinese had put into practice the same close co-operation of intellectuals and the government which Pound himself always sought to achieve. That co-operation embodied a higher principle of identity. The Chinese state provided Pound with the ideal of a cultural-political identity in which forces were balanced and political thought became one with political power. As long as rulers adhered to the principles developed by thinkers, Pound claimed, the state prospered and order was maintained. The latter implied a perfect harmony of the ruler and his advisors, of the ruler and his subjects, of the ruler and the foundations of nature itself – identity turned total. It is in relation to this concept of identity that we read Pound's dictum "Confucian is totalitarian."[77]

European Models: Tuscany, Napoleon

In Europe, the concept of rational government has a tradition of its own. Beginning with the administrative reforms of the medieval emperor Frederick II and continuing through the Italian Renaissance, as mentioned by Burckhardt, it reached a new peak in the Age of Enlightenment, when political discourse moved another step away from the old metaphysics of power, towards a more secular order. Even an age-old institution like the death penalty now became subject to discussion, as in Cesare Beccaria's works. Some rulers of the period gave moderate support to such tendencies and implemented administrative reforms that were influenced by Enlightenment theorists. Pound was openly impressed by that spirit of reform. He even discovered some 18th-century model monarchs who seemed to continue a tradition of good government that went back to ancient China. The poet focused his attention on the rulers of Tuscany, a region ravaged by

74 Confucius, The Great Digest, 19, similarly 89.
75 Giles, Herbert A., A History of Chinese Literature, 10ff.
76 Pound, Ezra, Forked Branches, 82-85.
77 "Mang Tsze (The Ethics of Mencius)" (1938), in: SP, 99.

foreign powers and transferred from one ruler to another in a sequence of rapid political changes and downright conquests. Once owned by the Habsburg family, it fell into the hands of Napoleon in 1799, to be regained by the Habsburgs in 1814, i.e. after Napoleon's defeat. Despite the political disruptions, however, the duchy witnessed some of the most innovative statemanship of the 18th and 19th centuries. Ruled by "enlightened despots," the territory was subject to administrative and legal reforms that would assume model character for other states. Reforms affected such areas as taxation, the penal code, religious liberty and tariff systems. The modernization of a state through its monarch had to appeal to a mind that appreciated strong state power and decisive rulers. And the fact that some Tuscan rulers were more rational or enlightened than other monarchs did not make them indifferent to power. As Pound took care to point out, Cosimo, first Duke of Tuscany, "was neither a liberal in his politics nor a soft-headed idiot."[78] The same applies to the major figures in Pound's version of Tuscan history in *The Fifth Decad.*

One of them is Pietro Leopoldo (1747-1792), later Holy Roman emperor Leopold II (1790-1792), who succeeded his father as duke of Tuscany in 1765. He is defined as a good ruler by his reforms, of which Pound provides a whole list (C44.227f.; from Monte VII.726ff.). Of special importance for Pound was Leopoldo's fight against public and private debt (also mentioned in C50.246). In the other reforms listed, we notice an emphasis on practical improvements, i.e. not merely administrative reforms, but such as affected the life of the people. E.g. guilds received a common tribunal, torture and death penalty were abolished, trade was enhanced. Pietro Leopoldo's reforms had their shortcomings, but they were imrpoved by the other important duke in *The Fifth Decad*, Ferdinando III (1769-1824), son of Pietro Leopoldo and grand duke of Tuscany from 1790. Innovative like his father, he sought to establish himself as a reformer in Leopoldo's tradition, but was hindered from carrying out his plans to their full extent by the conquests of Napoleon. Pound remembers him for his integrity. When forced to leave the duchy, he

> refused to take with him objects of small bulk which he
> held to be the property of the nation. Ferd III. 1796
> that the sovereign be il più galantuomo del paese
>
> (C44.225)

Ferdinando's state-centered policies attracted Pound to such an extent that the poet praised him as an early predecessor of Douglas's Social Credit

[78] "Banking Beneficence and..." (1935), in: P&P VI.247.

theories: "he went ON *into* managed economy, *à la* Douglas in some features, *à la* Corporate State with its control of import and export." Thus he started an Italian tradition of economics that extended to the 1850s, when Zobi wrote on state debt "in phrases to warm any Douglasite heart."[79]

The invasion of the French severed the enlightened ruler from his territory. The reformist "movement of castigation" was interrupted by "the French disturbances and by the chaos brought about by the Jews, who took part in the French chaos."[80] But although interrupted by Napoleon, the Tuscan brand of political Enlightenment remeined vital. For Pound, it belonged to one phase of a historical process that spanned several centuries and embraced, first, the "slow unfolding from Pietro Leopoldo to Ferdinando Terzo of Tuscany" and, more broadly, "the organic movement from pre-Napoleonic Tuscany into the American colonies."[81] In other words, the reforms initiated by the dukes of Tuscany culminated in the civic sense of Jefferson and Adams. Such arguments create an impression of Pound as an advocate of political reason. But while working on the Cantos about Siena and Tuscany in the mid-1930s, Pound was also conducting verbal attacks on Jews and bankers. It is one of the Poundian paradoxes to embrace both the reason of the European Enlightenment and populist extremism at the same time.

Although he admired some moderate rulers like Leopoldo, Pound was equally fascinated by imperial characters. We mentioned Mussolini, who embodied the contemporary ideal, and we must not forget another historical figure, Napoleon. Several of Pound's favorite writers treated the French emperor in their books, with different results. McClellan's overall assessment of Napoleon is mixed.[82] He pays him all due respect as a political talent, but at the same time stresses his human limits. Robert M. Wilson adopted an economic perspective that comes close to Pound's view. Several persons were generally claimed to have defeated Napoleon, among them Talleyrand, Metternich, Alexander I of Russia, the Duke of Wellington or the House of Rothschild. But as Wilson claims, Napoleon was "defeated by usury."[83] Wilson portrays Napoleon as an enemy of finance, who clearly understood stock exchange methods and the possible consequences of loans. He quotes his hero as saying "Loans were not part of my system."[84] Therefore Napoleon became the target of financiers who saw their assets threatened by his plans for economic reforms. They had to destroy him, or would otherwise have to

---

[79] "A Social Creditor Serves Notice" (1936), in: P&P VII.94f.

[80] Pound on 24 May 1943, in: Pound, Ezra, "Ezra Pound Speaking," 320.

[81] "The "Criterion" Passes" (1939), in: P&P VII.429.

[82] McClellan, George B., Venice and Bonaparte, 277ff. Item 79 contains an excerpt from the book.

[83] Wilson, Robert McNair, The Mind of Napoleon, xi.

[84] Wilson, Robert McNair, The Mind of Napoleon, 126.

bear the loss of their business and wealth. The financiers were also responsible for posterity's image of Napoleon as a dictator and suppressor, which they created because they found themselves menaced by Napoleon. Wilson points out the success of Napoleon's economic policy. The emperor borrowed money from himself, without relying on bankers, he granted loans to the public sector at low interest rates and he kept prices at a steady level. As a consequence, industry prospered and the standard of living rose continually. Wilson even has Napoleon praise his own achievements, such as new harbours, roads, bridges and factories.[85] This is not very far from Pound's eulogies on Mussolini. Wilson portrays Napoleon as a political economist and his enemies as international usurers. For Christopher Hollis, too, Napoleon impersonated the anti-usurer: "the force which he challenged was the force of usury; the society for which he fought was a Christian society; the society which conquered him, if ever such a word may be used of any society, anti-Christian. It was a society, whose very fundament was usury."[86] Wilson's and Hollis's terminology more than resembles Pound's.

Pound's own image of Napoleon was ambivalent. For him, the emperor represented once a dictator, once a liberator.[87] The early Pound was hardly enthusiastic about Napoleon and regarded him as an incarnation of provincialism who fought for old-fashioned political ambitions like a "belated condottiere."[88] On the other hand, Pound would later praise the Napoleonic law code for its sense of justice and proclaim it a lasting achievement.[89] As in the case of the Tuscan dukes, Pound applauded the administrative and legal reforms affected by the ruler. In economic terms, Pound's position comes close to Wilson. As Pound believed, Napoleon set out to fight evil in his time (item 304, [55]), but was ultimately cheated by usurers because he neglected economics.[90] Napoleon was Pound's counter-image to "usurious" 19th-century Britain, in which only few politicians found Pound's approval.[91] After Napoleon's defeat, the rise of Metternich and Wellington, presumably usurers' champions, marked the decay of Europe.[92] As Pound feared, the same might happen in contemporary Italy. To make his case, Pound quoted an

---

[85] Wilson, Robert McNair, The Mind of Napoleon, 181f.

[86] Hollis, Christopher, The Two Nations, 133f. The same tendency can be found in: Nelson, Benjamin, The Idea of Usury, 111.

[87] Wilhelm, James J., Ezra Pound: The Tragic Years (1925-1972), 121.

[88] "Provincialism the Enemy" (1917), in: SP, 171.

[89] Thus on 10 July 1942, see Pound, Ezra, "Ezra Pound Speaking," 197.

[90] "Waiting on M. Blum" (1936), in: P&P VII.59. Similarly "Economia Ortologica" (1937), in: P&P VII.253.

[91] Palmerston, for instance; compare "Demarcations" (1937), in: P&P VII.117.

[92] As Chace claims, Pound's notion follows Brooks Adams; see Chace, William M., The Political Identities of Ezra Pound and T. S. Eliot, 88f.

apocryphal dictum by financier Robert Mond: "it took us 20 years to crush Napoleon, but it will not take us 20 years to crush Mussolini."[93]

The U.S.A.

In 1937 Pound divided American national life into four periods:

> 1. American civilisation, 1760 to 1830.
> 2. The period of thinning, of mental impoverishment, scission between life of the mind and life of the nation, say 1830 to 1860.
> 3. The period of despair, civil war as hiatus, 1870 to 1930. The division between the temper, thickness, richness of the mental life of Henry Adams, and Henry James, and that of say U. S. Grant, McKinley, Harding, Coolidge, and Hoover.
> 4. The possibilities of revival, starting perhaps with a valorisation of our cultural heritage [...][94]

We will not analyze Pound's detailed views on events in American history, which plays a much more prominent role in the Adams Cantos than it does in *The Fifth Decad.* But we would like to emphasize some points of general importance. First, Pound's idea of "American civilisation" included a democratic element and was not as ruler-centered as his concepts for Italy. C50 opens with a quotation from John Adams, which highlights the importance of the populace:

> Revolution' said Mr Adams 'took place in the
> minds of the people
> in the fifteen years before Lexington'[95]

The American revolution was made possible by intellectual preconditions which led the people to seek political changes. This idea is different from the concept Pound developed for Italy, where he wanted the ruler to assume power by taking the role of an organizer in a top-to-bottom process. The historical example that Pound presents for the U.S. illustrates a process in which changes arise from the mass of the people.

---

[93] Pound, Ezra, Ezra Pound and Japan, 175.
[94] "The Jefferson-Adams Letters as a Shrine and Monument" (1937-38), in: SP, 117.
[95] C50.246. From John Adams: "What do We mean by the Revolution? The War? That was no part of the Revolution. It was only an Effect and Consequence of it. The Revolution was in the Minds of the People, and this was effected, from 1760 to 1775, in the course of fifteen Years before a drop of blood was drawn at Lexington." Letter from Adams to Jefferson, 24 Aug 1815, in: Adams, John / Jefferson, Thomas, The Adams-Jefferson Letters, 455. Comp. C33 and drafts of C33.161 in BL 43 / 73 / 3252.

But despite such slightly democratic tendencies, Pound remained focused on strong leaders: America's well-being depended on its heads of state, and a strong president like John Adams would increase the wealth of the nation by opposing the vested interests of private business and banking. The Jefferson and Van Buren of C46.234 are mentioned for their fight against "hyper-usura" and "money-lenders." Pound shared Jefferson's preference for a meritocracy, as opposed to an aristocracy of wealth and birth.[96] He interpreted Jefferson as a patrician not unlike Malatesta – which allowed him to praise revolutionary America as "the heir to a classical, Roman, republican tradition transmitted to eighteenth-century America via the Italian city states of the Renaissance period."[97] It might not have been the "strong man" of fascism whom Pound expected to govern the U.S., but it was a leader with the power of a European monarch (by merit, not by heritage). Wilson suspects Pound of personally identifying himself with Adams, as both were conservative patriots who set the public good over popularity, opposed the financial interests of a powerful minority and an American involvement in European wars.[98]

Our brief account of Pound's idea of leadership in U.S. politics would not be complete without mentioning Franklin D. Roosevelt, the president who led America into World War II against the fascist states and thus lost all of Pound's sympathies. When Pound wrote about his home country in a series of articles for the *New English Weekly* from 1932 to 1940, his attitude towards Roosevelt was not fully negative from the beginning, but became increasingly fanatic after 1936.[99] Pound's sympathy for Roosevelt waned when he felt that the President's policies did not adhere to the principles of Social Credit. The less Roosevelt attempted to control the banks, the less Pound supported him. This process began in 1935. When, on 4 July 1935, N. M. Rothschild & Sons announced their co-operation with the Silver Market, Pound wrote: "Roosevelt is fundamentally the usurer's champion."[100] It was basically two issues that estranged Pound from Roosevelt: national debt and monetary reform. As Pound claimed, Roosevelt tolerated the former and failed to

---

[96] Jefferson: "*I* think the best remedy [against an artificial aristocracy] is exactly that provided by all our constitutions, to leave the citizens the free election and separation of the aristoi from the pseudo-aristoi, of the wheat from the chaff. In general they will elect the real good and wise. In some instances, wealth may corrupt, and birth blind them; but not in sufficient degree to endanger the society"; see Jefferson to Adams, 28 Oct 1813, Adams, John / Jefferson, Thomas, The Adams-Jefferson Letters, 388f.

[97] Wilson, Stephen, "Pound's American Revolutions," 185.

[98] As Pound demanded, the U.S. should not intervene with the internal affairs of any country; see "A Civilising Force on the Move" (1936), in: P&P 58. This was an attempt to cut back American interventionism by resurrecting the Monroe Doctrine.

[99] Comp. Davis, Earle, Vision Fugitive, 188f.

[100] Quot. in Flory, Wendy S., The American Ezra Pound, 110.

achieve the latter. If government expenditure was really necessary, it should be paid in stamp scrip to the citizens of the state, which would leave the nation debt-free. The accumulation of debt, however, would mean selling the nation's children into slavery.[101] When Pound's image of Roosevelt became increasingly negative, so did his image of Morgenthau, and conspiracy theories abounded. As we saw in the preceding chapter, many populists believed that Morgenthau represented a shadow government which threatened the legitimate government and sovereignty of the state. Pound's image of Morgenthau shows how his perception of American history changed towards a paranoid perspective: "The great evil is Morgenthau, or the force that keeps it in office. WHEN is the public going to be TOLD efficiently that the U.S. was sold up the river in 1863 by traitors and the agents of Rothschild and their gang???"[102]

Conclusion

We have so far outlined several dimensions of Pound's political ideas that play a role in *The Fifth Decad*. Four aspects are particularly crucial, as they embrace the major part of Pound's thought. First, Pound promotes a state-centered model of government in which the state performs distributive and administrative functions. At the top of the political hierarchy, a head of state with far-reaching executive powers rules. This applies both to the dictatorial regime of Italian fascism and the (more moderate) presidential regime of the U.S.[103] According to Pound, the actual form of government depends on national tradition. Whereas America found its national solution in a strong presidency, Italy's imperial heritage contributed to Mussolini's fascist system.

Second: Pound's ideas, although unusual for an American, were conventional in some respects, which is why he cannot simply be condemned as an excentric. Originally not given to radicalism during his first years in Europe,[104] Pound had ties to Republican conservatism and was deeply aware of his American roots. In a letter to Senator Borah of 2 June 1934, Pound stressed that Cantos 31 to 41 summarized "some of the country's glory" and were supposed to support a reform of the Republican party.[105] In 1928 he

[101] Pound, „The Individual in His Milieu" (1935), in: SP, 280; also comp. Redman, Tim, Ezra Pound and Italian Fascism, 57.
[102] From a letter of 19 July 1940, quot. in: Redman, Tim, Ezra Pound and Italian Fascism, 203.
[103] "Regime" is here used in its neutral sense, denoting a system of government.
[104] Surette: "from his arrival in England through to the immediate postwar period, Pound was conventional in his political and economic opinions" and less radical than the *New Age* group. See Surette, Leon, Pound in Purgatory, 28.
[105] Quot. in Redman, Tim, Ezra Pound and Italian Fascism, 155f.

exclaimed: "Anything is preferable to having another democrat in the White House."[106] The same type of conventional, partisan patriotism informed his references to Adams, Jefferson and Van Buren in *The Fifth Decad*.

Third, Pound's political traditionalism is complemented by a distinctly irrational dimension that expresses itself in a metaphysics of power. Pound glorifies monarchs as godlike individuals of superior intellect, "doers" who are put high above common individuals by a blend of instinct and inspiration. Fourth, Pound's irrationality also came to dominate his perception of power relations within the state. The populist tradition provided Pound with a deep distrust of alleged shadowy forces behind politics, a distrust he shared and through which he increasingly radicalized himself.[107] The fight against the international "usurocracy" became the major criterion for Pound's assessment of politicians. It was for their opposition, respectively non-opposition, to usury that he championed Napoleon and despised F. D. Roosevelt. Other criteria moved to the background. More and more, Pound's obsession with economics overshadowed his interest in politics and culture, until it infected his poems.

[106] "The Exile" (1928), in: P&P V.17.

[107] The expression is appropriate, because Pound was solely responsible for his opinions and was not under direct pressure from a party or an individual. It is untrue that he "was radicalized," as some scholars claim.

III.4 Money as Nemesis, Economics as History

> *A notion prevails that the Money Market is something so impalpable that it can only be spoken of in very abstract words, and that therefore books on it must always be exceedingly difficult. But I maintain that the Money Market is as concrete and real as anything else; that it can be described in as plain words; that it is the writer's fault if what he says is not clear.*
>
> (Walter Bagehot, *Lombard Street*)

> *Probably there is nothing so universally used and so little understood as money.*
>
> (James P. Warburg, *The Money Muddle*)

Introduction

Pound has sometimes been scorned for his obsession with economics, particularly for introducing such a dry matter into poetry, which is still expected by some critics to be "lyrical." We should not forget, however, that Pound's interest in economics was not an exception, but a sign of the times. During the early decades of the 20th century, many authors were concerned with economic issues. Writers addressed such mundane issues like the power of finance and the stock exchange. Dos Passos wrote *U.S.A.* (1930-1936), Dreiser *The Financier* (1912) and *The Titan* (1914), while G. K. Chesterton published a collection of essays called *Utopia of Usurers* (1917). In short, Pound was not the only writer who would have agreed with Robert M. Wilson that money was the "greatest of all international powers."[1] What gives Pound's interest in economics a more individual accent is his historical perspective, particularly the inclusion of certain historical periods, persons or institutions in his work. Another inidividual trait is his fixation on usury, which he condemned not only as an important economic problem, but as a universal evil. This fixation led scholars to conclusions like Maud Ellmann's

[1] Wilson, Robert McNair, The Mind of Napoleon, ix.

melodramatic statement that "Pound's obsession with the 'usurocracy' was to lead to his downfall."[2]

As a young man, Pound was not yet an obsessive amateur economist, but rather a poet mainly interested in poetry. Gradually, however, he underwent a conversion that is not to be overestimated. According to Redman, Pound's shift of interest from *l'art pour l'art* to economics seems to have occured in about 1920. Pound, after he had met Douglas, now used his *New Age* articles to praise Douglas's attacks on „usury", and announced a new interest in economics – not because he had abandoned art, but because he felt an increasing sense of urgency about economic issues.[3] In a review of 1920, Pound explains the triumph of man over animals in terms of usury and exploitation He argues within a broad framework of economic conditions – "A bloated usury, a cowardly and snivelling politics, a disgusting financial system, the sadistic curse of Christianity work together" to create "milkable human cows, the shearable human sheep."[4] In the same year he proclaimed usury "the basis of our alleged civilization."[5] Thus Pound crossed his personal Rubicon, with consequences he could not foresee at that time. To him, usury was now no longer a minor aspect of economic morals, but a socio-historical, if not anthropological, phenomenon that undermined society as a whole.

Over the next years, Pound's continuing relations to editor A. R. Orage and reformers like C. H. Douglas sustained his interest in economics. After Orage had returned to England and founded the *New English Weekly* in 1932, Pound started to contribute articles on economics. When Orage died in November 1934, Pound seems to have lost a stabilizing influence. He now adopted increasingly extreme notions on economics and revered Mussolini stronger than before.[6] By 1934, most of Pound's writings were concerned with economic issues. At that time, Pound wrote the "Volitionist Economics" questionnaire that covered subjects like the distribution of purchasing power, currency and taxation. He was now convinced of "the bearing of econ/factor on every bloody human activity."[7] His opinions became inceasingly populist and he would sometimes evade rational discussion. When Roosevelt's industrial adviser Woodward asked Pound how C. H. Douglas would prevent inflation, Pound responded with verbal attacks on Jews and bankers.[8] By 1937, obviously, Pound's resentments had become as obsessive as his interest

---

[2] Ellmann, Maud, The Poetics of Impersonality, 163f.
[3] Redman, Tim, Ezra Pound and Italian Fascism, 31.
[4] "Hudson: Poet Strayed into Science" (1920), in: SP, 400.
[5] "A Letter From London" (1920), in: P&P XI.4.
[6] Flory, Wendy S., The American Ezra Pound, 42f.
[7] Quot. in: Tytell, John, Ezra Pound: The Solitary Volcano, 235.
[8] Tytell, John, Ezra Pound: The Solitary Volcano, 238.

in economics. More than that, both fueled each other, as will become clear in this chapter.

We will isolate several important aspects of Pound's economic theories: his general concept of money, his definition of usury and his criticism of banking. We will then outline an economic history according to Pound, a history stretching from classical Rome to 20th-century monetary reformers and their fight against economic orthodoxy. As should be emphasized, we will only deal with economic theories in their relation to Pound. The purpose of this study is to understand the foundations of Pound's ideas, not to give an objective assessment of the virtues or flaws of certain economic theories. Pound's subjective fascination with them is much more interesting, and a lot more telling.

Money

As Pound once noted, few treatises on economics began with a definition of money;[9] and even Marx was guilty of ignoring the nature of money.[10] Hence, Pound was not surprised about the persistence of economic problems, which could only be fought by using terminological precision: "With a clear and exact definition of money, a clear understanding of the nature of money, years of economic bewilderment and stupidity will be avoided."[11] For Pound, justice was the chief criterion for a sound economic system, and monetary theory, if understood properly, led to the required contemplation of justice.[12] With his insisting on terminological precision, Pound moved along the same lines as monetary reformer C. H. Douglas, who pointed out the importance of defining the exact nature of money.[13]

Usually money is attributed two functions: first, as a means of payment and medium of exchange, and second as a unit of account.[14] Bacon regarded money as a means of exchange, which has to be kept in distribution, "that the

[9] Pound, Ezra, Ezra Pound and Japan, 171.

[10] "History and Ignorance" (1935), in: SP, 238; also "The Individual in His Milieu" (1935), in: P&P VI.318f. The notion that Marx did not understand the nature of money was not an original idea of Pound's. Gesell and Kitson shared the same view, see Redman, Tim, Ezra Pound and Italian Fascism, 132, 147. Compare Gesell, Silvio, The Natural Economic Order, 4; Kitson, Arthur, "The Root of All Evil," in: *New Age* (27 Feb 1913), 400.

[11] Pound, Ezra, Impact, 61.

[12] Pound, Ezra, Impact, 68f.

[13] Hutchinson, Frances / Burkitt, Brian, The Political Economy of Social Credit and Guild Socialism, 36.

[14] On common definitions of money see Kindleberger, Charles P., A Financial History of Western Europe, 19f. In order to establish a connection to Pound's background reading on economics, the following definitions have been chiefly taken from a book he knew, Montgomery Butchart's *Money*.

treasure and monies in a state be not gathered into few hands, for otherwise a state may have a good stock and yet starve; and money is like muck; no good except it be spread."[15] Here we already encounter an idea later endorsed by Pound, namely that money was not to be hoarded by the happy few. Locke was an adherent of the commodity theory of money and defined it as a commodity used for exchange.[16] For Hume, money was a means to facilitate the exchange of one commodity for another[17] and a representation of labour and commodities.[18] According to John Gray, money was "merely a commodity, the price of which rises and falls, like every other commodity, in proportion as the demand for it is great or small."[19] W. T. Foster regarded it as suspended purchasing power,[20] while Angell defined it as "a medium of exchange, a measure of value, a standard of deferred payment and a store of value."[21] James Warburg called money a medium of exchange and a common denominator of value.[22] Hattersley saw it as a title to goods and services – "a social mechanism to facilitate their orderly production and distribution."[23]

Many of the above definitions endorse the commodity theory of money, in which, as Kitson explains, money functions as a medium of exchange, a common measure and standard of value. Kitson calls it absurd to define money as a commodity,[24] because a commodity "is the *end* desired by exchange; money is only a *means* to that end, the mechanism by which exchanges are affected."[25] For him, the value of money does not equal the value of the metal of which the money is made. Treating money as a commodity gives rise to hoarding, while it must actually be kept in circulation in order to fulfill its functions. Kitson's view represents what we could call the monetary reformers' perspective. It criticized the positions of earlier economists, who claimed that the value of money was a function of its supply and of the costs of its production, and that paper money was only a certificate of claim on true commodity money (i.e. gold). Reformers like Gesell and Douglas both based their economic assumptions on the quantity theory of

---

[15] Francis Bacon in 1625, in: Butchart, Montgomery, Money, 37.
[16] Locke, John, "Some Considerations of the Consequences of the Lowering of Interest," 34.
[17] "On Money," in: Hume, David, Essays Moral, Political and Literary, 289.
[18] Hume, David, Essays Moral, Political and Literary, 292f.
[19] John Gray in 1831, in: Butchart, Montgomery, Money, 122; similarly Archibald Alison in 1849, in: Butchart, Montgomery, Money, 22.
[20] William T. Foster in 1924, in: Butchart, Montgomery, Money, 109.
[21] Norman Angell in 1930, in: Butchart, Montgomery, Money, 26.
[22] Warburg, James P., The Money Muddle, 9.
[23] C. Marshall Hattersley in 1934, in: Butchart, Montgomery, Money, 132.
[24] Kitson, Arthur, A Scientific Solution of the Money Question, 164, also 146, 171f., 188f., 222.
[25] Kitson, Arthur, A Scientific Solution of the Money Question, 172.

money.[26] At the beginning of the 20th century, that theory had not yet achieved full credibility and therefore met the resistance of orthodox economists. The theory assumes that the prices of goods and services are a function of the costs necessary to produce and maintain these commodities, the supply and demand for them, as well as of the supply of money. If demand remains stable, prices depend on the supply of money.

Pound, too, contradicted the commodity theory of money as proposed by Marx and others. For Marx, money expressed the universal value of commodities. For Pound, it denoted the prices created by bankers. True money represented goods or services, not gold, whereas a commodity was a durable, "material thing or substance."[27] Pound defines money as a "measured claim" of general nature (i.e. including more than one type of goods or services). It does not bear interest and can bee freely transferred from one person to another. Money is "good" when its issuer possesses an amount of goods or services fully adequate to the quantity of money issued. As soon as more money is issued, inflation occurs.[28] Pound expected money to be a "certificate of work done,"[29] a means of exchange issued against goods: "for every ten shillings paper actually set in circulation there would be in existence the product."[30] Pound quotes Schacht as saying "Money that doesn't represent commerceable goods, meaning goods you can buy and sell, is mere paper *valuta*."[31] Pound himself could have written that sentence. How much Pound despised the commodity theory of money becomes clear from his obsessive "Christmas litanies" (items 246f.), in which he repeats his statement on money being no commodity over and over again. As Pound argues, neither money nor work are commodities, because you cannot eat or wear them.

What Pound generally aimed at was a close relation between money value and production. Gold, on the other hand, only served the financiers and bankers. We find the same thought concisely stated by Warburg: "The quantity of money created by the agreed authority must bear a direct relationship to the amount of work done or things exchanged in the community."[32] Accordingly, Pound's ally Orage wanted to equate the nation's purchasing power to available goods.[33] Purchasing power was vital for both Orage and Pound. The poet therefore called for the introduction of the

---

26 On the quantity theory of money see Kindleberger, Charles P., A Financial History of Western Europe, 27f.

27 Pound, Ezra, Pound/Zukofsky, 168, letter of 28 May 1935.

28 "Defining Money" (1937), in: P&P VII.177.

29 "Economics" (1933), in: P&P VI.13.

30 "The Depression Has Just Begun" (1932), in: P&P V.336.

31 "United States of Europe?" (1938), in: P&P VII.393. Also in "Communications" (1939), in: P&P VII.439.

32 Warburg, James P., The Money Muddle, 10, also 31.

33 "In the Wounds (Memoriam A. R. Orage)" (1935), in: SP, 421.

"commodity dollar," a dollar of varying gold content, but of fixed purchasing power.[34] General purchasing power was to be enhanced by sustained distribution.[35] What was needed, Pound believed, was a certain amount of perishable or diminishing money, "Schwundgeld," i.e. unhoardable money that had to be spent within a given period of time.[36]

Another means of achieving economic justice was the introduction of the "just price," a concept endorsed by many monetary reformers of the early 20th century.[37] Even earlier, Christopher Hollis, one of Pound's favorite writers, had claimed that money-power was best broken by keeping the price-level stable.[38] Similarly, economist Frederick Soddy called on the state to "smoothly and automatically distribute wealth without limit at a constant price-level."[39] For Pound, the just price was "basic in all economics."[40] The just price was to function as a regulatory mechanism to preserve the purchasing power of the populace. As Odon Por pointed out, it was not the same as a fixed price, but "should bear a certain definite relation to the cost of production, measured by a unit of labour."[41] Por advocates the concept of the just price as a particularly *moral* concept, a perspective shared by Pound.

In addition to money, Pound was also interested in other economic problems he regarded as crucial – the equal distribution of goods, legislation as a means of freeing the economy from private interests and the problem of how to combine the right to private property with the need for controlling governance. But money always remained the most basic problem for Pound. As long as no clear definition of money was agreed upon, economic problems would persist. Few countries had managed to settle the money issue in a satisfying way, and Pound left no doubt as to where he saw his monetary concepts realized. In 1939 he said: "War against Germany in our time, would be war against an honest concept of money."[42]

---

[34] For a definition of the "commodity dollar" see Warburg, James P., The Money Muddle, 69.

[35] J/M, 69; also "In the Wounds (Memoriam A. R. Orage)" (1935), in: SP, 419.

[36] "The Individual in his Milieu" (1935), in: SP, 247.

[37] On the concept of the just price see Hutchinson, Frances / Burkitt, Brian, The Political Economy of Social Credit and Guild Socialism, 50-54.

[38] Hollis, Christopher, The Two Nations, 246.

[39] Soddy, Frederick, "The 'Pound for Pound' System of Scientific National Monetary Reform," in: Butchart, Montgomery (ed.), To-Morrow's Money, 98.

[40] Pound on 6 Nov 1941, in: Pound, Ezra, "Ezra Pound Speaking," 18.

[41] Por, Odon, Guilds and Co-operatives in Italy, 64f.

[42] Pound, Ezra, Ezra Pound and Japan, 172.

Natural Abundance versus Usury

In some old cities you can still find medieval tower-clocks from which moving figures emerge when the hour strikes. Often you will see a wooden Everyman fleeing from the pursuing figure of Death. *The Fifth Decad*, too, has its Death figure to appear at regular intervals and even at the most idyllic moments: Usura. We often encounter it in the shape of Geryon, originally a monster with three bodies and three heads that guards the eighth circle of hell in Dante.[43] For Pound it became the symbol of fraud[44] and of destruction, "Gerion that passeth mountains and crusheth down walls and towers."[45] It raises its head in C49 and C50, but also appears as Usura itself in C45. Pound even stressed that the "point of that Fifth [Decad] is the Usura."[46] To fight it is one of the driving forces behind *The Fifth Decad*, which makes it necessary to reconstruct Pound's general concept of usury. As in our analysis of the populist and sensationalist aspects of Pound's thought, we will benefit from a look at the historical discourse, in this case about usury, a tradition Pound deliberately continued.

Usury has undergone countless definitions[47] in texts that range from religious classics to obscure pamphlets. Classical Greece condemned usury, and Aristotle is one of the major authorities on the subject (Politics I.10). The philosopher distinguished two ways of acquiring wealth, one natural (earnings from fruits or animals), the other unnatural:

> The most hated sort, and with the greatest reason, is usury, which makes a gain out of money itself, and not from the natural object of it. For money was intended to be used in exchange, but not to increase at interest. And this term interest, which means the birth of money from money, is applied to the breeding of money […]

Starting from Aristotle's definition, Marx would later oppose "natural" circulation (from commodity to money to commodity) with "chrematistic" circulation (money to commodity to money), which he condemned.[48]

---

[43] See Dante, Divine Comedy, Inf. XVII.7-10, 93, 133.

[44] Pound, Ezra, The Spirit of Romance, 133f.

[45] "Italy's Frame-up" (1936), in: P&P VII.23.

[46] Letter to Zukofsky of 29 Nov 1937, in: Pound, Ezra, Pound/Zukofsky, 194.

[47] To mention the present standard: The OED defines usury as the "fact or practice of lending money at interest; esp. in later use, the practice of charging, taking, or contracting to receive, excessive or illegal rates of interest for money on loan." On the Latin "foenore" see Salmasius, Claudius, Dissertatio de foenore trapezitico, 560.

[48] Shell, Marc, The Economy of Literature, 94, mentions the passage in Marx, Contribution to the Critique of Political Economy, ed. Maurice Dobb, New York 1970, 137n.

The Qur'an threats usurers that they "shall be given over to the fire; therein shall they abide for ever" (Sure 2.275.). The Old Testament forbids lending on usury to one's "brother" (i.e. fellow-tribe member) and permits it towards strangers (Ex 22:25, Lev 25:36f., Dt 23:19f.). In many source texts, the Christian usurer is called *usurarius* or *fenerator* (i.e., he who lands at interest, from *fenus* = interest).[49] Usury itself was often referred to in the plural (*usurae*), as if to hint at the multitudinous forms in which the vice appeared. The form *usura* denoted the totality of illicit financial businesses. Lending money at interest was not generally deemed illicit, nor was it regarded as usurious from the start. Lending became usury only when no real goods were involved and the principle of reciprocal barter for the mutual good was undermined. As St Thomas stated, the usurer sold something which did not exist, and hence created inequality, as opposed to justice. As Le Goff points out, usury both opposed the just price and nature, two aspects also stressed by Pound. The usurer wants his money to breed, whereas the Christian philosophers stress its sterility. Money is unable to bear fruit, as Bonaventura says. Hence, the usurer commits an unnatural act.[50] In the *Inferno*, Dante expresses a similar opinion, when he says: "e perché l'usuriere altra via tene, / per sé natura e per la sua seguace / dispregia, poi ch'in altro pon la spene" (Inferno 11.109ff.). In the stoneworks of medieval churches, the usurers had their places among sinners. In Chartres, for instance, a usurer is depicted with his swollen purse in his hands and the devil standing behind him, his claw on the man's arm. The church councils of the 12th to the 14th centuries, and the canonic law created by them, aimed at a containment of usury, which was now defined as a species of theft that was forbidden by the Seventh Commandment, "Thou shalt not steal." Usury was interpreted accordingly by the teachers and philosophers in their *summae*. Whether Bonaventura, Thomas or William of Auxerre, they all condemned usury as an expression of idleness and greed, while Stephen of Bourbon and William of Auxerre regarded usury as a form of avarice.

Chaucer's *Canterbury Tales* cultivated the image of the Jewish usurer.[51] Marx, who also knew "the usurer, that old-fashioned but ever renewed specimen of the capitalist," quoted a passage from Martin Luther, who regarded usury as a devastating monster stronger than Dante's Geryon.[52] Bacon quoted the Aristotelian – and later Poundian – opinion that usury was "against Nature, for *Money* to beget *Money*." According to Bacon, usury

---

[49] Le Goff, Jacques, Wucherzins und Höllenqualen: Ökonomie und Religion im Mittelalter, 102, n. 11.

[50] Le Goff, Jacques, Wucherzins und Höllenqualen: Ökonomie und Religion im Mittelalter, 27-31.

[51] On medieval notions of usury see chapter 3 of Watts, Cedric, Literature and Money.

[52] See Marx, Karl, The Capital vol. I, part 7, chapter 24.3, n. 20.

decreases the number of merchants and, second, makes them poorer, which, third, reduces customs. Fourth, "it bringeth the Treasure of a Realme or State, into a few Hands," fifth, it reduces the price of land, and sixth, it stalls progress in industry and invention. Seventh, "it is the Canker and Ruine of many Mens Estates." However, usury is not totally destructive of assets, "*Usury* doth but gnaw upon them."[53] We find repercussions of Bacon's language in C45, in which "Azure hath a canker" and usury "gnaweth the thread" (C45.230). Similarly, Chamberlen spoke of "that corroding and destructive Canker, Usury."[54]

Criticism of usury continued after the Early Modern period. At the beginning of the 19th century, the Irish priest Jeremiah O'Callaghan devoted his life to the fight against usury, a fight, however, which only secured him the suspicion of his superiors, who ordered him more than once to stop his increasingly quixotic crusade against usury.[55] O'Callaghan is representative of what could be called the Old Testament fraction of anti-usury fanatics. He interpreted usury as a vice that opposes the Mosaic law. A trace of this belief can also be found in Pound. Christopher Hollis accused usury of keeping borrowers under a constant tyranny of debt and of resulting in cultural and social sterility – "For under usury life withers, and the worship of the sterile metals spreads sterility over the whole life of society."[56] For Kitson, usury was a cancer eating into politics and society like a parasite.[57] And because America's wealth rested on debt and credit, interest devoured everything.[58] Kitson concluded on usury: "our modern so-called Christian Civilization is practically built on it."[59] This corresponds with Pound's 1920 statement mentioned earlier.

The recurring feature in many attacks on usury is its allegedly "unnatural" increase, as opposed to the reproduction of living beings. In Kitson's words, "*Wealth is wholly unproductive. Man and nature are alone productive.*"[60] Pound shared this view and condemned "the injustice of

---

53 Bacon, Francis, "Of Usurie," 125f.

54 Hugh Chamberlen in 1696, in: Butchart, Montgomery, Money, 72.

55 For his story see Nelson, Benjamin, The Idea of Usury, 124-132.

56 Hollis, Christopher, The Two Nations, 252.

57 Kitson, Arthur, A Scientific Solution of the Money Question, 334.

58 For notes on Kitson see Finlay, John L., Social Credit, 23-26. A thinker in the tradition of Proudhon and Spencer, he fought for a silver standard and founded the *Credit Reform League* in 1905 (later called *Banking and Currency Reform League*). He was increasingly given to conspiracy theories, arguing that some economic crises had been engineered by Jewish financiers. In fact, he showed a marked anti-Semitic tendency.

59 Kitson, Arthur, "Political Economy or The Science of Robbery," in: Butchart, Montgomery (ed.), To-Morrow's Money, 76. Coughlin also commented on usury, see Coughlin, Charles, Money!, 90f.

60 Kitson, Arthur, A Scientific Solution of the Money Question, 311.

supposing that money 'grows' (*vide* Shylock, etc.), while goods perish."[61] The "unnatural" character of usury led Pound to associate it with sodomy.[62]

Accordingly, the increase of wealth is not productive, but, by hoarding, deprives society of available resources. Usurers benefit from creating an artificial scarcity of money, grain, and merchandise.[63] The counter-concept, as favored by Pound, is sharing or the "increment of association,"[64] i.e. distribution and exchange. As opposed to usury, it is not sterile, as it enhances circulation and thereby helps to produce new commodities. As Proudhon said, "*productive industry is the only real basis of credit.*"[65] More specifically, Pound saw the basis of real wealth in natural resources refined by labor.[66] What Pound had in mind as an ideal were, literally, the "fruits of nature." He believed in fecundity and natural abundance and also interpreted usury in similar terms, so when he claimed that "Shylock was after Antonio's means to fecundity."[67] The references to "5 % fruitage" (C43.221) are in the same line of argument.[68] The fruit analogy was not new. For Ruskin, capital was sane only if acting as a "root" from which "fruit" would spring..[69]

As these remarks show, Pound experienced usury not only as a legal, but also as an ethical, moral and cultural issue.[70] Pound believed that the prevalence of usury would entail cultural long-term consequences, i.e. the decline of art.[71] As he claimed in 1935, usury penetrated everything from music to brick-making.[72] The rise of usury also went hand in hand with a decline of the *perception* of art.[73] Affecting the commercialization of art, usury obscured perception and the senses, because it was more interested in financial gain than in good art: "Any form of 'entertainment' that debases

[61] "The Individual in his Milieu" (1935), in: SP, 247; following Hollis's "eternal lie of Shylock" in: Hollis, Christopher, The Two Nations, 245; refers to Shakespeare, *Merchant* I.3.96f.
[62] Pound, Ezra, Impact, 144.
[63] "An Introduction to the Economic Nature of the United States" (1944, orig. Italian), in: SP, 142.
[64] "The Individual in his Milieu" (1935), in: SP, 251.
[65] Proudhon in 1850, in: Butchart, Montgomery (comp.), Money, 239.
[66] Pound in 1942, Pound, Ezra, "Ezra Pound Speaking," 196.
[67] "Banks Are a Blessing" (1939), in: P&P VII.404.
[68] Marsh, Alec, Money and Modernity, 120.
[69] Comp. Finlay, John L., Social Credit: The English Origins, 27.
[70] Pound, Ezra, Polite Essays, 55.
[71] Another interesting parallel between Pound and a contemporary writer. Like Pound, Corey establishes links between the rise of a money aristocracy and the decline (or downright non-existence) of culture: "Art collections adorned the masters of money, but beneath was an emptiness of creative cultural life," in: Corey, Lewis, The House of Morgan, 239.
[72] Pound, Ezra, Ezra Pound and Music, 375.
[73] "Musicians" (1938), in: P&P VII.363.

perception, anything that profanes the mysteries or tends to obscure discrimination, goes hand in hand with drives toward money profit."[74] Pound thinks that Henry Adams should have wondered why the design of the church of Mont St. Michel appeared so "neat and tidy," why San Zeno "has a column signed by the architect himself and WHY he cd. *afford* to cut it by hand Meaning with his OWN hands," and why St Trophime and St Hilaire were so different from the "opera house" style of St Peters in Rome. The answer is economics – one economic system created Romanesque cathedrals, the other merely garish façades.[75]

An important complementary term to usury is debt. Public debt was condemned by economists from all periods as a burden ultimately imposed on the populace. For Hume, public debt meant "to mortgage the public revenues, and to trust that posterity will pay off the incumbrances contracted by their ancestors," a "practice which appears ruinous beyond all controversy."[76] Accordingly, Warburg warned that excessive borrowing would increase taxation for future generations or else prepare the way for repudiation.[77] Pound regarded debt as the modern version of slavery, as it aimed at "keeping the debtor in debt perpetually or at least for the longest possible period."[78] Government bonds caused financial burdens for just the people who actually should not pay, because they had little money.[79] Pound was convinced of the state's right to borrow money without paying interest, a notion he asserted in the first lines of C48 ("And if the money be rented"), which we mentioned in chapter II.1.b. Pound followed Jefferson in demanding that debts should not continue beyond a generation.[80] He praised Pietro Leopoldo for his fight against state debt and for the abolition of gaolings for debt (C44.227). The extinction of debt was for Pound among the highest goals a politician could achieve, because it meant a victory over the financiers, whose only objective was the creation of debt, even by wars.[81] Pound combined his chief dislikes (usury, debt, financiers) in one sentence, when he said: "Usury is *not* sharing. Usury is the root of all wars. Nothing but wars makes debts fast enough to suit 'great' financiers."[82]

In Pound's work, usury represents a timeless force that permeates history. It vitiates the pace of history at the same time that it perverts the

---

[74] GK, 281f.
[75] "How to Save Business" (1936), in: P&P VII.14.
[76] "Of Public Credit," Hume, David, Essays Moral, Political and Literary, 355f.
[77] Warburg, James P., The Money Muddle, 201.
[78] Pound on 25 March 1943, Pound, Ezra, "Ezra Pound Speaking," 261.
[79] "Ezra Pound on Gold, War, and National Money" (1939), in: P&P VII.446.
[80] Comp. Murray, David, "Pound-Signs: Money and Representation in Ezra Pound," 186.
[81] Pound in about 1941, in: Pound, Ezra, "Ezra Pound Speaking," 382 and 383, referring the reader to pp. 206f. (actually 208) in Hollis, Christopher, The Two Nations.
[82] "Reviews" (1935), in: P&P VI.333.

sacraments. Pound included it among the most powerful and determinant impulses that shape the course of history. It reigned the Roman Empire as much as the 19th century, when it governed the actions of politicians like Metternich and Wellington (C50.248). Usury is a chimera that haunts the *Cantos* in several disguises. In Pound's poems, usury is not only a "mistress of many tongues," but also a monster of many metaphors. It is identified as a disgusting animal, "the beast with a hundred legs" (C15.64), as a murrain, cancer, slayer and old man (C45.229f.), a sepulchre (C46.234), Geryon (C49.245, C51.251) and Seramis (C51.251). In Pound's ultimately non-Christian work, usury takes the place of anti-Christ. However, as opposed to Christian apocalyptics, Pound suuggested not a religious, but a political solution to this universal problem, as he stressed in one of his money pamphlets: "USURY is the cancer of the world, which only the surgeon's knife of Fascism can cut out of the life of nations."[83]

Banking

In *Time and Western Man* Wyndham Lewis remarked with his usual sarcasm: "The question may have sometimes occurred to people why what goes on in the bed or upon the battlefield should be more 'romantic' than what happens in the bank."[84] As the Siena Cantos show, banks may even be a suitable subject for poetry, and we will soon discuss the role of the *Monte dei Paschi* within the framework of Poundian economic history. First, however, we should clarify Pound's general attitude towards banking. He was influenced by an American tradition of long standing: Jefferson had already envisioned powerful banks as a threat to society. He feared they would control the issuing of money and, through their greed, make many people homeless. The Agrarian Taylor regarded banking power as stronger than civil power, which it tended to enslave. Taylor used the history of the Roman Empire to demonstrate the negative influence of moneyed interests on the state. He mentioned usury as a particularly pernicious device: "Compound usury and an usurpation of national credit are two of the means used by the system of banking. [...] The patricians enslaved individuals with usury; banking, nations."[85] Pound's paternal grandfather Thaddeus Pound argued against the powerful position of private banks in state politics.[86] And C. H. Douglas warned in 1924 that the citizens' money deposited in the banks was

---

83 Quot. in Tytell, John, Ezra Pound: The Solitary Volcano, 245.

84 Lewis, Wyndham, Time and Western Man, 21.

85 Taylor, John, An Inquiry into the Principles and Policy of the Government of the United States, 281.

86 Tytell, John, Ezra Pound: The Solitary Volcano, 13.

"constantly created and destroyed by the banking system for its own financial advantage."[87]

Pound claimed he had no aversion to banking as such, only against "stranglers."[88] He discovered two types of banks in history, "banks built for beneficence, for reconstruction; and banks created to prey on the people."[89] The good banks were represented by the *Monte dei Paschi*, the others by the Banca San Giorgio.[90] Pound also distinguished between banks as *issuers* and *lenders* of money.[91] True economic power rested on the latter, the lending or control of credit, that is, control of the currency.[92] Lending contributed to the "legalisation of usury via the banks."[93] Banks were only legitimate if their transactions reflected the actual productivity of a community, as did the *Monte dei Paschi*.[94] As we will soon discuss the *Monte*, we should first take a closer look at one of the chief "evil" banks in the Pound cosmos, the Bank of England. Pound considered it the usurper of currency power, the originator of public debt and the prototype of usurious practice. As Hollis (one of Pound's sources) explains, the Bank of England was founded to collect money from the public and supply William III with it. The Bank had the privilege of issuing notes. If a creditor demanded cash, the Bank possessed the right to ask the government to raise the required amount of money by taxation, "as Paterson, the originator of the Bank, himself explained with charming simplicity, 'The bank hath benefit of the interest on all moneys which it creates out of nothing.'."[95] Pound later called Paterson's statement the formative moment of the usury system.[96]

---

[87] Quot. in: Hutchinson, Frances / Burkitt, Brian, The Political Economy of Social Credit and Guild Socialism, 39.

[88] "Banking Beneficence and..." (1935), in: P&P VI.247.

[89] Pound, Ezra, Impact, 147; also "Ecclesiastical History" (1934), in: SP, 61. For Pound and his ideas on historical banks see Chace, William M., The Political Identities of Ezra Pound and T. S. Eliot, 58 passim.

[90] Pound, Ezra, "Banking Beneficence, and ...," BL 43 / 69 / 3034. See Lobero, Antonio, Memorie sulla banca di S. Giorgio, Genoa 1822; also Rota, Pietro, Storia delle banche, 120f.

[91] Pound in one of his less modest moments: "After a good deal of research I can say that so far as I know I am the first person clearly to state what service the *issuer* of money performs, and why he should receive a just recompense for it. On that point at least I claim place among serious economists and assert the value of my writings on money," in: Gordon, David M. (ed.), Ezra Pound and James Laughlin: Selected Letters, 117f., letter of 9 Oct 1940.

[92] "Provincialism the Enemy" (1917), in: SP, 175f.

[93] "Ecclesiastical History" (1934), in: P&P 186.

[94] Comp. Flory, Wendy S., The American Ezra Pound, 61.

[95] Hollis, Christopher, The Two Nations, 30, also 36. Comp. "The Root of Evil" (1935), in: P&P VI.250.

[96] Pound on 30 March 1943, Pound, Ezra, "Ezra Pound Speaking," 265.

For Belloc the foundation of the Bank of England was the beginning of national debt. When the Bank issued a promise to pay, "all the resources of England were to be put at its disposal to enable it to keep that promise – in other words, its credit was not private but public" and existed as long as it was possible to tax the citizens. But although the Bank rested on public credit, it was not a fully public institution and not responsible to the government. Hence, it offered private money-lenders the opportunity to levy a constant tax on the public for the payment of national debt.[97] Jarvie, a pamphleteer and one of Pound's sources, calls the Bank of England a "private and long-sustained effort in lucrative mumbo jumbo."[98] He suggests connections between the Rothschilds and the Bank and mentions links of the Bank's directors to firms and concerns.[99] Here we encounter once more a marked antipathy to the mysterious "money-lenders" of American populism, on which we commented in an earlier chapter.

Centuries of Usury: An Economic History

Pound wrote extensively on several periods in European and American economic history. In addition to the events in his home country, he focused mainly on the ancient Romans, the Middle Ages, Early Modern Tuscany and the "usurious" 19th century. In this chapter, we will present a survey of Pound's ideas on economic history. It will contain some of the elements which are by now well-known to readers – usury, banking and a clear-cut set of villains.

Appian reports how, in about 111 BC, money lenders and their creditors were involved in violent disputes. The praetor Asellio, one of the opponents of the lenders, was murdered while making a libation. Appian leaves no doubt that the murder of Asellio was a sacrilege and mentions that the assassins even entered the forbidden area of the Vestals.[100] The connection between usury and sacrilege is quite obvious, as it is in Pound's C45. As Hume points out, the Roman state declined in the wake of Constantine's introduction of new tax laws.[101] Brooks Adams analyzed the subject in *The Law of Civilization and Decay*, which Pound read in the late 1930s. Adams's approach to Roman society is governed by a strongly economic perspective. He interprets usury and politics as instruments of oppression, used by the wealthy class of landowners to maintain their status and exploit the non-

---

[97] Hilaire Belloc in 1934, in: Butchart, Montgomery (comp.), Money, 46ff.
[98] Jarvie, J. R., The Old Lady Unveiled, 7.
[99] See Jarvie, J. R., The Old Lady Unveiled, 40, 24-30, passim.
[100] Appian, The Civil Wars, I.54.
[101] "Of Taxes," in: Hume, David, Essays Moral, Political and Literary, 352.

patrician part of the population. He thus adopts the notions of Macauly who, in his preface to *Virginia*, analyzed Roman society in terms of credit, debt, landowners, serfdom and usury. Adams concludes that "slavery was the ulcer which ate into the flesh, and the Roman fiscal system, coupled as it was with usury, was calculated to enslave all but the oligarchy who made the laws."[102] The predominance of an economic mentality in Roman society is here seen as a sign of social decay, which caused family disintegration and a decline in births – thus economic tendencies affected fertility, and hence society as a whole.

Like Adams, Pound attributed the fall of the Roman Empire to the influence of malevolent economic agents who used the system for their own interests, "the same follies that your kikes, your Rothschilds, Beits, Sieffs, Schiffs, and Goldsmids have squirted into your veins."[103] Whether Pound looked at ancient or contemporay economic systems, he always discovered financiers who manipulated society. Pound even linked the beginnings of the Roman Empire to a historical shift in the European usury system. The empire was able to emerge as a dominant force "when the Greek (maritime) usury system gave way to the more moderate agrarian usury of the Romans."[104] Whereas the Greek economy supposedly rested on financial hegemony at sea, Rome gained it pevalence through the consolidation of sea law and a transfer of usurious practices to the land. Pound sketched that historical moment in C46:

> 'I rule the Earth' said Antoninus 'but LAW rules the sea'
> meaning, we take it, lex Rhodi, the Law Maritime
> of sea lawyers.
> usura and sea insurance
> wherefrom no State was erected greater than Athens.[105]

With the introduction of marine insurance, usurers were forced to search new sources of income in the agrarian sector, as the sea was now governed by law.[106] High interest rates were now found in the mortgage system, as Pound suggests in C48: "12% interest in Bithynia; [/] for home Romans interest 6."[107]

---

102 Adams, Brooks, The Law of Civilization and Decay, 24.
103 Broadcast of 15 March 1942, Pound, Ezra, "Ezra Pound Speaking," 61.
104 "Europe MCMXXXVI" (1937), in: P&P VII.191f.; "The Individual in his Milieu" (1935), in: SP, 243.
105 C46.234.
106 "The Individual in his Milieu" (1935), in: SP, 242f.; "The Church of Rome" (1936), in: P&P VII.37.
107 C48.241f. From Hume: "In Trajan's time, money lent on mortgages in Italy bore 6 per cent., on common securities in Bithynia 12," see "On Interest," in: Hume, David, Essays

After the Roman age of usury, the Middle Ages seemed to Pound like an anti-usurious paradise, because they created a philosophical and theological environment which condemned usury and distinguished between productive and destructive investments.[108] The canonists propagated what Pound called *partaggio*, the principle of fair sharing, which Pound also discovered in Social Credit theory, as we will see later.[109] Among the medieval poets, Dante possessed the same sense of justice and an aversion to the power of wealth. As Pound noted in 1934, Dante's hell "reeked" with money and was full of usurers who had perverted natural increase and production, which, for Pound, included particularly agricultural production – "and for ten cantos thereafter the damned are all of them damned for money."[110]

Pound's idea of medieval economic history shows interesting parallels to arguments proposed by one of his favorite writers, Robert McNair Wilson. According to Wilson, the canonists and St. Thomas condemned money-lending at interest and called usury an offense to the Christian doctrine. They centered their teachings on the production of goods for the benefit of the community, as opposed to the money-lender's non-productive raising of interest. Lending was thus considered an anti-social activity, because creditors were not obliged to adopt a socially responsible behaviour. They were allowed to seize their securities even in times of crises, regardless of their debtors' economic situation. As Wilson points out, the creditor, by granting or withdrawing loans, was also able to control the price level. Wilson calls this "the power of life and death."[111] The Canonists clearly saw the potential dangers inherent in lending. But the credit business was so profitable that it never ceased to exist and even began to prevail during the 15th and 16th centuries, when "usurers laid siege to Christianity."[112] As Wilson claims, doctrine now adhered to money, and what was formerly regarded as a deadly sin became an accepted principle. By and by, governments in need of money turned to those who seemed apt to satisfy their financial needs. Thus, usury gained access to the inner circles of political power.

Similarly, Pound defined the medieval sense of economics partly *ex negativo*, i.e. by analyzing its decay. Pound dated the rise of usury to about 1200 or after 1221[113] and in 1936 attributed it to Jewish influence. Pound

---

Moral, Political and Literary, 314f.; comp. Pound, Ezra, The Selected Letters of Ezra Pound, 262.

108 Pound, Ezra, Polite Essays, 43; identically in "Hell" (1934), in: LE, 211.

109 "The Church of Rome" (1936), in: P&P VII.37; also in: Pound, Ezra, BL 43 / 66 / 2897.

110 Pound, Ezra, Polite Essays, 42.

111 Wilson, Robert McNair, The Mind of Napoleon, 14, also 125: "the strength of hoardable money (irreplaceable money) lies in its influence on the level of prices."

112 Wilson, Robert McNair, The Mind of Napoleon, 15.

113 See the Pound letter quoted in: Ellmann, Maud, The Poetics of Impersonality, 179.

quoted L. P. Cairoli to claim that "the Jew was the divulgator of usury, and thereby helped to break down an economy whereof MAN was the centre and to substitute one whereof MERCHANDISE is the centre," while canonists like Aquinas or Duns Scotus had measured goods only by their actual use value. The old canonists' system was anthropocentric, and rightly so, as Pound clearly states. But the mercantilists replaced man by goods. Merchandise assumed a major role in the economy.[114] Three factors participated in the destruction of the economic sanity of the Middle Ages. First, "the rise of old-testament-olatry;" second, the commodity theory of money; third, "the elevation of usury to pre-eminence, with the cant about parity, the kow-tow to sterility."[115]

It was not only the Jews who injected the virus of sterility into the veins of European culture, but also the Protestant reformation. The iconoclasts "destroyed the mystery of fecundity, bringing in the cult of sterility" and "destroyed the unity of the Catholic Church."[116] Spirituality was replaced by a commercial attitude that damaged medieval art, because steady development was replaced by the accelerated cycles of commerce and the "hyper-usury of the financial system."[117] Once more, Pound's ideas on usury and medieval architecture have their parallels in the writing of other authors, particularly Brooks Adams.[118] According to Adams, medieval monks were not affected by economic matters. They were able to cultivate the arts and therefore were able to create Gothic architecture as a pure and dignified expression of their time. The reformation brought about an economic turn, and now "wealth is the form in which energy seeks expression: therefore, since the close of the fifteenth century, architecture has reflected money."[119] As we can see, both Adams and Pound were not immune to an economic romanticism that celebrated a pre-industrial world of independent craftsmen.

From the Middle Ages Pound moved forward to the Early Modern period, when Tuscany experienced an era of reforms and Siena witnessed the foundation of a bank that was to become Pound's prime model of sound banking, the *Monte dei Paschi*. We will not repeat the multiple details Pound lists in the Siena Cantos and the Tuscan Canto. Rather, we will explain the overall economic framework in which his admiration for that special period of Tuscan history flourished. Before the founding of the bank in Siena, the

[114] "Man v. Merchandise" (1936), in: P&P VII.61f. Pound slyly praises Cairoli for not being an anti-Semite, but a "fair" historian.

[115] "John Buchan's 'Cromwell'" (1935), in: SP, 235f.

[116] "A Visiting Card" (1942), in: SP, 287.

[117] Pound, Ezra, Impact, 274.

[118] Which is not to suggest that Pound derived his theories directly from Adams. The parallel, but independent development of theories by different writers is far more interesting than immediate influence.

[119] Adams, Brooks, The Law of Civilization and Decay, 294.

monte di pietà, or mount of piety, had developed in Italy and France as a "pawnbroking establishment instituted and carried on by the state for the purpose of affording loans to the poor at low interest."[120] Originally established in the 15th century, some of the old pawnshops were transformed into savings banks, of which the most famous was the *Monte dei Paschi*, as Clough states.[121] It was the same bank on which Pound concentrated his attention during the second half of the 1930s. As Pound saw it in 1936, when he was working on the Siena Cantos, the creation of the *Monte* was driven by the productive impulse to "to re-establish the good life in Siena."[122]

The *Monte dei Paschi* was founded when Siena experienced financial problems in the wake of the Florentine conquest.[123] The Medici contributed their expertise and capital to the enterprise, which was to result in a bank of reconstruction, as Pound called it. Cosimo Medici, first duke of Tuscany, allocated a capital of 200,000 ducats to the bank, to be lent at 5.5 per cent, with profits used for the public good. Cosimo's security, and the ultimate source of credit, were the Sienese grazing lands and grazing rights to an annual amount of 10,000 ducats.[124] The bank's reliance on the Sienese grazing lands furnished Pound's conviction that true credit rested "on the abundance of nature, on the growing grass that can nourish the living sheep,"[125] and on the responsibility of the people.[126] As Makin emphasizes, the *Monte* was indeed founded on land, land which created a product that would certainly stay in demand: wool.[127] Pound points out the *Monte's* stability which helped it to survive the financial crashs of the Napoleonic era. The *Monte dei Paschi* achieved this large amount of stability, because it adhered to three principles. First, its credit rested on the abundance of nature, particularly the grazing lands. Second, credit was based on "the will or at least

---

120 OED, s.v. "mount of piety." On forms of Early Modern banking in Italy see Kindleberger, Charles P., A Financial History of Western Europe, 136ff.

121 Clough, Shepard B., The Economic History of Modern Italy, 22n.

122 Pound, Ezra, Impact, 250.

123 For a general account of Early Modern Sienese history, including the *Monte*, see Repetti, Emanuele (comp.), Dizionario geografico fisico storico della Toscana, vol. V, Florence 1843, 339-355.

124 "Mug's Game?" (1935), in: P&P VI.244. Similarly "Banking Beneficence and..." (1935), in: P&P VI.247. Also see "Ecclesiastical History" (1934), in: SP, 61f.; Pound, Ezra, Impact, 147.

125 Pound, Ezra, Impact, 147; also see "Mug's Game?" (1935), in: P&P VI.244. Also see Pound, Ezra, Ezra Pound and Japan, 187; "Moneta fascista" (1936), in: P&P VII.4.

126 GK, 194.

127 Makin, Peter, Pound's Cantos, 200. On the *Monte dei Paschi* also see Kenner, Hugh, The Pound Era, 427ff.

the formal consent of the whole people" and, third, on the responsibility of the people.[128]

As should be noted, the *Monte* could lend only what had been deposited with it and could therefore not "create" money.[129] This form of credit, together with moderate interest rates, allowed Pound to promote the *Monte* as a non-usurious institution and conclude C44 with the assertion "The foundation, Siena, has been to keep bridle on usury" (C44.228). The association of mounts and non-usurious practices was not new. Peter Beckford wrote in 1805 that the "*Monte di Pietà* was established first at Florence, in the year 1496, to restrain the usury of the Jews."[130] In C42 Pound lists several of the *Monte's* assets. First, its liberal credit policies, which not only benefitted a few citizens, but "folk of [/] ANY CONDITION" (C42.211), as "the specie [was] lent to whomso can best use it USE IT" (C42.209f.). The *Monte* offered its money and credit for productive purposes, "to the good of their houses, to benefit of their business [/] as of weaving, the wool trade, the silk trade" (C42.209f.). Second, it was non-usurious in its debt policies, for its regulations stated "that the borrowers can pay up before the end of their [/] term whenso it be to their interest." Of vital importance was the fact that the *Monte* refrained from a banking practice harshly criticized by Pound, i.e. from continually enslaving its debtors: "No debt to run more than [/] five years" (C42.209f.). Third, the profits, or "overabundance," of the *Monte* were not seized by bankers, but distributed "to workers of the contrade (the wards)" (C42.209f.).

The economic history of the U.S. was another of Pound's preoccupations. It included the same shift from economic sanity to usury like the Middle Ages, and like the other periods treated by Pound, it featured heroes and villains. The years to 1860 were a paradisal era praised by Pound for its sane sense of commerce "which continued an Italic tradition of the great City Republics of Venice and Genoa, the Superba and the Dominante," before Americans began to waste the natural abundance given to them.[131] American "honesty" was once a virtue, but the open country spaces which had shaped the development of the U.S. were soon in need of manpower, which resulted in the import of slaves, the accumulation of debts and a fierce competition between what Pound called "free craftsmanship" and the "slave

[128] "Built for Stability" (1936), in: P&P VII.84. Similarly "L'Economia Ortologica" (1937), in: P&P VII.220.

[129] Reynolds, Lloyd G., "Economics in History: The Poetic Vision of Ezra Pound," 396.

[130] Beckford, Peter, Familiar Letters, I.231.

[131] "An Introduction to the Economic Nature of the United States" (1944, orig. Italian), in: SP, 146.

system." Before the rise of finance, the country had prospered under personal commerce.[132]

According to Pound, John Adams still possessed a real sense of credit, which he based on the workforce of the colonists.[133] Adams was convinced that the division of society into rich and poor, gentleman and common man, was natural and sane. He distinguished between industrious acquirers of property and idle, and therefore poor, people. Both groups were important and a balance had to be maintained between them. Hence, predatory rich were dangerous to the general economy. Andrew Jackson and Martin Van Buren were two other model presidents praised by Pound for their fight against the "monopolists." As Pound kept repeating during the 1930s, Jackson's debt policy proved that national debt could be defeated.[134] Under Jackson's presidency, "the people beat the banks between 1830 and 1840,"[135] when Jackson prevented the renewal of the charter of the second Bank of the United States (1816-1836). Van Buren actively supported Jackson's war against "Biddle's traitorous bank" in the 1830s.[136]

Those were America's golden days, yet Pound assures us that, like the economic history of the Roman Empire and the Middle Ages, the economic history of the U.S. underwent a process of decay. An American "usurocracy" came to the fore after 1861.[137] In Pound's a chronology of the American economy from 1620 to 1939, the years from 1829 to 1841 were marked by a conflict between the banks and the people, in which the latter gained the upper hand when Jackson managed to reduce national debt. Then finance achieved supreme control after 1861.[138] Originally, Congress was supposed to issue money and regulate its value, but the banks assumed that power after the National Bank Act of 1863.

Pound shared Jefferson's doubts about banking, and like Jefferson he could have asserted "I have ever been the enemy of banks; not of those discounting for cash; but of those foisting their own paper into circulation,

---

[132] Comp. "An Introduction to the Economic Nature of the United States" (1944, orig. Italian), in: SP, 145. For a chronology of American economic history see "A Visiting Card" (1942), in: SP, 279f.

[133] "An Introduction to the Economic Nature of the United States" (1944, orig. Italian), in: SP, 138.

[134] "Intellectual Money" (1937), in: P&P VII.151; "Commentary on W. C. Williams" (1934), in: P&P VI.139.

[135] Pound, Ezra, Ezra Pound and Japan, 170f.

[136] "Ezra Pound, Silvershirt" (1936), in: P&P VII.35.

[137] "National Culture: A Manifesto 1938," in: SP, 131. Later Pound dated the beginning of America's economic downfall to 1863, see broadcast of 3 February 1942, in: Pound, Ezra, "Ezra Pound Speaking," 29.

[138] "An Introduction to the Economic Nature of the United States" (1944, orig. Italian), in: SP, 150, 153.

and thus banishing our cash."[139] But then the banks assumed power over American money, and "Usury ruined the Republic."[140] Until the time of F. D. Roosevelt, the U.S. never regained its former glory. Instead, the country plunged into new depths of depression. Pound sketched the 1935 economic situation of the U.S. in the final lines of C46:

> FIVE million youths without jobs
> FOUR million adult illiterates
> 15 million 'vocational misfits', that is with small chance for jobs
> NINE million persons annual, injured in preventable industrial
> accidents
> One hundred thousand violent crimes. The Eunited States ov
> America
> 3rd year of the reign of F. Roosevelt, signed F. Delano, his uncle.
>
> (C46.235)

The reasons for this decay were to be found, Pound believed, as far back as the 1860s, when finance gained power over the republic.

From the 19th century onward, not only the U.S. experienced a phase of decay. Pound recognized the same phenomenon in European history. Both contributed to his image of the 19th century as a particularly dark period of cultural degradation and usurers' hegemony. Pound extended his judgement to include ethics and concluded in 1937: "Western ethics were a consummate filth in the middle of the last century." Art, too, had degenerated with the progress of usury, and words had lost their clear definitions.[141] All this happened after the European usurers and their allies had established their predominance in 1815. With unrestrained contempt, Pound named them in C50: Franz Josef, Metternich, Wellington, "in their soul was usura [/] and in their hand bloody oppression" (C50.248). Indeed, wars were expensive and Wellington had to borrow money from international bankers in order to pay the military.

Pound and other conspiracy theorists passed a clear judgement on the European superpowers of the 19th century. Britain, for instance, pursued a "suicidal financial policy adopted by ignorant statesmen at the bidding of one or two orthodox economists and Bankers."[142] It was their fault when the 19th

---

139 Jefferson to Adams, 24 Jan 1814, Adams, John / Jefferson, Thomas, The Adams-Jefferson Letters, 423. On Jefferson's economic thought see Marsh, Alec, Money and Modernity, 11-41.

140 "An Introduction to the Economic Nature of the United States" (1944, orig. Italian), in: SP, 144.

141 "Immediate need of Confucius" (1937), in: SP, 90.

142 Kitson, Arthur, "Political Economy or The Science of Robbery," in: Butchart, Montgomery (ed.), To-Morrow's Money, 58.

century lost its sense of justice in economics, as Pound complained, and even Marx had to fail, because he was infected with the same spirit. With some resignation, Pound summarizes the complex history of the century in the statement "Marx found nothing to criticise in money" and thus represented the general ignorance of the period towards a crucial issue.[143] It was the monetary reformers from which Pound expected a decisive turn in western economics.

Reformers

The influence of C. H. Douglas and other reform economists on Pound has gained increasing attention in recent years. We will therefore not enter into a detailed discussion of Douglas's reform schemes, but will highlight those aspects which attracted Pound's particular interest and were relevant for *The Fifth Decad.* Pound became interested in C. H. Douglas and the Social Credit movement during the years of his involvement in the *New Age* group around Orage.[144] T. S. Eliot, too, wrote a number of articles on Social Credit in his position as co-editor of *The New English Weekly* after Orage's death in 1934.[145] At that time, Pound was already losing his interest in the Social Credit movement. By 1937, as Laughlin recalls, Pound was no longer an orthodox Douglasite, but disenchanted with the lack of success of the group's endeavours.[146] When he published *The Fifth Decad*, it was only a number of Douglas's ideas, rather than a fully-fledged theory, that Pound still found useful. These ideas concerned credit, the "increment of association" and the power of finance.

Douglas developed the so-called "A + B theorem" – A are payments made by an organization to individuals, like wages, salaries or dividends. B are payments to other organizations in order to purchase raw materials and cover other costs. Individuals only benefit from A payments. The price they pay when they buy goods, however, is calculated as to cover A and B costs. The price includes A and B, but consumers only receive A. Hence, Douglas concludes, they need additional purchasing power, which must be distributed

[143] "The Individual in his Milieu" (1935), in: SP, 243.

[144] For a history of the Social Credit movement 1918-36 see Finlay, John L., Social Credit: The English Origins, 119-144. For a brief first-hand description of Social Credit see Douglas, Clifford Hugh, "The Cause and Curse of Economic Malady," in: Butchart, Montgomery (ed.), To-Morrow's Money, 155-174. On Social Credit also comp. Flory, Wendy S., The American Ezra Pound, 56ff.; Surette, Leon, Pound in Purgatory, 29-38; Kenner, Hugh, The Pound Era, 301-308. On the *New Age* group and its influence on Pound see Surette, Leon, Pound in Purgatory, 49 passim.

[145] On Eliot's support for Social Credit see Ackroyd, Peter, T. S. Eliot: A Life, 220f.

[146] Laughlin, James, Pound as Wuz, 154.

in the form of loans, bank overdrafts or export credit.[147] As people are dependent on borrowing money, credit institutions and financiers are the really powerful actors on the money market, because they control the distribution of credit. What banks usually offer, however, is not credit in its actual sense, as Douglas distinguishes "real" from "financial" credit. The former is the creative capacity of a society to produce required goods. For Douglas, it is the only sane form of credit. The other form of credit merely concerns the supply of money for the purpose of creating a financial return. By the creation of "financial credit," as Douglas puts it, "industry becomes mortgaged to the banking system."[148] It is artificial credit and hence interest based on mere paper calculations, not goods. According to Douglas, credit-lending is very much like coining new money, i.e. the creation of fresh purchasing power.[149] For Douglas, credit granted by a financial institution is rather the creation of a mortgage on future production than the allocation of past savings of an industry.[150] It is this line of argument which Pound so feverishly adheres to throughout his economic writings of the 1930s.

Several Douglasite principles for the reform of financial systems were concerned with credit. First, cash credits available to citizens should equal cash prices for available and consumable goods. Purchase of such goods cancels the credits. Second, credits used to finance production are not to be supplied from savings. Investments should be based on new credits for new production. Third, cash credits to citizens (i.e. incomes) should cease to depend upon employment, which would turn wages and salaries into dividends. The higher goal was the creation of purchasing power to end underconsumption. If the private economy fostered "the creation of PRICES in excess of the amount of purchasing power which it distributes (as wages, dividends etc.),"[151] as Pound formulated the problem, then the state would have to supply money to enhance purchasing power. Hence, Douglas proposed to create more money in order to strengthen purchasing power by paying a national dividend.[152] This would be achieved by the state's borrowing money from itself, an idea Pound regarded as revolutionary: the state as lender, not borrower. Ideally, this scheme would eliminate the

[147] See Douglas, Credit-Power and Democracy, 21ff.; Finlay, John L., Social Credit: The English Origins, 107f.
[148] Douglas, Clifford H., Social Credit, 95.
[149] Douglas, Credit-Power and Democracy, 31f.
[150] Hutchinson, Frances / Burkitt, Brian, The Political Economy of Social Credit and Guild Socialism, 37.
[151] "More On Economics" (1933), in: P&P VI.34. Also see "Pro" (1933), in: P&P VI.49.
[152] Redman, Tim, Ezra Pound and Italian Fascism, 61. On the problem of inflation see Redman, Tim, Ezra Pound and Italian Fascism, 150f.

problem of capitalists usurping state functions as creditors.[153] Therefore Pound constantly asserted that the state had credit. The scheme also affected his statement at the beginning of C48 about the state "renting" its money. If the state adhered to Douglas's proposal, it would be able to avoid national debt and payment of "rent" to private institutions.

Another Douglasite idea in which Pound was highly interested during the mid-1930s was the "increment of association." Pound defined it as the surplus of joint workforce and the result of combined working efforts,[154] which may take place on many levels: as a group of workers, a co-operation based on ideas, or other forms of association. On a higher level, the sum of increment becomes cultural heritage. As Pound stated:

> 1. The "increment of association" means the overplus of what a lot of men acting together can do, above what they could do acting each one on his own. This economic concept dates back to tribal hunting.
> 2. Douglas's term "the cultural heritage," applied to economics is an extension of the "increment of association." It is our increment of *association with* all past human inventiveness [...] mechanical correlations, improved agricultural methods, habits of civilised order.[155]

The value arising from work is based on the achievements of a long row of dead inventors (individual and collective), who developed ideas from decade to decade, from generation to generation, and thus "rendered it needless to get up water from wells with buckets, to put oil into individual lamps."[156]

The fragment also hints at a link between monetary reformism and anti-finance aversions. This connection was not yet acute during Pound's early years in Europe. In 1920 Pound still pointed out the civic nature of Douglas's ideas and his lack of fanaticism.[157] Douglas's theories, he claimed, were based on the principle of equity, credit existed for mankind and salvation was to be reached by "honest accountants working in a plate-glass room under communal supervision," which was by then Pound's idea of an administrative *paradiso terrestre*. Pound regarded Douglas as a realist who fought the concentration of credit-capital in a few hands.[158] Pound's insistence on the

---

[153] "Probari Ratio" (1920), in: SP, 178. On Douglas's idea that the state could borrow money from itself see Davis, Earle, Vision Fugitive, 105f.

[154] "In the Wounds (Memoriam A. R. Orage)" (1935), in: SP, 413.

[155] "The Douglas Social Credit Scheme" (1934), in: P&P VI.207. Similarly "Towards Orthology" (1935), in: P&P VI.276. For Orage's definition of the "increment of association" see Butchart, Montgomery (comp.), Money, 208f.

[156] "The Individual in His Milieu" (1935), SP, 248.

[157] "Probari Ratio" (1920), in: SP, 179, 182.

[158] "Economic Democracy" (1920), in: SP, 181.

non-fanatical character of Social Credit theory should be noted. The Pound of the years around 1920 was not yet the ardent and increasingly grim preacher of the Rome radio broadcasts. Social Credit, however, was not without paranoid traits. In the 1930s they found their way into Pound's economic ideas.

The Social Credit movement sought to increase the transparency of finance. Often enough, this resulted in suspecting the protagonists of the financial world of secret schemes. Even Orage's magazine was not immune against conspiracy theories and anti-Semitism. Finlay notes a certain anti-Semitic tendency in the *New Age*, despite some Jewish contributors: "Correspondents on monetary reform could not resist the chance of accusing Jewish money lenders of being worse than Gentiles. The claim was made that the white slave traffic was a Jewish monopoly."[159] According to Douglas, it is mainly the financiers who benefit from war. The purchase of arms requires credit, which creates debt and entails interest. In cancelling public debt, the state pays interest, thus taking "credit" (that is, purchasing power) from its citizens. To regain purchasing power, further loans are necessary, but new loans entail new interest and create a vicious circle of debts and loans. Debt is here seen as a mortgage on future earnings. Citizens are expected to contribute to the payment of national debt without benefitting from it. But if the state can afford to pay unearned money to bankers and financiers, Douglas claims, it can as well pay it to the people in form of a national dividend. Both debt and dividend are based on future incomes. Whereas debt increases the profits of international finance, national dividend is supposed to support the whole populace.

Douglas himself saw Jewish interests dominate the Treasury and seemed to think that Hitler was related to the Rothschilds.[160] Douglas even believed in "a very deeply laid and well considered plot of enslaving the industrial world to the German-American-Jewish financiers" and regarded Zaharoff with the same suspicion as Pound did.[161] Douglas's attitude was moderate towards individual Jews and he tried to keep downright anti-Semitism out of his movement. On the other hand, he attacked Jewish financial business and established a connection between Jews and Europe's economic problems. Although Douglas did not share Pound's fixation on "usurers," he and the Social Credit movement were not immune to the lure of predjudice.

Pound received a second, substantial part of his economic ideas from Silvio Gesell.[162] In brief, Gesell proposed "the gradual repossession of land by

---

159 Finlay, John L., Social Credit: The English Origins, 72.
160 Finlay, John L., Social Credit: The English Origins, 96.
161 Quot. in Finlay, John L., Social Credit: The English Origins, 103.
162 Comp. chapter I.1, n. 1, of this study.

the state on behalf of the community through the issue of 'free money' by the state."[163] Gesell advocates a moderate economic egotism embedded in a socially corrected Manchester liberalism, which should at the same time provide for a large amount of individual liberty, without granting privileges (especially on land) only to the few. Gesell's "natural economic order" is to rest on self-interest, as self-interest is not negative in itself, but may lead to altruistic acts, if unspoilt by privilege. This system is based on notions of natural selection and free competition as beneficient priciples. Leadership of the fittest is as inevitable as competition is necessary, but it must accord to the principle of equality. Private property is a crucial foundation of Gesell's concept, although the state plays an important role, too. It is responsible for the currency, the equitable distribution of agricultural land and the reduction of interest for the benefit of the populace. The state is to act as a security guard, not as a bureaucratic leviathan. Land plays a central role in Gesell's theory. His reform proposals aim at the abolition of national borders, free trade and "Free-Land." The distribution of land is to be executed strictly according to the needs of its cultivators, i.e. large families require large portions of land, small families smaller portions. The state is to act as a distributing instance in the service of the community, putting the rent on the land into a large wage fund.[164]

Throughout his book, Gesell criticizes the ignorance people – and particularly economists – have displayed towards the nature of money, which resulted in the "lack of a sound theory of money,"[165] a notion Pound fully agreed with. Like Pound, Gesell claims that even Marx did not pay due attention to money.[166] Gesell attacks gold, but praises paper money. He seeks to distinguish between money and its material, trying to make the former as independent as possible of the latter.[167] The next step is to separate money not only from any durable material, but from the idea of durability itself. If money were a perishable good, it would require to be kept in constant circulation. Excessive hoarding and speculation would become impossible. In Gesell's words: "Money is an independent commodity and its price must be determined afresh, by the sale itself, every time it changes hands."[168] If money is a medium to facilitate the exchange of products, then it must be kept in circulation, as exchange is only complete when the money received for a product is re-invested in another product. Thus, the correct use of money

163 Hutchinson, Frances / Burkitt, Brian, The Political Economy of Social Credit and Guild Socialism, 26.
164 Gesell, Silvio, The Natural Economic Order, 80.
165 Gesell, Silvio, The Natural Economic Order, 99, also 98, 209.
166 Gesell, Silvio, The Natural Economic Order, 99, also 301f.
167 Gesell, Silvio, The Natural Economic Order, 102.
168 Gesell, Silvio, The Natural Economic Order, 105, note 5.

implies a constant sequence of sale and purchase, earning and spending. Economic agents that save large amounts of money in order to lend them at interest only obstruct circulation by their hoarding policy. They act in opposition to the criteria Gesell considers necessary for a healthy economy – free exchange of money, accelerated purchase cycles, cheap and stable prices.

Gesell champions stamp scrip as the best form of money, because it supposedly fits all of the above criteria.[169] Stamp scrip is perishable money. The longer a stamp scrip note is retained by its possessor, the less its monetary value. The owner is obliged to attach stamps to it regularly, stamps which are themselves worth a small amount of money. So people who insist on keeping a money note actually have to "pay" for keeping it by putting stamps on the note. Without stamps, the note will not be valid after a certain date and must be exchanged at a state institution for a new note, which again requires stamps to keep its value. The only way of avoiding this procedure and the payment affected by "stamping" is to hold one's money in constant circulation.[170] Stamp scrip has some features of conventional money, as it can be banked, invested or spent, but other than normal money, it cannot be hoarded. Apart from this intervention, the money market is to remains relatively liberal, because Gesell supposes that many economic problems will disappear after the introduction of stamp scrip.

The "usurer" also figures in Gesell's world. Usury, in Gesell, is an economic constant, but one with negative consequences. He mentions the small farmer driven from his property by the "usurer." He also includes a fictive monologue by somebody presented as a generic type of "The Usurer,"[171] a person identified as a Jew who is defeated by the newly introduced "free-money" proposed by Gesell. As we can see, even economic reformers are not free from clichés.

Following Gesell, Pound called for the introduction of a stamp scrip of monthly validity, with the stamp as a state fee for providing the money.[172] Besides Douglas's reform schemes, Pound considered stamp scrip the only serious solution to financial problems.[173] He expected Roosevelt to introduce it in the U.S..[174] The poet was particularly impressed by the Woergl experiment,[175] which was based on Gesell's proposal of a tax on money.[176]

---

[169] Gesell, Silvio, The Natural Economic Order, 210, passim.
[170] Gesell, Silvio, The Natural Economic Order, 217.
[171] Gesell, Silvio, The Natural Economic Order, 81, 240ff.
[172] "Intellectual Money" (1937), in: P&P VII.149.
[173] "Hel ... up !!!" (1933), in: P&P VI.111f.
[174] Gordon, David M. (ed.), Ezra Pound and James Laughlin: Selected Letters, 39f., 12 Jan 1935.
[175] For details see the commentary on item 82.
[176] "The Individual in his Milieu" (1935), in: SP, 245f.

In addition to the comprehensive reform schemes of Douglas and Gesell, we should not forget to mention two other infuences on Pound. Father Coughlin applied his populist ideas not only to politics, but also to economics. Like Pound, he fought debt, certain credit policies and the privatization of monetary privilege. Coughlin demanded "the abolition of the privately owned Federal Reserve Banking System," the establishing of a state-owned Central Bank with the chief duty "to maintain the cost of living on an even keel," and the restoration of the right to coin money from private individuals to the Congress.[177] Like Pound, Coughlin mentioned the Constitution's statement about the right of Congress to coin money. Public debt caused the government to collect interest through taxation, because public debts were a mortgage on the citizen's property. Like Pound, Coughlin criticized that banks "create money out of nothing."[178] He attacked the international bankers for their "unsound" and "unmoral" policies and called them the "rulers of the world."[179]

An economic publication Pound referred to several times was the "Loeb report," the *Chart of Plenty* (1935). The report states a discrepancy between "buying power" and "producing power" and addresses the problem of over-production.[180] It also favours fixed prices for certain goods and services.[181] In some important points, however, the Loeb report differs from Pound's ideas. As the report states, a modern economy makes it difficult to hoard money or withhold it from the market. Hoarding itself is not regarded as a serious issue, not even interest, which the report considers merely a method of "redistributing buying power."[182] Rather, the problem is production. Despite the differences, Pound appreciated the report and made it one of the few statistical documents in his economic canon.

Conclusion

Pound's economic thought during the 1930s was based on a set of basic assumptions. He postulated a powerful international elite of, mostly Jewish, bankers and financiers (the "usurers") with far-reaching influence on politics and journalism. Their chief interest was the creation of debt as an interest-bearing mechanism designed to increase their wealth. For this objective, they would even start wars. They cemented the hegemony of usury over western

---

[177] Coughlin, Charles, Money!, 7.
[178] Coughlin, Charles, Money!, 35.
[179] Coughlin, Charles, Money!, 115, 159, 160.
[180] Loeb, Harold et.al., The Chart of Plenty, 3f.
[181] Loeb, Harold et.al., The Chart of Plenty, 162.
[182] Loeb, Harold et.al., The Chart of Plenty, 138, 142.

culture, established an unnatural credit system and incurred the decay of art and language. Their influence was combatted by Napoleon, who was finally defeated by usurious politicians. Napoleon's century, in general, represented a paramount symbol of the predominance of usury, which has grown since the Roman Empire. Only few periods had experienced some freedom from usury, like the Middle Ages and Tuscany under the reformist rulers Pietro Leopoldo and Ferdinando III. The fate of the 20th century was still undecided, because monetary reform, as proposed by Douglas and Gesell, still had a chance to gain general acceptance. Fascist politicians set out to put economic reforms into practice, and while France, Britain and the U.S. were lost to "regents" and usurers, Italy and Germany were able to resist the powers of finance, as Pound hoped.

Pound's attention was focused on the state, rather than on private initiative. He considered it the prime function of the government to guarantee the economic welfare of its citizens.[183] Pound expected governments to create new money if they needed it; at the same time, though, they should only issue so much money as corresponded to the amount of existing wealth. He called on the state to control the value of goods and keep prices on a steady level, to check interest rates and take care that only as much money was lent as private lenders really owned.[184] Paradoxically, Pound argued in favor of individual freedom, but demanded more goverment control of the economy and a Keynesian deficit financing he usually despised.[185] As Murray criticized, Pound basically imagined an "ordered and largely static society" with a centralized authority controlling the economy.[186]

Reality, however, seemed to lag far behind the reform schemes envisioned by Pound, and his attacks on Roosevelt show his dissatisfaction with the state of economic affairs in the western world. Mussolini was the only politician to earn Pound's acclaim for his economic policies. In them, Pound saw a potential to reach the high standards set by the U.S. founding fathers and by Social Creditors.[187] This combination of fascism, monetary reform and a distinctly American tradition must seem odd to the educated economist. But it offers an important hint at a key mode of thinking in Pound's work: eclecticism. His economic ideas were anything but original. His major ideas can be found in the writings of other, more or less professional, economists – the just price, the polemics against debt, the anti-Semitic conspiracy theories. A look at the notions and arguments of Pound's

183 "A B C of Economics" (1933), in: SP, 231.

184 Makin, Peter, Pound's Cantos, 112. On Pound's basic economic assumptions also see Davis, Earle, Vision Fugitive, 116f.

185 Tytell, John, Ezra Pound: The Solitary Volcano, 225.

186 Murray, David, "Pound-Signs: Money and Representation in Ezra Pound," 174f.

187 "Great Comfort of Latin Mind" (1936), in: P&P VII.43.

allies in economic reformism shows common predjudices and assumptions. Yet Pound, as Redman has noted, was not systematic in his eclecticism, but attempted to merge positions usually considered as singular doctrines by their adherents.[188] His interpretation of Mussolini's econonomic policies in the light of American virtues and Social Credit reformism exemplifies this tendency.

Pound's economic thought moved in repetitious patterns. He was among those obsessive intellectuals who, as Lewis defined them, "found *debt* – and so *credit*, of course – to be at the root of the evil."[189] Debt, credit and usury were indeed counted by Pound among the forces of evil. Pound's litany about money not being a commodity (items 246f.) and about the Jewish bankers resembles some parts of his radio speeches, as both mirror his obsessions.[190] Yet Pound's economic ideas were not simply eccentric, but sometimes close to what American Senators like Brookhart and Frazier proposed.[191] And although he was eclectic in his merging of different ideas, those ideas existed before him and were adopted not only by Pound, but also by other people with an interest in economic reforms.

Two aspects are vital in the framework of Pound's economic obsessions. First, his absolute concentration on usury as the chief economic evil. We may state, without exaggeration, that Pound substituted usury for what the Christian Church knows as the anti-Christ, with all its apocalyptic implications. Not even populists like Coughlin or pamphleteers like Jarvie showed the same fixation on usury. They always attacked the group of "international financiers," i.e. persons, however weakly defined that group might be. Never did they target an abstract force like usury, which, despite the many metaphors used by Pound to describe it, is difficult to grasp – is it a vice, a sin, a psychological habit, a supernatural force or simply lending at an excessive amount of interest? An unequivocal answer remains difficult. The second idea Pound promoted with speacial vigor, particularly in the mid-1930s, was his linking of usurious practices and culture. The deacy of the arts could ultimately be "traced to maladministration of credit," as "Most social evils are at root economic."[192] When the age of baroque failed to distinguish between usury and *partaggio*, art entered a state of decay.[193] The results of this development are listed in C45.

---

[188] Redman, Tim, Ezra Pound and Italian Fascism, 109.

[189] Lewis's definition of "credit-cranks," in: Lewis, Wyndham, Hitler, 160f.

[190] Comp. e.g. Pound, Ezra, "Ezra Pound Speaking," 21, 61.

[191] As pointed out by Redman, Tim, "An Epic Is a Hypertext Containing Poetry," 139, passim.

[192] "Murder by Capital" (1933), in: SP, 199.

[193] "The Individual in his Milieu" (1935), in: SP, 244.

What is noteworthy about Pound's economic reformism is that it remained largely confined to his prose. Although the poet transferred several of his obsessions into *The Fifth Decad* (like the evil financiers and usury), he did not write a philosophical poem in the traditional sense (like Lucrece, for example) to develop a clear-cut reform scheme. Rather, the poems in *The Fifth Decad* present a non-systematic sequence of positive and negative examples of economic (mal-)practice in history. But why no comprehensive economic theory? Maybe because Pound regarded his interest in economics as temporary. He wrote to Odon Por in May 1936: "1937!!! do you expect ME to be still an economist by 1937? It ought to be DONE by then."[194] As a matter of fact, it *was* to some extent "done" by then – the 1937 *Fifth Decad* is the most economically charged section of the *Cantos*, with economic elements and allusions in every Canto except C47. Surely Pound regarded it as his most comprehensive non-prose statement on economics, although he did not abandon economics immediately after its publication. Pound's attitude to economics at about the time of *The Fifth Decad* is neatly summarized in a passage from a letter to Laurence Binyon of 29 September 1938:

> I hope yr/ country isn't going to war to keep up the price of gold; i.e., help the Rothschild and squander another five million anglo-saxon lives. At any rate, I have worked 20 years to prevent it and refer the lot of you to Canto 45 and a few others [...] War against Germany would be war AGAINST a clean concept of money.[195]

The quotation contains some of the key elements of Pound's economic ideas: the close connection between politics and economics, the notion that wars are waged for economic reasons, the aversions to Jewish bankers, and the image of fascist states as champions of monetary reform. The letter asserts Pound's investigative approach which had kept him, as he expressed it in C46, "on the case" for 20 years.

[194] Quot. in: Surette, Leon, Pound in Purgatory, 46.
[195] Quot. in Redman, Tim, Ezra Pound and Italian Fascism, 182.

III.5 "What is a god?": Ritual, Nature, Mythology

What I do wish to affirm is that the whole of modern literature is corrupted by what I call Secularism, that it is simply unaware of, simply cannot understand the meaning of, the primacy of the supernatural over the natural life: of something which I assume to be our primary concern.

(T. S. Eliot, *Religion and Literature*)

Eliot's statement, as quoted above, does certainly not apply to Pound. Although he was deeply immersed in secular issues like economics and although, in religious terms, Pound had a notion of the supernatural which differed strongly from Eliot's dogmatic Anglicanism, he nevertheless integrated allusions to what he called the "fourth dimension" into the *Cantos*. It is true, Pound did not adhere to any traditional creed or confession. At the same time, though, the *Cantos* include a distinct vertical axis that leads upwards to a metaphysics of light, as already mentioned in my remarks on Pound's concept of government. In the course of this chapter, I will outline this axis as it appears in Pound's work. Beginning with Pound's criticism of organized religion, I will analyze which alternatives he proposed to religious institutions. This includes aspects like nature worship and the observance of rituals. While both are not completely different from Christian concepts, we will also discuss some more pagan aspects of the *Cantos*. Based on a mythologizing notion of ritual, the ideas of sacrifice and initiation, Adonis and Eleusis, are particularly important, Eleusis being a key to Pound's concept of Eros. After that, I will move beyond what Pound conceived of as terrestrial expressions of the divine, towards a level on which religion and philosophy are merging in a realm of light.

Organized Religion

As early as 1914, Pound criticized the institutions of the Catholic church as petrified and too static.[1] Some years later he adopted an even bleaker perspective and claimed: "the organisation of religions has usually been for

[1] "Allen Upward Serious" (1914), in: SP, 380.

some ulterior purpose, exploitation, control of the masses, etc."[2] Pound's skepticism did not simply derive from subjective disappointment or suspicion towards institutions. Rather, he criticized the modern church for neglecting a crucial area it had originally held in firm control – economics.

This opinion came to the fore during the 1930s, when Pound drew the firm conclusion that "when religion was real the church concerned itself with vital phenomena in ECONOMICS."[3] But after the "Albigensian crusade," corruption spread and Christian ethics fell into a state of decay, as the medieval distinction between "sharing" and "usury" became blurred.[4] At about the time of Leo X (1475-1521), the Church lost its ruling power and economic competence, while Leo himself was remarkable only for his greed for taxes.[5] In the Middle Ages, the church had assembled the best intellectuals,[6] but then lost its vital *dogmatic* profile at a time when the papacy concentrated on strengthening the *administrative* aspects of the church: Improving its organization and enhancing its secular power deprived the church of its religious essence. The more imperial it became, the more it stood in opposition to Pound's actual religious ideal, Eleusis. Whereas the church was immersed in the process of secularizing itself politically, the Eleusian cult had always shown "indifference to empire."[7] Pound thus diagnosed a decay of the church in political, dogmatic and economic terms. He went so far as to state that financiers and the Christian church had reached the same level of infamy, because the church no longer opposed usury and finance, the latter being "nothing but a concatenation of usuries."[8]

As should be noted, Pound's anti-Semitism played a role in his diagnosis of the degenerated state of the church, but primarily on the theological, not on the economic level. One year after the publication of *The Fifth Decad*, he called the Hebrew scriptures the documents of a "servile" tribe and left no doubt that he considered them the seed of decay: "Jehovah is a semitic cuckoo's egg laid in the European nest. He has no connection with Dante's god."[9]

---

[2] "Axiomata" (1921), in: SP, 50.
[3] "Mr. Eliot's Mare's Nest" (1934), in: P&P VI.140.
[4] "Ecclesiastical History" (1934), in: SP, 61.
[5] "Ecclesiastical History" (1934), in: SP, 62.
[6] "Ecclesiastical History" (1934), in: SP, 62.
[7] "Terra Italica" (1931-32), in: SP, 56.
[8] "Hudson: Poet Strayed into Science" (1920), in: SP, 401.
[9] "Mang Tsze (The Ethics of Mencius)" (1938), in: SP, 105. In an essay for *The Criterion*, Pound called for a new Paganism without Semitic elements, a position similar to that of Hitler and many Nazis; see Tytell, John, Ezra Pound: The Solitary Volcano, 248.

Pound once distinguished two kinds of religion, first, the "Mosaic or Roman or British Empire type," which maintains order by using a frightening god. Second, "forms of ecstatic religion," built on a strong confidence in "life-force" and the natural order.[10] The idea of a natural order governs a substantial part of Pound's view of the world. Natural order manifests itself in several forms: first, in political hierarchies; second, the natural generation and distribution of goods (as opposed to usury); third, the rhythms of nature; fourth, the observance of rituals. The latter two are of special importance for Pound's religious views.

In his prose texts, Pound is a proponent of organicism, i.e. he believes in an organically grown (social, political, cultural etc.) order that, ideally, also forms an organic whole. Adopting what he calls a "totalitarian" perspective, he denies the possibility of dissecting natural phenomena into atomic parts, not because he thinks this is scientifically impossible, but because it would destroy the inner coherence of nature. Rather, nature must be recognized as an organic whole. Once more, Pound takes his inspiration from Chinese philosophy when he states: "at no point does the Confucio-Mencian ethic or philosophy splinter and split away from organic nature. [...] Any attempt to deal with it as split, is due to ignorance and a failure in the direction of the will."[11] An example of "splitting" nature would be the Catholic contempt for the body and its emphasis on the soul. Organicism also governs Pound's model of human life in accordance with the rhythms of nature, an ideal repeatedly commented on by scholars. Pound conceives of the virtuous human being as adhering to the rhythms of the natural world and thus to the "divine intellect."[12] Pearlman finds this notion grounded in an opposition of linear versus cyclical time, that is, a mechanically measurable succession of moments versus the "seasonal and cosmic rhythms of nature."[13] The two concepts express different senses of history. One the one hand, the chronocentric exactness of the modern age; on the other hand, an imagined "unceasing present" with an equally unceasing presence of divine forces, as experienced by primitive peoples.

Pearlman also points out the emphasis Pound puts on harmony with the organic rhythms of nature, a harmony that serves as a foundation of social order.[14] This argument is supported by several points in Pound. As we have noticed in the previous chapter, the poet condemns certain economic practices

---

[10] Pound, Ezra, The Spirit of Romance, 95.
[11] "Mang Tsze (The Ethics of Mencius)" (1938), in: SP, 101.
[12] Comp. Dante's Inferno XI.98-111; see Flory, Wendy S., Ezra Pound and the Cantos, 33.
[13] Pearlman, Daniel D., The Barb of Time, 22.
[14] Pearlman, Daniel D., The Barb of Time, 211.

because they seem to contradict or distort nature. Usury, for instance, is understood by Pound as the unnatural multiplication of a sterile matter, money. Finance represents a whole system based on this unnatural increase and "sin against nature" (C45.229). When this system prevails, society is doomed to decay. Similarly "unnatural" was the intrusion of Christianity into China in the 17th and 18th centuries. As Pound stresses, the new religion disrupted family life, brought unrest into the order of the empire, induced disrespect for the dead and undermined the well-established Confucian ethics.[15] The belief in a naturally grown order in society or politics and in the necessity to preserve it is a typical indication of conservative thought and can already be found in the works of writers like Edmund Burke.

In the *Cantos*, natural order and ritual occur in many constellations. C46 entertains us with a "camel driver," the stubborn representative of a culture that strongly depends on tradition and lives in a rhythm of its own (C46.232). The camel driver resists all attempts to force him into an abstract discussion about religion. Instead, he interrupts missionary arguments by hinting at the necessity to perform certain ritual actions. Obedient to the biological rhythms his closed culture still adheres to, his only aim is to fulfill his ritual obligations. Other parts of the *Cantos* draw more serious, and more positive, images of "natural" life, often with rural scenes and peasants at the center.[16] Rural life is of course traditionally associated with fertility, which is one aspect of nature celebrated by Pound: Before Siena could found the *Monte dei Paschi*, "there first was the fruit of nature" (C43.218) and the abundance praised in St. Francis's *Cantico del Sole*, as translated by Pound:

> Praisèd be the Lord by our mother
> The Earth that sustaineth,
> That feeds, that produceth
> Multitudinous grasses
> And flowers and fruitage.[17]

As Flory notes, fertility, sexuality, husbandry, religious observance and ritual all constitute positive values in Pound's poems.[18] The observance of rites denotes decency and honor of the gods,[19] a notion derived from the oldest times of religious worship. In fact, rituals not only secure society's adherence to natural rhythms, but also serve to create a historical continuity. This underlines the organicist-conservative side of Pound's image of history.

[15] "On the Degrees of Honesty in Various Occidental Religions" (1939), in: SP, 65.
[16] Hatlen claims that Pound believed in the "myth of the peasant free-holder," see Hatlen, Burton, "Ezra Pound and Fascism," 168.
[17] Pound, Ezra, The Spirit of Romance, 102.
[18] Flory, Wendy S., Ezra Pound and the Cantos, 34.
[19] "Religio or, The Child's Guide to Knowledge" (1918), in: SP, 47f.

As Pound claimed, the cultural spirit of the Provence was, in its essence, Hellenic and therefore pagan. The rites of May Day speak through Provençal song with "its half memories of Hellenistic mysteries," i.e. Eleusis.[20] Pound discovered the same continuity in Christianity and stressed its affinities to the ancient worship of sun and fire.[21] In fact he explicitly praised the church's potential to preserve the rites.[22] Pound's chief attention was focused on the mediterranean religions of classical times, hence he concentrated on finding their relics in Christianity, whereas he despised other influences in it, e.g. its Semitic roots. Therefore Pound's esteem for Christian rituals was highly selective:

> What we really believe is the pre-Christian element which Christianity has not stamped out. The only Christian festivals having any vitality are welded to sun festivals, the spring solstice, the Corpus and St. John's eve, registering the turn of the sun, the crying of 'Ligo' in Lithuania, the people rushing down the sea in Rapallo on Easter morning, the gardens of Adonis carried to Church on the Thursday [...].[23]

Christian rituals are only a small part of the religious ceremonies present in the *Cantos*. The section following *The Fifth Decad*, for instance, is dominated by the rites of China. Once more, we are taught lessons about the vital importance of observing the rituals for the well-being of the state, including detailed instructions for preparing sacrifices. C49 takes place in the same well-governed world, a world also described in the Chinese *Classic Anthology*, in which the seasons of nature, human laws and political hierarchy are in full accordance with each other:

> May is for grass seed,
> June, Cicada's joy;
> September, harvest, November to destroy
> dead leaves,
> Badger's in season when the year goes out,
> wild-cat can make a young lord's coat.
> In great hunts (March) that ready men for wars,
> commons get piglets; nobles, the full-size boars.[24]

This order is mirrored in the rural idyll of C49. If C49 seems to some scholars paradisal,[25] it is for the quietness created by its framework of rituals,

---

[20] Pound, Ezra, The Spirit of Romance, 90.
[21] "The Divine Mystery" (1913), in: SP, 374.
[22] Pound, Ezra, "I Cease Not to Yowl," 43.
[23] "Statues of Gods" (1939), in: P&P VII.457.
[24] Pound, Ezra, The Classic Anthology Defined by Confucius, 75.

which give form and order to society. Some lines describe the slow seasonal changes of the landscape, others the regular tolling of the "monk's bell" (C49.244) and the repetitious daily routine of peasant life from dawn to dusk, with its "Sun up; work [/] sundown; to rest" (C49.245). The distant, regular movement of ships (C49.244) and the remote but undeniable presence of the ruler (C49.245) contribute to an ideal irreality. C49 is a paramount symbol of Pound's organicism, which becomes even more apparent in the elements it aims to exclude – the unnatural accumulation of debt and the figure of Geryon (C49.245) lurking behind the idyll.

A specific form of semi-religious, in fact rather social, ceremonies are initiation rites, which are introduced in C48:

> DIGONOS; lost in the forest; but are then known as leopards
> after three years in the forest; they are known as 'twice-born'.
>
> (C48.241)

The initiation of the young men by sending them into the forest prepares them for a life in accordance with the laws of nature. Item 12 mentions the same initiation together with the rites of St. John's Eve, embedded in a pagan-mediterranean idyll of cypresses and sparks of fire. Digonos, i.e. Dionysos[26] is identified with Mussolini in the *Pisan Cantos*,[27] which once more hints at the close connection of politics and religion-mythology in the *Cantos*. Mythology, then, has two functions in the text: first, to symbolize a higher state of mind (e.g. the initiated and therefore more experienced person as an image of Dionysos); second, to glorify the political ruler by associating him with timeless forces. The continuity of rituals is not infinite, though. The thread of ceremonies is threatened by the disrespect of secular groups (like bankers), by profanation, decay and a loss of interest in the execution of the sacred act. The procession with oxen in C43 figures as a once sacred, now profaned ritual, in which candles are used to make money and holy chants are quoted only ironically.[28]

An important, although now extinguished, type of ritual is the sacrifice. Pound neither excluded it from the *Cantos*, nor condemned it as archaic. Instead, C47 carries it as a core element of its structure in the figure of

---

[25] Like Flory, Wendy S., Ezra Pound and the Cantos, 148.

[26] Hesse mentions the reference to "Dionysos (Zagreus, Iacchus, Bacchus), who was given the epithets *dithyrambos* and *digonos* (Twice Born), having been born once on earth and once in heaven," in: Hesse, Eva, "Introduction", in: Hesse, Eva (ed.), New Approaches to Ezra Pound, 42.

[27] Casillo, Robert, The Genealogy of Demons, 400, n. 42.

[28] Comp. Casillo, Robert, The Genealogy of Demons, 247f.

Adonis, "the yearly slain, 'victima paschalis,'."[29] Pound developed an early interest in the myth and mentioned Bion's "Lament for Adonis" in 1922.[30] Pound's evocation of Adonis has provoked several interpretations. Emphasizing the conflict between fertility and sterility, Babette Deutsch reads the myth of Adonis's resurrection as a counter-motif to usury.[31] In this sense, it serves to balance the negativity of C45. Guy Davenport integrates Adonis into a sexual reading of C47, which aligns Odysseus with Adonis and Osiris. They embody the male principle as discontinuous and prone to violence, whereas the female element is associated with caves, fecundity and earth.[32] On the same level, Pearlman interprets the reunion of Ulysses and Penelope in C39 as a vegetation rite that evokes Frazer's gods of the seasons, as represented by Adonis in C47.[33] Peter Makin finds a fusion of coition, death and rebirth in the image of Persephone's eating of the pomegranate, which is colored with the blood of Adonis in C47 and C25.[34] Whatever the exact interpretation, Adonis's close ties both to the ritual and the natural element in the *Cantos* are undoubted. More than once, Pound strikes us with a dense and hymnic interplay of ritual, mythology and sexuality.

Rituals are often public, but sometimes gain their particular power from secrecy. This applies especially to the Eleusinian Mysteries. When represented as closed ceremonies, rites are the counterpart of such public procedures as the procession in C43. In a questionable act of simplification, Pound promoted them as the historical source of all western religious thought.[35] At the same time, he stressed the erotic connotations of the Eleusis myth, taking for granted a sexual ceremony as the core of the mysteries.[36] Together with Pound's preference for sun worship, the erotic-sacral element symbolized by Eleusis constitutes part of the central cluster of the poet's religious ideas. He was interested in Christianity because it supposedly derived its rites from solar worship, but Eleusis represented the original center of myths. In the Eleusis myth, several crucial layers combine, namely the observance of rites, fertility and exclusiveness (the exclusion of the profane from the mysteries). Fertility is here intended to include sexuality as well as

---

29 Pound, Ezra, The Spirit of Romance, 98.

30 Letter of 9 July 1922, in: Pound, Ezra, The Selected Letters of Ezra Pound, 181.

31 Deutsch, Babette, "Speech and Song," 136.

32 Davenport, Guy, "Persephone's Ezra," in: Hesse, Eva (ed.), New Approaches to Ezra Pound, 168.

33 Pearlman, Daniel D., The Barb of Time, 163.

34 Makin, Peter, Pound's Cantos, 96.

35 Pound: "all the dogma worth a damn came from greek mysteries etc/ everything that built the cathedrals"; Pound, Ezra, "I Cease Not to Yowl," 40.

36 Although this has never been fully proven. For more information on Eleusis see Mylonas, Georgios E., Eleusis and the Eleusinian Mysteries, Princeton 1974.

fecundity in nature.[37] The sexual act is conceived of as a sacrament, which of course implies the danger of profanation, as hinted at in C45, where Pound mentions the "whores for Eleusis" (C45.230).[38]

In *The Fifth Decad*, it is chiefly C47 in which Eros reigns supreme. Among a whole group of classical mediterranean myths and fertility rites, the encounter of Circe and Ulysses takes place and is celebrated with the inevitability of a natural process – like the "moth is called over mountain" and the bull "runs blind on the sword," Ulysses is called to the cave of Circe (C47.237). While C39 describes a sensual scene with overtly sexual connotations, C47 frames the meeting of Ulysses and Circe in a set of natural processes and periodic acts like plowing, fertility rites and the growing of grass. Thus the erotic encounter transcends the secrecy of Eleusis and becomes part of a comprehensive sequence of natural phenomena.

Pound believed in a historical continuity created by rituals. Accordingly, he attributed a lasting infuence to the Eleusian mysteries.[39] As opposed to T. S. Eliot, who had a strong inclination towards *askesis*,[40] Pound favored Eros, which expressed itself in the Eleusinian rituals, Troubadour poetry and the mating of Ulysses and Circe.[41] Eros, in the *Cantos*, has two functions. First, it serves to integrate humanity into natural life, as becomes obvious in C47. Second, it enhances religious experience: in a dialectics of religious sentiment, Pound saw religious feelings arise from the tension between two charged poles. Whereas monks and hermits sought to create the second pole within themselves, others would find it in the erotic attraction of another person (which Pound calls the saner alternative).[42] Eros would then serve to elevate the human mind towards the center of Pound's belief – the light.

---

[37] Both aspects are coupled in Pound's claim that "Paganism included a certain attitude toward; a certain understanding of, coitus, which is the mysterium. The other rites are the festivals of fecundity of the grain and the sun festivals, without revival of which religion can not return to the hearts of the people," see Pound's "Religio" (1939), in: SP, 70, also compare P&P VII.470.

[38] Pound commented on C45: "'Eleusis is *very* elliptical. It means that in place of the sacramental [fuck] in the Mysteries, you 'ave the 4 and six-penny 'ore. As you see, the moral bearing is very high, and the degradation of the sacrament (which is the coition and *not* the going to a fat-buttocked priest or registry office) has been completely debased largely *by* Xtianity, or misunderstanding of that Ersatz religion."; see Pound, Ezra, The Selected Letters of Ezra Pound, 397.

[39] "Credo" (1930), in: SP, 53; "Terra Italica" (1931-32), in: SP, 59.

[40] See my essay "Checks and Balances: Functions of Mysticism in T. S. Eliot's Prose," in: *ZAA* 51.2 (2003), 113-122.

[41] P&P V.330f.

[42] Pound, Ezra, The Spirit of Romance, 94.

In Pound's case, religious sentiment has an important function, because even when we approach the more abstract levels of Pound's belief,[43] we are still confronted with a very subjective approach to religion at the core. Subjective is here defined as related to individual experiences. As Kenner has remarked in connection with French cave drawings, to "see gods was a way to see nature."[44] It rested on immediate sensations experienced by a person, who explained certain natural phenomena as divine. This took place within a framework of societal traditions and customs, but nevertheless affected the individual. Religious subjectivism also prevailed in medieval visionary works like *The Cloud of Unknowing* or in the ecstasies of Spanish mystics like St John of the Cross and Theresa of Avila. When subjectivity submits to the mythologies prescribed by dogma, it becomes mysticism; when it prefers the individual vision to dogma, it is condemned as heretic.

Avoiding the popular mythologies of Dryden's age, Blake introduced into post-medieval literature a way of perceiving the gods that had more in common with the prophets of the Old Testament and the mystics of the Middle Ages than with English classicism. Blake's visions may have a strong systematic bend, but what really separates them from the classicist approach to mythology is their origin in the poet's immediate perception, like he himeself was "walking among the fires of hell."[45] Blake claimed he sometimes saw the giant figures of his larger-than-life heroes with his own eyes. In Hölderlin, too, gods are experienced as an immediate sensual sensation. What Pound experienced was the power of light.

Pound's subjectivism becomes obvious in his reading of the Greek myths. He saw them as psychic experiences and as expressions of personal moods that were really intelligible only to the persons who had experienced them as reality. What classical Greece practiced was interpreting the universe by reading signs of gods in subjective perceptions.[46] This is a concept Pound adopted very early. In 1918 he clearly stated: "What is a god? A god is an eternal state of mind." The god manifests itself when this state takes form; and man becomes god by entering it. Divine forms are recognized by their beauty and a sense of subjective vision.[47] Pound's vocabulary becomes slightly exuberant when he laments the loss of a world in which philosophical

---

[43] We will not call it religion, for religion demands a developed system of dogmas and rites, also a substantial amount of the organization Pound mistrusted.

[44] Kenner, Hugh, The Pound Era, 30f.

[45] From *The Marriage of Heaven and Hell*, in: Blake, William, The Complete Poems, ed. Alicia Ostriker, London et.al. 1977, 182.

[46] Pound, Ezra, The Spirit of Romance, 92f..

[47] "Religio or, The Child's Guide to Knowledge" (1918), in: SP, 47f.

thought expressed itself in visions that were untouched by what he calls the "Hebrew disease":

> We appear to have lost the radiant world where one thought cuts through another with clean edge, a world of moving energies *'mezzo oscuro rade', 'risplende in sè perpetuale effecto'*, magnetisms that take form, that are seen, or that border the visible, the matter of Dante's *paradiso*, the glass under water, the form that seems a form seen in a mirror, these realities perceptible to the sense, interacting.[48]

Pound sought to re-enact this sense of vision in some passages of the *Cantos*, where the divine light is experienced in subjective moments beyond the boundaries of mythology or religion:

> On past the palazzi,
> in the stillness,
> The light now, not of the sun.
> Chrysophrase,
> And the water green clear, and blue clear;
> On, to the great cliffs of amber.
>
> (C17.76)

Light signifies the divine, which, if perceived in all its brightness, will challenge the human mind:

> and the light became so bright and so blindin'
> in this layer of paradise
> that the mind of man was bewildered.
>
> (C38.190)

These visions are governed by a mode of contemplation Pound defined in his notes on the terminology of philosopher Richard of St. Victor: While cogitation is the mere unsystematic viewing of a subject and meditation is a slightly more comprehensive form of perception, contemplation makes its subject radiate "as light from the sun reaches out in an infinite number of ways to things that are related to or dependent on it. [...] Poetry in its acme is expression from contemplation."[49]

We now reach the next level of Pound's subjectivist and unorthodox mysticism. What a person perceives by concentrated contemplation is not a chaotic multitude of forms, for this is what we experience only on lower

---

48 "Cavalcanti" (1910-1931, publ. 1934), in: LE, 154.
49 Pound, Ezra, The Collected Early Poems, 99; also comp. GK, 77.

levels of perception. Rather, the advanced mind discovers the unmoved mover. While Pound was skeptical about any definite description of the "intimate essence of the universe" and its unity,[50] the unmoved mover is a construct frequently used in the *Cantos*. Originally an Aristotelian concept, it denoted the idea of nine heavenly spheres set into motion by a prime mover, God, which remained unmoved. But Pound gives the concept a twist of his own. Led by his focus on Eros, he associates the unmoved mover with love, i.e. *eros*, not *agape*. As Pearlman points out, the immobile stillness of love, as opposed to human fickleness, informs the *Cantos* from their early stages (C2, C17) over C49 and C50 to the very end.[51] The erotic dimension of stillness is present in Cavalcanti's "Donna mi priegha," which claims: "None can imagine love / that knows not love; / Love doth not move, but draweth all to him."[52] In the *Cantos*, this becomes a hymn to the power of stillness:

> Unskilled can not form his image,
> He himself moveth not, drawing all to his stillness,
> Neither turneth about to seek his delight
> Nor yet to seek out proving
> Be it so great or so small.
>
> (C36.178)

In C50, it shines through the imagined figures of a classical courtesan and a cruel queen:

> Lalage's shadow moves in the fresco's knees
> She is blotted with Dirce's shadow
> dawn stands there fixed and unmoving
> only we two have moved.
>
> (C50.249)

In C51, the concept of the unmoved mover gains a Neoplatonic quality, so when Pound translates from stanza 5 of the poem "Al cor gentil repara sempre amore" by the poet Guido Guinizelli (c. 1230-1276): "Splende 'n la 'ntelligenzia del cielo / Deo Cr'iator piu che 'n nostr' occhi 'l sole" – "Shines [/] in the mind of heaven God [/] who made it" (C51.250). Guinizelli united Aristotelian and Neoplatonic concepts, combining Aristotle's First Mover

---

[50] "Axiomata" (1921), in: SP, 49.
[51] Pearlman, Daniel D., The Barb of Time, 159.
[52] Pound, Ezra, Pound's Cavalcanti, 174f.

with a Neoplatonc imagery of perception.[53] In "Al cor gentil," love results from an inner movement of the soul. It starts with sensual apprehension based on sight and with the inner contemplation of images, which causes the senses and appetites to impinge on the faculties of imagination, intellect, and memory – "Thus the eyes, spirits, and heart enact a drama of apprehension that joins the sensitive soul to reason."[54] We find Guinizelli's influence in Dante and Cavalcanti, discernible in the theme of praise and in the imagery of light and the eyes.[55] Again, Cavalcanti's "Donna mi priegha" can contribute to our understanding of Pound. Cavalcanti emphasizes the close connection between the visual and the intellect: "From form seen doth he start, that, understood, / Taketh in latent intellect."[56] Pound's concept of Eros has two poles – one is the ritual, Eleusis, which embeds Eros into a societal framework of sacred procedures; the other is inner experience, as described by Guinizelli and Cavalcanti.

Eros is not the only component of Pound's mysticism. Intellect is equally important and can hardly be conceived of without Eros. As should be noted, the combination of love and intellect is not an exclusively Neoplatonic theorem. In his copy of the *The Sacred Edict* Pound marked the old Chinese teaching "heaven has the virtue of loving production; man is the spiritual intelligence of creation."[57] Pound was aware of the possibility of ecstasy through contemplation and exact perception.[58] T. S. Eliot stressed that the same goal could be found in Richard of St. Victor, Aquinas and Dante, namely contemplation of the divine, and the "development and subsumption of emotion and feeling through intellect into the vision of God." Eliot quotes St. Thomas as saying: "it results evidently that it is only in the divine vision that intelligent beings can find the true felicity."[59] In Pound, perceiving the divine elevates the perceiver. The completeness of perception generates a god-like power in a human being. The person envisioning the divine becomes godlike, by assuming the "light of the doer" from C51, and then radiates a higher light that can illuminate others.

Here we encounter once more the metaphysics of light which permeates the *Cantos* as a whole. Whether in the sensual visions of Lalage and Dirce at dawn (C50) or in the radiant intellect of the political genius (C51) – whenever

---

[53] Edwards in Guinizelli, Guido, The Poetry of Guido Guinizelli, 113; also compare pp. 41ff. in: Guido Guinizelli, Rime (= Testi 5), ed. Pietro Pelosi, Naples 1998. For some early Poundian remarks on Neoplatonism see Pound, Ezra, Gaudier-Brzeska, 135.
[54] Edwards in Guinizelli, Guido, The Poetry of Guido Guinizelli, xxii.
[55] Edwards in Guinizelli, Guido, The Poetry of Guido Guinizelli, xlviii.
[56] Pound, Ezra, Pound's Cavalcanti, 172f.; also see "Cavalcanti" (1910-1931, publ. 1934), in: LE, 164 and 156.
[57] Comp. the BL copy of Baller, F. W., The Sacred Edict, 172, n. 1.
[58] Pound, Ezra, The Spirit of Romance, 91.
[59] Eliot, Thomas S., The Varieties of Metaphysical Poetry, 103f.

Pound wants to signify that we are about to witness a moment of higher inspiration, an imagery of light abounds. The divine is unthinkable without a clothing of light, a concept which has left its traces in texts ranging from the visions of Moses to the writings of Blake and later Pound. As Richard of St. Victor wrote of the divine: "de Deo scriptum est quia inhabitat *lucem inaccessibilem*."[60] Pound was quite aware of the tradition constitued by his philosophical and literary predecessors, by Aristotle, Albertus Magnus, Grosseteste and Guinizelli.[61] Whether he sought to explain political genius or the experience of love, he adhered to what Robert Grosseteste wrote in *De Luce*: "Et species et perfectio corporum omnium est lux: sed superiorum corporum magis spiritualis et simplex, inferiorum vero corporum magis corporalis et multiplicata."[62]

Coated in an imagery of light, moments of vision elevate the *Cantos* to occasional glimpses of purity. Within the poem, however, those moments are at the same time the most significant points of tension for the readers: If they bear in mind the verbal excesses and resentments present in so many of Pound's texts, they are not likely to be blinded by the lights of paradise. It is only a small step from the celebration of divine intelligence to the glorification of a dictator. This vertical tension is an inseparable part of the *Cantos* and should prevent the poems (and their readers) from slipping away into metaphysical exile.

---

60 Richard of St. Victor, Les Douze Patriarches, ch. XXII.

61 "Cavalcanti" (1910-1931, publ. 1934), in: LE, 158.

62 "The form and perfection of all bodies is light, but in the superior bodies it is more spiritual and simple, whereas in the inferior bodies it is more corporeal and multiplied." – Grosseteste, Robert, De Luce 56f.

III.6 “These fragments..” – Explaining *The Fifth Decad*

There is in inferior minds a passion for unity, that is, for a confusion and melting together of things which a good mind will want kept distinct.

(Ezra Pound, *Instigations*)

III.6.a Cantos 42 to 51

In the preceding chapters of this study we highlighted issues and concepts in which Pound was interested when he composed the *Fifth Decad*. In the process of writing, those subjects, from economics to religion, would then ramify and develop sub-elements in which Pound’s general ideas assumed specific forms and historical manifestations. This chapter will discuss how *The Fifth Decad* combines, synthesizes or juxtaposes those elements, how it establishes parallels between them and uses them to convey a message. While this chapter is not intended as a full synopsis of the decad, it will nevertheless outline those narrative threads and structural patterns that give inner coherence to the text. As Pound said, the “charge of obscurity has been raised at regular or irregular intervals since the stone age.”[1] We will do our best to contradict this charge and to decrypt the layers of meaning in the poem, encoded as they may be.

An identification of Cantos based on their content can help us to discover aspects of their structure. In addition to the standard or customized names applied to the ten Cantos (e.g. Seven Lakes Canto), we will also introduce three functional designations, i.e. names denoting the affiliation of a Canto to a group of Cantos. First, those Cantos which are mainly concerned with historical events and adhere more closely to historiographical narrative patterns than other Cantos (History Cantos). In the Cantos of this group, the fiction of historicity is created by means of an imitation of authenticity (transcriptions of documents) and by narrative devices (chronology, recurring characters). Second, a sub-group within the History Cantos that concentrates on collecting evidence to prove the negative influence and powers of usury in history (Evidence Cantos). These Cantos are distinguished from the other History Cantos by their strong use of apocryphal elements and by their fragmented, more argumentative than narrative, structure. Third, Cantos with

[1] Pound, Ezra, “Preface,” v.

a reduced number of historical references and a more lyrical style and content, i.e. a predominance of the poetical over the historical, of the metaphor over the plain fact and of the image over the event (Lyrical Cantos). We will use this categorization as an additional tool to describe the structure of *The Fifth Decad*, because the decad is distinguished by a constant shifting between the lyrical and the historical, both on the micro- and the macro-level.

In addition to the aspect of lyrical versus historical, the decad includes other, even more antagonistic contrasts. We already highlighted the economic tendency of *The Fifth Decad*. According to Davis, Cantos 31 to 51 are used by Pound to develop economic ideas and to establish Pound's distinction between institutions/persons assuming social responsibility and those engaged in increasing their own profit at the public's cost.[2] The juxtaposition of economic responsibility with reckless profiteering is one of the recurring binary oppositions in *The Fifth Decad*, while the contrast of natural fertility and sterility is another. Cantos 42 to 51 also confront political-economic disorder with order. Disorder is signified by war (C46.231, C50.246) and debt (C46.231, C49.245). Order is defined by the presence of strong rulers (C49.245, C50.246) and of a higher, metaphysical power (C49.245, C51.250). The poems of the decad develop in constant tension between those opposites. In fact, juxtaposition is one of the decad's major stylistic devices. It testifies to Pound's antithetical mode of thinking, which became increasingly more contrastive during the 1930s and early 1940s.

Canto 42-44

The three Siena Cantos constitute History Cantos 1 to 3. Their unity has thematical and bibliographical reasons. All three Cantos deal with Sienese history from the 1620s to 1814 and are derived from the same sources, as excerpted in Pound's Siena notebooks (items 301-305). The unity of the three Cantos is supported by authorial evidence: Pound himself regarded them as one block.[3] They represent the first, massive cluster of historical units in *The Fifth Decad* and show examples of good economic government, as realized in Early Modern history and now remembered through the filter of archival documents. The latter were reproduced in historiographical works whose essence Pound transferred to his notebooks and finally into the poem.

The beginning of Canto 42 is a British curse towards the U.S., followed by a cluster of references to the history of Britain and to empires in general. The allusion to different laws of monarchic succession creates an association

[2] Davis, Earle, Vision Fugitive, 69, 84.

[3] Gordon, David M. (ed.), Ezra Pound and James Laughlin: Selected Letters, 69, letter of 12 Oct 1936.

to Roman emperor Antoninus, whose presence is a first hint at the development of sea law, which marked an important shift in the historical usury system according to Pound. The combination of allusions to the anti-American British attitude, Queen Victoria and a Roman emperor serves to remind readers of the imperial periods of European history. In addition, Victoria embodies the 19th century that Pound detested so much. The brief overture provides us with some first motifs, but does not prepare readers for what immediately follows: a shift towards Early Modern Sienese history. An unidentified narrator introduces the new subject, the *Monte dei Paschi*. The following lines explain the administrative procedures for the foundation of the bank and list some of the conditions and provisions under which it was constituted. The narrator maintains an explanatory, insistent and eulogizing tone throughout this section: the facts listed by the narrator are all "important" (C43.209); the "contrade" is explained as "(the wards)" (C43.210). The validity of the administrative acts is confirmed by a notary (C43.210), which creates an atmosphere of officialdom, but in a positive sense. Some lyrical lines are inserted as a *memento mori* between the documents (C43.210). Together with the shorter comments by the narrator, they interrupt the administrative jargon of the major part of the poem and create a contrast to the subsequent transcriptional quotations (C43.211f.).

Pound's interpolation, reminding readers of their limited lifespan, also rhymes with the authoritative, almost proverbial, lines in C45 and C49. The lines "to be young is to suffer. [/] Be old, and be past that" (C43.213) are another proverbial moment among documentary artefacts. Another lyrical interpolation, "Saw cities move in one figure" (C43.213), describes a vision which combines several paramount symbols of Italian culture in one revelation that foreshadows the cultural peaks in C45 (Duccio, San Zeno etc.), where they are threatened by usury. What Pound grasps in this passage is a brief glimpse of the spirit of Italian culture, which embraces architecture and works of art as well as responsible economic practice. After details about the involvement and commitments of the Duke of Tuscany, regent Maria Magdalena's approval of the *Monte*, its actual foundation and an account of the conditions for shareholders, C42 ends with a positive accent, assuring us that the foundation of the *Monte* happened "out of sure knowledge and [/] ex certe scientia et in plenitude of their powers" (C43.214), followed by a reference to the capital of the *Monte*. The final lines affirm the positive intention behind the bank.

History Canto 2 is distinguished from C42 by its reduced use of administrative documents in favor of more narrative elements, like public events and town life in general, including the city prostitutes. The Canto covers a period from 1622 to 1749, continuing the sequence of events established in C42. The foundation of the *Monte* is again praised as a benefit for the people, and more administrative proceedings take place, supplemented by bibliographical references to the original documents from which Pound derived his information ("1251 of the Protocols marked also [/] X, I, I, F, and four arabic"; C43.216). The direct allusion to the bibliographical source of the poem serves to avoid a closed narrative and instead hints at the historicity of the material.

After mentioning Siena's economic problems, ranging from shortage of coin to usury, another Poundian interlude describes the traditional running of the *palio* (name of a prize banner) of the *contrade* or wards, including the *carrocio*, a painted wagon drawn by oxen.[4] Pound was generally interested in this type of public event. In *The Spirit of Romance*, Pound quotes a 17th century description of the Fiesta of Corpus to decribe the general atmosphere in which Vega's plays were staged, including a procession with a cardboard serpent carried through the streets.[5] He also read Dante's *Divine Comedy* as a cycle of mystery plays.[6] Pound's use of colloquial language and scatological details marks a strong contrast to the official language of the documents and underlines the presence of a narrator, who describes occasional events "under my window" (C43.216) in an appropriate occasional language.

We then return to the year 1622 and the documents with their provisions for the financial responsibility of the monarch and the security of the citizens. The historical focus of the poem is widened by a brief reference to fraud at sea in antiquity and modern times, from Syracuse to Standard Oil. The association is called up by the preceding reference to responsibility as a virtue, which is denied by those who commit fraud. Back in 1622, Pound lists further provisions for financing the *Monte dei Paschi* and re-enacts the official celebration of the founding act in the "hall of World Map" (C43.218). Celso Cittadini's wheat reform plans conjure up associations with fertility and evoke a remark on the beneficience of nature: "Grass nowhere out of place" (C43.219), a pseudo-proverbial remark later repeated in combination with the godlike ruler and a speech by Rudolf Hess (C51.251). After more financial transactions, Pound introduces a detail that underlines the power and efficiency of the Sienese administration: it even kept books about the town prostitutes, one of whom is then removed from the register (C43.219).

Then illegal "black money" from Florence is brought into Siena, ruler Pietro de Medici and his illegitimate children appear, and in 1624 another prostitute is punished by the Magistrate. That two prostitutes and Pietro's "fertility" are mentioned so close to each other serves to create an allusive field of sexual connotations, which enhance the History Cantos' preoccupation with the "fruit of nature" and foreshadow the fertility rites and

---

[4] Kearns, George, Guide to Ezra Pound's *Selected Cantos*, 113.

[5] Pound, Ezra, The Spirit of Romance, 212f.

[6] Pound, Ezra, The Spirit of Romance, 154.

sexual encounters in C47. From the 1622 preparations for the foundation of the *Monte* we move forward to 1626 and a new load of "black money." Despite the Grand Duke's ignorance of economic affairs, the 1670s and subsequent years bring economic reforms, people are no longer imprisoned for debt and financial support for the Tolomei foundation is raised. Back in 1622, we learn more about financial provisions for the *Monte* and the Duke's illegitimate children. Official credentials by Maria Magdalena and Orazio Grcolini are provdided. In 1749 money is spent on several improvements, before we reach the end of the Medici reign.

C44 (History Canto 3) continues the strategy of C42 to supplement official documents with descriptions of public events. Returning to Sienese history in 1766, we learn that Pietro Leopoldo abolished severe punishments of debtors and facilitated grain imports. He is succeeded by Ferdinando III. In 1792 the Sienese witness a public parade in praise of Ferdinando and the installation of a tablet in his honor. Ironically, the parade interrupts the dry administrative proceedings like an eventful narrative, but is itself only a slightly modified quotation from a history book. Less ironical is the tone in which the celebration is described. As opposed to the oxen in C43, the event is rendered far less colloquially and is placed between hints at Ferdinando's reasonable ideas ("thought grain was to eat"; C44.223) and a description of the duke as a model gentleman ("il più galantuomo del paese"; C44.225).

Due to the invasion of the French, Ferdinando III has to leave the country in 1796. Tuscany now undergoes a phase of political unrest, with uprisings in Arezzo, progroms and acts of sabotage against the French troops, who, in 1800, have an increasing demand for money. Louis becomes king of Etruria, while the population suffers from heavy taxes. In 1807 Napoleon writes a letter to former queen Maria Luisa, asking her to leave Tuscany. Quoted in detail, the document supplements the other letters incorporated into the Siena Cantos. After Maria Luisa's departure, Napoleon's sister Maria Anna is received as the new grand duchess, but has to leave the country in 1814. At the end of the Canto, Pound remembers Napoleon's achievements, which are surpassed by the reforms of Pietro Leopoldo and Ferdinando III. A visit by Napoleon's mother finishes C44, together with Pound's final assertion that the *Monte dei Paschi* was a non-usurious institution. The final lines stress the lasting achievement of the *Monte dei Paschi*, as opposed to the numerous, constantly changing rulers who governed the duchy.

Because Pound thought that Pietro Leopoldo and Ferdinand III were wiped out by a "Napoleonic flurry"[7] and that the traces of the Leopoldine Reforms had been forgotten,[8] he attempted to re-discover those traces by

[7] GK, 263.
[8] "An Introduction to the Economic Nature of the United States" (1944, orig. Italian), in: SP, 147.

providing a detailed account of their history in the Siena Cantos. Cantos 42 to 44 reconstruct the achievements of "Enlightened Despots," but also the virtues of a whole Italian city: we must not forget that, in the poem, the monarchs and aristocrats are not solely responsible for the *Monte*, as the magistrate plays an equally important role: an efficient balance of power. The positive example provided by Siena is constantly threatened by political forces, whose presence adds narrative momentum to the poems and complements the positive with a negative counterpart. The challenge threatening the ideal creates a narrative tension, which reaches its climax with the litany of C45, the counter-statement to the Siena Cantos. After emphasizing the "bridle on usury" of the *Monte*, Pound now confronts us with the consequences of unrestrained usury.

Canto 45

C45, the well-known Usura Canto, is the first Lyrical Canto in the decad – at this point, Pound replaces the documentary-archival emphasis of the Siena Cantos with a warning complaint about usury and its threats. Historical references are of course used in the poem, but do not govern its overall structure as the Sienese documents do in the first three Cantos. C45 presents the counterpart of the rich town life of Siena: a diverse, artistically refined Italian culture which is, however, endangered by sterility. Whereas the Siena Cantos provide the positive example of a well-governed bank, we are now warned against the negative powers of finance.

The Canto begins with the decay of design and painting. Usury affects the funding of the arts and hence, under an usurious system, Gonzaga would not have been painted with his concubines, who in turn indicate the presence of fertility and Eros, the opponent of Usura.[9] The concubines rhyme with the Pietro di Medici's illegitimate children in C43. Villon's "*harpes et luz*" (C45.229) establishes a link to the Middle Ages and underlines the medieval tone of the poem. The paradise alluded to in the "painted paradise" and the quotation from Villon will be irrevocably lost, Pound implies, if usury prevails and destroys both culture and spirituality. Food will become stale and sterile; design, building and stonecutting will degenerate. Weaving and the wool-trade, symbols of "natural" craft and commerce, will be impaired, as will be painting, church architecture and craft itself. "Azure hath a canker" may refer to the bad condition of blue skies in frescoes and paintings, e.g. in

[9] As Twitchell suggests, Pound used "concubines," with aristocratic undertones, in contrast to the more ordinary "whores"; see Twitchell, Jeffrey, "Art and the Spirit of Capitalism," 16.

della Francesco's Temio fresco, for which a quick, but perishable method of painting was used.[10]

From art, the poem moves to the elemental forces of fertility, which are also affected by usury: pregnancy, courting and sexuality. Usury, Pound claims, separates bride and groom, even in bed. Emphasizing (as expressed by capital letters) that this is against nature, Pound confronts the reader with ultimate profanations: prostitutes in the place of sacred mysteries (Eleusis) and dead bodies set for a banquet (C45.230). We already mentioned the importance of Eleusis for Pound, who considers the destruction of the sacred ritual of coitus by commercial sex an imminent threat. As the "dead bodies" signify, respect for the dead is equally threatened by usury. I would not go so far as to claim that "the last lines, implicitly scolding against abortion and contraceptives, are alarmingly in accord with the demographic policies of fascism."[11] Pound was not so much interested in social policies as in the consequences of an unrestrained usurious system that would affect every area of human life.

Structurally, C45 is the least complex Canto in the decad. Its stylistic and structural unity, however, contribute to the power of the poem. As has been noted by several scholars, C45 is of an almost medieval simplicity and organized like a tableau: "the commanding figure of Usury, like the figure of Death in the mediaeval tableaux, appears in one scene after another," as Dekker states.[12] In fact, usury really *acts* in the poem. While some negative consequences occur *with* Usura, usury figures as a subject in the other parts of the poem, where it actively "rusteth" and "slayeth."[13] As should be noted, however, it is not usury, but some unspecified "they" who introduce prostitutes to Eleusis. We can only identify "them" indirectly by using item 55 as evidence. In that draft, "they" are accused of having built vaults and cellars. These cellars constitute the private, i.e. *closed* counterpart of the medieval cathedrals (*public* expressions of a superior spirit). They are the safes of international financiers and bankers, like the "bomb proof, gas-proof cellar beneath the Rothschild private palace in Paris, whereto the works of art (as having commercial VALUE, monetary worth) are transported when the great chief usurer leaves the fatal and mentally foetid city."[14] "They" are revealed, once more, as the aristocrats of money.

---

[10] Twitchell, Jeffrey, "Art and the Spirit of Capitalism," 18.

[11] Bacigalupo, Massimo, The Formèd Trace, 61.

[12] Dekker, George, Sailing After Knowledge, 175.

[13] An aspect pointed out in: Brooke-Rose, Christine, A Structural Analysis of Pound's Usura Canto, 13.

[14] "John Buchan's "Cromwell"" (1935), in: P&P VI.295.

Evidence Canto 1 was written after Orage's death in 1934[15] and was published during the Spanish Civil War.[16] The moderate narrator of the Siena Cantos now assumes the role of an inspector and proseutor, who travels through history to unearth evidence for a far-reaching conspiracy, while occasionally adding personal reminiscences. As the first lines make clear, there is no simple language to help us get "through hell in a hurry" (C46.231), i.e. no "poetic" language like T. S. Eliot's. Instead, the narrator insists, we must cope with economics. In literary terms, this passage is almost programmatic. It underlines the shift away from 19th-century poetics Pound achieved even before he started working on the *Cantos*. It also stresses the priority of subject matter over lyrical expression, of economic issues over conventional ideas of poetic beauty. Pound criticizes those readers who think "that this tale teaches… [/] a *lesson*" (C46.231, my italics), i.e. who feel intimidated by Pound's overt didacticism. Teaching his readers the "truth" about history is exactly what he intends.

After a lyrical interlude in the form of a landscape scene, we encounter for the first time that insistent "Seventeen [/] Years on this case, nineteen years, ninety years [/] on this case" (C46.231), the *leitmotif* of this Canto. It establishes the central fiction and persona of C46, the investigator looking for evidence. It also refers us to the beginnings of Pound's interest in economics and usury: "In 1918 I began an investigation of causes of war, to oppose same."[17] Adding 17 years to 1918, we reach 1935, the year mentioned at the end of C46. Thus, the persona of the investigator is almost completely interchangeable with Pound himself. His insisting on those almost twenty years of commitment underlines the personal dimension of the Canto, an aspect that should not be overlooked among all the historical details in the text. C46 shows elements of an intellectual autobiography.

The following passage of the poem recounts one of Pound's earliest conversations with C. H. Douglas. Authorial evidence suggests that it took place in about 1919/1920, for in 1934 Pound referred to "a statement I made 14 years ago, namely that: Any government worth a damn COULD pay dividends instead of levying taxes."[18] The same statement occurs in the conversation with Douglas. In the next section, the fascist Decennio exposition calls up memories of Orage's office, of the people killed in World War I, war debts of the Civil War and – we now move from the historical to

[15] Subsequently, Pound also wrote the essay "In the Wounds (Memoriam A. R. Orage)" in 1935.

[16] As emphasized in: Deutsch, Babette, "Speech and Song," 152.

[17] Quot. in Tytell, John, Ezra Pound: The Solitary Volcano, 146.

[18] "As to Sprague" (1934), in: P&P VI.129; the same phrase occurs in SP, 417.

the autobiographical – the pictures on the wall of Orage's office. By a reference to British prime minister Balfour we are reminded of Pound's conviction that the politician was a scoundrel, as he remarked to Yeats in 1934.[19] The narrator quotes Orage's strong opinions on other journalists and writers, but juxtaposes the remarks with disparaging statements by the novelist Marmaduke about Greeks and Arabs. The anecdote about Abdul Baha and the obstinate camel driver, who will not give up his daily routine for discussion, is another reference to the role of rituals. Yet in this case, the ritual does not have connotations as positive as those in C47 and C49, but is rather satirized. Both Orage and Marmaduke utter strong opinions; Orage proves a sarcastic intellectual, while Marmaduke show his ignorance. Maybe Pound mentions him as an example of the type of writer Orage despised.

After another repetition of the *leitmotif* ("17 years on this case," C46.233) we reach a turning point at which the autobiographical is replaced by the historical. After encountering Pound's allies Douglas and Orage, we now meet their opponents. The Paterson quotation of 1694 about the creation of money out of nothing is followed by an arrogant statement by (allegedly) Rothschild on the benefits of the economic system for the few (1860s), a reference to desolate houses (pointing back to C45) and to Regius Professors as advocates of a usurious system. Pound follows Hollis in his interpretation of the Regius Professorship as an institution established to promote Whig history and to justify the (Walpole-dominated) present. As Hollis remarks, the attempt was successful and the Whig concept of history became generally accepted.[20]

In C46, the narrator now loudly calls for a jury to convict the mentioned criminals, another hint at the legal dimension of this Canto. As we are assured, the case approaches its conclusion (C46.233) and we are presented with more evidence: St Peter's (its architecture a symbol of the decay of art), slums, coffee and nitrate trade. Paterson's statement is called the first, but not last, case and revision is demanded. The narrator again names the enemy, even stronger than in C45: what was mere "usura" before, now becomes "hyper-usura" (C46.334), which was once fought by the American presidents Jefferson and Van Buren. In a narrative acceleration of history, "seventy four red revolutions" and ten empires pass, before we encounter Antoninus again, whose sea law is already present in the first lines of *The Fifth Decad*.

A chronological sequence of condemnations follows: Athens was built on usury, papal Rome ignored Luther, baroque style was a decay of art. After repeating the *leitmotif*, the narrator conludes that the first part of the evidence has now been presented. Usury is called a tomb and Geryon a destroyer,

[19] Quot. in Surette, Leon, Pound in Purgatory, 86.
[20] Hollis, Christopher, The Two Nations, 38-41.

transferring destructive and derogative connotations of Helen to usury.[21] The Latin and Greek language of the curses sets them apart from the colloquial language of other parts of the Canto. But the timeless appeal of the classical languages is quickly disturbed by a sudden leap into the reality of 1935 and the social problems of the U.S. under Roosevelt: unemployment, illiteracy and crime. The U.S. situation is one case, but the narrator points out the even more desolate condition of Britain and France, which are governed by usurers. Against this background, Cummings's personal ambition – as mentioned in the final line – appears as an ironical counterpoint to the seriousness of the overall situation. The final passage (C46.235) of the poem testifies to Pound's frequent use of large figures, a habit Elias Canetti found prevalent among people with paranoid tendencies: "FIVE million youths without jobs [/] FOUR million adult illiterates [/] 15 million 'vocational misfits', [/] NINE million persons annual, injured."[22] We can note the same obsession with such numbers in the lines "5 millions bein' killed off […] Debts of the South to New York, that is to the [/] banks of the city, two hundred million" (C46.231).

C46 is one the one hand a clear statement about U.S. economic history: bankers usurped the money of the colonists, while only Jackson and Van Buren seriously opposed private privilege.[23] The Civil War is interpreted as an economic conflict, from which the New York bankers profited. The downward spiral ended in the 1929 crash, when it became obvious that the Roosevelt administration had not been able to stabilize the country, as pointed out at the end of the Canto. At the same time, the Canto is a prosecutor's address: "it gives the damage inflicted by the economic crime (fetid brickwork; mass unemployment), the steps by which the investigator was led to track the crime down, and the documentation as to the time and the place where it was perpetrated."[24] The evidence presented in the text reconstructs the history of usury and economic infamy in general with all its consequences, going back to the Greeks and Romans.

After the presentation of the evidence, Pound assures us that the "case draws to a conclusion." Hence Pearlman reads C46 as the end of the first phase of the *Cantos*.[25] Yet C48, using similar arguments and strategies as C46, is still to come, which is why C46 is not the only turning point in *The Fifth Decad*, but rather part of a conclusive process unfolding throughout the section.

---

[21] Pearlman, Daniel D., The Barb of Time, 164f.

[22] Comp. the entry "million" in the Pound concordance; Dilligan, Robert J. / Parins, James W. / Bender, Todd K., A Concordance to Ezra Pound's *Cantos*, 215.

[23] Davis, Earle, Vision Fugitive, 133.

[24] Makin, Peter, Pound's Cantos, 107.

[25] Pearlman, Daniel D., The Barb of Time, 135.

Because of its absence of overt economic and political contents, C47 is here referred to as Lyrical Canto 2. Maintaining a full unity of style, it is a dithyrambic hymn to Adonis and constantly refers to ritual and mythology. Its tension results from the interaction of intellect (mind) on the one hand with Eros and sacred coitus/ritual on the other. The intellect is represented by Tiresias, whose presence marks the beginning of the poem. Although he is dead, his mind is still complete enough to foresee the fate of Odysseus, which is why Circe urges Odysseus in the first lines of C47 to visit the blind seer. Circe symbolizes the, for Pound, irrational female principle and Eros; Tiresias is the controlled and rational intellect. Tiresias is a central figure in the *Cantos*, because without him Odysseus would never have found his way home.[26] Then a new vision overlaps Circe and Tiresias and introduces the Adonis section of the poem. The lamps drifting in the water are the votive lights set adrift in the *Golfo di Tigullio* every July for the festival of the Montallegre Madonna.[27] This seasonal ritual is linked to the cyclic death and rebirth of Adonis, whose blood is a "red flame" of lights moving on the sea (C47.236). Greek fragments lament the loss of Adonis. The sacrifice of shoots on an altar completes the annual ritual.

The Adonis section is followed by a general characteristics of women in lyrical terms, complemented by the male principle, as embodied by Odysseus. The sexual instinct of man is likened to that of moth and bull. Man can control his instincts by Moly, which allows Odysseus to move from Circe's to Penelope's bed. Pearlman concludes that the herb symbolizes effective will and refined intelligence. Women, on the other hand, do not "count," i.e. they do not seek to impose human order on the rhythmes of nature, while man does measure time, as in the subsequent Pleiades passage.[28] From it emerges a rural landscape with hills, olives and shadows on the sunny terrace. With the sexual image of man's planting of seed in the female womb, as opposed to the transience of human life, the poem reaches a state of euphoric illumination, culminating in the moment of the light entering the cave (C47.238). The lyrical I becomes one with the grass and the roots, i.e. nature. The death of Adonis, his "falling," is followed by the growth of fruit. The final section repeats some major elements of the poem (drifting lights, plowing, sacrifice, Adonis) and concludes with a general praise of those elements. The word "that" comprises all of the above elements and the "healing" and the "power over wild beasts" can both be put into relation to the story of Odysseus. The beasts represent the transformed victims of Circe,

[26] Martz, Louis L., "Pound: The Prophetic Voice," 383.
[27] Comp. Kenner, Hugh, The Pound Era, 368f.
[28] Pearlman, Daniel D., The Barb of Time, 180f.

Scylla's dogs, the wild bull and Adonis's boar, all of which symbolize unconstrained passion.

Odysseus not only stands for Pound's erring or forgotten heroes from the troubadours to Mussolini,[29] but, in this poem, incarnates the male principle itself, without allusions to historical figures. Together with Adonis, the hero constitutes Circe's counterpart. The "action" of the poem results from the erotic tension between the two, which is described as a natural competition. Pound's blend of classical beauty and sacredness on the one hand, and sexual laguage on the other, was not unprecedented. Guilhem's Provençal songs, filled with spiritual desire as they are, at the same time sing of sexual pleasure, which they describe in a perfectly frank language.[30] C47 celebrates the harmony of sexuality and natural order. Undisturbed by economic realities, the Canto indulges in the mystification of the sexes and religious rituals. Dekker follows Espey in calling C47, not C49, the "bedrock" of the Cantos.[31] We find one point to support Dekker's case – the absence of economics in the Canto. As we have noted before, every other Canto in *The Fifth Decad* contains some reference to economic subjects, even the more "lyrical" Cantos, C49 (debt, Geryon) and C51 (usury, Geryon). C47, however, with its mythological world of ritual, is driven by elemental, positive forces, not by Pound's hatred of usury.

Canto 48

Like its twin C46, Evidence Canto 2 undertakes another journey through history to search for traces of fraud and rare moments of reason. The introductory lines with their reference to one of Pound's favorite phrases put the poem's focus on economics. The rhetorical question as to who should pay the "rent," i.e. interest, is posed to suggest one specific answer: the wealthy should pay. As an illustrative example, the reader is then immediately confronted with an "ex-sultan" in what reads like an excerpt from a newspaper clipping. The reference to Kolschitzky implies the fact that the Viennese coffee-houses were originally founded as reward for the services of a spy. They represent a doubtful practice, as does the sergeant who arranges the soldiers' corpses for emperor William's visit at Verdun. That Pound saw this event in an economic framework is shown by a 1935 statement: "The meaning of capitalism became clear to a minority between 1914 and 1919 (vide Fritz von Unruh's description of the sergant tramping down the corpses

[29] As stated by Kenner, Hugh, Gnomon, 286.

[30] See, for instance, "Companho, Tant Ai Agutz," in: Whigham, Peter (ed.), The Music of the Troubadours, 144-147.

[31] Dekker, George, Sailing After Knowledge, 97.

to get the place tidy for William)."[32] More symbols of decay follow: the lack of good conversation in London at Charles F. Adams's time, the suppression of Van Buren's memoirs, tuberculosis; interrupted by Marx's warning that children suffering from the severe conditions of child labor would "become fathers of the next generation." Anti-Semitic allegations and apocryphal quotations now enter the poem, like Bismarck's suspicious statement about the Jews and the American Civil War, and a Rothschild's remark to Disraeli about the foolishness of nations paying "rent." The Rothschild remark points back both to the "rent" at the beginning of C48 and to another Rothschild passage in Evidence Canto 1 (C46.233).

Greek symbols announce a brief positive interlude between the evidence, alluding to Dionysos (here: Digonos) and a ritual of initiation for young men (C48.241). But breeding and initiation are perverted, as the next section signifies. A letter about a young dog is juxtaposed with the appointment of a Secretary of State by drunken Senators. The point of this passage are not "cheap shysters and ignorant people who place the welfare of their pet dogs over that of their brothers," as Wilhelm suggests.[33] Rather, the traditional initiation ritual is put into opposition to the breeding of dogs as an aristocratic hobby ("Your Highness"), to which the obscure and unjustified appointment of a politician adds a new degree of perversity. Real excellence, Pound seems to say, is neither found among rich dog-breeders, nor among irresponsible politicians. In the next lines, the provincial ignorance of a voice condemning Galileo is contrasted with attempts to support or merit contact with other countries (foreshadowing Hess's *modus vivendi* in C51), like the trustees of Salem Museum and their voyages (which conjures up a brief vision of sea and clouds), Athelstan's theigns and their foreign trade, or whale hunters. On the opposite side, Pound notes economic issues like high interest rates and the printing of stock.

The reader then witnesses a genuinely modern ritual, shopping. Syntactically continuing the sentence about the whale hunters, a shopping tour is described ("watching the stars [/] 'while she bought," C48.242). Note the artificial orchid, which may be understood as a comment on shopping culture in general. Shopping is an artificial ritual if compared to traditional rituals like those in C47, the initiation in C48 or the subsequent procession with priest, lights and flowers. The procession enacts ritual correctly and signifies renewal, both elements missing from the ritual of shopping. Pound's description contains several allusions to light and fire, as in C47. The "new mass" is a communal feast of fascism, presented through the naïveté of young Mary de Rachewiltz's voice, which serves to give the feast a positive accent.[34]

---

[32] "Waiting" (1935), in: P&P VI.257.

[33] Wilhelm, James J., Ezra Pound: The Tragic Years (1925-1972), 119.

[34] Casillo, Robert, The Genealogy of Demons, 272.

The ritual ends with the child's wish to "go back there" (C48.242), i.e. to re-enact the ritual.

The ritual gives way to a sequence of historical visions and natural phenomena. On the one hand, memories of Provence and its faded glory, as experienced by Pound during his journey to France in 1919. He comes across the ruins of the temple-citadel of Montségur, reminding him of the extinction of the Albigensians in the 13th century, and at San Bertrand de Comminges finds merely a village instead of the flourishing town of Roman times.[35] The altar to Terminus is a last reminder of the mythological world of C47; Savairic and Gaubertz embody the time of the troubadours and their opposition to French centralism, as symbolized by "Paris." A vision of insects in agony concludes the Canto, pointing out the natural intelligence and *directio voluntatis* Pound attributed to animals.[36] The destroyed "great worm" (C48.243) is usury, a reference to C15 with its "beast with a hundred legs, USURA" (C15.64). The three ants have been interpreted as "three warring fascist nations" (Germany, Italy, Japan) and the helpless ox as a sacrificial victim.[37] The final image of the Canto is a reminiscence, through the words of an "elderly lady," of Venice beach at a time when women were not supposed to show much of their legs, so an old man would bring stones to prevent the ladies' skirts from being blown up by the wind. Like the references to Provence, this element constitutes a memory of a vanished period.

The chief stylistic device of C48 is contrast. The text confronts us with constant oscillations between positive and negative images. On the one hand, it is a list of what Pound considered infamies: a rich sultan, a spy, World War I, the hollowness of English society, the arrogance of the Rothschilds, the dubious appointment of a politician, high interest rates, stock-printing, rich women on shopping trips, the destruction of Provence, French centralism. On the other hand, the Canto contains the Digenes ritual, the well-travelled trustees of Salem Museum, Athelstan's theigns, the whale navigators, proper ritual, memories of the glory of Provence, nature's instinctive intelligence and the defeat of the "great worm." The poem is very broad in its scope, covering history, economy, society and nature. But it does not reconstruct a history of usury like C46, nor does it praise the integrity of ritual like C47. Rather, it merges both elements, combines the two preceding Cantos and thus creates a heightened tension between ideal and corruption, a tension which is resolved and transported to a higher level in C49.

---

[35] Flory emphasizes this aspect; see Flory, Wendy S., Ezra Pound and the Cantos, 147.
[36] Comp. chapter III.3 of this study.
[37] Casillo, Robert, The Genealogy of Demons, 147f., 271f.

Canto 49

After the multiple infamies and rare rays of light in C48, a more ideal world is envisioned in C49. The text moves from the beauty of nature to rural routine and finally to Pound's idea of a political-empyrean arcanum, distorted only slightly by glimpses of Geryon. With C49, i.e. Lyrical Canto 3, the reconciliation of society, politics and nature is achieved. On the one hand, we encounter the sublime landscapes which Pound described as early as 1919: "the mist clots about the trees in the valley [/] the gt. drops of mtn. rain break thru the heat about me."[38] On the other hand, Pound extends his gallery of good rulers. In addition to Pietro Leopoldo and Ferdinando III, Chinese emperors now receive some praise. Because we have repeatedly commented on C49 before, we will concentrate on the most vital aspects of the poem.

The poem's initial "by no man" (C49.244) refers both to Ulysses and the anonymous source manuscript. It suggests the absence of a narrator, who, however, will remain present throughout the text. The subsequent rural idyll is a collection of diverse phenomena that range from "weeping" to "leisure," from natural events (weather) to human activities (cultivation, fishing). The fading sails and boats contribute to an atmosphere of remoteness, while the allusions to the weather, the fishermen and the shrimp-divers evoke the hardships of rural life and the necessity to make a living. The narrator, who denounced himself at the beginning of the poem, returns with the question whether a well-governed state needs debts to sustain its economy. The answer follows instantly and condemns debt as "infamy" (C49.245). With the naming of Geryon, the idyll is disrupted; associations with other Cantos emerge, and by using that name Pound reminds us of the contrasting worlds of C45 and C46. But the appearance of Geryon is merely a threatening interlude: the monster is banned by a good ruler and the enduring achievements he has left to the people. The canal once constructed for the king's private purposes is still in use and shows that the ruler has reached a level of supreme order, at which even private desires are no longer antisocial.[39]

After a hymn to the sky, the "Auspicious Cloud Song," and an almost abstract rendering of the routines of country life (work, sleep, eat, drink), we approach a definition of imperial power as the "fourth dimension" and the control over wild beasts. Beyond all possible allusions to Einstein and mathematics,[40] that dimension is primarily one of fixed relations. As Pound

[38] Sieburth, Richard (ed.), A Walking Tour, 77.

[39] Pearlman, Daniel D., The Barb of Time, 202.

[40] Pearlman reads the phrase as an allusion to Einstein. This position has not remained unchallenged; comp. Tryphonopoulos, Demetres P., "The Fourth; the Dimension of Stillness," 117f. According to Taylor, some philosophers of Pound's period conceived of the fourth dimension as "a transcendence of physical reality and its representation in art to

wrote in a note: "Sacrum coitus est, inluminatio coitu [...] The 4th the dimension of stillness [/] The dimension of [/] fixed relations" (BL 43 / 73 / 3258). It is a sphere that is governed by the permanent, not by the ever-changing flux of the ordinary world. Following Pound's claim that the *Cantos* "should establish an hierarchy of values,"[41] the end of C49 is dedicated to the upper parts of that hierarchy: imperial order, static society, absence of debt. Whereas Lyrical Canto 1 (C45) confronts us with the consequences of usury as the great evil and Lyrical Canto 2 (C47) praises ritual and Eros, Lyrical Canto 3 depicts the civic paradise of a balanced society that reconciles the metaphysical and the ordinary. Like in the ritualistic context of C47, the power over beasts denotes the victory of permanent laws over the incalculable impulses of debased instinct. And whereas C45 offered only occasional glimpses of paradisal harps and lutes or sacred mysteries, C49 reverts the negative emphasis of C45 by concentrating on the ideal.

Canto 50

History Canto 4 continues the narrative thread of the Siena Cantos. As opposed to the serenity of C49, it leads us back into the conflict and flux of the 18th and 19th centuries in Europe. But whereas History Cantos 1 to 3 were mainly concerned with the micro-level of Italian history, concentrating on the city of Siena, the narrative of C50 is located on the macro-level of the Tuscan duchy and Italy in general.[42] The text is marked by the presence of *Risorgimento* historian Antonio Zobi as a historical authority and complementary narrator, whose opinion is continually evoked by the primary narrator with short remarks like "says Zobi" or "wrote Zobi."

Before we enter Italian history, a quotation from John Adams serves to emphasize the character of the U.S. as a "people's republic," whose founding revolution was preceded by a revolution in the minds of the populace in the years between 1760 and 1775. By a chronological parallel – Pietro Leopoldo became duke of Tuscany in 1765 – we return to Italy, where Count Orso and his heirs receive administrative powers in 1624. We learn about the accumulation of an enormous state debt under the Medici and about the economic and cultural decline of the duchy. Pietro Leopoldo, however, affected some changes. He initiated tax and interest cuts and fought the

---

a higher consciousness or intuition, a higher reality"; Taylor, Richard, "Canto XLIX, Futurism, and the Fourth Dimension," 347.

[41] "Mr. Ezra Pound's 'Cantos'" (1933), in: P&P VI.46.

[42] The geo-political term "Italy" can of course only be properly applied to the country as a whole after the unification of separate territorial entities in 1861. It should therefore be used with caution.

Jesuits. A luminous detail of intellectual history is the 1782 Italian translation of Locke's essay on interest (C50.246). Trade problems are combined with Zobi's praise of the U.S. as the home of democracy and civic virtues. Like any good ruler in the Poundian sense, Leopoldo seeks to abolish public debt, but is then made emperor and moves to Vienna. Pound's strong and scatological vocabulary leaves no doubt as to his negative image of the city and its politicians. Franz Josef and Metternich are exposed as the villains of the poem, embodying "absolute rottenness" (C50.247).

After the French Revolution and the succession of Ferdinando III to the Tuscan duchy, Zobi complains about the lack of economic experience in Tuscany. Another villain is introduced, the reactionary pope Pius VI. With Napoleon's *coup d'état* of 1791 and his victory at Marengo in 1800, the general establishes political hegemony over France and Italy. Tuscany meanwhile suffers from high interest rates and languishing commerce, but the ruling triumvirs still support Leopoldine laws. Then Napoleon is defeated and exiled to Elba, and Ferdinando regains Tuscany as a debt-free state, as Pound emphasizes. The restoration policy of England and Austria is condemned as the expression of the usurious spirit of the new masters of Europe, who divide Poland and attempt to enslave the Tuscans.

The villains in the text include Europe's monarchs and their aides, like Wellington and Metternich, who symbolize the corruption of politics by money. The return of Napoleon from exile raises new hopes, but unfortunate circumstances prevent him from regaining his power. As we learn, Napoleon attributed his defeat to his rebellion against the spirit of his time. After his death (mentioned in connection with Dante's death) Italy continues suffering from its main intellectual problem, "abstractions" (i.e. the prevalence of theory over practice), and sees two of its major figures go into exile, the pope and a nationalist. The English envoy Earl of Minto arrives in Arezzo and is welcomed by a cheering crowd. In a concluding vision, Lalage and Dirce, the courtesan and the cruel queen, move in shadows, but vanish against the "unmoved" dawn, which stands like a symbol of the permanent, as opposed to the historical events unfolded in the Canto. It is unlikely that dawn here symbolizes the beginning of a "new age," as Pound was critical of both the late 19th and the 20th century. It may allude to the founding of an Italian national state in 1861, but that is just one possibility.

Like other Cantos, C50 creates a marked contrast between positive tendencies and negative developments. Positive are Adams's American revolution, Leopoldo's measures, Napoleon's and Ferdinando's fight against usurers, finally the dawn. Negative are economic failures, trade problems, unreliable political allies, the defeat of Napoleon and the subsequent restoration of European monarchism. Pound, although a supporter of strong rulers, gives no praise to the 19th-century monarchs of England and France.

Rather, his choice of Zobi as an authority governs the political tendency of the poem. Pound includes Zobi's political opinions in the Canto and thereby adopts his perspective: we read Italian history through the eyes of a patriotic liberal with a strong admiration for the U.S.

Canto 51

C51 is the conclusion of *The Fifth Decad*, and as such combines and rephrases the central ideas of the section. Usury, politics, economics and the metaphysics of light all appear in the poem and prepare the transition to C52. After finishing C50 with the dawn, Pound begins C51 with the now fully risen sun as an image of the divine mind, which is immediately juxtaposed with mud. The two opposites formed a complementary pair in Pound's thought. In a 1936 letter he asked: "do you think mud, mind or will is the determinant in form?"[43] In C51, the ideal of the divine intellect is affected by mundane mud, just like Napoleon (who talks about mud in the text) was destroyed by the powers of usury. To emphasize that element even more, the next section of the poem contains a new warning against usury. The section is stylistically and syntactically identical with C45, but the motifs have been slightly modified. Again, Pound preaches against the effects of usury on art, design, craft and fertility. In Pound's typical contrastive style, a positive counter-image follows the threat of usury: the fly-fisher, a "skilled maker" who knows the rules of nature and uses them for his benefit; not against nature, like usury, but in accordance with natural rhythms.[44]

The fly-fisher is praised as a "doer" in which the divine intellect culminates. The passage is therefore not merely a "pastoral interlude,"[45] but a preparation for the now emerging ruler who is more than human: godlike. Rudolf Hess embodies the inspired politician trying "to work out a system of living together, meaning between European peoples"[46] in order to re-establish a set of common values and culture. The idea that Europe lost its unity in the time after the Middle Ages was not originally Poundian, but shared by others, like T. S. Eliot, who stated:

> in Dante's time Europe, with all its dissensions and dirtiness, was mentally more united than we can now conceive. It is not particularly the Treaty of Versailles that has separated nation from nation; nationalism was born long before; and the process of disintegration

---

[43] Letter to W. C. Wilson, 28 Nov 1936, in: Pound, Ezra, Impact, 273.

[44] Similarly Bacigalupo, Massimo, The Forméd Trace, 62f.; Pearlman, Daniel D., The Barb of Time, 217f.

[45] Wilhelm, James J., Ezra Pound: The Tragic Years (1925-1972), 122.

[46] "United States of Europe?" (1938), in: P&P VII.393.

which for our generation culminates in that treaty began soon after Dante's time [47]

As if to propose a cure for inner-European tensions, Pound wrote as early as 1917: "What peace Europe acquired she acquired by an enlargement of nations, by coalitions, such as that of Castille, Leon and Aragon."[48] It is therefore not surprising to find Pound support a seemingly peaceful statement made by Hess as the representative of an extremely expansive nation, given Pound's naïve belief in the truth of such claims. His inclusion of Hitler's deputy in the poem was probably influenced by early political moves towards a Rome-Berlin axis. After Mussolini's presence in C41, Hess now serves to establish the other end of that axis.[49]

Hess, implicitly presented as an inspired politician, is followed by another opposite, the group of 12 "regents," i.e. the presidents of the *Banque de France*, who fly on the "oily" wind like apocalyptic riders (C51.251). Finally Geryon himself appears and, for the first time, speaks. While at first claiming to help the aged, Geryon finally exposes himself and admits influencing politicians with money, knowing many tongues (the "international" banker again) and trading in chalcedony. Finally, he confesses to be the twin of usury and directly addresses the readers, ridiculing them as inhabitants of an artificial cardboard world. From item 211 we learn that this statement addresses the same people who thought (at the beginning of C46) they would be able to move through hell quickly and who now have the misperception of living in a harmless environment, while Geryon rises from the Inferno with ten thousand dead behind him. The image of the eel-fisher, initially a simple metaphor, gains a different accent in the final version of the poem, in which the fisher may now be identified with Geryon himself, or some greater evil, like Dante's Lucifer. The final line transports us back into history with a veiled hint at the League of Nations as a counterpart to the League of Cambrai, the historical alliance that "extinguished the light of Venice."[50] As Bacigalupo suggests, Cambrai in 1508 parallels Geneva in 1936.[51] Thus the poem, although it celebrates the divine intellect and godlike politicians, ends on a pessimistic note: Pound does not envision a future reign of fascism or of the divine, but rather the supremacy of an evil, apocalyptic power. The conclusion of C51 is one of the darkest moments of the *Cantos*.

[47] "Dante" (1929), in: Eliot, Thomas S., Selected Essays, 240.
[48] "Provincialism the Enemy" (1917), in: SP, 171.
[49] Bacigalupo, Massimo, The Forméd Trace, 64.
[50] Makin, Peter, Pound's Cantos, 198.
[51] Bacigalupo, Massimo, The Forméd Trace, 65.

The drafts of *The Fifth Decad*, up to the setting copies, are marked by an absence – the absence of a crucial element that would appear only during the editorial process preceding publication, i.e. on the page proofs corrected by Pound: the sign at the end of C51, the Chinese ideogram denoting the "rectification of terms." For Pound, this included terminological definition as well as the collection of facts. In the finished Canto (C51.252), the ideogram appears like a final, comprehensive message under which Pound subsumed *The Fifth Decad* – the clarification of terminology through the presentation of presumably unassailable facts. The Seven Lakes Canto, for example, shows how Pound tried to define good government by citing facts from Chinese history. Similarly, the Sienese History Cantos define Pound's idea of sound economics by unearthing long-buried facts about the *Monte dei Paschi*. The Evidence Cantos, on the other hand, concentrate on historical manifestations of usury. This connection of metahistorical terminology and historical facts also affects the structure of the decad, as will be discussed in the next chapter.

The ideogram in C51 is not the only reference in Pound's work to the problem of terminology. In fact, the definition of terms was one of his major preoccupations during the 1930s, when he was thoroughly convinced of the necessity to find clear expressions. As Pound stated in a letter to the historian Woodward of 5 June 1934: "JOB is to find the RIGHT idea, and its clearest possible formulation."[52] For Pound, this principle was not limited to poetry, but extended towards culture, economics and even ethics. Pound found a strong interest in terminological clarification among the Romans, whose civilization seemed to him "imprinted with the struggle for definition."[53] Roman attempts to define words were guided by notions of sincerity, which made the act of perfecting terminology almost ethical. Pound found similar concepts in Chinese philosophy, particularly in Confucius, from whom he derived the ideogram later incorporated into C51. The identification of sincerity with the perfection of the word, according to Pound, "comes out of the Confucian answer when asked about the first act of government: 'call things by their right names'," a remark followed by the same ideogram.[54] Pound saw the precise definition of terms as one of Confucius's most vital achievements.[55]

---

[52] Quot. in Surette, Leon, Pound in Purgatory, 146.
[53] "To-day and To-morrow" (1936), in: P&P VII.82.
[54] "Mang Tsze (The Ethics of Mencius)" (1938), in: SP, 99. For Pound's explanation of the ideogram for the "precise definition of terms" see Confucius, The Great Digest, 20. For a definition of sincerity as the precision of terms see Confucius, The Great Digest, 167.
[55] "Immediate need of Confucius" (1937), in: SP, 91, 93.

The Middle Ages continued the Roman pursuit of exact definition. According to Pound, medieval philosophers were chiefly interested in finding precise expressions for their ideas, a precision also present in the architecture of the period.[56] Pound himself sought to achieve the scholastic terminological precision of Dante, who wrote, as Pound translated it, that "Knowledge of a definite thing comes from a knowledge of things defined."[57] By its terminological clarity, the medieval Church was superior to its less precise heirs. In a letter to the Mother Superior of Mary de Rachewiltz's school, Pound complained about the "lack of precise statement" in modern church books – "There is no beauty in inexactitude, and the church was most holy when its theologians attained the greatest clarity of expression."[58] After the Middle Ages, terminological precision declined. The Renaissance had the merit of an immediate approach to natural phenomena, but was unable to use "exact descriptive terms," as the Middle Ages had done.[59] With the rise of the experimental method in science, "the Occident lost the habit of verbal definition," as Pound put it.[60]

Precise definition was as necessary in economics as it was in art. Like good art, any well-dsigned economic theory must start from verbal definition in the Chinese sense.[61] What economics needed was the simplification and articulation of terminology to "distinguish the root from the branch."[62] From economics, the "castigation of the word" would spread to other fields and accompany political reforms. In fact, Pound even went so far as to base political order on clear terminology: "An administration that can not or dare not define money, credit, debt, property, capital, is unlikely to provide a durable solution of national chaos or evolve a durable system of national order."[63] A clear terminology was the basis of sound philosophy[64] and was necessary to achieve the ideal of justice,[65] whereas the decline of language, e.g. in the press, only destroyed belief.[66] If, as Pound claimed, "thought hinges on the definition of words,"[67] then any work of art which was

---

56 "Mediaeval Music and Yves Tinayre" (1936), in: Pound, Ezra, Ezra Pound and Music, 395.
57 "Immediate Need of Confucius" (1937), in: P&P VII.240.
58 Rachewiltz, Mary de, Discretions, 108.
59 "How to Read" (1927/28), in: LE, 21f.
60 "Immediate need of Confucius" (1937), in: SP, 91.
61 Pound, Ezra, Ezra Pound and Japan, 91.
62 Pound, Ezra, Impact, 152.
63 "National Culture: A Manifesto 1938" (publ. 1960), in: SP, 132.
64 "The Dam' Nigger and the Banana Tree" (1936), in: P&P VII.113.
65 Letter of December 1935, Pound, Ezra, The Selected Letters of Ezra Pound, 277.
66 Letter of 5 October 1951, Pound, Ezra, "I Cease Not to Yowl," 78; similarly "A Visiting Card" (1942), in: SP, 277.
67 "Gold and Work" (1944), in: SP, 306.

committed to exactitude would influence general thought positively and prove useful to the community.[68] As the word itself reached out into ethics and politics, its castigation would heal human society as a whole.[69]

Flory has diagnosed an exaggerated notion of the power of clarity in Pound's texts, as Pound believed that precise definitions would cure all ills. This tendency increased during the 1930s: As Pound assumed, everybody would understand and advocate Social Credit, if the theory was only communicated properly.[70] The same applies to *The Fifth Decad*. Pound expected his readers to understand the usurers' plots and the mechanisms of history in general, if readers were only provided with enough evidence or facts to broaden their perspective. The ideogram concluding C51, by being placed at the end of the section, radiates back on the whole of *The Fifth Decad* and offers a perspective for the reading of the section. Unfortunately, its insertion at a late point in the writing process leaves us with questions we can hardly answer. Whether Pound simply forgot to include the ideogram earlier or rather had the idea to include it only when he had already finished the Canto, must remain undecided. We are left with a sign that both concludes *The Fifth Decad* and already hints at the message and ideogramic brevity of the next Canto in the subsequent section:

> Call things by the names. Good sovereign by distribution
>
> (C52.261)

---

[68] "How to Read" (1927/28), in: LE, 22.
[69] Pound, Ezra, Polite Essays, 52.
[70] Flory, Wendy S., The American Ezra Pound, 88f.

III.6.b The Art of the Fugue? The Structural Dimension

> *The motive and end of any art whatever is to make a pattern [...] a web at once sensuous and logical, an elegant and pregnant texture.*
>
> (Robert Louis Stevenson, *On Some Technical Elements of Style in Literature*)

One of the riddles of the *Cantos* is their structure. Even a modernist critic like F. R. Leavis made his case against the poem in structural terms, claiming that its design lacked the definition, form and direction he praised as qualities of Eliot's *The Waste Land.*[71] Later critics did not express themselves that harshly about the structural aspects of Pound's epic, but were equally puzzled by what they read as incoherences in the poem. Hence, they attempted to find comprehensive explanations and applied existing structural models to the *Cantos,* like Dante's *Divine Comedy* or the fugue, while some scholars reached the conclusion that the one key to the structure of the poem was either not existing or extremely well-hidden. We regard it as a more promising approach not to apply, by force, some comprehensive model to the poem, but to identify partial coherences. Accordingly, this section will point out crucial influences and authorial inventions that govern the structure of the decad's Cantos and sub-groups of Cantos. We will particularly endeavour to develop a functional analysis of their structure and describe elements and counter-elements used by Pound. Possible musical influences on the poem will be dealt with in order to highlight some aspects of the general question whether *The Fifth Decad* was contructed according to a definite set of structural principles or simply represents a collection of separate units. The unusual character of the Cantos makes this a more than urgent question to consider.

What we can define from the beginning is the poem's montage character.[72] This definition does not postulate overall criteria according to which Pound wrote the text, but creates theoretical clarity and helps to place the *Cantos* in a specific literary framework. In fact, describing Pound as a montage writer is one of the few generalizing statements about the structure of the *Cantos* we can make with some validity. In articles on montage and collage in literature, Joyce is usually mentioned as one chief representative of

---

[71] Leavis, Frank R., New Bearings in English Poetry, 155f.

[72] For definitions of the umbrella-term "montage" and the sub-term "collage" see Möbius, Hanno, Montage und Collage, 28f.

montage art,[73] often together with Pound. While some scholars see writers like Dickens and Flaubert as forerunners of montage writing, this style became prevalent only in the era of Futurism and modernism.[74] Typical of Futurist texts was their condensation of conventional sentence structures, a condensation that went together with a negation of narrative linearity and typographical conventions.[75] Montage and ellipsis created a density designed to transport the activism and dynamics the Futurists aimed to express. To simulate the multiplicity and synchronicity of events, for example, writers often incorporated newspaper excerpts into literary texts.[76]

This use of texts in other texts hints at one of the major features of montage, intertextuality. As Espagne claims, the montage of source texts and their melting into a literary text is a fusion of monadic elements grown out of a collective discourse. A system of separate intertextual elements is created to form a second, more organized system. Reading the first system allows the author to write the second one, as *lecture* and *écriture* subsequently follow each other.[77] This describes e.g. Pound's approach in the Siena Cantos, his reading of source texts and their incorporation into the poems, an approach that can be specified in the context of montage writing. In his standard work on montage and collage, Möbius introduced the term *quotational montage* to describe works in which whole passages consist fully or chiefly of quotations from other, literary or non-literary works.[78] In *The Fifth Decad*, we find no Canto to which the principle of montage in general and quotational montage in particular does not apply. This is obvious in some Cantos in which the use of quotations is immediately apparent, like the Siena Cantos or C46, C48, C50 and C51, but also applies to the Lyrical Cantos. C45 is a montage of direct quotations ("*Adamo…*") and indirect references to works or art. C47 uses elements from Homer and Bion, while C49, as we pointed out earlier, borrows from Chinese poetry.

Apart from being montage texts, some of the Cantos are also collages. The word "collage" is derived from the French "coller," i.e. paste, stick, glue.[79] As David Antin defined it, a collage is the "dramatic juxtaposition of disparate materials without commitment to explicit syntactical relations

[73] For a reading of Joyce as a montage artist see Möbius, Hanno, Montage und Collage, 431-438.
[74] On Dickens und Flaubert as montage writers see Möbius, Hanno, Montage und Collage, 31-42.
[75] Möbius, Hanno, Montage und Collage, 147f.
[76] Möbius, Hanno, Montage und Collage, 237-241.
[77] Espagne, Michel, De l'archive au texte, 119.
[78] Möbius, Hanno, Montage und Collage, 58.
[79] Perloff, Marjorie, "The Invention of Collage," 6.

between elements."[80] According to Perloff, collagist art was governed by two assumptions: First, linear discourse cannot fully convey the meaning intended by the artist; second, transferring words into a collage can create new modes of signification.[81] The collage developed in the years between 1910 and the outbreak of World War I. It came into use on several continents at the same time, when the boundaries between genres and media became increasingly blurred and writers experimented with new forms of literature.

The "Mr Rhumby" passage in C48 perfectly illustrates the collagesque aspect of the poem (C48.241). Pound develops two distinct narrative threads in a parallel movement. As demanded in Antin's definition of the collage, those separate elements are not connected by full syntactical relations. Instead, they form independent sentence clusters. The text jumps from one element (the letter about the pedigree dog) to the other (Mr Rhumby's appointment) and back again, thus etsablishing a dense oscillatory sequence without syntactical links between the two threads. The initial lines of C51 adhere to a similar pattern – a quotation from a poem by Guinizelli is followed, without transitional remarks, by Napoleon's statement about mud and, equally without transition, by the re-phrasing of a passage from C45.

Defining *The Fifth Decad* as a montage and collage text allows us to create a terminological framework to analyze the use of individual structural elements in Pound's texts. We can postulate a multiple-units structure and then attribute functions to those units. In the next section, we will discuss particularly Cantos 42, 43, 45, 51 and 49 as separate examples, and C48 in the context of musical elements in the *Cantos*.

Structural Functionalities in the Work

Traditional historiography shows a strong bias in favor of narrative. Historians like Croce considered any historical account not written in a narrative form incomplete.[82] Modernism, on the other hand, developed a strong skepticism towards conventional narrative structures, which had up to then been organized chronologically. Some early exceptions exist, of course, but even the flashbacks in *Melmoth the Wanderer* did not really deconstruct chronology. Maybe the first text to seriously damage traditional narrative was Sterne's *Tristram Shandy*. Later, modernism set out to undermine a

---

[80] David Antin, "Modernism and Postmodernism," in: *Boundary* 2.1 (1972), 106; quot. in Perloff, Marjorie, "The Invention of Collage," 6.

[81] Perloff, Marjorie, "The Invention of Collage," 10.

[82] On historiography and narrative see White, Hayden, "The Value of Narrativity in the Representation of Reality," 10.

storytelling it thought "vulgar," as Antonia Byatt says.[83] Some authors used epiphanies and streams of consciousness to deconstruct chronology and reveal hitherto neglected layers of reality. Writers with a particular interest in history employed other strategies to achieve the same goal. Like some modern historians, Pound refused to construct historical narratives in the traditional sense. He belongs into one group with Burckhardt, Huizinga or Braudel, historians who replaced the diachronic view of history with a synchronic vision that substituted chronological sequence with structural criteria. Similar tendencies can be found in *The Fifth Decad*, particularly in the Siena Cantos.

Notable about the narrative structure of the Siena Cantos is their lack of linear chronology in detail. From 1624 (C42.209) we move to 1623 (C42.210) and even further back to 1622 (C42.211). And from 1622 we jump forward in time to 1749 and 1766 (C42.222, C43.223). This may at first come as a surprise, given Pound's relatively linear work with his sources. As is discernible from Pound's Siena notebooks, he worked through his sources in a straightforward manner, generally following the sequence of events as described in the sources. While composing the Siena Cantos, he was obviously not primarily interested in the actual sequence of events and therefore granted priority to other structural criteria. Even if the sequence of events in the Siena Cantos is partly determined by the sequence of Pound's excerpts, it still was Pound's deliberate decision to adopt that sequence, because he considered it revealing.

This is especially true for Cantos 42 and 43, while C44 is the most chronological of the triad. We have provided an outline of the two Cantos in the previous chapter, where we pointed out the combination, as prevalent throughout the Siena Cantos, of documentary quotations and interpolations from the narrator. Although I acknowledge the presence of a narrator as a structuring instance in the poem, however, I do not think this entails conventional narrative structures. Rather, the narrator handles chronology in a deliberately flexible way. After an exposition, C42 begins with a list of the positive qualities of the *Monte* (C42.209f.). This part is concluded by some proverbial lines. The next passage continues to list qualities and adds details on the historical situation of Siena in the 1620s ("Siena had no income" etc., C42.211). The quotation from a document of 30 December 1622 (C42.212) concludes the founding provisions for the bank in concentrated form, whereas the following paragraphs add more details on the actual act of foundation. With "OB PECUNIAE SCARCITATEM" we learn about the reasons for the foundation of the bank. The final passage of C42 (C42.214) is an explanatory conclusion – "get that straight" – of financial details and an affirmation of the good intentions of the bank. The overall sequence thus reads: exposition –

[83] Byatt, Antonia S., On Histories and Stories, 166.

qualities and historical context – foundation – reasons for the foundation – affirmative conclusion.

C43 repeats some motifs already used in C42. It first confronts the readers with a cluster of administrative acts that culminate in a repeated assertion of good intentions, and then again mentions the economic problems of Siena, interrupted by a Sienese ritual, which is followed by another collage-like cluster of details and an assertion of responsibility. After an interlude concerning maritime fraud, we learn about the founding act and its aftermath. As a sub-motif, fertility comes to the fore with the "fruit of nature" (C43.218) and the "Grass" (C43.219), as well as with the previously mentioned prostitutes and illegitimate children. The following passages offer several references to the capital and the beneficient interest rates of the bank (see particularly C43.221), repeating some previously quoted parts. The final lines, starting with 1749, then guide us into the more chronological C44.

The overall pattern of C43 is much more fractured than that of C42. The structure of C42 is argumentative, designed to convince us of the beneficience of the *Monte dei Paschi*. From the beginning, we learn about the qualities of the bank and are provided with such details as make its foundation seem reasonable. This is emphasized throughout the poem to the affirmative conclusion. Pound uses the first Canto in the sequence to state his point and leave no doubt about the importance of the *Monte*. The structural emphasis on the benefits of the bank, which is created by listing them at the beginning of C42, clearly underlines Pound's intention. C43, with its clusters of repetitious details, one the one hand reinforces the case made in C42. Repetition is here used for intensification. On the other hand, C43 introduces a new element to counter-balance the administrative emphasis of the Cantos: the running of the *palio* and other details from Sienese town life serve to compensate some of the poem's documentary dryness. C43 is actually the center of the triad, if read in relation to Siena in particular, because it draws the most complete picture of Siena as a city, including the economic, administrative and social aspects of town life. The *palio* race foreshadows later events like the celebration in C44 or the procession in C48. C43 is also the last Canto to be fully dedicated to Siena, whereas C44 opens the view for historical events beyond the city and for the political upheavals and battles of C50. In total, Siena Cantos I and II show how Pound avoided chronological narrative in favor of argumentative or intensifying structures.

In *The Fifth Decad* we also encounter intensification in a different, more contrastive form. As was pointed out repeatedly in the previous chapter, contrasts are an integral part of the structure of many Cantos. Contrasts sometimes appear as antitheses, while at other times we find dualisms in the form of parallelisms. The Usura Canto may serve to exemplify parallel composition in *The Fifth Decad*. Its main subject is usury, as introduced in the first line. In the poem, that subject is unfolded in two leitmotifs, first, usury as a destroyer of art and craftsmanship, and second, usury as a "sin against nature." C45 begins with the first leitmotif, conjuring up the decay of art under usury. With "sell quickly" the second leitmotif is introduced – unnatural usury as affecting the quality of food. The "against nature" motif is here presented in a restrained form, with fewer lines than the art and craftsmanship motif. With "line," "demarcation" and "Stonecutter" the text returns to the first leitmotif, here referring to crafts in particular. After "WITH USURA" the crafts motif continues and then broadens again to cover works of art, with additional references to craftsmanship. Repeated, more specific references to stoneworks establish an additional sub-motif ("house of good stone," "Stonecutter," "rusteth the chisel"). In the final passage, after "Memling," the "against nature" motif recurs in extended form and with stronger images than before, until the victory of the profane in the end. In the final passage, the "CONTRA NATURAM" serves as a structural node around which two sub-units of the passage center: one about the loss of procreative powers and another about profanation.

The dual leitmotif structure of the poem can be represented as: art – contra naturam – art – contra naturam. The two motifs form a parallel sequence. A concluding return to the initial motif, art, is denied. Instead, the poem ends with an urgent warning about the spiritual evils of usury. Structurally, the parallelism rests on the art leitmotif (which occupies the major part of the poem), out of which the more fundamental threat of unnaturalness and profanation emerges in two steps: first as a hint, finally as a fully-fledged danger to fertility and religion. The latter element is emphasized by the two-fold, parallel structure.

Whereas C45 uses parallel structures to intensify complementary aspects, C51 is more antithetical. The structure of C51 is determined by the function of the poem as a recapitulation of the whole *Decad*. Therefore we cannot read C51 as a fourth Lyrical Canto, despite some lyrical passages like the Usura section, an imitation of C45 (C51.250),[84] or the song of the fly-fisher, whose georgic wisdom refers back to the Pleiades passage in the Adonis Canto (C47.237). Lyrical as these passages may be, the final stanzas of C51 (after "Granham") strongly disrupt the unity of style and language we find in all three of the Lyrical Cantos. As opposed to them, the final passage of C51 has a marked collagesque character, because it combines several references to historical and philosophical sources in what is only a small part of the poem. From a Latin quotation we move to proverbial wisdom ("Grass…"), a political speech, a Dantean vision, Geryon's monologue, and finally to a political alliance. The density of those diverse references is far

[84] As should be noted, Pound does not repeat the direct quotations used in C45, "*harpes et luz*" and "*Adamo me fecit*," but uses only allusions.

more typical of the Evidence Cantos than of the Lyrical Cantos. C51 may therefore be called a structurally and stylistically antithetical composite of elements used throughout *The Fifth Decad*. Pound contrasts them in order to avoid any impression of reconciliation at the end of *The Fifth Decad*. As C51 states, the gap between the ideal of enlightened government and usury-ridden reality is still wide. A dialectical resolution is not part of the structure of the poem; the fractured narrative represents a conclusion, but not a perfect synthesis in the traditional, Hegelian sense.

Some elements in the *Cantos* seem, at a first glance, to be identifiable as structural borrowings, simply for their closeness to existing poetical traditions. This applies to parts like the Cavalcanti poem in C36 or Pound's translations from the Chinese. The Chinese tradition provides a suitable starting point for an analysis of C49, as Pound's relation to the admired model provided by Chinese poetry is more complex than his borrowing from some anonymous poems might suggest. Formally, old Chinese poetry often used strict patterns and exactly positioned parallelisms. Poets sought to create semantic juxtapositions or complicated parallel structures.[85] This included parallelisms between lines. If one line read noun – verb – noun, the next line would repeat this sequence. This could even apply to things (e.g. animals) or properties (parallelization of colors). The result were dense and intricately designed poems. At the same time, though, the structures of Chinese poetry are not completely different from their European counterpart. The *lü shih*, for instance, was a delicate, but regular form with eight lines per stanza and five or seven words per line, including two rhymes.[86] Pound offers a glimpse of Chinese regularity in the layout of the "KEI MEN RAN KEI" passage in C49 (C49.245). His condensed style of writing found its counterpart in the dense brevity of Chinese poetry. Pound tried to imitate it in the elliptical verses of C49 with their frequent lack of articles ("hills rise about lakes [/] against sunset," C49.244) and syntactically minimalistic sentences ("Sun up; work [/] sundown; to rest," C49.245). On this surface level, the structure of the Canto is imitative of Asian grammar, syntax and stanza form. Yet we should not be deceived by the outward simplicity of the poem.

C49 is more challenging in terms of structure than its surface suggests. On the one hand, the major part of the poem consists of complex references to and quotations from Asian painting and poetry, and presents them in a coherent whole by creating a rural idyll of political and economic tranquility. Vocabulary, motifs and even typographical conventions of Chinese literature are reproduced. On the structural level, however, C49 is less uniform. While

---

[85] Wang Wei / Li Po / Tu Fu / Li Ho, Four T'ang Poets, 12f. and Hawkes, A Little Primer of Tu Fu, offer many remarks on the particularities of sentence structure and meaning in Chinese poetry.

[86] For a more detailed rhyme and verse pattern see Lu Yu, The Wild Old Man, xvii.

chiefly constructed from excerpts borrowed from Asian poetry, its internal coherence is interrupted by Poundian interpolations. Although it simulates the imitation of a Chinese poem, C49 does therefore not fully embrace the illusion of authenticity. The poem uses Chinese literature merely as a style, not as a full structural model. Its Chinese style is used as a façade for the political message Pound makes explicit in the final stanzas of the poem – the fight against debt and Geryon (i.e. usury), and the endorsement of a strong ruler who will control the powers of finance. Functionally, the rural idyll serves as the opposite pole to the powers symbolized by Geryon. Pound integrates these elements into a tripartite structure, in which the depiction of an ideal world is juxtaposed with the infamy of finance, which is finally resolved in the definition of imperial power at the end of the poem.

I do not claim that Pound degraded the Chinese quotations to mere illustrations of his point. But as I want to emphasize, the genuinely Asian passages in C49 only gain their full functionality when read in combination with the veiled political statements. When Pound seems to indulge in references to beautiful landscapes, he is in fact making his case against economic malpractices like state debt, and against bankers. And although Chinese poetry of course transports and teaches political ideals, the reference to the fourth dimension and the "power over wild beasts" are specifically Poundian concepts unfolding in the context of the *Cantos*. It is this double dimension of the poem, not its perfect imitation of the Chinese style, which makes C49 important. Pound's hovering between beauty and polemics reveals more about the inner mechanisms of the *Cantos* than the craftsmanship shaping their surface.

Musical Aspects

As Pound stated, "any given work of art is bad when its content could have found more explicit and precise expression through some other medium."[87] At the same time, though, Pound constantly drew connections from poetry to other arts. During his vorticist phase, Pound eulogized "the picture that means a hundred poems, the music that means a hundred pictures."[88] When talking about his own work, music was Pound's preferred point of reference. As Walter Pater said, "All art constantly aspires towards the condition of music."[89] Accordingly, Pound once explained that poetry was situated

[87] "I gather the limbs of Osiris" (1911-1912), in: SP, 36.
[88] Pound, Ezra, "Vortex. Pound.," 153.
[89] Walter Pater, "The School of Giorgione," in: Studies in the History of the Renaissance, quot. in: Borges, Jorge Luis, This Craft of Verse, 77.

between music and prose, as Sisley Huddleston recalls in his memoir of the poet.[90]

The musical form most widely used to describe the Cantos is the fugue, an association to which Pound himself contributed substantially. His interest in music manifested itself in descriptions of poetry in musical terms. In the early "A Retrospect," he called the "musical phrase" his rhythmic goal and spoke of "rhythm waves," claiming that the same laws applied to poetry and music.[91] In 1921 he used the fugue and the sonata as explanatory references: "Where Gaudier had developed a sort of form-fugue or form-sonata by a combination of forms, Brancusi has set out on the maddeningly more difficult exploration toward getting all the forms into one form."[92] Pound did not state whether he himself tried to follow one of the two models, but as the quotation shows, he used music as a general structural concept. As Pound once admitted, he started the Cantos "in a way fugal" by working with parallel arrangements of themes.[93] He explained the Cantos to his daughter in similar terms:

> You know how a fugue of Bach is composed, one instrument comes in and the others repeat the theme. The Cantos start with Homer, the descent into hell. Then a theme of Ovid – Dafne, my own myth [...]. And then Dante – Dante has said everything there is to be said, so I start with Malatesta...[94]

For Pound, the contrapuntal harmony of themes meant "that a number of melodic lines carry on and, by carrying on, interact."[95] As can be discerned from Pound's remarks, his idea of the fugue centered on the parallel arrangement and interaction of themes. Fugues were still on Pound's mind when, in 1934, he complained about not being able to write a fugue or continue C42.[96]

But despite Pound's numerous remarks on fugal structures, we should bear in mind his use of the fugue as an *explanatory* model, not as a clearly identifiable *compositional* model. What Pound offers us in his statements are mere analogies[97] and it would be a methodological flaw to analyze the *Cantos* fully in Pound's terms. Pound's occasional hints at the fugue show his preference for a particular analogy and model, but do not convey certain facts

[90] Huddleston, Sisley, Paris Salons Cafés, 84.
[91] LE, 3, 6.
[92] "Brancusi" (1921), in: LE, 442.
[93] Statement of April 1937, in: Pound, Ezra, The Selected Letters of Ezra Pound, 294.
[94] Rachewiltz, Mary de, Discretions, 159.
[95] Pound in 1936, see Pound, Ezra, Ezra Pound and Music, 403.
[96] Pound, Ezra, "Italy 1934," BL 43 / 108 / 4551, 1.
[97] A point also acknowledged by Kay Davis in Davis, Kay, Fugue and Fresco, 79.

about the structure of the *Cantos*. Kay Davis has followed Pound's hints at his possible use of fugue elements, but found the fugue only one possible model among several which might be applied to the text. If we discuss the fugue in this chapter, it is only as an analogy, not as a universal key to the poem.

Pound's allusions to the fugue were taken seriously by various scholars who proclaimed the fugue a partial[98] or chief structural model of the *Cantos*. Albright understands the early parts of the poem as a fugue, as opposed to readings of the *Cantos* as satire and Dada.[99] Earle Davis, too, prefers to discuss the *Cantos* in musical terms, rather than as the expression of an "ideogramic method." The latter seems to lack precision, whereas the former allows the reader to explore the multiple layers of the poem. Davis compares the structure of the text to a fugue based on polyphony and counterpoint.[100] As a basic structural unit, Davis uses the "theme," an umbrella term that covers both the short *motif* and the more complex *subject*. In a Canto, a theme is introduced, contrasted with other themes, maybe restated in alternative terms or simply repeated. This description, however, could also be applied to other, clearly non-fugal poems. We have to be more specific as to what a fugal structure would imply.[101]

The fugue is composed in counterpoint and rests on one main theme, or *subject*, which is introduced first and then developed in other voices. They join the main theme successively and repeat the subject in modified form. Forms of development include *imitation* (e.g. by canon or inversion) as one of the most important devices. In the *exposition*, the subject is introduced and answered by a second voice, which is supported by the *countersubject* (often continuing throughout the fugue). The exposition is followed by *episodes*, i.e. parts between the different entries of the subject during its development. Crucial for the organization of the fugue are the subject, the countersubject and their transformations during development.

One likely candidate for fugal form in the *Cantos* is Evidence Canto II (C48) with its densely interwoven elements. We find an obvious exposition at the beginning of the poem ("if the money be rented"), introducing debt and interest as the main issues. Together, they form the subject. What follows is a development of the subject with additional "voices," i.e. transformations and sub-elements of the subject: war (Turkish war, World War I, American Civil War) and decline (London conversation, tuberculosis). They develop the

[98] For a fugal reading of the Adams Cantos see Davis, Kay, Fugue and Fresco, 82-92.

[99] Albright, Daniel, "Early Cantos I – XLI," 82f.

[100] Davis, Earle, Vision Fugitive, 18.

[101] For introductions to the history and form of the fugue see Imogene Horsley, Fugue: History and Practice, New York / London 1966; Paul Mark Walker, Theories of Fugue: From the Age of Josquin to the Age of Bach, Rochester 2000. On standard fugue structures see Davis, Kay, Fugue and Fresco, 72ff.

subject in a modified form, as demanded in the definiton of the fugue. The Rothschild passage (C48.241) combines the war and interest motifs. Rothschild's remark about nations paying "rent" points back to the beginning of the Canto. The Digonos passage introduces a new element, which we could read as a countersubject, setting nature, exploration and ritual against the financial and other infamies listed before. By its Greek letters and the reference to Dionysos, the passage is linked to C47. The subsequent appointment of "Mr Rhumby" and the parallel letter about the dog affect a new transformation of the subject, now focusing on decline in politics.

The definition of the Galileo passage in fugal terms is difficult (possibly an episode between the entries of the subject), as is that of the Salem trustees. The latter may function as a countersubject to the preceding passage: while the politicians merely drink, the Salem trustees have actually sailed the seas. On the other hand, if we decide to call the trustees a continuation of the Digenes countersubject, we have to extend our concept of what a countersubject includes. Then it cannot be defined by any unity of place or time, but embraces diverse phenomena from all periods. In this case, it expands the already introduced idea of exploration from the Salem trustees to the reign of Saxon king Athelstan, while at the same time containing the ideal of ritual, represented by intitiation rites (Digenes) and a modern Italian procession. The Bithynia passage returns to the main subject, interest, followed by a countersubject rhyming with the Salem trustees: king Athelstan who demands of his theigns to travel the world. The stock-printing president signals a brief return to the subject, whereas the whale sailors continue a specific aspect of the countersubject (nature and exploration). In contrast to the shopping ritual ("while she bought...") stands the proper ritual described in the procession passage. With the concluding Provence passage and the insects in agony, attributions become finally difficult. Pound's description of the vanished glory of Troubadour times and his vision of the towers over the fighting insects has only thin thematic ties to either subject or countersubject. The same applies to the old man with the basket at the end of the poem. Reading the final passages of the poem in fugal terms would call for daring interpretations. We may establish a number of serious analogies between the Canto and a fugue, but applying the fugue model in full is difficult.

In order to balance the fugue thesis, we should also look for poetic analogies to another musical form mentioned by Pound in his mentioned remark on Gaudier-Brzeska, the sonata.[102] The sonata form governs the structure of a single musical movement (often within a multiple-movement framework), dividing it into *exposition*, *development* and *recapitulation*. While the exposition introduces contrasting musical elements (tonal

[102] For a general introduction see Cecil Hill, Sonata Form: An Introduction, Calgary (Alberta) 1987.

contrasts), the development sets these elements into dialectical relations to each other, by means of combination, conflict or modulation. The recapitulation is a reformulation of the themes – what begins as a contrast in the exposition is then reconciled tonally in development and recapitulation. As should be noted, the sonata form does not exclude contrapuntal structures. The development, which is the most flexible part of the sonata, may reduce the main themes to smaller elements and establish contrapuntal relations between them. In addition, the themes, or their fragments, are modulated or combined to new melodies. We may test this definition on a complex example, C48. The first passages of the poem can be interpreted as the contrasting elements required by definition, which are then developed through combination or modulation. But this still leaves us without a proper recapitulation, as the end of the poem does not reformulate and reconcile the main themes (interest, war, ritual etc.). Rather, they remain in contrast to each other. If the exposition of C48 is concerned with money, the end of the poem is not. It does not establish any close link to the beginning of the text. The final passages of C48 defy both the fugue thesis and the sonata model.

What cannot be applied to a single Canto may at least be true for *The Fifth Decad* as a whole, we might assume. However, the section cannot simply be likened to a sonata. Rather, it contains several movements. It is true, there certainly are a development and a recapitulation (C51) in the section, with recurring themes being juxtaposed or modified. For instance, the motif of the soul, "nell' anima," which we find at the beginning of C42 (C42.209), is restated in C51 as God shining in the "mind of heaven" (C51.250). But the Siena Cantos are not an exposition, for two reasons. First, they not only introduce, but already develop one of the major subjects of *The Fifth Decad*, i.e. Sienese and Tuscan political-economic history. By their mere length, the Siena Cantos occupy a more prominent part of the section than C50. Hence, it would be wrong to call the Tuscan Canto the development of the theme, when the Siena Cantos have already stated many of its aspects in detail. Second, if the Siena Cantos were an exposition, they would emphasize the central subjects of the whole section, one of which is usury. Usury, however, is only marginally present in the Siena Cantos and only comes to the fore in C45. Cantos 42 to 44 contain several references to interest, i.e. the generous interest rates of the *Monte*, but in a sonata, the exposition would already set this element in contrast to another element. That element, however, i.e. the power of usury and of the usurers, not yet plays the crucial role it will play from C45 onwards.

Obviously, a reading of *The Fifth Decad* as a whole in musical terms has its limits. While some elements show partial analogies to the fugue and the sonata, none of the two musical forms can be applied comprehensively to *The Fifth Decad* without terminological dificulties. The analogies work for some of the more collagesque texts, but not completely. Alternative structural models need to be considered in order to understand the section.

Other Aspects of Structure in the Cantos

Pound had a strongly developed and broad sense of structure. Whether he discussed the Ptolemaic, concentric system of spheres[103] or musical structures, he proved this sense in the most diverse fields integrated a variety of structures and structural devices into *The Fifth Decad*. We mentioned contrast / juxtaposition, parallelism, fugue-like polyphony, repetition and others. We have not applied popular structural characteristics of modernism to the section, like alogical structure, spatial form, fluidity of consciousness and myth as an organizing principle.[104] In fact we should keep the use of a somewhat blurred popular terminology as limited as that of musical terms. The number of explanatory attempts by scholars, and their repeated failure to explain the structure of the *Cantos* with one comprehensive model, show that structure in the poem remains an unresolved issue.

Kay Davis's book *Fugue and Fresco* explains some of the most widely used models applied to the poem. According to Davis, the most simple pattern in the *Cantos* is the transition "from dromena to epopte, darkness to light, terror to grace, […] human error to divine wisdom."[105] It is the initiation process once undergone at Eleusis. Davis also finds a "nesting organization" in the poem, a system of intricate units and sub-units, the most basic among which Davis calls "subjects." They are connected by subject rhymes, of which Davis offers the following definition: "If two words rhyme because they sound the same, two ideas or images will rhyme because their meaning is the same."[106] Accordingly, two periods or persons may "rhyme" if they played similar roles or formed similar constellations under different historical circumstances. Davis also finds instances of ring composition in some Cantos, i.e. symmetric parallels centering around a node.[107] In addition, some scholars have championed the Dantean sequence of Hell, Purgatory and Paradise as a structuring principle,[108] while others emphasized Pound's sometimes very close work with his sources and his adhering to their structures. In the Adams Cantos, for instance, Pound reduced 8,000 pages of Adams to 80 pages of poetry, borrowing fragments of text from Adams exactly in the sequence in

[103] Pound, Ezra, Pound's Cavalcanti, 13.
[104] Perloff, Marjorie, "Modernist Studies," 158.
[105] Davis, Kay, Fugue and Fresco, 19.
[106] Davis, Kay, Fugue and Fresco, 31.
[107] On ring composition in the *Cantos* see chapter 3 of Davis, Kay, Fugue and Fresco.
[108] Comp. Makin, Peter, Pound's Cantos, 65.

which the pieces appear in the works.[109] As Moody points out, Pound not just chose random elements, but sought to create inner coherence.[110] In portraying, for instance, Adams shortly before the presidency, Pound employed the strategy of extracting from the politician's writings and diaries certain elements not explicitly stated, yet brought to light in the Cantos. As far as the total structure of the Adams Cantos is concerned, however, Pound was largely derivative and depended on the edition he quoted.

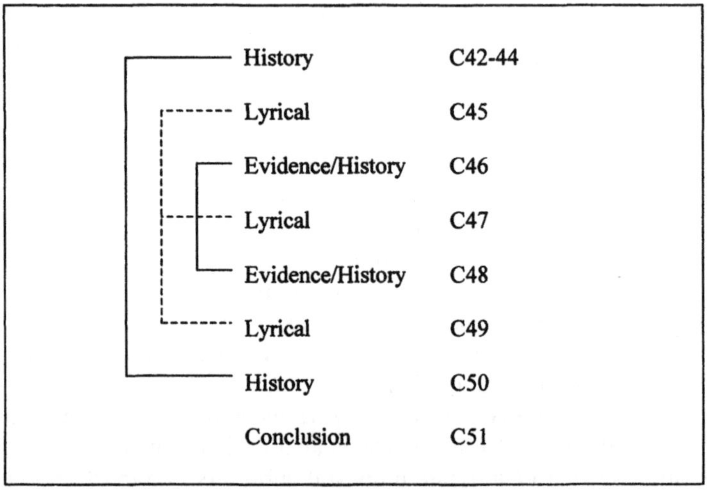

Fig. 11: An overall structure of Cantos 42 to 51.

Other scholars have explained the overall structure of the *Cantos* in terms defined by the subjects and functions of textual units, like Kenner did with reference to the earlier Cantos, which he divided into an overture (C1-3), a phantastikon group (C4-7), the Malatesta Cantos (C8-11), moral exempla (C12-13) and a hell group (C14-16).[111] Surette mentions Pound's tendency to group a block of cantos around a "single individual or historical period".[112] The sketch for Cantos 31 to 38 on item 120 seems to support Surette's notion. It refers to individuals like Thomas Jefferson or John Adams and to a historical period: The subject of C38 is called contemporary. In another sketch, too, Pound classifies C38 as contemporary.[113] But not only individuals or periods serve as structuring nodes. Institutions like the *Monte dei Paschi*,

[109] Moody, A. D., "Composition in the Adams Cantos," 79.
[110] Moody, A. D., "Composition in the Adams Cantos," 85.
[111] Kenner, Hugh, The Pound Era, 416f.
[112] Surette, Leon, A Light from Eleusis, 18.
[113] Pound, Ezra, BL 43 / 73 / 3268.

too, provide the basis for structural clusters, as do political-geographical entities. On item 120, we find central Europe as another heading. Basing one's structural analysis on function and subject-content is a pragmatic way of reading the *Cantos*. On a more abstract level, we have applied it to *The Fifth Decad* in the previous chapters, as displayed in the diagram (fig. 11). Suddenly, we become aware of symmetries.

Although Pound acknowledged, in 1912, that "most symmetrical forms have certain uses," still a "vast number of subjects cannot be precisely, and therefore not properly rendered in symmetrical forms."[114] The *Cantos* as a whole do not share the clear-cut symmetries used by conventional poetry, for instance regular stanza structures. Symmetrical parts can be found in the poem, yet not as general models, but as local solutions, like the couplets in C80: "Tudor indeed is gone and every rose, [/] Blood-red, blanch-white that in the sunset glows" (C80.516). The regularity of the lines is not a genuinely Poundian symmetry, but establishes a link to a specific tradition, whereas most of Pound's *vers libre* remains irregular. As our analysis of Cantos 42 to 51 showed, structures in the 1937 Cantos are equally incalculable. On the macro-level, however, some readers may be surprised to discover obvious symmetries in the overall structure of *The Fifth Decad*, as represented in figure 3. But what looks like a perfectly mirrored ring structure (except for C51) requires a cautious reading.

The fact that C47 is at the center of the structure of *The Fifth Decad* does not make it the acme of the section. Rather, C47 is one step in a threefold dialectical process: C45 confronts us with pure evil, i.e. unrestrained usury, with no balancing force to contain it. After that, C47 guides us into an ideal realm of sacred rituals and natural rhythms. Whereas C45 describes what is ultimately unnatural, C47 eulogizes nature itself, its processes of dying and renewal, as symbolized by Adonis and the returning constellations. C45 is a warning against profane (and profanizing) economic thinking that wants to corrupt Eleusis, while C47 is a hymn to fertility and to mysteries like those celebrated in Eleusis. Foreshadowed by the georgic Pleiades passage in C47, C49 then presents a less ecstatic, rural world of balanced forces. On the one hand, it includes a glimpse of the Geryon of C45, but only as a short warning briefly disturbing the Canto's balance between humanity and nature. The people in the poem live in accordance with the rhythms of nature and move harmoniously within landscapes governed by rhythmical processes, like harvests or changes of weather. Not only are humanity and nature in balance. The monarch and his subjects form a perfect symbiosis, too. C49 combines and transforms the main elements of C45 and C47 in a societal context. The dialectical progress from one Lyrical Canto to the next gains its momentum from the Evidence Cantos placed between them. By their abundance of

[114] LE, 9.

historical references and quotations, they stand in contrast to the thematic clarity of the Lyrical Cantos and at the same time complement them. The Evidence Cantos unfold historical and contemporary reality, as Pound perceived it, while the Lyrical Cantos show a timeless panorama of those forces Pound thought vital in a negative or positive sense – usury, ritual, nature, good government. The Evidence Cantos are not simply the opposite of the more lyrical Cantos, for the three Lyrical Cantos themselves are not merely concerned with ideal worlds. Rather, Cantos 46 and 48 form one level of a tripartite structure, in which the four History Cantos represent a second level and the Lyrical Cantos the center.

If we try to establish a terminological framework for this mode of description, we may find a partial key to this structure in another descriptive model by Pound, the division of elements in the *Cantos* into permanent, recurrent and casual.[115] The three-fold concept interested Pound particularly in the 1930s. In a letter to John Drummond of 18 February 1932, Pound distinguished the three elements.[116] As Pound stated in 1933, his poem "should establish an hierarchy of values, not simply: past is good, present is bad [...] If the reader wants three categories he can find them rather better in: permanent, recurrent and merely haphazard or casual."[117] The quotation shows one of the characteristics of the modernist epic, as outlined by Conte: a desire for hierarchy,[118] which manifests itself in structural and political terms. At the top of the hierarchy we find the permanent, followed by the recurrent and finally the casual. Yeats may help us to understand this concept. In *A Packet for Ezra Pound*, Yeats refers us to Cosimo Tura frescoes in the Palazzo Schifanoia, which depict virtues and values at the top (e.g. the Triumph of Love), astrology and cosmology in the middle, particulars and contemporary details at the bottom. Pound showed Yeats the frescoes to explain the structure of the *Cantos*. In his memory of the event, Yeats mentions "emotions or archetypal events"[119] to characterize the timeless features, and continues: "The descent and the metamorphosis [...] his fixed elements, took the place of the Zodiac, the archetypal persons [...] that of the Triumphs, and certain modern events [...] that of those events in Cosimo Tura's day."[120]

If applied to *The Fifth Decad*, the above concept immediately raises some basic questions. First, whether only positive values or archetypes are

[115] See e.g. Laughlin, James, Pound as Wuz, 111f.

[116] From this and other evidence, Pearlman derives his theory about a three-fold movement in the *Cantos* subsumed under one central idea, time. See Pearlman, Daniel D., The Barb of Time, 12f.

[117] "Mr. Ezra Pound's 'Cantos'" (1933), in: P&P VI.46.

[118] Conte, Joseph M., Unending Design, 37.

[119] Yeats, William B., A Packet for Ezra Pound, 3.

[120] Yeats, William B., A Packet for Ezra Pound, 3.

among the permanent forms, or whether we can also include such persistent evils like usury among them. After all, C45 portrays a timeless evil, despite its references to specific historical periods. It is not clear from Pound's hints whether we have to define usury as permanent or merely recurrent. And Yeats, in his description of the permanent, only refers to the Triumphs, i.e. positive ideals. Second, while we may claim that the Evidence Cantos are filled with casual elements, they at the same time contain the banker Rothschild, who, for Pound, embodied the abstract vice of usury. Hence, a permanent or recurring evil is present in the poem through a historical figure. Is this a combination of the permanent and the casual? The different elements appear mixed and hardly discernible in their property as permanent, recurrent or casual. This is not a fault of the concept itself, but is rather caused by a lack of explanatory definition of the scope of the three terms.

Still, the three-fold model is helpful for an understanding of the inner structure of the whole section, as long as we avoid oversimplifications. I argue that *The Fifth Decad* makes use of certain archetypal subjects, which are presented and developed on different levels of a hierarchy ranging from the abstract-permanent to the historical realization. The archetypal subjects do not succeed each other in a progressive, linear movement from level to level. Instead, we have to imagine them as always present throughout the poem, sometimes in a pure form, sometimes clouded by dense references or by complex historical details. One subject is usury, which appears in its pure and permanent form in C45 and assumes a historical shape in other Cantos, e.g. in Rothschild's remarks in C48 and in Metternich and Wellington in C50. The same applies to the idea of good government. The beneficient ruler as an eternal ideal is praised in C49, while he enters the historical stage as Pietro Leopoldo in the Siena Cantos. The two levels run immediately parallel in C51, where the Latin quotation about the godlike intellect (permanent) appears near the reference to the speech by Hess (historical). As we can see here, the archetypal subject is developed and modulated in the Cantos like a musical theme. Another major subject is ritual, which we encounter in its most pure and ecstatic form in C47. It is preceded by the historical *palio* celebration in C43 and succeeded by the equally historical processions in C48. C49 then transcends those historical manifestations in a realm of idealized images.

The archetypal subjects determine the structure of the text indirectly, in terms of priority. Pound created a Usura Canto, and hence a sequence of lyrical patterns, because he was committed to the fight against usury. Starting from what he considered the most pressing issue and presenting it in its unveiled form in C45, he supplied developments and variations of the subject, following its trails through history. Pound wrote the Seven Lakes Canto as another key node, because he put a strong emphasis on good government, a concept he isolated in C49 and treated in historical context in the Cantos about Leopoldo and Ferdinando III. Although Pound's general montage method, as used in C48, is not genuinely Poundian or derived from a particular subject, we claim that the subjects govern the overall structure of the section, as the textual units determine its micro-structure.

One the one hand, Pound had a thoroughly modernist sense of structure, a sense that led him to the use of montage and collage, patchwork techniques and multiple layers. On the other hand, he was very much a programmatic and rhetorical writer and broke rules for expressive purposes, which distinguished him from other modern poets. Symbolists like Georg Trakl composed poetry that, in many parts, contained sequences of visionary images with no explicit political or other "messages" attached to them. Although Pound, too, included many visionary moments in his Cantos, he permeated them with an ideological zeal that reminds one of Early Modern writers like Blake or Milton, whose major works are inseparable from their personal ideologies. In composing and structuring the Fifth Decad, Pound was just as programmatic; a poet with a mission.

III.6.c Coda II: The Historical Method

> ***Poets themselves, though liars by profession, always endeavour to give an air of truth to their fictions; and where that is totally neglected, their performances, however ingenious, will never be able to afford much pleasure.***
>
> (David Hume, *A Treatise of Human Nature*)

We have so far followed Pound through the remains of history, and have reconstructed traces of historical sources and of their authorial manipulations. Yet the basic question for Pound's approach to history, as discernible from his use of historical units, has not yet been answered comprehensively. What I will outline in this chapter are aspects of Pound's method of perceiving and describing history – not so much as a comprehensive Poundian theory of history, but as a cluster of assumptions about the nature and representation of history. We have to take into consideration the compressed nodes of historicity Pound calls "luminous details," including the transmissional capabilities of those nodes; the narrative strategies employed in the *Cantos*; Pound's notion of "contemporaneous ages;" and his firm belief in the degeneration of culture as affected, throughout history, by usury.

The first important aspect about Pound's method is his concentration on "luminous details." This highly flexible term includes both complex historical narratives and concentrated units of discourse. The account of Tuscan history presented in C50 is a collection of such details in the form of a dense, coherent narrative. The multiple quotations occurring throughout the *Cantos* are brief narrative excerpts from history and provide details in a more fragmented form. Both groups of details illustrate Pound's faith in the transmissional capability of words, i.e. their function as transmitters of information about the past. Words function as a node around which history condenses itself. Pound wrote in 1940:

> In one sense history, not merely ideological history, is built out of phrases. It is built out of crystallizations of words into very brief groups, say five, six, or a dozen words. These words become fact. And it is impossible to exaggerate their force.[121]

[121] Pound, Ezra, Ezra Pound and Japan, 186.

What Pound found in the traces of the past, i.e. in his sources, was a multiplicity of implications, which allowed even single words to represent parts of that now fragmented past. Pound substituted the piece for the whole and then sought to reconstruct history *ex ungue leonem*. His belief in the transmissional force of single units of historical discourse explains his condensed style of writing. When, in 1936, Pound supposes "it to be premature to try any compressed history on N. Americ. YET.,"[122] the important point in this sentence is his idea of *compressed* history. What Baudrillard wrote about history is strikingly true for Pound's notions: that history is "the dispersal of the dense and hieratic nuclei of previous civilizations."[123] Those nuclei are the "luminous details" collected by the poet as an editor of history, as someone who selects and arranges remains of the past.

Pound did not consider his own approach very innovative, but firmly believed that historiography had not adavanced methodically "since the days when Confucius selected the documents of the old kingdoms, and condensed his conclusions in the Testament."[124] Although written some years after the publication of *The Fifth Decad*, Pound's statement about the historian-as-collector describes exactly the method he used in the Siena Cantos. Like Chinese historiography before it,[125] Pound's text combines economic facts (e.g. tax laws, currency issues), political history and moral judgements. Its typical, compressed style of narrating historical events is also found in Chinese poetry, which in some passages resembles Pound's condensed epicisms. The poem "Fighting South of the Ramparts" by Li Po begins:

> Last year we fought
> at the headwaters
> of the Mulberry
> this year we're fighting
> on the Onion River Road[126]

The quotation is likely to remind the reader of a passage in the Malatesta Cantos (C9.34: "One year floods rose, [/] One year they fought in the snows").

The obvious historical-narrative elements in the *Cantos* are only the starting point for questions concerning the role of the author-narrator who

---

[122] Gordon, David M. (ed.), Ezra Pound and James Laughlin: Selected Letters, 67, 26 Sept 1936.

[123] Baudrillard, Jean, "The Illusion of the End," 42.

[124] "An Introduction to the Economic Nature of the United States" (1944, orig. Italian), in: SP, 137. Again note the idea of compression.

[125] See Giles, Herbert A., A History of Chinese Literature, 102-109.

[126] Wang Wei / Li Po / Tu Fu / Li Ho, Four T'ang Poets, 61.

edits the historical discourses in the poem. Longenbach accuses Pound of removing all signs of authorial presence from *The Cantos* and calls this a "political strategy designed to make his idiosyncratic interpretations of history and economics seem as inevitable as nature itself."[127] Accordingly, Bernstein argues that Pound, as a traveller in history, surely dominates some of the Cantos, while most parts of the poem are "generated with no locatable or definable narrative source."[128] But in fact we can discover many hints at Pound the narrator in the *Cantos*. Some parts of the text include clear references to biographical events, even in the conventional sense of chronological references. C41 carries the "ad interim 1933" at the end, while the final line of C46 establishes "1935" as the historical place of the poem. C46 at the same time exemplifies the presence of a biographical narrator in the poem. The comments in the Siena Cantos (e.g. the "damn good bank" in C42.209) are undoubtedly the comments of a narrator who is different in style and historical place from the presented pieces of historical discourse. C48 may consist largely of borrowed units of text, but remarks like "sixteen hundred, I think, and whenever" identify a narrator behind the collection of luminous details (C48.240).

The historical units of discourse never fully overshadow the voice of their collector, who maintains his control over the ramifications of the text.[129] It is the narrator who determines the patterns developed in the text. Generally speaking, a narrative structure figurates those events to which it primarily refers "and transforms these events into intimations of patterns of meaning that any literal representation of them as facts could never produce."[130] But whereas conventional historians assume a sequential, universal time in order to impose a pattern on events,[131] Pound, although mentioning some dates, structures his narrative according to argumentative, rather than chronological, criteria. C48, with its quick leaps from San Remo in 1926 to World War I and back to the Civil War, demonstrates Pound's narrative flexibility. He achieved it by applying the diachronic method, i.e. by locating a phenomenon in different constellations, places and times.

---

[127] Longenbach, James, Modernist Poetics of History, 142f.

[128] Bernstein, Michael André, "Identification and Its Vicissitudes," 547.

[129] Note that we do neither generally nor naïvely identify a narrator in a text with its author. In Pound's case, however, many hints in the text allow for such a conclusion. In *The Fifth Decad*, this is most obvious in the initial passage of C46 with its autobiographical references to the beginnings of Pound's interest in economics.

[130] White, Hayden, The Content of the Form, 45.

[131] Berkhofer, Robert F., Beyond the Great Story, 109f. For narrative models applied to historiography also see Robert Berkhofer, "The Challenge of Poetics to (Normal) Historical Practice," in: Jenkins, Keith (ed.), The Postmodern History Reader, London / New York 1997, 139-157, here 144ff.

This method is based on the Poundian concept of history. Pound's approach to chronology is specific in its assumption of the contemporaneous existence of ages: "It is dawn at Jerusalem while midnight hovers above the Pillars of Hercules. All ages are contemporaneous."[132] Lewis calls this an attitude of "timelessness" and quotes the passage on the "homology principle" from Spengler's *Decline of the West* to provide a more exact definition of Pound's notion.[133] Spengler is indeed an important key to our understanding of Pound's method, especially because Spengler exemplifies a typical attitude of the 1930s. The German philosopher of culture advocated an organicist view of world history, defining cultures as organisms with similar structures and developments.[134] What Spengler applies to history is basically Goethe's morphological method, which searched for the ur-form behind individual flowers and aimed at discovering the laws that governed the growth of every single flower. Spengler's concept implies a non-centralistic view of civilization. If all cultures are contemporaraneous and subject to identical laws, no single culture can claim superiority. Their achievements are homologically identical, because they "occur in exactly the same – relative – positions in their respective Cultures, and therefore possess exactly equivalent importance. [...] Classical coinage and our double-entry book-keeping; the first Tyrannis and the Fronde; Augustus and Shih-huang-ti; Hannibal and the World War."[135] Spengler's perspective, if applied to poetry, would result in exactly the multi-referential and non-linear texts Pound created.

Spengler's theory also directs our attention to another aspect implied in his concept, the decline of cultures. This notion was very common among early 20th-century philosophers of history. Brooks Adams, for instance, proposes a theory similar to Spengler, Toynbee and others. Like Spengler, he undertakes to formulate universal laws that govern the rise and fall of states, societies and races. In their early stages, societies tend to be energetic, martial and governed by fear. An increasing level of concentration and consolidation leads to centralization. Now the ruling principle of fear yields to greed, as "the economic organism tends to supersede the emotional and martial."[136] The economy increasingly uses up all surplus energy of the race for competition, while the arts degenerate and die. In Pound, this cyclic concept of history applies to the rise and fall of Rome, the Catholic Church, the Renaissance, and to the decline of the U.S. The idea of decay is always present and in 1938 Pound wrote: "Run your eye along the margin of history and you will observe great waves, sweeping movements and triumphs which fall when their

---

[132] Pound, Ezra, The Spirit of Romance, 8, written in 1910.
[133] Lewis, Wyndham, Time and Western Man, 23.
[134] Spengler, Oswald, The Decline of the West, I.104.
[135] Spengler, Oswald, The Decline of the West, I.112.
[136] Adams, Brooks, The Law of Civilization and Decay, vii.

ideology petrifies."[137] The one force Pound held responsible for degenerative processes in culture was usury, and as we have seen, not only C45 testifies to this position.

Given Pound's assumption of an aggressive, evil force in history, the historical "fact" is logically assigned a special role in the historiographical poetry which results from that pessimistic view of events. Facts become instrumental in making the case against the multiple intrigues and alleged machinations of secretive powers. The history that needs to be written is an underground version of history, which seeks to excavate hidden and less-known facts, if they help to restrain the power of that intangible force Pound called by such names as usury and Geryon. Pound's attempt to turn what he deemed secret history into poetry is illustrated by a statement in a letter of 1939:

> We are having a LOAN-Capital war. Some say a jew war against the aryan population of Europe. Mc N. Wilson sees American finance as the real enemy of England. [...]
> At any rate there is no understanding of the present wars without understanding of war loans/ loans by the SAME MEN to the Same men. De Wendel the banker, pays the <*french*> people's money to De Wendel the gunmaker. And SO FORTH.
> and all this is subject matter for literature. [138]

We could call this an investigative approach to history. When Pound quotes an apocryphal remark by a Rothschild banker in C46, he does so to reveal a certain mentality and at the same time an influential force behind historical events. And when he denounces the Regius professorships as propagandistic institutions, he demonstrates his awareness of the fact that, to a certain extent, to communicate history means to control history. Pound's approach comes close to what Veeser defined in a New Historicist context as the pragmatic view of history, the notion that "history is not merely a chronicle of the past, but rather a pragmatic weapon for explaining the present and controlling the future."[139] T. S. Eliot makes a similar point in "The Method of Mr. Pound:"[140] For Pound, he states, the present is the present significance of the past, and by acquiring the past, the poet reveals the present. The danger inherent in this approach is obvious – while accusing others of instrumentalizing facts, Pound himself comes dangerously close to the instrumentalization of history for the purpose of illustrating a particular point, i.e. the power of usury. As Wyndham Lewis stressed, historians are

[137] GK, 52.
[138] Pound, Ezra, Ezra Pound and Japan, 79.
[139] Veeser, Harold A., "The New Historicism," 11.
[140] See bibliography.

anything but disinterested. They are intellectual politicians who try to provide their generation with what is often a downright partisan, or at least moralist, perspective determined by the historian's temper.[141] Accordingly, they may edit history to argue a case.

We mentioned Pound's tendency to de-contextualize quotations. The reason for this was a flawed historical perception. Pound regarded the information provided by populists like Coughlin or by politicians like Rudolf Hess as historical fact when it was no more than political or polemical propaganda. What they presented as facts were really arguments created for specific purposes. Because Pound himself was inclined to instrumentalize information, he did not notice the difference between actual historical facts and arguments disguised as historical facts. Hence, the "evidence" he compiled in poems like C46 reveals more about Pound's own historical and intellectual background than about history itself, even if Pound believed the opposite. *The Fifth Decad* perfectly illustrates, and is perfectly illustrated by, a statement by Pound about his idea of history, published one year after the *Fifth Decad*:

> Secret history is at least twofold. One part consists in the secret corruptions, the personal lusts, avarices etc. that scoundrels keep hidden, another part is the 'plus', the constructive urges, a *secretum* because it passes unnoticed or because no human effort can force it on public attention.[142]

The Fifth Decad is the realization of this idea. Cantos 42 to 51 constantly hover between, first, the revelation of hidden "truths" or "facts" to indicate the presence of destructive forces in history, and second, the suggestion of alternative forces which may curtail evil: the *secretum* of fertility, Eros, ritual, good government. Between them, areas of history wait to be unearthed by the poet-archeologist, areas buried in the course of time, just like "the thought of Van Buren, A. Johnson, A. Jackson and the story of Tuscany under Pietro Leopoldo, have been buried."[143] Pound balances on a narrow edge between the pragmatic reformism of those model leaders and apocalyptic sermons against the sin of usury. He evokes both the circles of a secular hell and mystical moments of vision and light. In between, history is edited.

[141] Lewis, Wyndham, Time and Western Man, 263.
[142] GK, 264.
[143] GK, 30.

IV. Mnemosyne 4 – Reading the Text

A textual critic engaged upon his business is not at all like Newton investigating the motions of the planets: he is much more like a dog hunting for fleas.

(A. E. Housman, *The Application of Thought to Textual Criticism*)

The world of documents is a world of imperfection.

(George Thomas Tanselle, *A Rationale of Textual Criticism*)

IV.1 Prospects: Genetic Editing and the *Cantos*

IV.1.a The Genetic Edition as a Hermeneutical Aid

Being asked about the immediate purpose of a genetic edition, a textual scholar might answer that it is important to establish a text based solely on the author's intentions, which can best be deduced from the original manuscripts. In order to understand their development, a genetic approach is required. The scholar could also hint at the visual appeal of manuscript editions, as obvious, for instance, in the facsimile pages of Reuss's Kafka edition, which gives readers an authentic feeling like they are actually browsing through the writer's original notebooks. Yet genetic criticism can affect the hermeneutics of literature beyond the teleological idea of the perfect text, beyond the deception of authenticity and the fallacy of authorial intention. It is a surgical tool for the vivsection of a work and the understanding of its anatomy. And it is well-suited for editing Pound's *Cantos*, as will be explained in this chapter, which outlines my proposals for a genetic edition of the decad.

The idea of editing as a hermeneutic act has its tradition. Finneran once remarked that one comma can alter the interpretation of a whole poem – and it is often the editor who decides about individual commas.[144] According to Hay, editorial analysis is necessary to make the interpretation of a work even possible.[145] For other critics, the idea of "editing as interpretation" has even become just another commonplace of textual criticism,[146] since it first appeared, among others, in a 1957 essay by Windfuhr.[147] Wollenberg claims that even a basic act like the deciphering of authorial handwriting is already an interpretation.[148] It is easy to agree with Wollenberg, given the margins of error that reading an untidy manuscript implies. The transcribing of manuscripts always involves subjectivity, because textual ambiguities, deficits in linguistic competence and other defects often lead to contaminated readings.[149] Transcribing difficult passages in manuscripts requires a high

[144] Finneran, Richard J., "Text and Intepretation in the Poems of W. B. Yeats," in: George Bornstein (ed.), Representing Modernist Texts, 26f.
[145] Hay, Louis, "Drei Randglossen zur Problematik textgenetischer Editionen," 69f.
[146] Kanzog, Klaus, Einführung in die Editionsphilologie, 50.
[147] Manfred Windfuhr, "Die neugermanistische Edition. Zu den Grundsätzen kritischer Gesamtausgaben," in: Dte. Vierteljahresschr. f. Lit.wiss. u. Geistesgesch. 31 (1957), S. 426-442.
[148] Wollenberg, Friedrich W., "Zur genetischen Darstellung innerhandschriftlicher Varianten," 252f.
[149] Kanzog, Klaus, Einführung in die Editionsphilologie, 50.

amount of imagination. Gellhaus even went so far as to claim that the editor is always a recipient who literally constitutes, if not creates, work and author.[150]

The points discussed by Wollenberg and others strongly center on the micro-level of textual genetics, i.e. the process of decoding and sequencing authorial documents.[151] But a genetic edition possesses an even broader scope that involves the macro-level of hermeneutic analysis. It allows for conclusions about, first, the meaning of difficult passages, second, the overall structure of the growing text, and third, the historical background of the text. Such conclusions have been reached in chapters II.1 and II.2 of this study. A brief recapitulation of some arguments will highlight their hermeneutic significance.

First, a genetic edition helps to clarify puzzling or obscure passages of the *Cantos*. As mentioned earlier, scholars have proposed different readings of a line in C49: "The fourth; the dimension of stillness." (C49.245), which some have applied to Einstein. As Pound's notes and drafts show, he understood the line in a very basic and simple sense. In an early note, he clarified that this dimension was one of fixed relations.[152] Similarly in another note (item 72). In the context of C49, the genetically extended reading underlines and clarifies the meaning of the poem: The dynastic-imperial world of C49 represents a historical utopia in which everything is assigned a proper place. A third note refers to the same dimension of fixed relations and mentions the "nous" as a supreme authority (item 293). This note adds another level to the poem, because "nous" links the text to the European tradition of philosophy. This becomes obvious only through genetic analysis. It therefore takes a genetic edition to provide the poem itself with a "fourth dimension."

Second, a genetic edition conveys important information about poetic structuring. In C48, for instance, a letter about a pedigree dog named "Dhu Ahil" runs parallel to an anecdote about the more than casual way a secretary of state called Rhumby is appointed (C48.241). The genesis of this passage originates from a letter by an A. E. Evans (item 114), to whose formulations Pound largely adheres, and from a draft version of the Rhumby anecdote (item 115). Pound deliberately deconstructed the very formal letter and, by contradicting its coherence and attaching it to a story about ridiculous politicians, gains an artistic effect from a structural transformation. We can only assess the full extent of such transformations if we reconstruct the genesis of C48. Another structural dimension of the Cantos is their use of

[150] Gellhaus, Axel, "Textgenese zwischen Poetologie und Editionstechnik," 314.

[151] I borrow the term "sequencing" from the field of biogenetics, in which it denotes the reconstruction of a DNA sequence. I use it to describe the process of establishing a genetic stemma.

[152] See BL 43 / 73 / 3258.

archival sources. An analysis of the writing process of Cantos 42-44 and 50, starting with the Siena notebooks (items 282-286), showed how Pound transformed reading notes into historically charged poetry and administrative documents into a modernist version of economic history. Genetic analysis provides a genuine method for understanding the historical fact-epic of the Siena Cantos.

Third, a genetic edition offers the possibility of obtaining information about the historical and biographical background of a poem. For Martens, that background, as the personal experience of the author, is encoded aesthetically as the genesis of a text progresses. Martens states that textual variants often communicate historical information about political and historical events, or name specific social circumstances that take on a general form in the process of aesthetization.[153] In some cases, an author starts with a personal experience and then transforms it into a piece of impersonal poetry, rendering its background incomprehensible by revising it. Thus, the dynamics of revision are employed for the purpose of impersonalization. A genetic edition allows for a virtual reversal of this process and can help us understand the personal and historical background facts involved in the poem. This is not intended to support any misguided claims for a romanticist revival of "authenticity" or "personality" as key criteria in literature. Impersonality, in poetry, is no less than a virtue; yet the historian is obliged to collect as much information about the background of a text as available.

The Hess quotation in C51 shows how a genetic edition can reconstruct both the dynamics of revision and authorial experience. The transformation of the quotation into a part of C51 grants insights into Pound's political ideas at the time of writing. It helps to identify a textual source and at the same time links it to a name with certain political connotations. It proves Pound's enthusiastic reception of fascist propaganda, in this case a speech by Hitler's deputy, Rudolf Hess. It also reveals how the original note underwent a process of compression and revision in order to hide the speaker's identity and Pound's enthusiastic reaction to Hess's speech. The Canto's seemingly impersonal humanitarianism has very personal roots.

Of course a genetic edition does not solve every problem of interpretation and might even face serious obstacles. In fact, a hermeneutic-genetic approach to the *Cantos* encounters several general difficulties by which many manuscript editions are plagued;[154] problems concerning both editorial decisions and the subsequent acts of interpretation that depend on them. First, how broad or narrow a selection of documents should be included in the edition? As the Hess example shows, even early reading notes might

[153] Martens, Gunter, "(De)Constructing Texts by Editing," 136, also 141.
[154] Comp. Gellhaus's remarks in "Textgenese zwischen Poetologie und Editionstechnik," 320.

help to understand a poem. Hence, an edition which focuses on the actual text of the poem and therefore excludes such notes might raise objections on grounds of its limited scope. On the other hand, practical reasons make it often necessary to confine the size of an edition. Editors have to decide on a case-by-case basis whether they edit the complete genetic dossier of a work or only a selection. The latter, however, might seriously limit the scope of possible interpretations.

The second problem is chronology. In order to reconstruct processes of aesthetization and impersonalization properly, editors have to establish genetic stages. Deficiencies in transmission, however, make the sequencing of drafts and fragments difficult. The loss or destruction of intermediate stages is one aspect of this problem. In other cases, the lack of revisions in documents, i.e. their almost identical looks, may prevent the editor from drawing conclusions about which document was written earlier. Or, for example, we have independent drafts of two passages of text (A and B) which were then combined to form a final text – in this case, too, it might be impossible to state clearly which draft preceded the other. When more than one sequence of drafts is possible, the editor can form hypotheses, but not make definitive statements.

As the above examples show, the *Cantos* call for a combined textual-editorial and critical-interpretative approach, a fact also pointed out by McGann.[155] In the process of constantly reshaping and revising the poem, Pound discarded, for the sake of conciseness, many lines and passages of hermeneutic value. A genetic edition is crucial for their reconstruction.

IV.1.b The Special Requirements of the Pound Papers

According to Housman, the textual critic is not occupied with unalterable laws of nature, but with erratic and imperfect textual histories. Despite generic similarities, not two of them are ever exactly alike, whether on the macro- or the micro-level. This is largely due to the specific writing methods and habits that authors develop in order to refine their style and achieve their literary goals. In part II of this study we highlighted Pound's particular habits. The material traces and witnesses left by Pound provide the framework for the following brief considerations, which are intended to set those habits in relation to the necessities of a genetic edition. We are not yet talking about solutions, but will outline some of the issues raised by the typical characteristics of the Pound papers.

[155] McGann, Jerome, "Pound's *Cantos*: A Poem Including Bibliography," 38.

The written record certainly represents an extension of memory.[156] At the same time, though, a manuscript is not only related to the secluded privacy of the individual mind, but also functions as a form of utterance. As any utterance, it either expresses itself spontaneously, with all the ruptures and incongruities occuring in the event, or as the cautious result of attentive thinking and planning. It is therefore appropriate when Hurlebusch distinguishes two types of writing processes: one which is founded on ideas already conceived in the writer's mind, realizes pre-developed concepts and strives for linear communication. In this case, revisions are often minimal, as the text is not developed while writing, but has already been *thought*. Second, a psycho-genetic type of writing, with the creative process at its center.[157] This process-oriented type can be recognized by the large number of revisions occuring in draft autographs.

As is obvious from the archival evidence, the latter applies to Pound. His manuscripts usually show several layers of writing that interact intricately. Pound made extensive use of several writing instruments and colors, and we mentioned his blue-ribbon typescripts and the different pencils he used for revisions. Those writing instruments served to create *physical* layers of writing. On the *textual* level, they resulted in overlapping and replaced utterances; multiple speech acts translated into writing gestures. What this complexity requires is an editorial approach that is not content with the constitution of a reading text, but makes the full diversity of Pound's manuscripts available (and legible). The challenge lies not in cleaning up the remains, but in preserving them and reducing them to their essentials. The particular character of Pound's errors and the individual architectures of his complicated drafts all form parts of the *historical* level of writing, which requires the accuracy of a diplomatic edition. Pound's use of newpaper clippings, for example, is not a feature that a conventional reading text can represent properly.

Textual and factual errors included in Pound's drafts are a substantial challenge the editor has to meet. Editing *The Fifth Decad* with diplomatic exactness implies a large amount of tolerance towards errors, if not their identical reproduction, which entails avoiding even cautious emendations.[158] As a result of these preconditions, the editor must consider diplomatic transcriptions as the possibly best representation of the individual character of

---

[156] Grésillon, Almuth, Literarische Handschriften, 183.

[157] Hurlebusch, Klaus, "Den Autor besser verstehen," 37. Hurlebusch's typology resembles Grésillon's concepts of product-oriented and process-oriented writing; see Grésillon, Almuth, Literarische Handschriften, 133.

[158] Emendations as defined by Scheibe and Zeller in: Scheibe, Siegfried, "Zu einigen Grundprinzipien einer historisch-kritischen Ausgabe," 43; Zeller, Hans, "Record and Interpretation," 36f. and 41.

the documents. Although diplomatic transcriptions preserve many "accidentals" of handwriting,[159] such as different types of corrections, they also have a strong editorial component which gives editors a broad range of possibilities. As we will see in a subsequent chapter, some editors use transcriptions to establish genetic processes, whereas others provide them as mere reading aids. Hence, diplomatic transcriptions possess an editorial depth which makes them suitable for Pound's complex manuscripts.

We also observed Pound's partly selective use of paper, for instance of yellow sheets for late genetic stages. If paper is used in such a non-arbitrary way, it gains editorial significance. Thus, to acknowledge the possible importance of physical and bibliographical details becomes a major editorial objective. To point out the significance of the paper type in selected cases only would be half-hearted and – what is more serious – bad scholarship, because it would keep readers from testing the editor's conclusions against the evidence. Hence, the only fully responsible way of dealing with the matter is a documentary approach that includes the bibliographical and physical properties of the edited documents. The editor must collect and store those data in an accessible part of the edition.

Starting from the material aspects, readers must be able to trace the history of the poem through the textual and physical development of the related documents. The display of their multiple layers, from physical paper to immaterial text, can provide the basis for an in-depth analysis. Rainey has shown how much information Poundian documents can convey. He dates the drafts of the Malatesta Cantos according to historical, intrinsic and extrinsic criteria. Historical criteria are based on "external documentation," as in the case of transcriptions of archival documents. Exact dates may be established by following Pound's correspondence or archival administrative records. Intrinsic characteristics are based on the contents of drafts (e.g. when an event in a specific year is mentioned), extrinsic ones on the material properties of the drafts (paper, ink, typing ribbon etc.). The latter can be collated with bibliographical features of Pound's correspondence.[160] Obviously, Pound's drafts call on editors to bridge the gap between hermeneutics and bibliography. The genetic edition may be a hermeneutical aid, but we cannot employ it fully unless it is turned into a bibliographical aid, too.

To conclude, we consider it necessary to develop a strongly documentary approach to genetic editing, an approach which, first, allows for the inclusion of physical and bibliographical details in order to provide readers with full information about Pound's pre-publication documents, so that readers may interpret their significance and check editorial findings.

---

[159] As Wollenberg calls them in: Wollenberg, Friedrich W., "Zur genetischen Darstellung innerhandschriftlicher Varianten," 252.

[160] Rainey, Lawrence S., Ezra Pound and the Monument of Culture, 229.

Second, it should reproduce the topographies of the autographs as witnesses of individual writing processes. In short, what the Pound papers require is an edition with archival emphasis and rich options for information retrieval: an electronic edition.

IV.1.c The Benefits of an Electronic Edition

Pound created the *Cantos* from an enormous amount of literary and historical sources. He included several languages, Chinese ideograms and Egyptian hieroglyphs in the text. Even a musical score found its way into the poem. The writing process was a constant re-shaping and re-locating of diverse material. Given these complex preconditions, a genetic edition of the *Cantos* must unfold multiple layers of text, identify paths of writing and provide annotations on both textual genesis and historical background. Some of these tasks have always been performed by the traditional print edition, chiefly the annotation of a text. The development of genetic editing, too, has taken place chiefly in the print medium. Even recent genetic editions, like Büchner's *Woyzeck*,[161] still rest on the printed text and offer the electronic version as a mere supplement with only a limited number of additional functions. Often released as PDF files, those versions are books turned electronic document, and hardly make use of the genuine possibilities of the electronic medium. They do not yet satisfy the playfulness which, as Gabler hopes, might increase scholarly interest in editing.[162]

In the case of the *Cantos*, the call for a – not necessarily genetic – edition is often accompanied by the call for an electronic approach. According to Redman, a "hypertext or hypermedia environment would best actualize all the various contexts of the poem and their relations to each other."[163] This can be applied to the poem's multi-layered background of historical-biographical contexts, and to its diverse levels of writing and publication. Even the problem of fragmentation, so acute in both genesis and published text, could be solved by an eletronic edition. Led by a genuinely genetic interest, Taylor calls for an electronic edition to allow readers to trace transformations of the text as it passed through the hands of Pound and others.[164] But what benefits can an electronic edition really offer?

[161] Georg Büchner, Woyzeck: Faksimile, Transkription, Emendation und Lesetext, ed. Enrico DeAngelis, Munich 2001; on CD-ROM.
[162] Gabler, Hans Walter, "Computergestütztes Edieren und Computer-Edition," 323.
[163] Redman, Tim, "An Epic Is a Hypertext Containing Poetry: *Eleven New Cantos* (31-41) by Ezra Pound," 119.
[164] Taylor, Richard, Variorum Edition of "Three Cantos" by Ezra Pound: A Prototype, 7.

Printed editions have quantitative limits which create a wide gap between the ideal edition and its realization. Scheibe's theoretical approach to the German historical-critical edition may serve as an example. As Scheibe states, a historical-critical edition should publish the complete material handed down from an author to posterity, including not only notes, but also marks and underlinings of passages in books, plus audio-visual material.[165] As a consequence, editors would be obliged to reproduce anything from the books read by an author to interviews offering hints at the work. Such an enormous amount of material would require a multi-volume edition with a multimedia supplement. It would only be usable with a complex reference system designed to navigate between the several parts of the edition. An electronic edition can fulfil Scheibe's requirements better than a printed edition. The integration of multimedia elements is one of the genuine virtues of the electronic medium, as is the use of databases and indices for referencing.

We now move to the structural level of editing. Referencing is substantial for annotating a text and for reconstructing its genesis. While the latter describes the analytical dimension of editing, the commentary is the result of a synthetic process.[166] It has to combine pieces of information that are rooted in contexts ranging from historical source documents to recordings of authors reading their work. The commentary connects those units of information, if they are related, and in addition establishes links between itself and the text, as most notes exist as references to a particular passage of the work. An electronic edition can establish such links in a more convenient way than printed reference systems. Existing forms of hypertext linking, for instance, seem extremely appropriate for editorial commentaries. They can assume forms such as unidirectional, bidirectional, string to lexia (linking a word to another element), string to string (word to word), or one-to-many.[167] The background of a work can be unfolded in multiple subscreens, including e.g. a quotation, a source bibliography and finally the source itself.[168] Some editors might want to sub-structure their commentary in order to distinguish different levels of annotations (intertextual relations, stilistics, non-literary allusions, etc.). Users can be offered the choice between a professional, database-oriented approach (providing access to textual data, e.g. paper descriptions) and a more reader-friendly layout that can be easily used by

---

[165] Scheibe, Siegfried, "Zu einigen Grundprinzipien einer historisch-kritischen Ausgabe," 9.

[166] Gabler, Hans W., "Naissance de l'édition: de l'ordinateur comme sage-femme," 54f.

[167] Landow, George P., Hypertext 2.0, 12f.

[168] Redman, Tim, "An Epic Is a Hypertext Containing Poetry: *Eleven New Cantos* (31-41) by Ezra Pound," 141.

students. This aspect is of special importance when designing an edition for educational purposes.

A particularly complex problem for any printed edition is the representation of the genetic stages of a text: The genetic stemma has to be translated into a comprehensible order and hierarchy of documents, documents of doubtful chronology have to be assigned a place in that hierarchy, multiple stages have to be reproduced – thus increasing the number of pages – and, after all, readers have to be guided through them without confusion. Serious difficulties arise for a printed edition, often resulting in complicated genetic apparatuses based on systems of diacritical signs that have to be thoroughly studied before they can be understood. As Almuth Grésillon has said, those apparatuses are deficient in presenting a multi-dimensional genesis in a two-dimensional space, mixing material findings and chronological interpretation.[169] An electronic edition, however, allows for the reconstruction of genetic stages down to the level of the single sheet as the smallest editorial unit. The electronic medium can fully mirror the processuality of writing, as it allows for the reproduction of dynamic sequences.[170] The textual genesis of single sheets can be reconstructed with multiple layers of images. The genesis of a complete text can be shown in an electronic stemma hyperlinked to the single drafts or sheets. The flexibility of the electronic medium in terms of design and layout supports those structural benefits.

Aspects of layout and usability are often mentioned first when describing the advantages of hypertext.[171] Gabler stresses the importance of an innovative user interface.[172] Lebrave mentions the user-friendly benefits of search options that allow readers to look for phrases or words, or to search an index.[173] It is particularly the use of flexible search strategies that makes an electronic edition likely to attain a balance between complexity and usability, because it allows users to apply their own criteria to the edition. For instance, by retrieving all blue ribbon typescripts or all drafts containing the word "usura." Readers could even be enabled to isolate what Gabler calls a "self-defined state of development of the text."[174]

Despite the danger of redundancy, the benefits of an electronic edition are many. It can use multiple graphical layers to reconstruct the micro-genesis of a text, and hyperlinked stemmata for the macro-genesis. The immediate linking of similar passages in remote documents is possible, as is complex

---

169 Grésillon, Almuth, "Bemerkungen zur französischen 'édition génétique'," 54.
170 Gabler, Hans W., "Towards an Electronic Edition of James Joyce's *Ulysses*," 115f.
171 Landow, George P., Hypertext 2.0, 5f.
172 Gabler, Hans W., "Towards an Electronic Edition of James Joyce's *Ulysses*," 115.
173 Lebrave, Jean-Louis, "Hypertext und textgenetische Edition," 344f.
174 Gabler, Hans W., "Towards an Electronic Edition of James Joyce's *Ulysses*," 118.

referencing of commentary and text. By the use of search options, enhanced data retrieval becomes a powerful tool. An extensive archive can be reproduced on one disk, while the archival material can be approached from different perspectives, depending on the users' level of proficiency. Different formats and media can be integrated, whether facsimiles, audio documents, or others.

Given the vast amount of options available in the electronic medium, it goes without saying that the editor's responsibility increases considerably. The more data can be integrated into an edition, the more important are, first, strict criteria for the selection of the included material, and second, clear principles guiding the structuring of an edition. After all, the limited amount of space offered by printed editions was not only a confinement, but much of a virtue.

IV.1.d Editorial Structuring

Within a genetic edition of *The Fifth Decad*, the *Canto* should serve as the prior structural unit. We consider this a natural designation, as the Canto constitutes the major unit to divide the published text and Pound wrote with the Canto structure in mind. Whenever possible, documents should be attributed to a Canto, sometimes on the evidence of a single phrase or other textual element. Item 288, for instance, includes a phrase that would later form a part of C48. On the other hand, item 289 does not contain any explicit reference to a part of *The Fifth Decad*, but is linked to the genesis of C48 in an indirect way. Hence, it should be filed under C48. Some sheets are related to more than one Canto, because they contain elements which were later incorporated into several Cantos. Item 293, for instance, mentions the old man on the beach who appears at the end of C48 and the "dimension of stillness" from C49.

On the same level as the Canto unit, we find miscellaneous documents, which the editor could collect in a Miscellaneous Section. These documents are notes and fragments which cannot be assigned at all, or only with difficulty, to individual Cantos. It might be asked why they should be included in an edition at all, if they have no relevance for the genesis of *The Fifth Decad*. The reason is documentary coherence: Most of the miscellaneous sheets can be found in document folders which also contain drafts of *The Fifth Decad*. In order to maintain archival completeness, those documents should be transcribed like the other sheets, but not be integrated into genetic structures.

The next level is constituted by *genetic stages*, i.e. compositional stages of individual Cantos. Each genetic stage consists of pages. On the content level, the *page* functions as the lowest unit, to which corresponds, on the document level, the sheet. The major part of Pound's drafts has survived as separate sheets, hence it is natural to choose them as the basic units of the edition. Genetically, the pages can be divided into what I call *sheet sub-stages*, i.e. genetic stages on the micro-level. These sub-stages reconstruct the layers of writing on one document, hence one sub-stage may include the typewritten contents of a page, followed by a second layer of ink or pencil corrections.[175]

All archival material related to the *Fifth Decad* should be listed in a database and be described by several columns of document properties. In general, the possibilities of modern photographic reproduction allow for a condensed form of manuscript descriptions. As Kraft suggests, descriptions should include details on writing materials, paper specifications (e.g. watermarks, color) and the condition of the paper (torn or cut sides, spots or stains etc.).[176] This proposal was adopted in the item list in the appendix of this study.

Stemmata

The complex ramifications of some Cantos (mostly C48 and C51) make it appropriate to use stemmata for their representation. The genetic stemmata used in chapter II.2 are, in some respects, the exact opposite of conventional editorial stemmata with their archetype-centered approach. According to Espagne, the traditional idea of the stemma developed in close connection with the Romantic concept of the archetype. Herder and others sought to discover the one original language behind the Babylonian multitude of the European tongues. 19th century textual critics hunted for the one "true" text behind the presumed corruptions later inflicted on the works of the classical authors.[177] Ironically, the highly desired archetype is usually lost and can only be reconstructed from corrupted texts. So the outwardly historicist construction of the stemma actually serves an idealistic purpose. We will not follow this traditional notion and instead establish a stemmatic concept more suitable for a genetic edition. As opposed to the search for the one archetype, we deal with stemmata whose origins cannot be traced back to only one text, but lose themselves in a number of textual roots – fragments, excerpts, torn and illegible sheets of paper. The direction of the stemmatic arrows moves from a multitude of early notes toward the concentrated form of the setting copies.

[175] For details on the sub-stages see the subsequent chapter diplomatic transcriptions.
[176] Kraft, Herbert, Die Geschichtlichkeit literarischer Texte, 81.
[177] Espagne, Michel, De l'archive au texte, 166.

The genetic stages (A, B, C etc.) and sub-stages (AA, AB, AC etc.) – which are not to be confused with the sheet sub-stages – were grouped and named according to the complexity of the genesis of a Canto. I have attempted to assign genetic stages to larger groups of drafts, and sub-stages to versions or carbon copies within those groups. Whether this makes the stemmata more usable is something the reader has to decide. The graphical arrangement of a complex stemma seeks to achieve groupings and threads based on textual units and their combinations. In the case of C51, for instance, Pound's excerpts on fly-fishing (A) develop into two different threads, one of which (PA/PB to TA/TB) assumes a final form integrated into the finished Canto, while the other thread (CA/CB to EA/EB and MA/MB) is short-lived and gradually disappears from the drafts. The two threads constitute two different genetic processes, both in textual terms (the formulations in CA differ from those in PA) and in referential terms (CA is related to EA; PA and TA lead to U). It was therefore appropriate to establish two different paths in the stemma to represent this aspect. I also created multiple paths when no clear genetic sequence could be established for a textual unit. The "grass" unit from C51 is one such case. BA and BB form one thread, BC another, as the "grass" unit appears in two totally different contexts, for none of which we can claim absolute priority: once in combination with the peasants' song later incorporated into C49 (BB), once together with references to taxes and usury (BC). BA and BB have different contexts, too, but are linked by the specific formulation "nowhere off base" occurring in both stages. In this case, the sub-stages (A to C) do not denote a chronological sequence, but differences in context and formulation.

Using criteria like "context" and "formulation" implies a certain amount of critical discernment and subjectivity by the editor. Hence, as should be pointed out, the stemmata represent hypotheses. Whereas Froula, in her stemma of C4, uses broken lines to signify indirect or uncertain descent,[178] our stemmata do not feature such lines, for we would have to use them almost all the time. The whole reconstruction of genetic processes rests on fragile, uncertain assumptions, because we never know whether Pound did not write another, intermediate draft between two drafts of seemingly certain descent. The draft might be lost, but we cannot claim it never existed. All we can do is to weigh probabilities and draw some feeble lines.

We can now move from the macro- to the micro-level. The genesis of a Canto does not only include different drafts and versions as witnesses of the structural ramifications of the poem. The physical act of writing, too, is of course anything but homogeneous. On the macro-genetic level, we are confronted with subsequent drafts replacing each other, and the same phenomenon occurs on the micro-genetic level with regard to individual

[178] Froula, Christine, To Write Paradise, 69.

formulations or shorter passages, which are revised or discarded.[179] A genetic edition must be aware of, and deal with, this dimension of the writing process. Hence, it should reconstruct the genetic sub-stages which are formed by the layers of writing on each sheet. This includes physical and textual layers, as both levels interact in revision. This can best be represented by the use of diplomatic transcriptions.

IV.1.e Diplomatic Transcriptions

Genetic editing mainly rests on the dissatisfaction of the writer. Whenever words are deleted, replaced or supplemented by alternative formulations, the textual critic comes to life and seeks to walk in the footsteps of the writer, but backwards. Unfortunately, few writers leave orderly trails we can easily follow. Most of the time, the genetic critic finds ruins and patchwork, if not mere fragments. Reconstruction is difficult, and even more difficult is the transmission of genetic conclusions to an impatient audience. It was not without reason that Zeller mentioned the feeling of resignation among editors who find their complex genetic apparatuses rarely used by readers.[180]

While it is true that an adequate representation of the facts should not be blamed for its complexity, it is equally true that complexity is not always user-friendly. Hence, some recent genetic editions shun genetic apparatuses like the one in Gabler's *Ulysses*, and have instead set their faith into diplomatic transcriptions as adequate means to reconstruct the genesis of literary works. Basically, this method is anything but avantgardist. The exact reproduction of the manuscript text, including all characteristics of irregular spelling and punctuation, is, after all, the most conservative editorial approach.[181] But diplomatic transcriptions satisfy a certain interest in "authenticity" and immediacy that has developed over the last thirty years. At the same time, they are suited very well for the description of complex manuscripts like Pound's, as we will see in this chapter, where we will discuss the assets, deficits and implications of diplomatic editing. Examples from existing editions will serve to illustrate our points.

Tanselle once made an important distinction with regard to posthumous materials: "When a poem, left in manuscript, is posthumously published in the form of an exact transcript, it is being treated like a historical document;

---

[179] Which proves what Espagne observes: "Les matériaux relevant de chaque strate constituent eux-mêmes un ordre, un système dont les éléments discrets entrent dans des relations complexes," see Espagne, Michel, De l'archive au texte, 109.

[180] Zeller, Hans, "Die Faksimile-Edition als Grundlagenedition für Philologie und Textgenetik," 87f., n. 14.

[181] Greetham, David C., Textual Scholarship, 224.

when it is published in a clear reading text, it is being treated like a work of literary art."[182] In more general terms: transcriptions may represent documents, but only reading texts are appropriate for representing a work of art. Tanselle also established a distinction between writing intended for publication, often best represented by a critical edition, and writing not intended for it, in which case diplomatic transcriptions are more suitable.[183] It is with reference to this statement that an edition of *The Fifth Decad* should contain a *format text*[184] that represents the state of the poem at the time when it left Pound's hands. Yet this conventional, normalized format text is only one end of a spectrum which ranges from the "work of art" to the stained and frail piece of paper from which the art first originated. A genetic edition has to consider both the document and the work of art, and especially a facsimile edition must document the text in all its historical phases. Between the facsimile and the format text, the diplomatic transcription has its place.

Diplomatic transcriptions serve to translate layers of writing into a legible form. We agree with Zeller who said: "The more complicated and ambiguous the manuscript and the more intricate its graphical appearance, the more important a typographical reproduction is for the user."[185] In addition to this, the diplomatic transcription is uniquely predestined to preserve what Grésillon called the "topography" of a document.[186] Writing as a gesture, as an at times hesitating, or freely flowing gesture, is best reproduced by diplomatic transcriptions, as is a writer's individual system of revisions. Diplomatic transcriptions, however, are not an exact science. According to Zeller, typographical representation is interpretation, and even the basic act of deciphering manuscripts has an interpretative component.[187]

It is for this subjective dimension that diplomatic transcriptions must be complemented by facsimiles. Although editing will not simply overcome its subjective dimension by relying on facsimiles, as Kittler and Neumann claimed,[188] facsimiles are indeed useful for the verification of editorial findings. The documentation of records as facsimiles offers the reader the

[182] Tanselle, George Thomas, Selected Studies in Bibliography, 347f.
[183] See Tanselle, George Thomas, "Historicism and Critical Editing," 113.
[184] I.e. the reading text. Whereas the term "reading text" is not very precise – there are in fact few texts which cannot be read –, I prefer the term "format text" because it clearly denotes a text formatted according to a set of editorial criteria, as opposed to what could be termed "diplomatic text."
[185] Zeller, Hans, "Record and Interpretation," 47.
[186] Grésillon, Almuth, Literarische Handschriften, 157.
[187] Zeller, Hans, "Record and Interpretation," 19, 47. Kraft used this argument to deny transcriptions the objectivity he finds in original documents, comp. Kraft, Herbert, Die Geschichtlichkeit literarischer Texte, 71f.
[188] Comp. Zeller, Hans, "Die Faksimile-Edition als Grundlagenedition für Philologie und Textgenetik," 80.

possibility to achieve some freedom from the editor's conclusions, whose decisions thus become more transparent and might be checked or contradicted by the reader. Documentation clarifies the *signifiant* without yielding to interpretation of the *signifié*.[189] Of course, any reproduction of a document, whether by photocopying or other means, creates a new document, which will always deprive readers of some of the physical aspects of the original. As Kanzog has pointed out, facsimiles always contain substantially less information than originals, whether in terms of paper properties (e.g. watermarks) or writing (e.g. illegible passages).[190] Reproductions are "reports," whose accuracy is debated by those persons who know the originals. It takes both the facsimile and the transcription to at least approximate the original document.

Aspects and Examples of Diplomatic Transcriptions

Diplomatic transcriptions have been in use for some time now in more or less refined and systematic forms. Some examples from different writers will provide us with a survey of different species of diplomatic transcriptions. Some remarks on the specific characteristics of the Pound autographs and their transcription will conclude this part.

We will first look at some, not strictly editorial, but rather supplementary transcriptions. In his book *From Writer to Reader*, Philip Gaskell uses diplomatic transcriptions as reading aids for facsimiles he reproduces. Unfortunately, he gives no explanation of the editorial conventions and signs employed by him. However, the transcriptions are simple, more simple than the editorial apparatuses so carefully explained in editions. On the one hand, Gaskell's transcriptions stay close to the originals. They adopt the writers' " ^ " (signifying an insertion) and also provide exact representations of individual signs, such as Richardson's serpentine lines.[191] On the other hand, the representation of irregular features remains abstract, that is, Gaskell does not aim at an exact graphical reproduction of what is written down. On one of Thackeray's manuscript pages, for instance, we find a large item number written rather carelessly across the page. The number, added after the actual text was written, is embraced by two almost diagonal lines, of which the upper one accidentally crosses a line of writing. In the transcription, the two lines are written horizontally and the item number is written in a typeface of much smaller size than the original, thus requiring

[189] Zeller, Hans, "Record and Interpretation," 44.
[190] Kanzog, Klaus, "Faksimilieren, transkribieren, edieren," 281f.
[191] Gaskell, Philip, From Writer to Reader, 86f.

substantially less space. Now the irregular line above the item number no longer crosses Thackeray's text.[192]

In the case of the Rosenbach manuscript of Joyce's *Ulysses*, Gaskell does not adopt the most distinct feature of the manuscript page: Joyce started the first line with a left margin of about one quarter of the page. Throughout the page the left margin increases, and whereas the first line occupies three quarters of the total page width, the last line merely occupies half of it.[193] Gaskell's transcription includes Joyce's indentations of single lines, but not the overall shift in the line beginnings. Here, Gaskell's abstraction excludes an element which might allow important conclusions about Joyce's writing habits, if the phenomenon occured on more than one page. Hence, Gaskell not only transforms the manuscript page into an abstract, if not strongly simplifying, representation of its individual elements, but also simplifies the overall topography of the page. Gaskell's rather plain approach is rendered even more controversial by his decision to attach line numbers to lines *in the facsimile*, that is, to type them into the image of the original page immediately in front of Joyce's text. It is left to the readers to decide whether they want to call this an illegitimate manipulation or a useful reading aid.

If Gaskell sometimes ignores what makes manuscripts original, i.e. their topography, we must bear in mind that authenticity is not a virtue by itself. Even a fully exact transcription is not really "authentic," and we should not fall victim to the naïve assumption that a diplomatic transcription just represents what is written on the original page. We must not forget that every transcription involves a chronological or, in editorial terms, genetic aspect. When we transcribe a typescript with corrections in ink, we already deal with a genetic process, as typing was followed by handwriting. Whereas manuscript pages with only two, clearly distinguishable layers of writing are indeed a simple case, other autographs are much more complicated. In order to make this complexity more transparent, many genetic editions provide complicated apparatuses now slighted by readers, which led to Zeller's abovementioned complaint. However, it is another naïve assumption to believe that only an inctricate apparatus can represent the genesis of a page appropriately. Rather, a diplomatic transcription can substantially contribute to our understanding of the writing process.

In a printed edition, the editor will have difficulties in covering all genetic aspects of a page in the context of a diplomatic transcription. In his Kleist edition,[194] Roland Reuss attempted the, in typographical terms, strongly refined combination of all genetic stages on one page, using different typefaces and character sizes to represent all alterations made on a sheet.

---

[192] Gaskell, Philip, From Writer to Reader, 162f.
[193] Gaskell, Philip, From Writer to Reader, 226f.
[194] Kleist, Heinrich von, Sämtliche Werke, ed. Roland Reuss, Basel et.al. 1988-.

Whereas the classic genetic apparatus lacks the topography of the page, Reuss maintains it. But, as Zeller remarked, encoding several layers of writing in one transcription is hardly reader-friendly.[195] In addition to this, the Reuss approach is problematic because the transcriptions no longer function as mere reading aids, but already interpret Kleist's writing. Every one of the transcriptions has a genetic perspective and suggests a genetic chronology, which means that readers are not able to read the pages in a more or less "neutral" form. Of course, even the diplomatic editor knows that neutrality is even more rare in editing than it is in politics. Instead, we are confronted with a constituted text in disguise, or rather, an odd combination of constitution and diplomatic transcription. The same applies to D. E. Sattler's, otherwise pioneering, edition of Friedrich Hölderlin's works.[196] Here, too, a system of typefaces is used to distinguish all genetic stages on one page. Hölderlin's often irregular lines are slightly regularized, so each line can be numbered. The Innsbruck edition of the works of Georg Trakl[197] takes a different approach. The genesis of the pages is not explicitly reproduced in the diplomatic transcriptions, which do not even distinguish typographically between typescript and handwriting. To spot the difference, readers must always consult the facsimiles. Hence, the Trakl transcriptions function as reading aids supplementing the facsimiles, without conveying additional genetic information, as in the other editions mentioned.

We should now move to the Pound papers and their difficulties. It may be true that Pound the writer often imagined the page like a painter or a book designer would.[198] Unfortunately, Pound's manuscripts show few signs of perfectly imagined designs, but rather of the practical aspects of the writer's craft, i.e. revising and discarding. Obviously, we have to be content with ragged drafts and ink spots, rather than William Morris-like perfection. The coarse appearance of the Pound papers poses particular problems when it comes to transcribing.

Non-textual elements are one difficulty editors must be aware of. Those elements demand a decision as to whether they should be reproduced in their exact shape or be replaced by a typographical standard sign that approximates their meaning. Pound's famous "Z," as it occurs so frequently between the lines of many drafts, is often read as a dash, but is not exactly like it, because Pound used conventional dashes, too, which suggests a difference. Rainey isolates two forms of the autograph sign – one version of about 2-3 mm in

---

195 Zeller, Hans, "Die Faksimile-Edition als Grundlagenedition für Philologie und Textgenetik," 98ff.

196 Friedrich Hölderlin, Werke. Frankfurter Ausgabe, ed. D. E. Sattler, Frankfurt/Main et.al. 1979-.

197 See part V.1.b of the bibliography.

198 McGann, Jerome, The Textual Condition, 142.

length which "usually appeared at the end of a phrase or line, placed in roughly the same position as would be a comma or period," also occuring with the same frequency. Rainey concludes that the smaller mark serves to mark the ending of a small unit of composition, a single line or even less. The larger version of the mark, of 5-6 mm size, is put near the left margin, between two lines and with a larger amount of interlinear space preceding and following. Occuring two or three times on one page, it "registered the completion or the new beginning of a larger unit of composition, most typically some five to six lines, or something resembling a stanza."[199] When moving on to typewritten drafts, Pound deleted the larger marks and most of the smaller ones, transforming the rest into commas. Hence, the z-sign cannot be translated adequately into some standard typographical sign and should be retained by the editor.

Another frequent instance of non-textual elements are drawings, as in the case of item 34, where a piece of text is supplemented by three straight lines with a small circle between them. The question whether and how this drawing is to be reproduced in the transcription must be answered even before we decide whether the drawing has any immediate connection to the text on the page. After all, we might overlook something that links the textual to the non-textual elements. If we want to keep our transcriptions as documentary and neutral as possible, we cannot avoid to incorporate the drawing into the transcription. The drawing is part of the topography of the page; if it was sketched before the text was written, it is even crucial for the form of the text. If a drawing has no connection to a literary work at all (e.g. a musical score), it should still be reproduced for documentary purposes and as a reading aid, an approach adopted, for instance, in Sattler's Hölderlin edition.

Sometimes drafts or notes contain textual, but non-literary elements. The newspaper clipping attached to item 116 is a good example of such an element. As an editor might argue, the text of the advertisement can be deciphered easily in the facsimile, was not written by Pound and should not be included in the diplomatic transcription. On the other hand, the newspaper clipping has been selected, in an authorial act, by Pound and does in fact contain an authorial element: the frame drawn by the poet. Hence, the editor is obliged to reproduce the advertisement in the transcription. Item 282 presents a slightly different case. Its left side bears the letter-head of an "Albergo Bristol" in Rapallo. The exact text of the letter-head can be ignored, as the Trakl editors did in similar cases.[200] A transcription of item 282, however, should contain a reproduction of the letter-head, because the facsimile is difficult to read.

---

[199] Rainey, Lawrence S., Ezra Pound and the Monument of Culture, 23.

[200] Comp. the postal stamp in: Trakl, Georg, Sämtliche Werke und Briefwechsel II.238f.

Other Poundian autographs include additions written into the margins at irregular angles (e.g. items 1, 2, 233). The angles of authorial additions can convey information about the sequence in which they were added to the manuscript. But the same can be learned from a facsimile, which is why the reproduction of irregular angles is usually at the editor's discretion. Their reproduction is reasonable when, for instance, a word was written diagonally across several lines and cannot be linked to one of them. Putting the word into an horizontal angle might then link the word to one specific line, which would create a wrong impression.

Objectives of Diplomatic Transcriptions

First, it must be emphasized that diplomatic transcriptions are only fully valid with proper documentation, as provided by facsimiles. According to Tanselle, a fully-fledged diplomatic edition should "provide full-size photographic reproductions, accompanied on facing pages by transcriptions and supplied (somewhere) with annotation explaining the physical details that are not evident from the reproductions."[201] Facsimiles not only allow readers to interpret the manuscript, but also create the possibility of controlling editorial decisions[202]. Second, diplomatic transcriptions should be governed by the principle of textual accuracy. We follow Tanselle's statement that the "text of a document is whatever it is, and any alteration to smooth out a presumed difficulty creates a different text."[203] Pound's textual errors, his misspellings and typos, should not be corrected.

In total, accuracy and legibility should reign supreme. However, transriptions, although textually accurate, do not have to provide photographic reproductions of the original documents. Hence, the size of characters may differ from the original, especially where handwriting is concerned. As a consequence, line lengths may vary and the overall topography of a page may look different in absolute terms, while identical with the original in relative terms. Re-sizing of fonts is legitimate for the sake of legibility. The editor may e.g. enlarge one letter in order to keep it clearly distinguishable from its context.

Two of the most characteristic features of Pound's drafts are spacing and indentations, which challenge any editor of a reading text. In Tryphonopoulos's and Surette's edition of Pound's letters to O. R. Agresti, standard spacing is used throughout and all marks of punctuation have been

[201] Tanselle, George Thomas, A Rationale of Textual Criticism, 60.
[202] Zeller, Hans, "Record and Interpretation," 44.
[203] Tanselle, George Thomas, A Rationale of Textual Criticism, 62.

moved close to the nearest letter.[204] The diplomatic transcriptions for *The Fifth Decad*, however, should retain the original spacing (always bearing in mind the above remarks on relative topologies) and indentations.

In order to reconstruct the genesis of individual manuscripts and typescripts, an edition of *The Fifth Decad* should make extensive use of the possibilities of the electronic medium. The temporal dimension of the writing process could find its representation in multiple graphical layers describing the relative chronology of Pound's autographs. Thus, readers would be allowed to view the usual full trancriptions as well as transcriptions of single genetic stages. For instance, a typescript page subsequently revised by Pound with ink and pencil could be dissolved into three different layers, offering readers three images: the plain typescript page, the typescript plus ink revisions, and the final genetic stage including the pencil revisions. As should be noted, this procedure cannot be applied to every sheet of the Pound papers. The first general exception are sheets with only one layer of writing. The second exception are sheets containing additional layers of a marginal nature, like a pencilled page number or bibliographical note in the upper right corner. The addition does not affect the textual genesis of the page and needs therefore not be represented as a genetic stage. In other cases, ink and pencil revisions exist sidy by side, but no genetic sequence can be established, because the two layers do not overlap each other. Hence, it is impossible to grant one of them priority and to establish a genetic sequence.

In total, diplomatic transcriptions of Pound autographs should seek to steer a middle course between the plain functionality of the mentioned Trakl edition and the large amount of editorial interventions in the Hölderlin and Kleist transcriptions. We want neither mere reading aids, nor combi-transcriptions mixing genetic interpretation and documentation. The reading aid cannot provide us with genetic interpretations,[205] whereas the German genetic-diplomatic approach deprives us of the possibility of viewing a more or less neutral transcription. It takes the electronic medium to achieve a compromise.

---

[204] Pound, Ezra, "I Cease Not to Yowl," xxvii.

[205] Comp. Grésillon's position in: Grésillon, Almuth, Literarische Handschriften, 157.

IV.2 Conclusion: Objectives of a Modern Genetic Edition

If we want to explain the aims of a genetic edition, we once more have to talk about history. According to Scheibe, the goal of any edition should be the visualization of the historical process of writing.[206] And Espagne called on editors to integrate into the study of texts their historical dimension.[207] This is particularly true of the genetic edition. It should represent a historical process: As opposed to the traditional edition, which aims at a stable reading text, it should be an open edition and not only constitute a text, but a process with many branches and dead ends. In Pound's case, as with other writers, we do not always encounter "texts" among the autographs. Often we find mere "writing," fragments or quotations; these, however, are a substantial genetic part of what will become the text of the poem. We also find, for instance, associative marginal notes which cannot be included into the text of a Canto, but still belong to the genesis of the work, as they accompany the creative process of writing.

Hence, what a Pound edition requires is not actual *textual* criticism, but the historization of the work's genesis – "work criticism" as a historical science. It has to rid itself of the finalistic assumptions that often go together with a teleological concept of what a work of literature is supposed to be (usually the published version in a book). In Pound's case, the published printing of *The Fifth Decad* constitutes a paradigmatic field around which all immediately related materials should be grouped. At the same time, though, an edition must include the small splinters and nameless fragments of writing in its editorial network. We demand an archeology of writing which acknowledges the historicity of the material Pound used and of the literary concepts he developed. This criticism has to work *diachronically*, by unfolding the multiple layers of writing in time, and *synchronically*, by exploring the links between the *Cantos* and Pound's essays, or between original thoughts and quotations. You could compare those two levels to the x and y axis in a mathematical graph: Both are necessary for exact descriptions.

We regard textual stability as a phantom and as no more than a theoretical aid. The creative process of writing is not a sequence of versions that are stable in themselves, as Scheibe seems to believe.[208] The genetic edition must instead adopt a notion of textual fluidity based on Gabler's concept of a continuous production text. We support McGann when he states:

---

[206] Scheibe, Siegfried, "Zu einigen Grundprinzipien einer historisch-kritischen Ausgabe," 7.

[207] Espagne, Michel, De l'archive au texte, 169.

[208] Scheibe, Siegfried, "Zu einigen Grundprinzipien einer historisch-kritischen Ausgabe," 4.

"If we define text as words in a certain order, then we have to say that the ordering of the words in every text is *in fact*, at the factive level, unstable. No text, either conceptually or empirically, can have the 'ordering of its words' defined or specified as invariant. Variation, in other words, is the invariant rule of the textual condition."[209] Stability is not a feasible concept for a genetic edition anyway, as genetic stability, too, is very fragile. Grésillon claims that a genetic edition should contain all textual witnesses in the sequence of their writing.[210] This objective is fairly idealistic, as chronology, especially in poetic drafts, is often not to be established. As Mitterand says about Zola, "Il est malaise de reconstituer l'ordre chronologique de ces sections, d'autant plus qu'à partir d'un certain moment, elles progressent en éventail, et simultanément."[211]

Only rarely does each draft carry a date and tell us when it was written. More often, we have to use intrinsic criteria to establish what are merely *relative* chronologies. Quite correctly, Hurlebusch distinguishes between absolute chronologies (the exact sequence of alterations of one passage) from relative chronologies (the temporal relation of alterations in different parts of the text). As regards Pound, we can speak of absolute chronologies only in a broad sense, as Scheibe defined it for the historical-critical edition, meaning the assignment of general work stages to the biography and contemporary history of an author.[212] We learn from Pound's letters about when he finished certain Cantos, but not when exactly he discarded an individual draft.

Therefore we cannot establish the chronology of the writing of *The Fifth Decad*, only its genesis. The difference is easily explained. Whereas "chronology" determines exact temporal relations based on absolute, extra-textual points of orientation (date, month, year), "genesis" is to be understood as a process located within a relative, textual frame of reference. Thus, each authorial or non-authorial act is defined in relation to other levels of the textual system, not as a point in time. The changing of a word must be read against the word written before in the same place and is defined on a textual basis. Strictly speaking, only if the author has attached a date to the correction can we postulate a rudimentary chronology.

To be established, the genetic dossier requires the reconstruction of a chronological process, but unfortunately, chronology is the weak point of genetic editing. According to Boetius, relative chronologies "are simplifications that contain a strong interpretive component."[213] Hence, one

---

209 McGann, Jerome, The Textual Condition, 185.
210 Grésillon, Almuth, Literarische Handschriften, 230.
211 Mitterand, Henri, "Programme et préconstruit génétiques," 196.
212 Scheibe, Siegfried, "Zu einigen Grundprinzipien einer historisch-kritischen Ausgabe," 6.
213 Boetius, Henning, "Preliminary Reflections on a Generative Theory of Editing," 154.

objective of any genetic edition must be to develop an awareness of its own relativity and of its strong narrative component. After all, a genetic edition is a narrative edition. What the editor tells is the story of the writing of the text, a story in which the editor, not the author, presents the plots and sub-plots of the tale.

In addition to this, the editor must identify the agents participating and intervening in the production of a text. What Shakespeare philology has been doing for more than a century now must be applied to genetic editing. If the paradigms of writing are as clearly separated as in Pound's case, in which the author writes the text virtually without interventions by a publisher, then the edition, despite its processual approach, has the obligation to create a clear-cut profile of the paradigm it edits. It must delineate the edges of the paradigm and therefore reproduce the final state of the text before it entered the next socio-cultural paradigm, i.e. the publication process. The paradigm of writing is governed by an interaction between the author and his texts and sources, whereas the subsequent paradigm is constituted by the interests of several social agents. An edition can display the difference between both paradigms. Hence, it should use the most advanced stages of composition to constitute a text which represents the poem at the edge of its first paradigm, when the text left the hands of its author. This serves to underline the distinctly individual character of the authorial text, as opposed to the social product of a publishing process.

To explore the authorial paradigm to its fullest extent, a genetic edition should realize the complete potential of the genetic dossier. In the case of a historically charged poem like the *Cantos*, the divisions between sources and authorial product are blurred, and reading notes occupy a curious position between source document and literary text. Using the capabilities of the electronic medium, the edition must represent the full range of authorial materials from marginal notes to final setting copy, and may even include relevant source documents. This emphasis on the documentary character of the edition leads to another important point.

A genetic edition of Pound's work has to intermediate between document and text. Editing the pre-publication materials, it must provide users with an overview of the relevant parts of the Pound archive. It should list the documents in the archive with their bibliographical, physical and textual properties. At the same time, the edition should approach textual form by establishing, between the separate documents, such links as allow for the reconstruction of textual coherence. An electronic genetic edition can include both the archival documentation and the text constituted from the documents. We therefore agree with Peter Shillingsburg's definition of a scholarly edition, which should be:

> 1. an archive of historical documents whose iconography is intact but whose words can be searched by computer aid; 2. an archive of edited texts, or at least one edited text, produced to reflect the work of a historian or of several [...]; and 3. an archive that is introduced historically, critically, and textually.[214]

The genetic edition not only has to inermediate between document and text, but also, on another level, between text and image. There are still huge differences between the traditional apparatus-based edition and recent diplomatic editions of the Stroemfeld group (Sattler, Reuss, Zwerschina). The former type centers on the constitued text, whose variants are often banished to an apparatus, which itself is marginalized by its position somewhere at the end of the edition. And often it only includes variants from printings of the text, not from manuscripts. Facsimile editions, on the other hand, offer source images and diplomatic transcriptions which can easily outweigh the constituted text. In both quantitative and qualitative terms, such editions are dominated by facsimiles and diplomatic transcriptions. Both types of edition have different objectives, which is legitimate: The apparatus edition is chiefly interested in text, whereas the diplomatic edition uses images to realize its notion of semi-authentic documentation. To reduce the gap between the two types, the modern genetic edition should use the electronic medium, which allows editors to present facsimiles, transcriptions, constituted and published texts as display modes of *equal* value.

For a genetic edition, to embrace the full spectrum from document to constituted text means to develop a liberal notion of text. Usually, the reading text is still edited in accordance with a statement by Housman: "Textual criticism is a science, and, since it comprises recension and emendation, it is also an art. It is the science of discovering error in texts and the art of removing it".[215] Housman's definition is the polished memorial of the traditional notion of textual criticism. The genetic edition, however, has to be aware of alternative concepts of how to edit textual errors. We know at least three such concepts.[216]

First, a *contextual concept* as championed by Kraft who states that textual errors are defined by a lack of meaning within the context of the work. For Kraft, meaning does not denote what the editor regards as factual correctness. Rather, it refers to the genetic conditions.[217] Hence, if an author gives a wrong date, because he was misinformed by a source, Kraft would not

---

[214] Shillingsburg, Peter L., Resisting Texts, 24.

[215] Housman, Alfred E., "The Application of Thought to Textual Criticism," 131.

[216] We will not consider any psychological concept of error. For a purely psychological typology of errors see Kay, Janice, "Psychological Aspects of Spelling," 1083f.

[217] See Kraft, Herbert, Die Geschichtlichkeit literarischer Texte, 46, also Scheibe, Siegfried, "Zu einigen Grundprinzipien einer historisch-kritischen Ausgabe," 43.

consider this an instance of error. Typing "New Yorick" instead of "New York," however, creates an error, because "Yorick" makes no sense in most contexts.

Second, we distinguish a *pragmatic concept* of error. Scheibe, while admitting that textual versions "should be reproduced in an edition in their transmitted form and that only this transmitted form as a whole represents the work as willed and arranged for by the author," nevertheless permits editors to correct "obvious textual faults,"[218] assuming that the author would not have authorized them. Hugh Kenner takes the same approach when he suggests the following editorial principles for a (conventional, not genetic) Pound edition: correct clear misprints, especially the printers'; forget encyclopedic accuracy, for it was not intended by Pound; record printed variants and indicate them by inserting a note.[219]

Third, we acknowledge a *diplomatic concept* of error. Commenting upon the irregularity of handwritten documents, Tanselle remarks: "The messiness of such documents is an essential part of their nature, and a documentary edition is not performing its function if it does not report as much of that untidiness as photographic reproduction, typographic transcription, and supplementary discussion can convey."[220] Emphasizing the documentary character of the genetic edition, we cannot but support Tanselle's notion.

However, being documentary is not without flaws. One danger inherent in a genetic edition of strongly documentary orientation is that the same methods used to conserve the irregularities of writing and the messiness of authorial documents can entail the aesthetization of manuscripts. In the wake of the Kafka edition by Reuss, reviewers praised the "beauty" and gesture-like character of Kafka's handwriting. But in order to analyze documents in neutral terms, we have to avoid what Espagne termed the "pan-aesthetization" of manuscripts.[221] The genetic edition must not create a new work of art. Rather, it should draw our attention to aspects of the work which, at their best, embrace both the bibliographical and the hermeneutical, the process and the result. It possesses the virtue of "bringing into focus a form or forms of the work not attained in publication."[222] It explores not only the production of a text, but also the writing mechanisms on which production rests. And it allows us to view the work from the perspective of the writer (in the literal sense of the word) by representing the author as a craftsman and an agent

---

[218] Scheibe, Siegfried, "Theoretical Problems of the Authorization and Constitution of Texts," 185.
[219] Kenner, Hugh, "Notes on Amateur Emendations," 28.
[220] Tanselle, George Thomas, A Rationale of Textual Criticism, 62.
[221] Espagne, Michel, "Pour une épistémanalyse des études génétiques," 37.
[222] Gabler, Hans W., "The Text as Process and the Problem of Intentionality," 108.

within a dynamic process which takes us beyond the concept of the stable, published text. We may know the final result of the author's efforts, but genetic editing can guide us to places, sources and words we have not known before. The editor can unearth them and plot some paths through unknown territory. After that, readers have to find their way alone, maybe with no point to begin with.

IV.3 A Genetic Chronology of *The Fifth Decad of Cantos*

The Roman numerals in brackets give the years according to the Italian fascist calendar as introduced by Mussolini and as used by Pound in many of his manuscripts and letters. The fascist year began in October. I am particularly grateful to Prof. Richard Taylor for providing me with his unpublished annals for *The Fifth Decad*, which have allowed me to clarify several dates.

1920-1930

- 1928 – Pound begins early work on C49: "1) Pound received a Chinese book from his parents some time before March 1, 1928. 2) A Miss Thseng (i.e. Tseng), a descendant of Tseng Tzu, visited Pound in Rapallo before May 17, and helped him to 'decipher' the poems. 3) Pound copied out the English paraphrase of the poems on July 30 for his father, but did not mail the letter" (Palandri, Angela J., "The 'Seven Lakes Canto' Revisited," 53).

1931 (year IX – X)

- Pound begins to date his letters according to the fascist calendar. As Stock claims, he does so from "Anno X" on (Stock, Noel, The Life of Ezra Pound, 299). But Pound starts earlier, in year IX, that is, before October 1931 (Pound, Ezra, Pound's Cavalcanti, 9; also, more general, Tytell, John, Ezra Pound: The Solitary Volcano, 224).

1932 (year X – XI)

- From 16 June 1932, Pound's letters to Zukofsky are dated according to the fascist calendar. From 1935-37, the letterhead includes both the Christian and the fascist year (Pound, Ezra, Pound/Zukofsky, xxiv).

1933 (year XI – XII)

- The ms. of J/M is finished in February 1933 (See Pound's introductory note in J/M).

- Pound travels and writes to Olga Rudge from Rome (March), Florence (March), Woking/Surrey (May), Paris (May), Bolzano (September).
- Pound spends July 1933 doing library research in Siena.
- C41 written.
- Pound reads Arthur Kitson's *The Bankers' Conspiracy.*
- Pound is granted an audience with Mussolini.

1934 (year XII – XIII)

- Pound travels to Venice, Salzburg, Rome.
- 2 December 1934: Pound is angry about his publishers, Farrar, because he thinks the firm is too slow in publishing his works; now he is uncertain about the publication date of the next group of Cantos (Gordon, David M. (ed.), Ezra Pound and James Laughlin: Selected Letters, 36).
- [24] December 1934: Pound writes a litany against usurers (items 246f.).

1935 (year XIII – XIV)

- Pound publishes J/M.
- Reads proofs of C31-41 in January / February.
- Pound reads Coughlin and Brooks Adams's *Law of Civilization and Decay* in May 1935 (see a letter to Olga Rudge of 29 May [1935], Rapallo, BL Rudge I, 54 / 16 / 408). At the same time, Pound reads Claudius Salmasius (See Surette, Leon, Pound in Purgatory, 200).
- Pound visits Wörgl in August 1935 (see letter to Homer Pound, 3 August [1935], BL Pound, II; also Flory, The American Ezra Pound, 72f.).
- In December 1935 Pound works on C45 and begins C47 (see letter to Olga Rudge, 28 [December 1935], Rapallo, BL Rudge, I).

1936 (year XIV – XV)

- On 31 January 1936 Pound sends C46 to Laughlin (see letter to J. Laughlin, 31 January [1936], in: Ezra Pound and James Laughlin: Selected Letters, 54ff.).

- On 4 February 1936 Pound sends a finished Canto (C46?) to Rudge (see letter to Olga Rudge, 4 February [1936], Rapallo, BL Rudge, I, 54 / 16 / 431).
- C45 is published as: "Canto – "With Usura"," in: Prosperity IV.3 (February 1936), London, 44 (P&P VII.21f.).
- C46 is published as: "Canto XLVI," in: New Democracy VI.1 (March 1936), 14-16 (P&P VII.28-31), without a date at the end of the Canto.
- According to Hesse, Pound finishes C51 in January 1936 (Hesse, Eva, Ezra Pound: Usura-Cantos XLV und LI, 82), but in a letter to Joseph Ibbotson he writes: "I havent yet got to the Fuhrer, but some lines on Rudolf Hess in a draft/ not yet settled on where it can go" ([20 April] 1936, Rapallo, in: Pound, Ezra, Letters to Ibbotson, 49ff.).
- From July to September 1936 Pound visits the library in Siena, where he reads about the history of the *Monte dei Paschi* and Antonio Zobi (see letter to Homer Pound, 12 Aug 1936, Siena, Beinecke 43 / 61 / 2699).
- In August 1936 Pound begins C42 (see letter to Dorothy Pound, [11 August 1936], Lilly Pound, III). He writes from Siena on 12 August 1936: "This is the only town where I have ever been able to live in a palace with a painted ceiling. With a pine tree and the cornice of a renaissance church under this window" (Pound, Ezra, Ezra Pound and Japan, 31).
- Pound spends September 1936 in Venice.
- He mentions his work on C50 in a letter to J. Laughlin of 2 September 1936 (in: Ezra Pound and James Laughlin, 64): "I have done canto carrying on to Marengo."
- On 5 September 1936 Pound finishes C44 and sends a copy to Dorothy Pound (see letter to Dorothy Pound, [5 September 1936], Lilly Pound, III; item 327).
- In a letter to Odon Por of 7 September 1936, Pound mentions that he has finished work on C42-44: "I have worked in Siena Tuscanyi Lorraine Hapsburg. 1765 to 1792. P Leopoldo and Ferd. III FURER along, more enlightened than any modern state. Free trade error corrected in controll at frontier. Nap. ended state debt. taxes halved. etc. etc. I have just done THREE CANTOS of shout about that and Monte dei Paschi so EZ SEZ and he KNOWZ." (quot. in Redman, Tim, Ezra Pound and Italian Fascism, 172).
- In a letter of 17 September 1936 Pound states: "my mind is on concrete things. Have shipped the three Sienese Cantos [C42-44], and have a fourth pretty well set [C50?]. but a few hunks of Orient and Adonis cult [C47]

<already drafted> must intervene" (see Ezra Pound and James Laughlin, 65).

- On 26 September 1936 Pound sends C42-44 to Harriet Monroe (see letter to J. Laughlin, 26 September [1936], in: Ezra Pound and James Laughlin, 67).
- On 30 October 1936 Pound sends C45 and C47-51 to Rudge (see letter to Olga Rudge, 30 October [1936], Rapallo, BL Rudge, I, 54 /17 / 448). He writes to Rudge about having drafted the rest of the decad except C42-44, C46 and C50 and expresses his hope that the remaining Cantos will fit in (30 October [1936], Rapallo, BL Rudge, I, 54 /17 / 447).
- C46 is published as: "CANTO XLVI," in: New Directions in Prose and Poetry, Norfolk (Ct.) [November] 1936, 25-29 (see P&P VII.1-3). The final line of the Canto is a date: "30 Jan XIV" (= 1936), the day before Pound sent C46 to Laughlin.
- On 2 December 1936 Pound sends C42-51 to Faber & Faber (see letter to Agnes Bedford, 2 December [1936], Lilly Pound, II).

1937 (year XV – XVI)

- In January / February 1937 Pound corrects the galleys of *The Fifth Decad of Cantos* (Redman, Tim, Ezra Pound and Italian Fascism, 176, also see a letter from Dorothy Cowling [F&F], 5 February 1937, BL Pound, I).
- On 28 February 1937 Pound finishes correcting the page proofs: "anyhow I have Korecte prooves of 42 / 5I" (Ezra Pound and James Laughlin, 75).
- GK is probably written between 2 March and 22 April 1937 (Surette, Leon, Pound in Purgatory, 200).
- Pound publishes "CANTOS XLII-XLIV," in: Criterion XVI.64 (April 1937), 405-423. (P&P VII.155-173).
- Pound publishes *The Fifth Decad of Cantos*, London: Faber & Faber 1937 [1st ed. of 3 June 1937].
- In August / September 1937 Pound reads Kung's *Ta Hio*, *Analects*, and *The Unwavering Middle*, as well as Mencius ("Mang Tsze (The Ethics of Mencius)" (1938), in: SP, 96).
- Pound publishes *The Fifth Decad of Cantos*, New York / Toronto: Farrer & Rinehart 1937 [1st American ed. of 29 November 1937].

V. Bibliography

Entries by one author are arranged in chronological order. For frequently cited titles, abbreviations are given in brackets. Rare and old titles have been provided with full bibliographical information including the publisher.

V.1 Primary Literature

V.1.a Ezra Pound

Editions of The Fifth Decad of Cantos *and included Cantos (except translations)*

(The entries in this section are mostly based on Gallup 1969.)

- "Canto – "With Usura"" [C45], in: *Prosperity* IV.3 (Feb. 1936), London, 44. (P&P VII.21f.)
- "Canto XLVI," in: *New Democracy* VI.1 (Mar. 1936), 14-16. No date at the end. (P&P VII.28-31)
- "CANTO XLVI," in: New Directions in Prose and Poetry, Norfolk (Ct.) [Nov.] 1936, 25-29. (P&P VII.1-3)
- "CANTOS XLII-XLIV," in: *Criterion* XVI.64 (Apr. 1937), 405-423. (P&P VII.155-173)
- The Fifth Decad of Cantos, London: Faber & Faber 1937. [1st ed., 3 June 1937]
- The Fifth Decad of Cantos, New York / Toronto: Farrer & Rinehart 1937. [1st American ed., 29 Nov 1937]
- The Fifth Decad of Cantos, Norfolk (Conn.): New Directions 1937. [2nd issue, summer 1940]
- "Canto XLV," in: A Selection of Poems by Ezra Pound, London: Faber & Faber 1940.
- Spearhead: 10 Years' Experimental Writing in America, New York: New Directions 1947. [incl. C45, C49, C51]
- The Cantos of Ezra Pound, New York: New Directions 1948.
- "If this be treason......," Siena: Tip. Nuova 1948. [incl. C45]

- Seventy Cantos, London: Faber & Faber 1950.
- The Cantos of Ezra Pound, London: Faber & Faber 1954.
- The Cantos of Ezra Pound, London: Faber & Faber 1964.
- The Cantos (1-95), New York: New Directions 1965.
- Stock, Noel (ed.), EZRA POUND Perspectives: Essays in Honor of His Eightieth Birthday, Chicago: H. Regnery 1965, 188. [incl. ms. opening of C45]
- Selected Cantos of Ezra Pound, London: Faber & Faber 1967. [incl. C42-45]
- The Cantos of Ezra Pound, New York: New Directions 1970.
- Cantos Scelti, Milano: Arnoldo Mondadori Editore [1973]. [incl. C43, transl. by Mary de Rachewiltz]
- Con Usura, [Milano: Locatelli 1974]. [C45]
- Selected Poems 1908-1959, London: Faber & Faber 1975. [incl. C45, C47, C49, C51]
- The Cantos of Ezra Pound, London: Faber & Faber 1976.
- "Blue Dun," in: Fly Fisherman, Dorset (Vt.) VIII.3 (Spring 1977), 28. [part of C51]
- The Cantos of Ezra Pound, New York: New Directions [13]1995. [this printing was used as a base text for quotations from the Cantos]

Other Poetry

- Pound, Ezra, The Collected Shorter Poems, London [2]1968.
- Pound, Ezra, The Collected Early Poems, New York 1976.

Prose

- Pound, Ezra, "Vortex. Pound.," in: *Blast* 1 (20 June 1914), 153-154.
- Pound, Ezra, Gaudier-Brzeska: A Memoir, London / New York: John Lane 1916.
- Pound, Ezra, Instigations, New York: Boni and Liveright 1920.
- Pound, Ezra, Indiscretions or, Une Revue de Deux Mondes, Paris: Three Mountains Press 1923.
- Pound, Ezra, "Preface," in: Oppen, George, Discrete Series, New York: The Objectivist Press 1934, v-vi.

- Pound, Ezra, Jefferson and/or Mussolini: L'Idea Statale, Fascism as I Have Seen It, New York: Liveright / London: Stanley Nott 1935.
- Pound, Ezra, Polite Essays, London: Faber & Faber 1937, repr. New York 1966.
- Pound, Ezra, The Spirit of Romance, Norfolk (Conn.) 1953 [1st ed. 1910].
- Pound, Ezra, Literary Essays, Norfolk (Conn.) 1954.
- Pound, Ezra, Impact: Essays on Ignorance and the Decline of American Civilization, ed. Noel Stock, Chicago 1960.
- Pound, Ezra, Guide to Kulchur, London 1966 [1st ed. 1938] (= GK).
- Pound, Ezra, Selected Prose 1909-1965, ed. William Cookson, London 1973.
- Pound, Ezra, Ezra Pound and Music: The Complete Criticism, ed. R. Murray Schafer, New York 1977.
- Pound, Ezra, "Ezra Pound Speaking": Radio Speeches of World War II, ed. Leonard W. Doob, Westport (Conn.) / London 1978.
- Pound, Ezra, Ezra Pound and Japan: Letters and Essays, Redding Ridge 1987.
- Pound, Ezra, Ezra Pound's Poetry and Prose Contributions to Periodicals, vol. V, eds. Lea Baechler / A. Walton Litz / James Longenbach, New York / London 1991 (= P&P V).
- Pound, Ezra, Ezra Pound's Poetry and Prose Contributions to Periodicals, vol. VI, eds. Lea Baechler / A. Walton Litz / James Longenbach, New York / London 1991 (= P&P VI).
- Pound, Ezra, Ezra Pound's Poetry and Prose Contributions to Periodicals, vol. VII, eds. Lea Baechler / A. Walton Litz / James Longenbach, New York / London 1991 (= P&P VII).
- Pound, Ezra, Ezra Pound's Poetry and Prose Contributions to Periodicals, vol. XI, eds. Lea Baechler / A. Walton Litz / James Longenbach, New York / London 1991 (= P&P XI).
- Pound, Ezra, Machine Art and Other Writings: The Lost Thought of the Italian Years, ed. Maria Luisa Ardizzone, Durham 1996.
- Sieburth, Richard (ed.), A Walking Tour in Southern France: Ezra Pound among the Troubadours, New York 1992.

Translations

- Pound, Ezra, The Classic Anthology Defined by Confucius, London s.d. [1954].
- Pound, Ezra, Ezra Pound's Cavalcanti Poems, London 1966.
- Confucius, The Great Digest – The Unwobbling Pivot – The Analects, New York 1969.

- Pound, Ezra, Pound's Cavalcanti: An Edition of the Translations, Notes, and Essays, ed. David Anderson, Princeton (N.J.) 1983.
- Pound, Ezra, Forked Branches: Translations of Medieval Poems, ed. Charlotte Ward, Iowa City 1985.

Letters

- Pound, Ezra, Letter to the Editor, in: Criterion XVII.66 (1937), 119.
- Pound, Ezra, Pound / Joyce: The Letters of Ezra Pound to James Joyce, with Pound's Essays on Joyce, ed. Forrest Read, New York 1967.
- Pound, Ezra, The Selected Letters of Ezra Pound, 1907-1941, ed. D. D. Paige, London 1971.
- Pound, Ezra, Letters to Ibbotson, 1935-1952, ed. V. I. Mondolfo / M. Hurley, Orono 1979.
- Pound, Ezra, The Letters of Ezra Pound and Wyndham Lewis, ed. Timothy Materer, New York 1985.
- Pound, Ezra, Pound/Zukofsky: Selected Letters of Ezra Pound and Louis Zukofsky, ed. Barry Ahearn, New York 1987.
- Pound, Ezra, Pound/The Little Review: The Letters of Ezra Pound to Margaret Anderson. The Little Review Correspondence, eds. Thomas L. Scott / Melvin J. Friedman / Jackson R. Bryer, New York 1988.
- Pound, Ezra, Selected Letters of Ezra Pound to John Quinn, 1915-1924, ed. Timothy Materer, Durham 1991.
- Pound, Ezra, Ezra Pound and James Laughlin: Selected Letters, ed. David M. Gordon, New York 1994.
- Pound, Ezra, Ezra Pound and Senator Bronson Cutting: A Political Correspondence, 1930-1935, eds. E. P. Walkiewicz / Hugh Witemeyer, Albuquerque 1995.
- Pound, Ezra, "I Cease Not to Yowl": Ezra Pound's Letters to Olivia Rossetti Agresti, ed. Demetres P. Tryphonopoulos / Leon Surette, Urbana / Chicago 1998.
- Sutton, Walter (ed.), Pound, Thayer, Watson, and *The Dial*: A Story in Letters, Gainesville u.a. 1994.

V.1.b Other Authors

- Adams, Brooks, The Law of Civilization and Decay. An Essay on History, London: Swan Sonnenschein / New York: MacMillan 1895.
- Adams, Charles Francis, A Cycle of Adams Letters, 1861-1865, ed. Worthington C. Ford, 2 vols., Boston / New York: Houghton Mifflin / The Riverside Press 1920.
- Adams, Charles Francis, Charles Francis Adams, 1835-1915: An Autobiography, New York 1968.
- Adams, Henry, Letters of Henry Adams (1858-1891), vol. I, ed. Worthington C. Ford, Boston / New York: Houghton Mifflin 1930.
- Adams, John, The Works of John Adams, Second President of the United States, ed. Charles Francis Adams, 10 vols., Boston: Little, Brown 1850-56, repr. New York 1971.
- Adams, John, Diary and Autobiography of John Adams, eds. L.H. Butterfield / Leonard C. Faber / Wendell D. Garrett, 4 vols., Cambridge (Mass.) 1961.
- Adams, John / Jefferson, Thomas, The Adams-Jefferson Letters, ed. Lester J. Cappon, 2 vols., Chapel Hill 1959.
- Adams, John Quincy, Memoirs of John Quincy Adams, comprising portions of his Diary from 1795 to 1848, ed. Charles Francis Adams, 12 vols., Philadelphia: J. B. Lippincott & Co. 1874-77.
- Anon., Marchands de canons, Paris: G. Mignolet et Storz 1933.
- Appian, The Civil Wars, transl. by John Carter, London et.al. 1996.
- Aristotle, On Politics, transl. Benjamin Jowett, Oxford: The Claredon Press 1885.
- Aspland, Clifford W. (ed.), A Medieval French Reader, Oxford 1979.
- Bacon, Francis, "Of Usurie," in: The Essayes or Counsels, Civill and Morall, ed. Michael Kiernan, Oxford 1985, 124-129.
- Walter Bagehot, Lombard Street: A Description of the Money Market, London: King 1873.
- Baller, F. W., The Sacred Edict, Shanghai: American Presbyterian Mission Press ^{2}1907 [Pound's copy, BL Za P865 Zz 907K].
- Beard, Charles A., Economic Origins of Jeffersonian Democracy, New York: MacMillan 1915.
- Beckford, Peter, Familiar Letters from Italy, to a Friend in England, 2 vols., Salisbury: J. Easton 1805.
- Bell, Herbert C. F., Lord Palmerston, 2 vols., London / New York / Toronto 1936.

- Bentham, Jeremy, Defence of Usury [...], Philadelphia: Mathew Carey 1796.
- Benton, Thomas H., Thirty Years' View; or, A History of the Working of the American Government for Thirty Years, from 1820 to 1850 [...], 2 vols., New York / London: D. Appleton 1856.
- Biel, Gabriele, Tractatus de potestate et utilitate monetarum, Oppenheim: J. Köbel 1516.
- Binyon, Laurence, The Flight of the Dragon: An Essay on the Theory and Practice of Art in China and Japan, Based on Original Sources, London: John Murray [3]1922.
- Borges, Jorge Luis, This Craft of Verse: The Charles Eliot Norton Lectures 1967-1968, ed. Calin-Andrei Mihailescu, Cambridge (Mass.) / London 2000.
- Brockway, Fenner, Bloody Traffic, London: Victor Gollancz 1933.
- Butchart, Montgomery (comp.), Money. Selected Passages Presenting the Concepts of Money in the English Tradition 1640-1935, London: Stanley Nott 1935.
- Butchart, Montgomery (ed.), To-Morrow's Money, by Seven of To-Day's Leading Monetary Heretics, London: Stanley Nott 1936.
- Byatt, Antonia S., On Histories and Stories: Selected Essays, Cambridge (Mass.) 2002.
- Chaucer, Geoffrey, The Canterbury Tales and Other Poems, ed. D. Laing Purves, Edinburgh: Nimmo 1870.
- Corey, Lewis, The House of Morgan: A Social Biography of the Masters of Money, New York 1930, repr. New York 1969.
- Coughlin, Charles, Father Coughlin's Radio Discourses 1931-1932, Royal Oak (Mich.): The Radio League of the Little Flower 1932.
- Coughlin, Charles E., The New Deal in Money, Royal Oak (Mich.): The Radio League of the Little Flower 1933.
- Coughlin, Charles, Money! Questions and Answers, Royal Oak (Mich.): The National Union for Social Justice 1936.
- Crevel, René, Les pieds dans le plat [1933], Paris: Jean-Jacques Pauvert 1974.
- Crevel, René, Les pieds dans le plat, Paris: Éditions du Sagittaire 1933.
- Del Mar, Alexander, History of Monetary Systems, Chicago 1896, repr. Orono (Maine) 1983.
- Dos Passos, John, U.S.A. (= Library of America 85), New York 1996.
- Douglas, C. H., Credit-Power and Democracy, London: Cecil Palmer 1920.
- Douglas, C. H., Economic Democracy, London: Ceceil Palmer 1920.
- Douglas, C. H., Social Credit, London: Cecil Palmer 1924.

- Douglas, C. H., The Monopoly of Credit, London: Chapman & Hall 1931.
- Douglas, C. H., The Use of Money, New York: New Economics Group 1934.
- Eliot, Thomas S., Ezra Pound: His Metric and Poetry, Chicago 1917.
- Eliot, Thomas S., "A Note on Ezra Pound," in: *Today* 4.19 (1918), 3-9.
- Eliot, Thomas S., "The Method of Mr. Pound," in: *Athenaeum* 4.669 (1919), 1065f.
- Eliot, Thomas S., Notes toward the Definition of Culture, London 1948.
- Eliot, Thomas S., Selected Essays, London [3]1969.
- Eliot, Thomas S., The Waste Land: A Facsimile and Transcript of the Original Drafts Including the Annotations of Ezra Pound, ed. Valerie Eliot, San Diego / New York / London 1971.
- Eliot, Thomas S., The Varieties of Metaphysical Poetry, ed. Ronald Schuchard, London 1993.
- Emerson, Ralph Waldo, "Quotation and Originality," in: Letters and Social Aims (= Complete Works 8), Cambridge: Riverside Press 1883, 169-194.
- Fisher, Irving, Stamp Scrip, New York: Adelphi Company 1933.
- Frazer, James George, The Golden Bough, 12 vols., London / New York: Macmillan / St Martin's Press 1963.
- Frobenius, Leo, Erlebte Erdteile: Ergebnisse eines deutschen Forscherlebens, vol. 7: Monumenta Terrarum. Der Geist über den Erdteilen, Frankfurt a.M.: Frankfurter Societäts-Druckerei 1929 [Pound's copy in the Beinecke Library, call no. Za P865 Zz925 F].
- Frobenius, Leo, Erlebte Erdteile: Ergebnisse eines deutschen Forscherlebens, vol. 1: Ausfahrt. Von der Völkerkunde zum Kulturproblem, Frankfurt a.M.: Frankfurter Societäts-Druckerei 1925.
- Frobenius, Leo, Erlebte Erdteile: Ergebnisse eines deutschen Forscherlebens, vol. 2: Erschlossene Räume. Das Problem Ozeanien, Frankfurt a.M.: Frankfurter Societäts-Druckerei 1925.
- Frobenius, Leo, Erlebte Erdteile: Ergebnisse eines deutschen Forscherlebens, vol. 3: Vom Schreibtisch zum Äquator. Planmässige Durchwanderung Afrikas, Frankfurt a.M.: Frankfurter Societäts-Druckerei 1925.
- Frobenius, Leo, Erlebte Erdteile: Ergebnisse eines deutschen Forscherlebens, vol. 5: Das sterbende Afrika. Die Seele eines Erdteils, Frankfurt a.M.: Frankfurter Societäts-Druckerei [s.d.].
- Gesell, Silvio, The Natural Economic Order, Berlin-Frohnau: Neo-Verlag 1929.
- Giles, Herbert A., A History of Chinese Literature [1901], Rutland (Verm.) / Tokyo 1973.

- Grosseteste, Robert, Die philosophischen Werke des Robert Grosseteste, Bischofs von Lincoln (= Beiträge zur Geschichte des Mittelalters 9), ed. Ludwig Baur, Münster: Aschendorffsche Verlagsbuchhandlung 1912.
- Guinizelli, Guido, The Poetry of Guido Guinizelli (= Garland Library of Medieval Literature A 27), ed. Robert Edwards, New York / London 1987.
- Henze, Hans Werner, Essays, Mainz / London / New York 1964.
- Hölderlin, Friedrich, Sämtliche Werke, ed. D. E. Sattler, 18 vols., Frankfurt a.M. 1975-2000.
- Hollis, Christopher, The Two Nations: A Financial Study of English History, London: G. Routledge & Sons 1935; Repr. New York 1975.
- Hume, David, Essays Moral, Political and Literary, London 1963.
- Iamblichus, On the Mysteries of the Egyptians, Chaldeans, and Assyrians... (= The Thomas Taylor Series 17), The Butts: Prometheus Trust 1999.
- Jarvie, J. R., The Old Lady Unveiled: A Criticism and an Explanation of the Bank of England, [s.l.]: Wishart & Co. 1933.
- Jeanroy, Alfred (ed.), Anthologie des Troubadours XIIme – XIIIme siècles, Paris ^{2}1974.
- Kafka, Franz, Beschreibung eines Kampfes, eds. Roland Reuss / Peter Staengle / Joachim Unseld, Frankfurt/Main / Basel 1999.
- Kitson, Arthur, A Scientific Solution of the Money Question, Boston: Arena Publishing 1895.
- Kitson, Arthur, The Bankers' Conspiracy! Which Started the World Crisis, London: Elliot Stock ^{2}1933.
- Lewinsohn, Richard, Zaharoff. L'Européen Mystérieux, Paris 1929.
- Lewis, Wyndham, Hitler, London: Chatto & Windus 1931.
- Lewis, Wyndham, The Art of Being Ruled, London: Chatto & Windus 1926.
- Lewis, Wyndham, Time and Western Man, London: Chatto & Windus 1927.
- Locke, John, "Some Considerations of the Consequences of the Lowering of Interest, and Raising the Value of Money. In a Letter sent to a Member of Parliament in the year 1691," in: The Works of John Locke, 10 vols., vol. 5, London: W. Sharpe & Son 1823, repr. Aalen 1963, 1-116.
- Loeb, Harold et.al., The Chart of Plenty: A Study of America's Product Capacity Based on the Findings of the National Survey of Potential Product Capacity, New York: Viking Press 1935.
- Lu Yu, The Wild Old Man. Poems of Lu Yu, transl. David Gordon, San Francisco 1984.
- Mark, Jeffrey, The Modern Idolatry, being an Analysis of Usury and the Pathology of Debt, London: Chatto & Windus 1934.

- Martineau, Harriet, Society in America, 3 vols., London 1837 (repr. New York 1966).
- Mayo, Robert, Political Sketches of Eight Years in Washington [...], Baltimore: Fielding Lucas, jr. et.al. 1839.
- McClellan, George B., Venice and Bonaparte, Princeton: Princeton University Press 1931.
- Mengozzi, Narcisco (ed.), Il Monte dei Paschi di Siena e le Aziende in Esso Riunite, 9 vols., Siena 1891-1925.
- Mencius, The Works of Mencius, transl. James Legge, New York 1970.
- Orage, Alfred R., Orage as Critic, ed. Wallace Martin, London / Boston 1974.
- Plethon, Georgius Gemistus, Opuscula de Historia Graeca, ed. Enrico Maltese, Leipzig 1989.
- Por, Odon, Guilds and Co-operatives in Italy, transl. E. Townshend, London: The Labour Publishing Company 1923.
- Renan, Ernest, Averroès et l'averroïsme: Essai historique, Paris: Michel Lévy Frères 1866.
- Richard of St. Victor, Les Douze Patriarches ou Beniamin Minor (= Sources Chrétiennes 419), ed. by Jean Châtillon / Monique Duchet-Suchaux, Paris 1997.
- Rock, Joseph F., The Ancient Na-khi Kingdom of Southwest China, Cambridge (Mass.) 1947.
- Rostand, Maurice, Les marchands de canons. Pièce en trois act en prose, Paris: Editions Eugène Figuière 1933.
- Rota, Pietro, Storia delle banche [1874] (= Collana di studi di economia e finanza 3), Palermo: S. F. Flaccovio 1964.
- Salmasius, Claudius, De Modo Usurarum Liber, Lugduni Batavorum: Ex Officina Elfeviriorum 1639.
- Salmasius, Claudius, Dissertatio de foenore trapezitico, Lugduni Batavorum: Ex Officina Ioannis Maire 1640.
- Schmitt, Carl, Positionen und Begriffe im Kampf mit Weimar – Genf – Versailles 1923-1939, Hamburg-Wandsbek: Hanseatische Verlagsanstalt 1940.
- Sorosina, Amedeo, Il Monte dei Paschi di Siena: Per il terzo centenario, Siena: Lazzeri 1925.
- Spengler, Oswald, The Decline of the West, 2 vols. in one, New York: Alfred A. Knopf 1932.
- Stevenson, Robert Louis, "On Some Technical Elements of Style in Literature," in: Essays of Travel and in the Art of Writing, New York: Charles Scribner's Sons 1923, 253-277.

- Taylor, John, An Inquiry into the Principles and Policy of the Government of the United States, ed. Loren Baritz, Indianapolis / New York 1969.
- The Greek Bucolic Poets, transl. J. M. Edmonds, Cambridge (Mass.)/London [11]1991.
- The Jade Mountain: A Chinese Anthology, transl. Witter Bynner, New York: Alfred A. Knopf 1930.
- Trakl, Georg, Sämtliche Werke und Briefwechsel, vol. 2, eds. Eberhard Sauermann / Hermann Zwerschina, Basel / Frankfurt a.M. 1995.
- Union of Democratic Control, The Secret International: Armament Firms at Work, London: Union of Democratic Control 1932.
- Wang Wei / Li Po / Tu Fu / Li Ho, Four T'ang Poets (= FIELD Translation Series 4), [s.l.] 1980.
- Warburg, James P., The Money Muddle, New York: Alfred A. Knopf 1934.
- Williams, William C., The William Carlos Williams Reader, ed. M. L. Rosenthal, New York 1966.
- Wilson, Robert McNair, Napoleon's Love Story, London: Peter Davies [s.d.].
- Wilson, Robert McNair, The Mind of Napoleon: A Study of Napoleon, Mr Roosevelt, and the Money Power, London: G. Routledge & Sons 1934.
- Yeats, William B., A Packet for Ezra Pound, Dublin: The Cuala Press 1929.
- Zach, Erwin von, Tu Fu's Gedichte, Cambridge (Mass.) 1952.
- Zappa, Paolo, Oro Cannoni Democrazie, Milano: Edizioni Corbaccio [s.d.].
- Zobi, Antonio, Storia Civile della Toscana dal MDCCXXXVII al MDCCCXLVIII, 5 vols., Florence 1850-53.

V.2 Secondary Literature

V.2.a Bibliographies

- Bischoff, Volker, Ezra Pound Criticism 1905-1985. A Chronological Listing of Publications in English, Marburg 1991.
- Gallup, Donald, A Bibliography of Ezra Pound, London [2]1969.
- Ricks, Beatrice, Ezra Pound: A Bibliography of Secondary Works (The Scarecrow Author Bibliographies 74), Metuchen (N.J.)/London 1986.
- Somer, John/Cooper, Barbara E., American and British Literature 1945-1975: An Annotated Bibliography of Contemporary Scholarship, Lawrence (Kans.) 1980.

V.2.b Reference

- American National Biography, general eds. John A. Garraty / Mark C. Carnes, 24 vols., New York 1999 (= ANB).
- Coppa, Frank J. (ed.), Dictionary of Modern Italian History, Westport (Conn.) / London 1985 (= DMIH).
- Encyclopaedia Britannica CD 99, [s.l.] 1999.
- Jones, Howard M. / Ludwig, Richard M., Guide to American Literature and its Backgrounds Since 1890, Cambridge (Mass.) 1974.
- Hornblower, Simon / Spawforth, Antony (eds.), Oxford Classical Dictionary, Oxford / New York 1996.
- Oxford English Dictionary 2nd edition on CD-ROM, Version 1.13, Oxford 1992 (= OED).
- Sestan, Ernesto (ed.), Dizionario Storico Politico Italiano, Florence 1971 (= DSPI).
- Terrell, Carroll F., A Companion to the Cantos of Ezra Pound, 2 vols., Berkeley / Los Angeles / London 1980 (= Companion).
- Wissowa, Georg et.al. (eds.), Paulys Realencyclopädie der classischen Altertumswissenschaft (+ suppl.), Stuttgart 1893-1978.

V.2.c Studies

- Ackroyd, Peter, T. S. Eliot: A Life, New York 1984.
- Albright, Daniel, "Early Cantos I – XLI," in: Ira B. Nadel (ed.), The Cambridge Companion to Ezra Pound, Cambridge / New York / Melbourne 1999, 59-91.
- Anis, Jacques, L'écriture: Théories et descriptions, Bruxelles 1988.
- Antos, Gerd, Grundlagen einer Theorie des Formulierens: Textherstellung in geschriebener und gesprochener Sprache (= Reihe germanistische Linguistik 39), Tübingen 1982.
- Antos, Gerd, "Ist es auch Ihr sehnlichster Wunsch, wie ein Schriftsteller schreiben zu können? Vorläufige Bemerkungen zu einer Ideologiekritik des Schreibens. Am Beispiel literarischer Produktion," in: *Zeitschrift für Literaturwissenschaft und Linguistik* 17.68 (1987), 21-32.
- Antos, Gerd, "Textproduktion: Ein einleitender Überblick," in: Antos, Gerd / Krings, Hans P., Textproduktion: Ein interdisziplinärer Forschungsüberblick. Tübingen 1989, 5-57.

- Assmann, Jan, "Text und Kommentar. Einführung," in: Assmann, Jan / Gladigow, Burkhard (eds.), Text und Kommentar (= Archäologie der literarischen Kommunikation 4), München 1995.
- Athans, Mary C., The Coughlin-Fahey Connection: Father Charles E. Coughlin, Father Dennis Fahey, C.S.Sp., and Religious Anti-Semitism in the United States, 1938-1954, New York et.al. 1991.
- Bacigalupo, Massimo, The Forméd Trace, New York 1980.
- Baier, Peter E., "Maschineschreiben und forensische Urheberidentifizierung," in: Günther, Hartmut / Ludwig, Otto, Schrift und Schriftlichkeit (Writing and Its Use). Ein interdisziplinäres Handbuch internationaler Forschung, 2 vols., Berlin / New York 1994-96, II.1056-1068.
- Baudrillard, Jean, "The Illusion of the End," in: Jenkins, Keith (ed.), The Postmodern History Reader, London / New York 1997, 39-46.
- Baurmann, Jürgen, "Empirische schreibforschung [sic!]," in: Antos, Gerd / Krings, Hans P., Textproduktion: Ein interdisziplinärer Forschungsüberblick. Tübingen 1989, 257-277.
- Bayor, Ronald H., "Klans, Coughlinites and Aryan Nations: Patterns of American Anti-Semitism in the Twentieth Century," in: Gurock, Jeffrey S. (ed.), Anti-Semitism in America 2 (= American Jewish History 6), 2 vols., New York / London 1998, 579-593.
- Beach, Christopher, ABC of Influence: Ezra Pound and the Remaking of American Poetic Tradition, Berkeley / Los Angeles / Oxford 1992.
- Beetz, Manfred / Antos, Gerd, "Die nachgespielte Partie: Vorschläge zu einer Theorie der literarischen Produktion," in: Finke, Peter / Schmidt, Siegfried (Hg.), Analytische Literaturwissenschaft, Braunschweig/Wiesbaden 1984, 90-141.
- Bell, Ian F. A., "Middle Cantos XLII – LXXI," in: Ira B. Nadel (ed.), The Cambridge Companion to Ezra Pound, Cambridge / New York / Melbourne 1999, 92-108.
- Berkhofer, Robert F., Beyond the Great Story: History as Text and Discourse, Cambridge (Mass.) / London 1995.
- Berkhofer, Robert, "The Challenge of Poetics to (Normal) Historical Practice," in: Jenkins, Keith (ed.), The Postmodern History Reader, London / New York 1997, 139-157.
- Bernstein, Michael Alan, The Great Depression: Delayed Recovery and Economic Change in America, 1929-1939, Cambridge et.al. 1987.
- Bernstein, Michael André, "Identification and Its Vicissitudes: The Narrative Structure of Ezra Pound's *Cantos*," in: *Yale Review* 69.4 (1980), 540-556.

- Bernstein, Michael André, "Image, Word, and Sign: The Visual Arts as Evidence in Ezra Pound's *Cantos*," in: Bloom, Harold (ed.), Ezra Pound. Modern Critical Views, New York / New Haven / Philadelphia 1987, 161-176.
- Bernstein, Michael André, The Tale of the Tribe: Ezra Pound and the Modern Verse Epic, Princeton 1980.
- Bieberstein, Johannes Rogala von, Die These von der Verschwörung 1776-1945: Philosophen, Freimaurer, Juden, Liberale und Sozialisten als Verschwörer gegen die Sozialordnung, Flensburg 1992.
- Binder, Harmut, "Kafkas Varianten," in: Deutsche Vierteljahrsschrift für Literaturwissenschaft und Geistesgeschichte 50 (1976), 683-719.
- Boetius, Henning, "Preliminary Reflections on a Generative Theory of Editing," in: Gabler, Hans W. / Bornstein, George / Pierce, Gillian B. (eds.), Contemporary German Editorial Theory, Ann Arbor 1995, 153-169.
- Bohnenkamp, Anne, "...das Hauptgeschäft nicht außer Augen lassend": Die Paralipomena zu Goethes 'Faust', Frankfurt a.M. 1994.
- Bolter, Jay David, Writing Space: The Computer, Hypertext, and the History of Writing, Hillsdale / Hove / London 1991.
- Bornstein, George, "Introduction," in: George Bornstein (ed.), Representing Modernist Texts: Editing as Interpretation, Ann Arbor 1991, 1-16.
- Bowers, Fredson, "Mixed Texts and Multiple Authority," in: *TEXT* 3, New York 1987, 63-90.
- Brannigan, John, New Historicism and Cultural Materialism, London 1998.
- Brinker, Klaus, "Die Konstitution schriftlicher Texte," in: Günther, Hartmut / Ludwig, Otto, Schrift und Schriftlichkeit (Writing and Its Use). Ein interdisziplinäres Handbuch internationaler Forschung, 2 vols., Berlin / New York 1994-96, II.1515-1527.
- Brooke-Rose, Christine, "Lay me by Aurelie: An Examination of Pound's Use of Historical and Semi-Historical Sources," in: Hesse, Eva (ed.), New Approaches to Ezra Pound, 242-279.
- Brooke-Rose, Christine, A Structural Analysis of Pound's Usura Canto: Jakobson's Method Extended and Applied to Free Verse, The Hague / Paris 1976.
- Brooke-Rose, Christine, A ZBC of Ezra Pound, London 1971.
- Bush, Ronald, "Excavating the Ideological Faultlines of Modernism: Editing Ezra Pound's *Cantos*," in: George Bornstein (ed.), Representing Modernist Texts: Editing as Interpretation, Ann Arbor 1991, 67-98.
- Bush, Ronald, "Late Cantos LXXII – CXVII," in: Ira B. Nadel (ed.), The Cambridge Companion to Ezra Pound, Cambridge / New York / Melbourne 1999, 109-138.

- Bush, Ronald, The Genesis of Ezra Pound's Cantos, Princeton 1976.
- Carrard, Philippe, The Poetics of the New History, Baltimore 1992.
- Casillo, Robert, The Genealogy of Demons: Anti-Semitism, Fascism, and the Myths of Ezra Pound, Evanston (Ill.) 1988.
- Chace, William M., The Political Identities of Ezra Pound and T. S. Eliot, Stanford 1973.
- Charles B. Faulhaber, "Textual Criticism in the 21st Century," in: *Romance Philology* XLV (1991), 123-148.
- Clough, Shepard B., The Economic History of Modern Italy, New York / London 1964.
- Cochrane, Eric, Florence in the Forgotten Centuries: 1527-1800, Chicago 1973.
- Cohen, Philip (ed.), Texts and Textuality: Textual Instability, Theory, and Interpretation, New York/London 1997.
- Conover, Anne, "Her Name Was Courage: Olga Rudge, Pound's Muse and the 'Circe/Aphrodite' of the Cantos," in: *Paideuma* 24.1 (1995), 7-23.
- Conte, Joseph M., Unending Design: The Forms of Postmodern Poetry, Ithaca / London 1991.
- Dasenbrock, Reed W., "Pound and the Visual Arts," in: Ira B. Nadel (ed.), The Cambridge Companion to Ezra Pound, Cambridge / New York / Melbourne 1999, 224-235.
- Davenport, Guy, "Persephone's Ezra," in: Hesse, Eva (ed.), New Approaches to Ezra Pound, 145-173.
- Davie, Donald, "The Poet as Sculptor",in: Hesse, Eva (ed.), New Approaches to Ezra Pound, 198-214.
- Davis, Earle, Vision Fugitive: Ezra Pound and Economics, Lawrence / London 1968.
- Davis, Kay, Fugue and Fresco: Structures in Pound's *Cantos*, Orono 1984.
- De Biasi, Pierre-Marc, "What is a Literary Draft? Toward a Functional Typology of Genetic Criticism," in: *Yale French Studies* 89 (1996), 26-58.
- Dekker, George, Sailing After Knowledge: The Cantos of Ezra Pound, London 1963.
- Demott, Robert, "Ezra Pound and Charles Bowlker: Note on Canto LI," in: *Paideuma* 1.2 (1972), 189-198.
- Deutsch, Babette, "Speech and Song," in: Poetry in Our Time, New York 1956, 119-151.
- Dilligan, Robert J. / Parins, James W. / Bender, Todd K., A Concordance to Ezra Pound's *Cantos*, New York / London 1981.

- Dilthey, Wilhelm, “Archive für Literatur,” in: Gesammelte Schriften, vol. 15, ed. by. Ulrich Herrmann, Göttingen 1970, 1-16.
- Ellmann, Maud, The Poetics of Impersonality: T. S. Eliot and Ezra Pound, Cambridge (Mass.) 1987.
- Espagne, Michel, “Pour une épistémanalyse des études génétiques,” in: *Etudes Françaises* 28.1 (1992), 29-48.
- Espagne, Michel, De l'archive au texte: Recherches d'histoire génétique, Paris 1998.
- Fenster, Mark, Conspiracy Theories: Secrecy and Power in American Culture, Minneapolis / London 1999.
- Ferguson, Niall, The World's Banker: The History of the House of Rothschild, London 1998.
- Ferkiss, Victor C., “Populist Influences on American Fascism,” in: Gurock, Jeffrey S. (ed.), Anti-Semitism in America 1 (= American Jewish History 6), 2 vols., New York / London 1998, 301-324.
- Ferrer, Daniel / Lebrave, Jean-Louis, “De la variante textuelle au geste d'écriture,” in: Hay, Louis et.al. (eds.), L'écriture et ses doubles. Genèse et variation textuelle, Paris 1991, 9-26.
- Finlay, John L., Social Credit: The English Origins, Montreal / London 1972.
- Finneran, Richard J., “Text and Intepretation in the Poems of W. B. Yeats,” in: George Bornstein (ed.), Representing Modernist Texts: Editing as Interpretation, Ann Arbor 1991, 17-47.
- Flory, Wendy S., “Pound and Anisemitism,” in: Ira B. Nadel (ed.), The Cambridge Companion to Ezra Pound, Cambridge / New York / Melbourne 1999, 284-300.
- Flory, Wendy S., Ezra Pound and the Cantos: A Record of Struggle, New Haven (Conn.) / London 1980.
- Flory, Wendy S., The American Ezra Pound, New Haven (Conn.) / London 1989.
- Fox-Genovese, Elizabeth, “Literary Criticism and the Politics of the New Historicism,” in: Jenkins, Keith (ed.), The Postmodern History Reader, London / New York 1997, 84-88.
- Froula, Christine, To Write Paradise: Style and Error in Pound's *Cantos*, New Haven (Conn.) / London 1984.
- Fuchs, Catherine / Grésillon, Almuth / Lebrave, Jean-Louis, “Flaubert: ‘Ruminer Hérodias’. Du cognitif-visuel au verbal-textuel,” in: Hay, Louis et.al. (eds.), L'écriture et ses doubles. Genèse et variation textuelle, Paris 1991, 27-110.

- Gabler, Hans W., “Introduction,” in: Gabler, Hans W. / Bornstein, George / Pierce, Gillian B. (eds.), Contemporary German Editorial Theory, Ann Arbor 1995, 1-16.
- Gabler, Hans W., “Naissance de l’édition: de l’ordinateur comme sage-femme,” in: Hay, Louis (ed.), La Naissance du Texte, Paris 1989, 53-62.
- Gabler, Hans W., “The Text as Process and the Problem of Intentionality,” in: *TEXT* 3, New York 1987, 107-116.
- Gabler, Hans W., “Towards an Electronic Edition of James Joyce’s *Ulysses*,” in: *Literary and Linguistic Computing* 15.1 (2000), 115-120.
- Gabler, Hans Walter, “Computergestütztes Edieren und Computer-Edition,” in: Martens, Gunter / Zeller, Hans (eds.), Textgenetische Edition (= Beihefte zu editio 10), Tübingen 1998, 315-328.
- Gabler, Hans Walter, „Genetic Texts – Genetic Editions – Genetic Criticism or, Towards Discoursing the Genetics of Writing“, in: Jansohn, Christa (ed.), Problems of Editing (= Beihefte zu Editio 14), Tübingen 1999, 59-78.
- Gaskell, Philip, From Writer to Reader: Studies in Editorial Method, Oxford 1978.
- Gellhaus, Axel, “Textgenese zwischen Poetologie und Editionstechnik,” in: Gellhaus, Axel u.a. (Hg.), Die Genese literarischer Texte: Modelle und Analysen, Würzburg 1994, 311-326.
- Germann, Dietrich, “Zur Erläuterung einiger editorischer Begriffe,” in: *Forschungen und Fortschritte* 38 (1964), S. 83-85.
- Giuriato, Davide / Stingelin, Martin / Zanetti, Sandro, “Eigensinnige Schreibwerkzeuge,” in: *Basler Zeitung* 28 (13 July 2002), 8-9.
- Glotz, G., Ancient Greece at Work. An Economic History from the Homeric Period to the Roman Conquest, Repr. London / New York 1996 (orig. 1926).
- Goldensohn, Barry, “Pound and Antisemitism,” in: *The Yale Review* 75.3 (1986), 399-421.
- Gordon, David M. (ed.), Ezra Pound and James Laughlin: Selected Letters, New York / London 1994.
- Greetham, David C., Textual Scholarship: An Introduction (= Garland Reference Library of the Humanities 1417), New York / London 1992.
- Grésillon, Almuth / Werner, Michael (eds.), Leçons d’écriture: Ce que disent les manuscrits. En hommage à Louis Hay, Paris 1985.
- Grésillon, Almuth, “Bemerkungen zur französischen ‘édition génétique’,” in: Martens, Gunter / Zeller, Hans (eds.), Textgenetische Edition (= Beihefte zu editio 10), Tübingen 1998, 52-64.
- Grésillon, Almuth, Literarische Handschriften (= Arbeiten zur Editionswissenschaft 4), Bern et.al. 1999.

- Grooden, Michael, "Contemporary Textual and Literary Theory," in: George Bornstein (ed.), Representing Modernist Texts: Editing as Interpretation, Ann Arbor 1991, 259-286.
- Gurock, Jeffrey S. (ed.), Anti-Semitism in America (= American Jewish History 6), 2 vols., New York / London 1998.
- Hamilton, Alastair, The Appeal of Fascism: A Study of Intellectuals and Fascism 1919-1945, London 1971.
- Hatlen, Burton, "Ezra Pound and Fascism," in: Korn, Marianne (ed.), Ezra Pound and History, Orono 1985, 145-172.
- Hawkes, David, A Little Primer of Tu Fu, Oxford 1967.
- Hay, Louis, "Die dritte Dimension der Literatur," in: *Poetica* 16 (1984), 307-323.
- Hay, Louis, "Drei Randglossen zur Problematik textgenetischer Editionen. Wünsche des Lesers," in: Martens, Gunter / Zeller, Hans (eds.), Textgenetische Edition (= Beihefte zu editio 10), Tübingen 1998, 65-79.
- Hay, Louis, "History or Genesis?," in: *Yale French Studies* 89 (1996), 191-207.
- Hay, Louis, "Über die Entstehung von Texten und Theorien. Deutsch-französische Randglossen zu einem Forschungsgebiet," in: *Zeitschrift für Literaturwissenschaft und Linguistik* 17.68 (1987), 9-20.
- Hesse, Eva (ed.), Ezra Pound: Usura-Cantos XLV und LI. Texte, Entwürfe und Fragmente, Zürich 1985.
- Hesse, Eva, "Introduction", in: Hesse, Eva (ed.), New Approaches to Ezra Pound, 13-54.
- Hill, C. William, The Political Theory of John Taylor of Caroline, Rutherford et.al. 1977.
- Hofstadter, Richard, The Age of Reform from Bryan to F.D.R., London 1962.
- Hofstadter, Richard, The Paranoid Style in American Politics and Other Essays, London 1966.
- Housman, Alfred E., "The Application of Thought to Textual Criticism," in: Selected Prose, ed. John Carter, Cambridge 1961, 131-150.
- Huddleston, Sisley, Paris Salons Cafés, Studios, Philadelphia / London: Lippincott 1928.
- Hurlebusch, Klaus, "Den Autor besser verstehen: aus seiner Arbeitsweise. Prolegomenon zu einer Hermeneutik textgenetischen Schreibens," in: Martens, Gunter / Zeller, Hans (eds.), Textgenetische Edition (= Beihefte zu editio 10), Tübingen 1998, 7-51.
- Hurlebusch, Klaus, "Deutungen literarischer Arbeitsweise," in: *Zeitschrift für Deutsche Philologie* 105 (1986) special issue, 4-42.

- Hutchinson, Frances / Burkitt, Brian, The Political Economy of Social Credit and Guild Socialism (= Routledge Studies in the History of Economics 14), London / New York 1997.
- Jenny, Laurent, "Genetic Criticism and its Myths," in: *Yale French Studies* 89 (1996), 9-25.
- Johnson, George, Architects of Fear: Conspiracy Theories and Paranoia in American Politics, Los Angeles 1983.
- Kantorowicz, Ernst H., The King's Two Bodies: A Study in Mediaeval Theology, Princeton 1957.
- Kanzog, Klaus, "Faksimilieren, transkribieren, edieren: Grundsätzliches zu Gerhard Schmids Ausgabe des Woyzeck," in: *Georg Büchner Jahrbuch* 4 (1984), 280-294.
- Kanzog, Klaus, Einführung in die Editionsphilologie der neueren deutschen Literatur, Berlin 1991.
- Kay, Janice, "Psychological Aspects of Spelling," in: Günther, Hartmut / Ludwig, Otto, Schrift und Schriftlichkeit (Writing and Its Use). Ein interdisziplinäres Handbuch internationaler Forschung, 2 vols., Berlin / New York 1994-96, II.1074-1094.
- Kearns, George, Guide to Ezra Pound's *Selected Cantos*, Brunswick (N.J.) 1980.
- Kenner, Hugh, Gnomon: Essays on Contemporary Literature, New York / Toronto 1958.
- Kenner, Hugh, "More on the Seven Lakes Canto," in: *Paideuma* 2.1 (1973), 43-46.
- Kenner, Hugh, The Pound Era, Berkeley / Los Angeles ^{2}1973.
- Kenner, Hugh, "Notes on Amateur Emendations," in: Lawrence S. Rainey (ed.), A Poem Containing History: Textual Studies in *The Cantos*, Ann Arbor 1997, 21-29.
- Kimpel, Ben / Eaves, T. C. Duncan, "The Sources of Cantos XLII and XLIII," in: Paid. 6.3 (1977), 332-358.
- Kimpel, Ben / Eaves, T. C. Duncan, "The Sources of the Leopoldine Cantos," in: Paid. 7.1/2 (1978), 249-277.
- Kimpel, Ben / Eaves, T. C. Duncan, "The Source of Canto L," in: Paid. 8.1 (1979), 81-93.
- Kimpel, Ben / Eaves, T. C. Duncan, "Pound's Use of Sienese Manuscripts for Cantos XLII and XLIII," in: Paid. 8.3 (1979), 513-518.
- Kindleberger, Charles P., A Financial History of Western Europe, London 1984.
- Kodama, Sanehide, "The Eight Scenes of Sho-Sho," in: *Paideuma* 6.2 (1977), 131-145.

- Kraft, Herbert, Die Geschichtlichkeit literarischer Texte. Eine Theorie der Edition, Tübingen 1973.
- La Capra, Dominick / Kaplan, Steven L. (eds.), Modern European Intellectual History: Reappraisals and New Perspectives, Itahca / London 1982.
- La Capra, Dominick, History and Criticism, New York 1985.
- Landow, George P., Hypertext 2.0, Baltimore / London 1997.
- Laughlin, James, Pound as Wuz: Essays and Lectures on Ezra Pound, Saint Paul 1987.
- Le Goff, Jacques, Wucherzins und Höllenqualen: Ökonomie und Religion im Mittelalter, Stuttgart 1988.
- Leavis, Frank R., New Bearings in English Poetry. A Study of the Contemporary Situation. London 1938, repr. New York 1978.
- Lebrave, Jean-Louis, "Hypertext und textgenetische Edition," in: Martens, Gunter / Zeller, Hans (eds.), Textgenetische Edition (= Beihefte zu editio 10), Tübingen 1998, 329-345.
- Levaillant, Jean / Bastet, Ned (eds.), Ecriture et génétique textuelle: Valéry à l'oeuvre, Lille 1982.
- Lipset, Seymour M. / Raab, Earl, The Politics of Unreason: Right-Wing Extremism in America, 1790-1977, Chicago / London ²1978.
- Longenbach, James, Modernist Poetics of History: Pound, Eliot, and the Sense of the Past, Princeton (N.J.) 1987.
- Loss, Archie, "Joyce's Use of Collage in 'Aeolus'," in: *Journal of Modern Literature* 9.2. (1982), 175-182.
- Makin, Peter, Pound's Cantos, London 1985.
- Marsh, Alec, Money and Modernity: Pound, Williams, and the Spirit of Jefferson, Tuscaloosa / London 1998.
- Martens, Gunter, "(De)Constructing Texts by Editing: Reflections on the Receptional Significance of Textual Apparatuses," in: Gabler, Hans W. / Bornstein, George / Pierce, Gillian B. (eds.), Contemporary German Editorial Theory, Ann Arbor 1995, 125-151.
- Martens, Gunter, "What is a Text? Attempts at Defining a Central Concept in Editorial Theory," in: Gabler, Hans W. / Bornstein, George / Pierce, Gillian B. (eds.), Contemporary German Editorial Theory, Ann Arbor 1995, 209-231.
- Martz, Louis L., "Pound: The Prophetic Voice," in: *The Yale Review* 75.3 (1986), 373-384.
- McGann, Jerome J., "History, Herstory, Theirstory, Ourstory," in: Perkins, David (ed.), Theoretical Issues in Literary History (= Harvard English Studies 16), Cambridge (Mass.) / London 1991, 196-205.

- McGann, Jerome, "Interpretation, Meaning, and Textual Criticism: A Homily," in: *TEXT* 3, New York 1987, 55-62.
- McGann, Jerome, "Pound's *Cantos*: A Poem Including Bibliography," in: Lawrence S. Rainey (ed.), A Poem Containing History: Textual Studies in *The Cantos*, Ann Arbor 1997, 33-62.
- McGann, Jerome, A Critique of Modern Textual Criticism, Charlottesville / London 1992.
- McGann, Jerome, The Textual Condition, Princeton 1991.
- McKenna, George (ed.), American Populism, New York 1974.
- Mendelson, Edward, "The Two Audens and the Claims of History," in: George Bornstein (ed.), Representing Modernist Texts: Editing as Interpretation, Ann Arbor 1991, 157-170.
- Mendelson, Edward, "Revision and Power: The Example of W. H. Auden," in: *Yale French Studies* 89 (1996), 103-112.
- Minton, Robert, John Law: The Father of Paper Money, New York 1975.
- Mitterand, Henri, "Programme et préconstruit génétiques: le dossier de L'assomoir," in: Hay, Louis (ed.), Essais de critique génétique, Paris 1979.
- Möbius, Hanno, Montage und Collage: Literatur, bildende Künste, Film, Fotografie, Musik, Theater bis 1933, München 2000.
- Montrose, Louis, "New Historicisms," in: Greenblatt, Stephen / Gunn, Giles (eds.), Redrawing the Boundaries: The Transformation of English and American Literary Studies, New York 1992, 392-418.
- Moody, A. D., "Composition in the Adams Cantos," in: Jacqueline Kaye (ed.), Ezra Pound and America, New York 1994, 79-92.
- Morrison, Paul, The Poetics of Fascism: Ezra Pound, T. S. Eliot, Paul de Man, New York / Oxford 1996.
- Muir, Edwin, Review: The Fifth Decad of Cantos, in: *Criterion* XVII.66 (1937), 148f.
- Murray, David, "Pound-Signs: Money and Representation in Ezra Pound," in: Korn, Marianne (ed.), Ezra Pound and History, Orono 1985, 173-198.
- Neefs, Jacques, "Manuscrits littéraires: Comparaisons et histoire littéraire," in: Bevan, D. G. / Wetherill, P. M. (eds.), Sur la génétique textuelle, Amsterdam / Atlanta (GA) 1990, 7-18.
- Neidhardt, Frances E., "From Apelles to Pound's 'Usury' Canto: Botticelli's *La Calumnia* goes modern," in: *Paideuma* 12.2+3 (1983), 427-445.
- Nelson, Benjamin, The Idea of Usury: From Tribal Brotherhood to Universal Otherhood, Chicago / London ^{2}1969.

- Nicholls, Peter, Ezra Pound: Politics, Economics and Writing. A Study of *The Cantos*, Atlantic Highlands 1984.
- Nichols, Stephen G., "The Old Provençal Lyric," in: Denis Hollier et.al. (eds.), A New History of French Literature, Cambridge (Mass.) / London 1989, 30-36.
- Nussbaum, Arthur, A Concise History of the Law of Nations, New York 1954.
- Nutt-Koforth, Rüdiger u.a. (Hg.), Text und Edition: Positionen und Perspektiven, Berlin 2000.
- Palandri, Angela J., "The 'Seven Lakes Canto' Revisited," in: *Paideuma* 3.1 (1974), 52ff.
- Payne, Stanley G., A History of Fascism, 1914-1945, London / Madison 1995.
- Pearlman, Daniel D., The Barb of Time: On the Unity of Ezra Pound's *Cantos*, New York 1969.
- Perloff, Marjorie, "The Invention of Collage," in: *New York Literary Forum* 10/11 (1983), 5-47.
- Perloff, Marjorie, "Modernist Studies," in: Greenblatt, Stephen / Gunn, Giles (eds.), Redrawing the Boundaries: The Transformation of English and American Literary Studies, New York 1992, 154-178.
- Preda, Roxana, Ezra Pound's (Post)Modern Poetics and Politics. Logocentrism, Language, and Truth (= Studies in Literary Criticism and Theory 14), New York et.al. 2001.
- Pugh, Anthony R., "Proust's working methods: The importance of structure," in: Bevan, D. G. / Wetherill, P. M. (eds.), Sur la génétique textuelle, Amsterdam / Atlanta (GA) 1990, 109-124.
- Rachewiltz, Mary de, "Afterword: *Ubi Cantos Ibi America*," in: Lawrence S. Rainey (ed.), A Poem Containing History: Textual Studies in *The Cantos*, Ann Arbor 1997, 267-273.
- Rachewiltz, Mary de, Discretions, Boston / Toronto 1971.
- Rainey, Lawrence S., " 'All I Want You to Do Is to Follow the Orders': History, Faith, and Fascism in the Early Cantos," in: Lawrence S. Rainey (ed.), A Poem Containing History: Textual Studies in *The Cantos*, Ann Arbor 1997, 63-114.
- Rainey, Lawrence S., "Introduction," in: Lawrence S. Rainey (ed.), A Poem Containing History: Textual Studies in *The Cantos*, Ann Arbor 1997, 1-17.
- Rainey, Lawrence S., Ezra Pound and the Monument of Culture: Text, History, and the Malatesta Cantos, Chicago / London 1991.
- Redman, Tim, "An Epic Is a Hypertext Containing Poetry: *Eleven New Cantos* (31-41) by Ezra Pound," in: Lawrence S. Rainey (ed.), A Poem Containing History: Textual Studies in *The Cantos*, Ann Arbor 1997, 117-149.

- Redman, Tim, “Pound’s Politics and Economics,” in: Ira B. Nadel (ed.), The Cambridge Companion to Ezra Pound, Cambridge / New York / Melbourne 1999, 249-263.
- Reiss, Timothy, The Discourse of Modernism, Ithaca / London 1982.
- Repetti, Emanuele (comp.), Dizionario geografico fisico storico della Toscana, vol. V, Florence 1843.
- Reynolds, Lloyd G., “Economics in History: The Poetic Vision of Ezra Pound,” in: *The Yale Review* 75.3 (1986), 385-398.
- Rosenthal, M. L., “Pound at his best: Canto 47 as a model of poetic thought,” in: *Paideuma* 6.3 (1977), 309-321.
- Sanders, Frederick K., John Adams Speaking: Pound‘s Sources for the Adams Cantos, Orono (Maine) [1975].
- Scheibe, Siegfried, “On the Editorial Problem of the Text,” in: Gabler, Hans W. / Bornstein, George / Pierce, Gillian B. (eds.), Contemporary German Editorial Theory, Ann Arbor 1995, 193-208.
- Scheibe, Siegfried, “Theoretical Problems of the Authorization and Constitution of Texts,” in: Gabler, Hans W. / Bornstein, George / Pierce, Gillian B. (eds.), Contemporary German Editorial Theory, Ann Arbor 1995, 171-191.
- Scheibe, Siegfried, “Zu einigen Grundprinzipien einer historisch-kritischen Ausgabe,” in: Martens, Gunter / Zeller, Hans (eds.), Texte und Varianten: Probleme ihrer Edition und Interpretation, München 1971, 1-44.
- Schmidt-Glintzer, Hedwig, Geschichte der chinesischen Literatur. Von den Anfängen bis zur Gegenwart, Munich ^{2}1999.
- Scholnick, Myron I., The New Deal and Anti-Semitism in America, New York / London 1990.
- Schwartz, Sanford, The Matrix of Modernism: Pound, Eliot, and Early Twentieth-Century Thought, Princeton 1985.
- Shalhope, Robert E., John Taylor of Caroline: Pastoral Republican, Columbia (SC) 1980.
- Shell, Marc, The Economy of Literature, Baltimore / London 1978.
- Shell, Marc, Money, Language, and Thought: Literary and Philosophic Economies from the Medieval to the Modern Era, Baltimore / London ^{2}1993.
- Shillingsburg, Peter L., Resisting Texts: Authority and Submission in Constructions of Meaning, Ann Arbor 1997.
- Shneiderman, Ben, “Reflections on Authoring, Editing, and Managing Hypertext,” in: Barrett, Edward (ed.), The Society of Text: Hypertext, Hypermedia, and the Social Construction of Information, Cambridge (Mass.) / London 1989, 115-131.

- Sicari, Stephen, "Reading Pound's Politics: Ulysses as Fascist Hero," in: *Paideuma* 17.2+3 (1988), 145-169.
- Sieburth, Richard, Instigations: Ezra Pound and Remy de Gourmont, Cambridge (Mass.) / London 1978.
- Stock, Noel, The Life of Ezra Pound, New York 1970.
- Stoicheff, Peter, The Hall of Mirrors: *Drafts and Fragments* and the End of Ezra Pound's *Cantos* (= Editorial Theory and Literary Criticism 3), Ann Arbor 1995.
- Surette, Leon, A Light from Eleusis: A Study of Ezra Pound's *Cantos*, Oxford 1979.
- Surette, Leon, Pound in Purgatory: From Economic Radicalism to Anti-Semitism, Urbana / Chicago 1999.
- Tanselle, George Thomas, A Rationale of Textual Criticism, Philadelphia 1989.
- Tanselle, George Thomas, Selected Studies in Bibliography, Charlottesville 1979.
- Tanselle, George Thomas, "Historicism and Critical Editing: 1979-85," in: Textual Criticism since Greg: A Chronicle 1950-1985, Charlottesville 1987, 109-154.
- Taylor, Richard, "Canto XLIX, Futurism, and the Fourth Dimension," in: *Neohelicon* 20.1 (1993), 337-356.
- Taylor, Richard, "Reconstructing Ezra Pound's *Cantos*: Variorum Edition – Manuscript Archive – Reading Text," in: Jacqueline Kaye (ed.), Ezra Pound and America, New York 1994, 132-147.
- Taylor, Richard, "The History and State of the Texts," in: Lawrence S. Rainey (ed.), A Poem Containing History: Textual Studies in *The Cantos*, Ann Arbor 1997, 235-265.
- Taylor, Richard, Variorum Edition of "Three Cantos" by Ezra Pound: A Prototype, Bayreuth 1991.
- Thorpe, James, Principles of Textual Criticism, San Marino 1972.
- Timpanaro, Sebastiano, Die Entstehung der Lachmannschen Methode, Hamburg [2]1971.
- Tryphonopoulos, Demetres P., "The Fourth; the Dimension of Stillness," in: *Paideuma* 19.3 (1990), 117-122.
- Twitchell, Jeffrey, "Art and the Spirit of Capitalism: Iconography and History in The Usura Canto," in: *Paideuma* 19.3 (1990), 7-31.
- Tytell, John, Ezra Pound: The Solitary Volcano, New York 1987.
- Veeser, Harold A., "The New Historicism," in: Veeser, Harold A. (ed.), The New Historicism Reader, New York / London 1994, 1-32.

- Viollet, Catherine, "Schriftlichkeit und Literatur," in: Günther, Hartmut / Ludwig, Otto, Schrift und Schriftlichkeit (Writing and Its Use). Ein interdisziplinäres Handbuch internationaler Forschung, 2 vols., Berlin / New York 1994-96, I.658-672.
- Vodicka, Felix, Die Struktur der literarischen Entwicklung, Munich 1976.
- Watts, Cedric, Literature and Money: Financial Myth and Literary Truth, New York et.al. 1990.
- Michael Werner, "Etudes de genèse et mythologie de l'écriture," in: Jean Bessière (ed.), Mythologies de l'écriture: champs critiques, Paris 1990, 23-40.
- Whigham, Peter (ed.), The Music of the Troubadours (= Provençal Series 1), Santa Barbara (Calif.) 1979.
- White, Hayden, "Historical Emplotment and the Problem of Truth," in: Jenkins, Keith (ed.), The Postmodern History Reader, London / New York 1997, 392-396.
- White, Hayden, "The Value of Narrativity in the Representation of Reality," in: *Critical Inquiry* 7 (1980), 5-27.
- White, Hayden, Metahistory: The Historical Imagination in Nineteenth-Century Europe, Baltimore / London 1973.
- White, Hayden, The Content of the Form: Narrative Discourse and Historical Representation, Baltimore / London 1987.
- Wilhelm, James J., Ezra Pound: The Tragic Years (1925-1972), University Park (Penns.) 1994.
- Wilhelm, James J., Il Miglior Fabbro: The Cult of the Difficult in Daniel, Dante, and Pound, Orono 1982.
- Wilson, Stephen, "Pound's American Revolutions," in: Jacqueline Kaye (ed.), Ezra Pound and America, New York 1994, 181-199.
- Wimsatt, W. K., "Genesis: A Fallacy Revisited," in: Peter Demetz et.al. (eds.), The Disciplines of Criticism: Essays in Literary Theory, Interpretation, and History, New Haven (CT) / London 1968, 193-225.
- Witemeyer, Hugh, "Ruskin and the Signed Capital in Canto 45," in: *Paideuma* 4.1 (1975), 85-88.
- Wollenberg, Friedrich W., "Zur genetischen Darstellung innerhandschriftlicher Varianten," in: Martens, Gunter / Zeller, Hans (eds.), Texte und Varianten: Probleme ihrer Edition und Interpretation, München 1971, 251-272.
- Woodmansee, Martha / Osteen, Mark, The New Economic Criticism: Studies at the Intersection of Literature and Economics, London / New York 1999.
- Xie, Ming, "Pound as Translator," in: Ira B. Nadel (ed.), The Cambridge Companion to Ezra Pound, Cambridge / New York / Melbourne 1999, 204-223.

- Zeller, Hans, “Die Faksimile-Edition als Grundlagenedition für Philologie und Textgenetik. Ein Vorschlag,” in: Martens, Gunter / Zeller, Hans (eds.), Textgenetische Edition (= Beihefte zu editio 10), Tübingen 1998, 80-100.
- Zeller, Hans, “Record and Interpretation: Analysis and Documentation as Goal and Method of Editing,” in: Gabler, Hans W. / Bornstein, George / Pierce, Gillian B. (eds.), Contemporary German Editorial Theory, Ann Arbor 1995, 17-58.
- Zeller, Hans, “Structure and Genesis in Editing: On German and Anglo-American Textual Criticism,” in: Gabler, Hans W. / Bornstein, George / Pierce, Gillian B. (eds.), Contemporary German Editorial Theory, Ann Arbor 1995, 95-123.
- Zwerschina, Hermann, “Die editorische Einheit ‘Textstufe’,” in: Martens, Gunter / Zeller, Hans (eds.), Textgenetische Edition (= Beihefte zu editio 10), Tübingen 1998, 177-194.

VI. APPENDIX: Autographs Related to *The Fifth Decad*

The following list comprises the archival items that constitute the pre-publication corpus of what was to become *The Fifth Decad of Cantos*. Autograph items include manuscripts, typescripts (with carbon copies), notebook materials and individual notes. The listed items are archived in BL and HRC. Note that the list represents the sequence of items as found in the two archives. The author has maintained the order of individual sheets in their folders in order to emphasize the documentary character of the list: It is not the result of an editing process, but of archival research.

The list includes a description of the physical and bibliographical properties of each item. This allows readers to identify individual items not only on the list, but also in the archives themselves. The following properties are included:

- Box/Folder. Identifies the item's location in the original archive.
- Sheet. This column lists page numbers written on individual drafts; numbers in square brackets have been supplied by the editor.
- Paper/Sheet Properties. To allow a more exact identification of individual items, this column provides physical details concerning the paper, such as paper color or damages.
- Watermark. Lists watermarks. In some cases, when watermarks are not visible on sheets whose paper, however, can be clearly identified, watermarks in square brackets have been supplied by the editor.
- Writing. This column identifies each sheet as a typescript and/or manuscript document by listing the writing instruments used by Pound. "Pc." denotes the gray standard pencil; where Pound used more than one type of pencil, the colors are specified.
- Contents. Supplementing the previous column, Contents lists the layers of writing on each sheet and classifies them and the contents of the document according to their function. Documents may function as notes or drafts, or as carbon copies of notes or drafts (simple "notes" and "drafts" listed are always top copies; carbon copies are indicated). These may contain additions (abbreviated as "add."), revisions/corrections ("rev.") and other layers.

Descriptions in square brackets have been supplied by the author, who partly had to work with photocopies. Items attributed to Canto 0 are miscellaneous items that are not clearly linked to the *Fifth Decad*, but are archived in folders related to the decad.

Item	Canto	Box	Folder	Sheet	Paper/Sheet Properties	Watermark	Writing	Contents
1	48	BL 43.73	3289		half of ls. + single perforation	"Papel Fluminense"	pc.	ms. note
2	50	BL 43.73	3289	"5"	ls. + clip left top + 2 letter-like folds + horizontal middle fold	"Extra Strong"	blue ts. + black ts. + pc.	ts. note + add.
3	50	BL 43.73	3289		back of cc. of cheque + clip left top + horizontal middle fold		black ink	ms. note
4	42	BL 43.73	3289	"A" [1]	ls. + clip left top + 2 letter-like folds	"Extra Strong"	blue ts. + black ink + red pc. + black pc.	ts. draft + rev. in ink
5	42	BL 43.73	3289	"2"	ls. + clip left top + 2 letter-like folds	"Extra Strong"	blue ts. + black ink	ts. draft + rev. in ink
6	42	BL 43.73	3289	"3"	ls. + clip left top + 2 letter-like folds	"Extra Strong"	blue ts. + black ink	ts. draft + rev. in ink
7	42	BL 43.73	3289	"4"	ls. + clip left top + 2 letter-like folds	"Extra Strong"	blue ts. + black ink + pc.	ts. draft + rev. in ink
8	42	BL 43.73	3289	"5"	ls. + clip left top + 2 letter-like folds	"Extra Strong"	blue ts. + bluish-black ink + pc.	ts. draft + rev. in ink
9	42	BL 43.73	3289	"6"	ls. + clip left top + 2 letter-like folds	"Extra Strong"	blue ts. + bluish-black ink	ts. draft + rev. in ink
10	42	BL 43.73	3289	"7"	ls. + clip left top + 2 letter-like folds	"Extra Strong"	blue ts. + bluish-black ink	ts. draft + rev. in ink + drawing of Monte
11	48	BL 43.73	3291	"1"	ls. + diagonal fold left bottom	"Extra Strong"	blue ts. + black ink + pc.	ts. draft + rev. + traces of p. "2"
12	48	BL 43.73	3291	"2"	ls.	"Extra Strong"	blue ts. + black ink + pc.	ts. draft + rev.
13	48	BL 43.73	3291	"3"	3/4 of ls. + bottom torn	"Extra Strong"	blue ts. + pc. + black ink	ts. draft + rev. + add.
14	47	BL 43.73	3292	[1]	ls. + clip left top + clip right middle + torn bottom	"Extra Strong"	blue ts. + black ink + black pc. + red pc.	ts. draft + rev.

Item	Canto	Box	Folder	Sheet	Paper/Sheet Properties	Watermark	Writing	Contents
15	48	BL 43.73	3292	"1"	ls. + perforation + clip left top + 2 letter-like folds	"Papel Fluminense"	blue ts. + black ink + red pc.	ts. draft + rev.
16	48	BL 43.73	3292	"2"	ls. + perforation + clip left top + 2 letter-like folds	"Papel Fluminense"	blue ts. + black ink + red pc.	ts. draft + rev.
17	48	BL 43.73	3292	"3"	ls. + perforation + clip left top + 2 letter-like folds	"Papel Fluminense"	blue ts. + black ink + red pc.	ts. draft + rev.
18	47	BL 43.73	3292	"4"	ls. + perforation + clip left top + 2 letter-like folds	"Papel Fluminense"	blue ts. + black ink + red pc.	ts. draft + rev.
19	47	BL 43.73	3293	[1]	yellow ls. + clip left top	[lily]	black ts. + black ink	ts. cc. of 338 + rev.
20	47	BL 43.73	3293	"2"	yellow ls. + clip left top	[lily]	black ts. + black ink	ts. cc. of 339 + rev.
21	47	BL 43.73	3293	"3"	yellow ls. + clip left top	[lily]	black ts. + black ink	ts. cc. of 340 + rev.
22	47	BL 43.73	3293	"4"	yellow ls. + clip left top	[lily]	black ts. + black ink	ts. cc. of 341 + rev.
23	47	BL 43.73	3293	"5"	yellow ls. + clip left top	[lily]	black ts. + black ink	ts. cc. of 342 + rev.
24	48	BL 43.73	3294		ls. + single perforation + bottom cut	"Papel Fluminense"	blue ts. + pc.	ts. draft + rev.
25	48	BL 43.73	3294		ls. + single perforation + bottom cut	"Papel Fluminense"	blue ts. + pc.	ts. draft + rev.
26	47	BL 43.73	3294	"1"	ls. + single perforation + bottom cut	"Papel Fluminense"	blue ts. + black ink + pc.	ts. draft + rev. in pc. + ink
27	47	BL 43.73	3294	"2"	ls. + single perforation + bottom cut	"Papel Fluminense"	blue ts. + black ink + pc.	ts. draft + rev.
28	47	BL 43.73	3294	"3"	ls. + single perforation + bottom cut	"Papel Fluminense"	blue ts. + black ink + pc.	ts. draft + rev.
29	47	BL 43.73	3294	"4"	ls. + single perforation + bottom cut	"Papel Fluminense"	blue ts. + black ink + pc.	ts. draft + rev.
30	47	BL 43.73	3294		ls. + single perforation + bottom cut	"Extra Strong"	blue ts. + black ink	ts. draft + rev.
31	47	BL 43.73	3294	[1]	ls. + single perforation + fold right top	"Papel Fluminense"	black ink	ms. draft

Item	Canto	Box	Folder	Sheet	Paper/Sheet Properties	Watermark	Writing	Contents
32	47	BL 43.73	3294	[2]	ls. + single perforation + fold right top	"Papel Fluminense"	black ink	ms. draft
33	47	BL 43.73	3294	[3]	ls. + single perforation + fold right top	"Papel Fluminense"	black ink	ms. draft
34	47	BL 43.73	3294	[4]	ls. + single perforation	"Papel Fluminense"	black ink + pc.	ms. draft + pc. drawing of lines
35	47	BL 43.73	3294	[5]	ls. + single perforation + torn at top	"Papel Fluminense"	black ink	ms. draft
36	47	BL 43.73	3294	[6]	ls. + single perforation + fold right bottom	"Papel Fluminense"	black ink	ms. draft
37	47	BL 43.73	3294	[7]	ls. + single perforation	"Papel Fluminense"	black ink	ms. draft
38	48	BL 43.73	3294	"1"	ls. + clip + diagonal fold right bottom	"Papel Fluminense"	purple ts. + pc.	ts. cc. of 100
39	48	BL 43.73	3294	"2"	ls.	"Papel Fluminense"	purple ts.	ts. cc. of 101
40	48	BL 43.73	3294	"3"	ls.	"Papel Fluminense"	purple ts.	ts. cc. of 15
41	48	BL 43.73	3294	"4"	ls. + bottom cut	"Papel Fluminense"	purple ts.	ts. cc. of 16
42	48	BL 43.73	3294	"5"	ls.	"Papel Fluminense"	purple ts.	ts. cc. of 17
43	48	BL 43.73	3294	"6"	ls.	"Papel Fluminense"	purple + blue ts.	ts. cc. of 18
44	44	BL 43.73	3295	"C" [1]	ls. + 2 clips left top + vertical fold left quarter	"Extra Strong"	blue ts. + blue ink + red pc. + black pc.	ts. draft + rev.
45	44	BL 43.73	3295	"2"	ls. + 2 clips left top	"Extra Strong"	blue ts. + blue ink + pc.	ts. draft + rev.
46	44	BL 43.73	3295	"3"	ls. + 2 clips left top	"Extra Strong"	blue ts. + blue ink	ts. draft + rev.
47	44	BL 43.73	3295	"4"	ls. + 2 clips left top	"Extra Strong"	black ts. + blue ink	ts. cc. of 325 + rev.

Item	Canto	Box	Folder	Sheet	Paper/Sheet Properties	Watermark	Writing	Contents
48	44	BL 43.73	3295	"5"	ls. + 2 clips left top	"Extra Strong"	blue ts. + blue ink	ts. draft + rev.
49	44	BL 43.73	3295	"6."	ls. + 2 clips left top	"Extra Strong"	black ts. + blue ts. + black ink + pc.	ts. cc. of 327 + line from top copy
50	45	BL 43.73	3296	[1]	notepad ls. + perforation + clip left top + vertical fold left quarter	"Extra Strong"	black ink + pc.	ms. draft
51	45	BL 43.73	3296	[2]	notepad ls. + perforation + clip left top + vertical fold left quarter	"Extra Strong"	black ink	ms. draft
52	45	BL 43.73	3296	[3]	notepad ls. + perforation (added after writing) + clip left top + vertical fold left quarter	"Extra Strong"	black ink	ms. draft
53	45	BL 43.73	3296	[4]	notepad ls. + perforation + clip left top + horiz middle fold	"Extra Strong"	black ink	ms. draft
54	45	BL 43.73	3296	[5]	notepad ls. + perforation + clip left top + horiz middle fold	"Extra Strong"	black ink	ms. draft
55	45	BL 43.73	3296	[6]	notepad ls. + perforation + clip + horiz middle fold	"Extra Strong"	black ink + red biro	ms. draft
56	45	BL 43.73	3297		yellow ls. + punched left	[lily]	black ts. + black ink	ts. draft + ms. add.
57	45	BL 43.73	3298		ls. + clip	"Papel Fluminense"	black ts. + black ink	ts. draft + rev.
58	45	BL 43.73	3298		ls. + clip	"Papel Fluminense"	blue ts. + pc.	ts. cc. of 57
59	45	BL 43.73	3298		yellow ls. + clip left top	[lily]	black ts. + black ink	ts. draft + rev.
60	45	BL 43.73	3298		yellow ls. + clip left top + vertical fold far left	[lily]	black ts. + black ink	ts. draft + rev.
61	45	BL 43.73	3299	[1]	yellow ls. + clip left top	[lily]	black ts. + black ink	ts. cc. of 329 + rev.

Item	Canto	Box	Folder	Sheet	Paper/Sheet Properties	Watermark	Writing	Contents
62	45	BL 43.73	3299	"2"	yellow ls. + clip left top + diagonal fold lower left quarter	[lily]	black ts. + black ink	ts. cc. of 330 + rev.
63	45	BL 43.73	3299	"3"	yellow ls. + clip left top	[lily]	black ts. + black ink	ts. cc. of 331 + rev. + add.
64	45	BL 43.73	3300	[1]	ls. + torn perforation + clip left top + stained bottom	"Extra Strong"	blue ts. + black ink + blue ink + red pc.	ts. cc. + rev. made on top copy
65	45	BL 43.73	3300	[2]	ls. + torn perforation + clip left top	"Extra Strong"	blue ts. + blue ink	ts. cc. + rev. made on top copy
66	45	BL 43.73	3300	[3]	ls. + torn perforation + clip left top	"Extra Strong"	blue ts. + black ink + blue ink	ts. cc. + rev. on top copy + rev. on cc.
67	45	BL 43.73	3301		photo copy ls. + perforation right	[three leaves]	blue ts.	Ital. transl. of 45, incl. "blue Dun"
68	45	BL 43.73	3302		ls. + perforation	[stripes]	black ts. + purple ts. + pc.	Germ. translation of C45 + pc. note
69	46	BL 43.73	3303		yellow ls. + clip left top	[lily]	black ts. + black ink	ts. draft + rev.
70	46	BL 43.73	3303		half of ls. + clip left middle	"Papel Fluminense"	pc.	Note enwrapping 69
71	51	BL 43.73	3303		yellow ls. + clip left middle	[lily]	black ts.	ts. draft
72	50	BL 43.73	3303		yellow ls. + clip left middle	[lily]	black ts. + ink	ts. cc. + add.
73	46	BL 43.73	3303	"1"	yellow ls. + horizontal middle fold + clip left middle	[lily]	blue ts. + black ink + pc.	ts. draft + rev.
74	46	BL 43.73	3303	"2"	yellow ls. + horizontal middle fold + clip left middle	[lily]	blue ts. + pc.	ts. draft

Item	Canto	Box	Folder	Sheet	Paper/Sheet Properties	Watermark	Writing	Contents
75	46	BL 43.73	3303	"4"	yellow ls. + horizontal middle fold + clip left middle	[lily]	blue ts. + pc.	ts. draft
76	46	BL 43.73	3303		yellow ls. + horizontal middle fold + clip left	[lily]	black ts.	ts. cc. of 75
77	46	BL 43.73	3303		yellow ls. + clip left middle	[lily]	black ts. + ink copy	ts. cc. of 69
78	51	BL 43.73	3303		yellow ls. + clip left middle + diagonal folds in bottom corners	[lily]	black ts.	ts. cc. of 71
79	0	BL 43.73	3304		photo copy of ls. + perforation right	"Pennalife"	ts. + ink	Excerpt from McClellan, Venice and Bonaparte
80	48	BL 43.73	3304	"1"	ls. + clip left top trace	"Extra Strong"	purple ts. + pc.	ts. draft + add.
81	0	BL 43.73	3304	"2"	ls. + clip left top trace	"Extra Strong"	purple ts.	ts. draft
82	48	BL 43.73	3304		ls.	"Extra Strong"	purple ts.	ts. cc. of 80 + pc. add.
83	0	BL 43.73	3304		ls.	"Extra Strong"	purple ts.	ts. cc. of 81
84	43	BL 43.73	3305	"B." [1]	ls. + clip left top + vertical fold in left quarter + 2 letter-like folds	"Extra Strong"	blue ts. + black pc. + red pc. + dark blue ink	ts. draft + rev.
85	43	BL 43.73	3305	"2"	ls. + clip left top + vertical fold in left quarter + 2 letter-like folds	"Extra Strong"	blue ts. + blue ink + dark blue ink	ts. draft + rev.
86	43	BL 43.73	3305	"3"	ls. + clip left top + 2 letter-like folds	"Extra Strong"	blue ts. + dark blue ink	ts. draft + rev.
87	43	BL 43.73	3305	"4"	ls. + clip left top + 2 letter-like folds	"Extra Strong"	blue ts. + dark blue ink	ts. draft + rev.
88	43	BL 43.73	3305	"5"	ls. + clip left top + 2 letter-like folds	["Extra Strong"]	blue ts. + dark blue ink + pc.	ts. draft + rev.

Item	Canto	Box	Folder	Sheet	Paper/Sheet Properties	Watermark	Writing	Contents
89	43	BL 43.73	3305	"6"	ls. + clip left top + 2 letter-like folds	"Extra Strong"	blue ts. + dark blue ink + pc.	ts. draft + rev.
90	43	BL 43.73	3305	"7"	ls. + clip left top + 2 letter-like folds	"Extra Strong"	blue ts. + dark blue ink + pc.	ts. draft + rev.
91	43	BL 43.73	3305	"8"	ls. + clip left top + 2 letter-like folds	"Extra Strong"	blue ts. + dark blue ink + pc.	ts. draft + rev.
92	43	BL 43.73	3305	"9"	ls. + clip left top + 2 letter-like folds	"Extra Strong"	blue ts. + dark blue ink + pc.	ts. draft + rev.
93	48	BL 43.73	3306	[1]	ls. + clip top left	"Papel Fluminense"	blue ts. + black ink + pc.	ts. draft + rev.
94	48	BL 43.73	3306	[1]	ls. + clip top left	"Papel Fluminense"	purple ts.	ts. cc. of 99 + rev.
95	48	BL 43.73	3306		ls. + clip top left	"Papel Fluminense"	blue ts. + black ink + pc.	ts. draft + rev.
96	48	BL 43.73	3306	[4]	ls. + clip top left	"Papel Fluminense"	purple ts.	ts. cc. of part of 104
97	48	BL 43.73	3306	[1]	ls. + clip top left	"Papel Fluminense"	purple ts. + pc. copy + pc.	ts. cc. of 93 + copy of pc. rev. in 93
98	48	BL 43.73	3306	[2]	ls. + clip top left + vertical fold left	"Papel Fluminense"	purple ts.	ts. cc. of 102
99	48	BL 43.73	3307	"1"	ls. + clip top left + perforation + 2 letter-like folds	"Papel Fluminense"	blue ts. + black ink + black pc. + red pc.	ts. draft + rev.
100	48	BL 43.73	3307	"1"	ls. + clip top left + perforation + 2 letter-like folds	"Papel Fluminense"	blue ts. + black ink + pc.	ts. draft + rev.
101	48	BL 43.73	3307	"2"	ls. + clip top left + perforation + 2 letter-like folds	"Papel Fluminense"	blue ts. + black ink + pc.	ts. draft + rev. Comp. 25

Item	Canto	Box	Folder	Sheet	Paper/Sheet Properties	Watermark	Writing	Contents
102	48	BL 43.73	3307	"2"	ls. + clip top left + perforation + 2 letter-like folds	"Papel Fluminense"	blue ts. + black ink + pc.	ts. draft + rev.
103	48	BL 43.73	3307	"3"	ls. + clip top left + perforation + 2 letter-like folds	"Papel Fluminense"	blue ts. + black ink	ts. draft + rev.
104	48	BL 43.73	3307	"4"	ls. + clip top left + perforation + 2 letter-like folds	"Papel Fluminense"	blue ts. + black ink + pc.	ts. draft + rev. Comp. 96.
105	48	BL 43.73	3307	"5"	ls. + clip top left + perforation + 2 letter-like folds	"Papel Fluminense"	blue ts. + black ink + pc.	ts. draft + rev. Comp. 96.
106	48	BL 43.73	3307	[5]	ls. + clip top left	"Papel Fluminense"	purple ts. + pc.	ts. cc. of 105
107	48	BL 43.73	3307	"6"	ls. + clip top left + perforation + 2 letter-like folds	"Papel Fluminense"	blue ts. + black ink + pc.	ts. draft + rev.
108	48	BL 43.73	3307	[6]	ls. + clip top left	"Papel Fluminense"	purple ts.	ts. cc. of 107
109	48	BL 43.73	3307		ls. + clip top left	stripes	pc.	ms. draft
110	48	BL 43.73	3307		ls. + clip top left	stripes	pc.	ms. draft
111	48	BL 43.73	3307		ls. + clip top left + diagonal fold right bottom quarter	"Papel Fluminense"	blue ts. + black ink + pc.	ts. draft + rev.
112	48	BL 43.73	3307		ls. + clip top left	"Papel Fluminense"	blue ts. + pc.	ts. draft + rev.
113	48	BL 43.73	3308		ls. + horizontal fold		black ts. + pc.	ts. draft + add.
114	48	BL 43.73	3309		DIN A5 + 2 cross-like folds		black ts. + black ink + pc.	letter by A. E. Evans

Item	Canto	Box	Folder	Sheet	Paper/Sheet Properties	Watermark	Writing	Contents
115	48	BL 43.73	3309		cut ls. + stained right bottom		blue ts. + pc.	ts. draft
116	48	BL 43.73	3309		ls.	"Extra Strong"	blue ts. + black ink + pc.	ts. draft + add. + newspaper clipping
117	48	BL 43.73	3309		ls.	"Extra Strong"	black ink + pc.	ms. notes
118	48	BL 43.73	3309		ls. + clip top left + brown stains	"Extra Strong"	black ts. + pc.	ts. draft + rev.
119	47	BL 43.73	3309		lined ls. + brown stain top right	"Extra Strong CCCM."	purple ts. + black ink	ts. draft + original rev.
120	48	BL 43.73	3309		ls. + torn right bottom + diagonal fold top right	"Extra Strong CCCM."	blue ts. + black ink + black pc. + red pc.	ts. draft + rev. + pc. note on back
121	48	BL 43.73	3309		ls. + brown stain top left	"Extra Strong"	black pc. + red pc.	ms. note
122	48	BL 43.73	3309		lined ls. + clip left top + torn top left (fixed)	"Extra Strong CCCM."	purple ts. + black pc. + red pc.	ts. draft + rev.
123	48	BL 43.73	3309		ls. + three diagonal folds	"Extra Strong"	black ts. + black ink + black pc. + red pc.	ts. draft + rev. + add.
124	48	BL 43.73	3309	"3"	ls. + clip top left	"Papel Fluminense"	blue ts. + black ink + pc.	ts. draft + rev. + add.
125	48	BL 43.73	3309	[3]	ls. + clip top left	"Papel Fluminense"	purple ts.	ts. cc. of 103
126	0	BL 43.73	3309		ls. + Pound's letter-head + middle fold	"1902 Extra Strong"	black ts. + pc.	ts. note + add.
127	48	BL 43.73	3309		ls. + clip top left	"Papel Fluminense"	purple ts. + pc.	ts. cc. of 104
128	51	BL 43.73	3309		ls. + torn right	"Extra Strong"	purple ts. + pc.	ts. draft + rev. + add.
129	48	BL 43.73	3309	[1]	ls. + folds left	"Extra Strong"	blue ts. + black ink + pc.	ts. draft + rev.
130	48	BL 43.73	3309	[2]	ls.	"Extra Strong"	blue ts. + black ink + pc.	ts. draft + rev.

Item	Canto	Box	Folder	Sheet	Paper/Sheet Properties	Watermark	Writing	Contents
131	0	BL 43.73	3309		ls.	"Extra Strong"	blue ts. + black ink + pc.	ts. draft + rev.
132	48	BL 43.73	3309		ls.	"Extra Strong CCCM."	blue ts. + pc.	ts. draft + rev. + add.
133	48	BL 43.73	3309	[2]	ls. + clip top left	"Papel Fluminense"	purple ts.	ts. cc. of 98
134	48	BL 43.73	3309	[3]	ls. + clip top left	"Papel Fluminense"	purple ts.	ts. cc. of 124
135	48	BL 43.73	3310	[1]	yellow ls. + clip top left	[lily]	black ts. + black ink	ts. cc. of 343 + rev.
136	48	BL 43.73	3310	"2"	yellow ls. + clip top left	[lily]	black ts. + black ink	ts. cc. of 344 + rev.
137	48	BL 43.73	3310	"3"	yellow ls. + clip top left	[lily]	black ts. + black ink	ts. cc. of 345 + rev.
138	48	BL 43.73	3310	"4"	yellow ls. + clip top left	[lily]	black ts. + black ink	ts. cc. of 346 + rev.
139	48	BL 43.73	3310	"5"	yellow ls. + clip top left	[lily]	black ts. + black ink	ts. cc. of 347 + rev.
140	48	BL 43.73	3310	[6]	yellow ls. + clip top left	[lily]	black ts. + black ink	ts. cc. of 348 + rev.
141	49	BL 43.74	3311		ls. + clip top left	"Extra Strong LJC"	blue ts. + pc.	ts. draft + rev.
142	49	BL 43.74	3311		ls. + clip top left	"Extra Strong LJC"	blue ts. + pc.	ts. draft + rev. + pc. note on back
143	49	BL 43.74	3312	[1]	ls. + clip top left + 2 letter-like folds + fold top	"Papel Fluminense"	blue ts. + black ink + pc.	ts. draft + rev. + add.
144	49	BL 43.74	3312	[2]	ls. + clip top left + 2 letter-like folds + fold top	"Papel Fluminense"	blue ts. + black ink + pc.	ts. draft + rev. + add.
145	49	BL 43.74	3312	[3]	ls. + clip top left + 2 letter-like folds + fold top	"Papel Fluminense"	blue ts. + black ink	ts. draft + rev.
146	49	BL 43.74	3313	[1]	yellow ls. + clip top left	[lily]	blue ts. + black ink	ts. cc. of 349 + rev.
147	49	BL 43.74	3313	[2]	yellow ls. + clip top left	[lily]	blue ts. + black ink	ts. cc. of 350 + rev.
148	49	BL 43.74	3313	[3]	yellow ls. + clip top left	[lily]	blue ts. + black ink	ts. cc. of 351 + rev.
149	49	BL 43.74	3314	[1]	ls. + perforation + clip top left	"Papel Fluminense"	blue ts. + black ink + black pc. + red pc.	ts. draft + rev.

Item	Canto	Box	Folder	Sheet	Paper/Sheet Properties	Watermark	Writing	Contents
150	49	BL 43.74	3314	"2"	ls. + perforation + clip top left	"Papel Fluminense"	blue ts. + black ink + pc.	ts. draft + rev.
151	49	BL 43.74	3314	"3"	ls. + perforation + clip top left	"Papel Fluminense"	blue ts. + black ink + pc.	ts. draft + rev.
152	49	BL 43.74	3314	"4"	ls. + perforation + clip top left	"Papel Fluminense"	blue ts. + black ink + pc.	ts. draft + rev.
153	49	BL 43.74	3314		ls. + clip top left	"Papel Fluminense"	blue ts. + black ink + pc.	ts. draft + rev.
154	49	BL 43.74	3314		ls. + clip top left	"Papel Fluminense"	blue ts. + black ink + pc.	ts. draft + add.
155	51	BL 43.74	3314		ls. + clip top left + vertical fold left	"Papel Fluminense"	blue ts. + black ink + pc.	ts. draft + rev.
156	49	BL 43.74	3314	[1]	ls. + clip top left	"Papel Fluminense"	purple ts. + pc.	ts. cc. of 149
157	49	BL 43.74	3314	[2]	ls. + clip top left	"Papel Fluminense"	purple ts. + pc.	ts. cc. of 150
158	49	BL 43.74	3314	"3"	ls. + clip top left	"Papel Fluminense"	purple ts. + pc.	ts. cc. of 151
159	49	BL 43.74	3314	[4]	ls. + clip top left	"Papel Fluminense"	purple ts.	ts. cc. of 152
160	49	BL 43.74	3314		ls. + clip top left	"Papel Fluminense"	purple ts. + pc.	ts. cc. of 153
161	0	BL 43.74	3315		half of ls. + perforation bottom + torn bottom + horizontal fold top	"Papel Fluminense"	blue ts.	ts. draft
162	0	BL 43.74	3315		ls. + perforation + vertical fold left + 2 vertical folds right half	"Extra Strong"	blue ts.	ts. draft

Item	Canto	Box	Folder	Sheet	Paper/Sheet Properties	Watermark	Writing	Contents
163	0	BL 43.74	3315		ls. + torn perforation + 1 vertical fold in left third + brownish stains	"Extra Strong"	black ts. + red pc.	ts. cc. of 162 + rev.
164	0	BL 43.74	3315		ls. + torn perforation + 1 vertical fold in left half	"Extra Strong"	blue ts.	ts. draft
165	0	BL 43.74	3315		ls. + perforation + 2 vertical folds in right half	"Extra Strong"	black ts.	ts. cc. of 164
166	0	BL 43.74	3315		ls. + perforation + 2 vertical middle folds	"Extra Strong"	blue ts. + red pc.	ts. draft + rev.
167	0	BL 43.74	3315		ls. + perforation + 2 vertical folds in right half	"Extra Strong"	black ts. + pc.	ts. cc. of 166 + rev.
168	46	BL 43.74	3315		ls. + perforation + slightly torn bottom + vertical middle fold	[Extra Strong]	blue ts.	ts. draft
169	46	BL 43.74	3315		ls. + perforation + vertical middle fold	[Extra Strong]	black ts.	ts. cc. of 168
170	0	BL 43.74	3315		ls. + perforation + vertical middle fold	"Extra Strong"	blue ts. + black ink	ts. draft + rev.
171	0	BL 43.74	3315		ls. + perforation + vertical middle fold	"Extra Strong"	black ts.	ts. cc. of 170
172	0	BL 43.74	3315	[2?]	ls. + perforation + vertical middle fold + 2 vertical black lines	[Extra Strong]	black ts.	ts. cc. of ???
173	0	BL 43.74	3315	[1?]	ls. + perforation + vertical middle fold	[Extra Strong]	blue ts.	ts. draft
174	0	BL 43.74	3315		ls. + perforation + vertical middle fold + 2 vertical black lines	[Extra Strong]	black ts.	ts. cc. of 173

Item	Canto	Box	Folder	Sheet	Paper/Sheet Properties	Watermark	Writing	Contents
175	51	BL 43.74	3315		ls. + perforation + vertical middle fold + 2 vertical black lines	[Extra Strong]	black ts.	ts. cc. of 176 + ts. Add.
176	51	BL 43.74	3315		ls. + perforation	"Extra Strong"	blue ts.	ts. draft
177	51	BL 43.74	3315		ls. + perforation + vertical fold left quarter + 2 vertical folds right quarter	"Extra Strong"	blue ts.	ts. draft
178	51	BL 43.74	3315		ls. + perforation + 2 vertical folds right quarter + 2 vertical black lines	"Extra Strong"	black ts.	ts. cc. of 177
179	0	BL 43.74	3315		ls. + torn perforation + vertical middle fold + brown stains left	"Papel Fluminense"	blue ts.	ts. draft
180	0	BL 43.74	3315		brown note-pad ls. + perforation		purple ts. + red pc.	ts. cc. of 179
181	51	BL 43.74	3315		brown note-pad ls. + perforation		blue ts. + black ink	ts. draft + rev. + add.
182	51	BL 43.74	3315		brown note-pad ls. + perforation		purple ts.	ts. cc. of 181
183	0	BL 43.74	3315	"1"	brown note-pad ls.		blue ts.	ts. draft
184	0	BL 43.74	3315	[2]	brown note-pad ls.		blue ts.	ts. draft
185	0	BL 43.74	3315	[3]	brown note-pad ls.		blue ts.	ts. draft
186	0	BL 43.74	3315		ls.	"Papel Fluminense"	blue ts.	ts. draft in prose
187	0	BL 43.74	3315		ls. + horizontal fold lower half + diagonal folds top right	"Papel Fluminense"	purple ts.	ts. cc. of 186
188	50	BL 43.74	3316	[1]	ls. + clip top left + horizontal middle fold + 2 vertical black lines	"Extra Strong"	black ts. + pc.	ts. cc. of 352

Item	Canto	Box	Folder	Sheet	Paper/Sheet Properties	Watermark	Writing	Contents
189	50	BL 43.74	3316	[2]	ls. + clip top left + horizontal middle fold + 2 vertical black lines	"Extra Strong"	black ts.	ts. cc. of 353
190	50	BL 43.74	3316	"3"	ls. + clip top left + horizontal middle fold + 2 vertical black lines	"Extra Strong"	black ts.	ts. cc. of 354
191	50	BL 43.74	3316	"4"	ls. + clip top left + horizontal middle fold + 2 vertical black lines	"Extra Strong"	black ts.	ts. cc. of 355
192	50	BL 43.74	3316	[5]	ls. + clip top left + horizontal middle fold + 2 vertical black lines	"Extra Strong"	black ts.	ts. cc. of 356
193	50	BL 43.74	3317	[1]	ls. + clip top left + horizontal middle fold + 2 vertical black lines + perforation	"Extra Strong"	black ts. + pc.	ts. cc. of 188
194	50	BL 43.74	3317	[2]	ls. + clip top left + horizontal middle fold + 2 vertical black lines + perforation	"Extra Strong"	black ts.	ts. cc. of 351
195	50	BL 43.74	3317	"3"	ls. + clip top left + horizontal middle fold + 2 vertical black lines + perforation	"Extra Strong"	black ts.	ts. cc. of 190
196	50	BL 43.74	3317	"4"	ls. + clip top left + horizontal middle fold + 2 vertical black lines + perforation	"Extra Strong"	black ts.	ts. cc. of 191
197	38	BL 43.74	3317		ls. + brown stains	"Extra Strong"	purple ts.	ts. draft

Item	Canto	Box	Folder	Sheet	Paper/Sheet Properties	Watermark	Writing	Contents
198	0	BL 43.74	3317		ls. + folds right bottom + brown stains top	"Extra Strong"	purple ts.	ts. draft
199	48	BL 43.74	3317		ls. + brown stain + slightly torn bottom	"Extra Strong"	blue ts. + pc.	ts. draft + add. + rev.
200	48	BL 43.74	3317		ls.	"Extra Strong"	purple ts.	ts. draft
201	48	BL 43.74	3317		ls. + 2 diagonal folds + 2 brown stains + slightly torn bottom	"Extra Strong"	blue ts. + pc.	ts. draft + rev.
202	48	BL 43.74	3317		ls. + 2 vertical folds	"Extra Strong"	purple ts. + black ink	ts. draft + add.
203	48	BL 43.74	3317		ls. + purple stains	"Extra Strong"	purple ts.	ts. cc. of 202
204	51	BL 43.74	3319		yellow ls. + clip top left	[lily]	blue ts. + black ink + black pc. + red pc.	ts. draft + rev.
205	51	BL 43.74	3319		yellow ls. + clip top left	[lily]	blue ts.	ts. cc. of 204
206	51	BL 43.74	3319		yellow ls. + clip top left	[lily]	blue ts. + black ink	ts. draft + rev.
207	51	BL 43.74	3319		yellow ls. + clip top left	[lily]	blue ts. + red pc.	ts. cc. of 206 + rev.
208	51	BL 43.74	3319		ls. + perforation	"Papel Fluminense"	purple ts. + black ink + red pc.	ts. cc. of 237 + rev.
209	51	BL 43.74	3319		yellow ls. + clip top left	[lily]	blue ts.	ts. draft
210	51	BL 43.74	3319		yellow ls. + clip top left	[lily]	blue ts.	ts. cc. of 209
211	51	BL 43.74	3319	[1]	yellow ls. + clip top left	[lily]	blue ts. + black ink + pc.	ts. draft + rev.
212	51	BL 43.74	3319	[1]	yellow ls. + clip top left	[lily]	blue ts.	ts. cc. of 211
213	51	BL 43.74	3319	[2]	yellow ls. + clip top left	[lily]	blue ts. + black ink	ts. draft + rev.
214	51	BL 43.74	3319	[2]	yellow ls. + clip top left	[lily]	blue ts. + pc.	ts. cc. of 213
215	51	BL 43.74	3320		ls. + perforation + 2 cross-like folds + torn bottom	"In Tritico Vis et Vita"	pc.	ms. draft + continued on verso
216	51	BL 43.74	3320		ls. + perforation + vertical middle fold + slightly stained bottom	"Extra Strong"	blue ts. + black ink	ts. draft + rev.

Item	Canto	Box	Folder	Sheet	Paper/Sheet Properties	Watermark	Writing	Contents
217	51	BL 43.74	3320		ls. + perforation + vertical black line left + slightly stained bottom	"Extra Strong"	black ts.	ts. cc. of 216
218	51	BL 43.74	3320		ls. + perforation + vertical middle fold	"Extra Strong"	blue ts. + black pc. + red pc.	ts. draft + rev.
219	0	BL 43.74	3320		ls. + perforation + vertical middle fold + torn bottom	"Extra Strong"	blue ts.	ts. draft
220	0	BL 43.74	3320		ls. + perforation + vertical middle fold + 2 vertical black lines	"Extra Strong"	black ts.	ts. cc. of 219
221	0	BL 43.74	3320		ls. + perforation + vertical middle fold + brown bottom	"Extra Strong"	blue ts. + pc.	ts. draft + rev.
222	0	BL 43.74	3320		ls. + perforation + vertical middle fold + vertical black line left	"Extra Strong"	black ts.	ts. cc. of 221
223	0	BL 43.74	3320		ls. + perforation + vertical middle fold	"Extra Strong"	blue ts. + pc.	ts. draft + rev.
224	0	BL 43.74	3320		ls. + perforation + vertical middle fold + vertical black line left	"Extra Strong"	black ts.	ts. cc. of 223
225	51	BL 43.74	3320		ls. + perforation + vertical middle fold + diagonal fold right bottom quarter	"Extra Strong"	blue ts. + pc.	ts. draft + rev.
226	51	BL 43.74	3320		ls. + perforation + vertical middle fold + diagonal fold right bottom quarter + vertical black line left	"Extra Strong"	black ts.	ts. cc. of 225 + top copy rev.

Item	Canto	Box	Folder	Sheet	Paper/Sheet Properties	Watermark	Writing	Contents
227	0	BL 43.74	3320		ls. + perforation + vertical middle fold + slightly torn right	"Extra Strong"	blue ts. + pc.	ts. draft + rev.
228	0	BL 43.74	3320		ls. + perforation + vertical middle fold + slightly torn right + vertical black line left	"Extra Strong"	black ts. + pc.	ts. cc. of 227 + new rev.
229	51	BL 43.74	3320		note-pad ls. + perforation + 2 vertical folds		blue ts. + red pc.	ts. draft + rev.
230	51	BL 43.74	3320		ls. + perforation	"Papel Fluminense"	purple ts. + pc.	ts. cc. of 229
231	51	BL 43.74	3320		ls. + perforation + 2 letter-like folds + black stain top	"Papel Fluminense"	blue ts. + black ink + pc.	ts. draft + rev.
232	51	BL 43.74	3320		ls. + perforation + 2 letter-like folds + black stain top	"Papel Fluminense"	purple ts.	ts. cc. of 231
233	51	BL 43.74	3320		ls. + perforation + 2 letter-like folds + stain left top	"Papel Fluminense"	blue ts. + black ink	ts. draft + add.
234	51	BL 43.74	3320		ls. + perforation + 2 letter-like folds	"Papel Fluminense"	purple ts.	ts. cc. of 233
235	51	BL 43.74	3320		ls. + perforation	"Papel Fluminense"	blue ts.	ts. draft
236	51	BL 43.74	3320		ls. + perforation + stained bottom	"Papel Fluminense"	purple ts.	ts. cc. of 235
237	51	BL 43.74	3320		ls. + perforation	"Papel Fluminense"	blue ts.	ts. draft
238	0	BL 43.74	3320		half of ls. + perforation + torn top + torn bottom	"Extra Strong"	pc.	ms. draft
239	0	BL 43.74	3320		ls. + perforation	"Papel Fluminense"	blue ts.	ts. draft

Item	Canto	Box	Folder	Sheet	Paper/Sheet Properties	Watermark	Writing	Contents
240	0	BL 43.74	3320		ls. + perforation	"Papel Fluminense"	purple ts.	ts. cc. of 239
241	0	BL 43.74	3320		ls. + perforation	"Papel Fluminense"	blue ts. + black ink	ts. draft + rev. + add.
242	51	BL 43.74	3320		half of ls. + 3 perforations + torn bottom	"Papel Fluminense"	blue ts. + pc.	ts. draft + rev. + add.
243	51	BL 43.74	3320		ls. + perforation + 2 letter-like folds	"Papel Fluminense"	blue ts. + black ink	ts. draft + add.
244	51	BL 43.74	3320		ls. + perforation + 2 letter-like folds	"Papel Fluminense"	blue ts. + pc.	ts. draft + rev.
245	0	BL 43.74	3320		quarter of brown ls. + perforation + torn bottom	[lily]	purple ts.	ts. note
246	0	BL 43.74	3320		note-pad ls. + perforation		blue ts. + pc.	ts. draft
247	0	BL 43.74	3320		note-pad ls. + perforation		blue ts. + red pc.	ts. draft + rev.
248	51	BL 43.74	3321	[1]	yellow ls. + clip top left + cut bottom + left bottom corner fold	[lily]	blue ts. + black ink	ts. cc. of 357 + rev.
249	51	BL 43.74	3321	"2"	yellow ls. + clip top left	[lily]	blue ts. + black ink	ts. cc. of 358 + rev.
250	51	BL 43.74	3321	"3"	yellow ls. + clip top left	[lily]	blue ts. + black ink	ts. cc. of 359 + rev.
251	46	BL 53.29	609	[1]	yellow ls. + horizontal middle fold + vertical middle fold	[lily]	black ts. + black ink	ts. cc. of 332 + rev.
252	46	BL 53.29	609	"2"	yellow ls. + horizontal middle fold + vertical middle fold	[lily]	black ts. + black ink	ts. cc. of 333 + rev.
253	46	BL 53.29	609	"3"	yellow ls. + horizontal middle fold + vertical middle fold	[lily]	black ts. + black ink	ts. cc. of 334 + rev.

Item	Canto	Box	Folder	Sheet	Paper/Sheet Properties	Watermark	Writing	Contents
254	46	BL 53.29	609	"4"	yellow ls. + horizontal middle fold + vertical middle fold	[lily]	black ts. + black ink	ts. cc. of 335 + rev.
255	46	BL 53.29	609	"5"	yellow ls. + horizontal middle fold + vertical middle fold	[lily]	black ts. + black ink	ts. cc. of 336 + rev.
256	46	BL 53.29	609	"6"	yellow ls. + horizontal middle fold + vertical middle fold	[lily]	black ts. + black ink	ts. cc. of 337 + rev.
257	45	BL 53.29	610	[1]	yellow ls. + clip left top + 2 letter-like folds	[lily]	black ts. + black ink	ts. cc. of 329 + rev.
258	45	BL 53.29	610	"2"	yellow ls. + clip left top + 2 letter-like folds	[lily]	black ts. + black ink	ts. cc. of 330 + rev.
259	45	BL 53.29	610	"3"	yellow ls. + clip left top + 2 letter-like folds	[lily]	black ts. + black ink	ts. cc. of 331 + rev.
260	47	BL 53.29	610	[1]	yellow ls. + clip left top + 2 letter-like folds	[lily]	black ts. + black ink	ts. cc. of 338 + rev.
261	47	BL 53.29	610	"2"	yellow ls. + clip left top + 2 letter-like folds	[lily]	black ts. + black ink	ts. cc. of 339 + rev.
262	47	BL 53.29	610	"3"	yellow ls. + clip left top + 2 letter-like folds	[lily]	black ts. + black ink	ts. cc. of 340 + rev.
263	47	BL 53.29	610	"4"	yellow ls. + clip left top + 2 letter-like folds	[lily]	black ts. + black ink	ts. cc. of 341 + rev.
264	47	BL 53.29	610	"5"	yellow ls. + clip left top + 2 letter-like folds	[lily]	black ts. + black ink	ts. cc. of 342 + rev.
265	48	BL 53.29	610	[1]	yellow ls. + clip left top + 2 letter-like folds	[lily]	black ts. + black ink	ts. cc. of 343 + rev.
266	48	BL 53.29	610	"2"	yellow ls. + clip left top + 2 letter-like folds	[lily]	black ts. + black ink	ts. cc. of 344 + rev.

Item	Canto	Box	Folder	Sheet	Paper/Sheet Properties	Watermark	Writing	Contents
267	48	BL 53.29	610	"3"	yellow ls. + clip left top + 2 letter-like folds	[lily]	black ts. + black ink	ts. cc. of 345 + rev.
268	48	BL 53.29	610	"4"	yellow ls. + clip left top + 2 letter-like folds	[lily]	black ts. + black ink	ts. cc. of 346 + rev.
269	48	BL 53.29	610	"5"	yellow ls. + clip left top + 2 letter-like folds	[lily]	black ts. + black ink	ts. cc. of 347 + rev.
270	48	BL 53.29	610	[6]	yellow ls. + clip left top + 2 letter-like folds	[lily]	black ts. + black ink	ts. cc. of 348 + rev.
271	49	BL 53.29	610	[1]	yellow ls. + clip left top + 2 letter-like folds	[lily]	black ts. + black ink	ts. cc. of 348 + rev.
272	49	BL 53.29	610	"2"	yellow ls. + clip left top + 2 letter-like folds	[lily]	black ts. + black ink	ts. cc. of 349 + rev.
273	49	BL 53.29	610	[3]	yellow ls. + clip left top + 2 letter-like folds	[lily]	black ts. + black ink	ts. cc. of 350 + rev.
274	51	BL 53.29	610	[1]	yellow ls. + clip left top + 2 letter-like folds	[lily]	black ts. + black ink	ts. cc. of 357 + rev.
275	51	BL 53.29	610	"2"	yellow ls. + clip left top + 2 letter-like folds	[lily]	black ts. + black ink	ts. cc. of 358 + rev.
276	51	BL 53.29	610	"3"	yellow ls. + clip left top + 2 letter-like folds	[lily]	black ts. + black ink	ts. cc. of 359 + rev.
277	50	BL 53.29	611	"1"	ls. + clip left top + 2 letter-like folds + torn right	"Extra Strong"	blue ts. + pc.	ts. draft + rev.
278	50	BL 53.29	611	"2"	ls. + clip left top + 2 letter-like folds	[Extra Strong]	blue ts. + pc.	ts. draft + rev.
279	50	BL 53.29	611	"3"	ls. + clip left top + 2 letter-like folds	"Extra Strong"	blue ts. + pc.	ts. draft + rev.
280	50	BL 53.29	611	"4"	ls. + clip left top + 2 letter-like folds	"Extra Strong"	blue ts. + pc.	ts. draft + rev.
281	50	BL 53.29	611	[5]	ls. + clip left top + 2 letter-like folds	"Extra Strong"	black ts.	ts. cc. of 356

Item	Canto	Box	Folder	Sheet	Paper/Sheet Properties	Watermark	Writing	Contents
282	46	BL 43.72	3243		part of sheet + perforation	"Poteie"	black ts.	ts. note on paper of "Albergo Bristol, Rapallo"
283	51	BL 43.72	3245		yellow ls.	[lily]	black ts. + black ink	ts. cc. note + add.
284	46	BL 43.72	3245		ls. + torn bottom	"Papel Fluminense"	black ts. + black ink	ts. note + rev.
285	51	BL 43.72	3245		yellow ls. + torn right	[lily]	black ts.	ts. cc.
286	51	BL 43.72	3245		yellow ls. + torn right	[lily]	black ts.	ts. cc. of 285
287	48	BL 43.72	3245		ls. + torn bottom + torn right	"Extra Strong C.C.C.M."	black ts. + pc.	ts. note + add.
288	48	BL 43.72	3245		ls.	"Extra Strong"	blue ts.	ts. note
289	48	BL 43.72	3245		ls.	"Papel Fluminense"	blue ts.	ts. note
290	0	BL 43.72	3245		ls.	"Papel Fluminense"	blue ts. + black ink + pc.	ts. note + rev.
291	49	BL 43.72	3245		ls.	"Papel Fluminense"	blue ts. + pc.	ts. note + rev.
292	48	BL 43.72	3245		ls.	"Extra Strong"	black ts. + pc.	ts. note + add.
293	49	BL 43.72	3245		ls. + torn right	"Papel Fluminense"	blue ts. + pc.	ts. note + rev.
294	51	BL 43.103	4298	"1"	ls. + torn bottom + black stain	"Extra Strong"	black ink	ms. note excerpt
295	51	BL 43.103	4298	"2"	ls.	"Extra Strong"	black ink	ms. note excerpt
296	51	BL 43.103	4298	"3"	ls.	"Extra Strong"	black ink	ms. note excerpt
297	51	BL 43.103	4298	"4"	ls. + torn top left	"Extra Strong"	black ink	ms. note excerpt
298	51	BL 43.103	4298	"5"	ls.	"Extra Strong"	black ink	ms. note excerpt
299	51	BL 43.103	4298	"6"	ls. + slightly torn bottom right	"Extra Strong"	black ink	ms. note excerpt
300	51	BL 43.103	4298	"7"	ls. + slightly torn bottom right	"Extra Strong"	black ink + pc.	ms. note excerpt

Item	Canto	Box	Folder	Sheet	Paper/Sheet Properties	Watermark	Writing	Contents
301	44	BL 43.115	4895	"1.st"	note-pad "Block Notes Essevuesse"		pc. + black ink	ms. reading notes + draft pieces
302	44	BL 43.115	4896	"2nd"	note-pad "Block Notes" squared		pc. + black ink	ms. reading notes + draft pieces
303	50	BL 43.115	4897	"III"	note-pad "Block Notes" squared		pc.	ms. reading notes + draft pieces
304	50	BL 43.115	4898	"IV"	note-pad "Block Notes" squared		pc. + black ink	ms. reading notes + draft pieces
305	50	BL 43.115	4899	"V"	note-pad "Block Notes" squared		pc. + black ink	ms. reading notes + draft pieces
306	42	HRC 1	9	"A" + "1"	ls. + clip left top	["Extra Strong"]	[black ts. + black ink + pc.]	ts. cc. of 4 + rev.
307	42	HRC 1	9	"2"	ls. + clip left top	["Extra Strong"]	[black ts. + black ink + pc.]	ts. cc. of 5 + rev.
308	42	HRC 1	9	"3"	ls. + clip left top	["Extra Strong"]	[black ts. + black ink + pc.]	ts. cc. of 6 + rev.
309	42	HRC 1	9	"4"	ls. + clip left top	["Extra Strong"]	[black ts. + black ink + pc.]	ts. cc. of 7 + rev.
310	42	HRC 1	9	"5"	ls. + clip left top	["Extra Strong"]	[black ts. + black ink + pc.]	ts. cc. of 8 + rev.
311	42	HRC 1	9	"6"	ls. + clip left top	["Extra Strong"]	[black ts. + black ink + pc.]	ts. cc. of 9 + rev.
312	42	HRC 1	9	"7"	ls. + clip left top	["Extra Strong"]	[black ts. + black ink + pc.]	ts. cc. of 10 + rev.
313	43	HRC 1	9	"B" + [1] + "8"	ls. + clip left top	["Extra Strong"]	[black ts. + black ink + pc.]	ts. cc. of 84 + rev.
314	43	HRC 1	9	"2" + "9"	ls. + clip left top	["Extra Strong"]	[black ts. + black ink + pc.]	ts. cc. of 85 + rev.
315	43	HRC 1	9	"3" + "10"	ls. + clip left top	["Extra Strong"]	[black ts. + black ink + pc.]	ts. cc. of 86 + rev.

Item	Canto	Box	Folder	Sheet	Paper/Sheet Properties	Watermark	Writing	Contents
316	43	HRC 1	9	"4" + "11"	ls. + clip left top	["Extra Strong"]	[black ts. + black ink + pc.]	ts. cc. of 87 + rev.
317	43	HRC 1	9	"5" + "12"	ls. + clip left top	["Extra Strong"]	[black ts. + black ink + pc.]	ts. cc. of 88 + rev.
318	43	HRC 1	9	"6" + "13"	ls. + clip left top	["Extra Strong"]	[black ts. + black ink + pc.]	ts. cc. of 89 + rev.
319	43	HRC 1	9	"7" + "14"	ls. + clip left top	["Extra Strong"]	[black ts. + black ink + pc.]	ts. cc. of 90 + rev.
320	43	HRC 1	9	"8" + "15"	ls. + clip left top	["Extra Strong"]	[black ts. + black ink + pc.]	ts. cc. of 91 + rev.
321	43	HRC 1	9	"9" + "16"	ls. + clip left top	["Extra Strong"]	[black ts. + black ink + pc.]	ts. cc. of 92 + rev.
322	44	HRC 1	9	"C"+ "1" + "17"	ls. + clip left top	["Extra Strong"]	[black ts. + black ink + pc.]	ts. cc. of 44 + rev.
323	44	HRC 1	9	"2"+ "18"	ls. + clip left top	["Extra Strong"]	[black ts. + black ink + pc.]	ts. cc. of 45 + rev.
324	44	HRC 1	9	"3" + "19"	ls. + clip left top	["Extra Strong"]	[black ts. + black ink + pc.]	ts. cc. of 46 + rev.
325	44	HRC 1	9	"4" + "20"	ls. + clip left top	["Extra Strong"]	[blue ts. + black ink + pc.]	ts. draft + rev.
326	44	HRC 1	9	"5" + "21"	ls. + clip left top	["Extra Strong"]	[black ts. + black ink + pc.]	ts. cc. of 48 + rev.
327	44	HRC 1	9	"6" + "22"	ls. + clip left top	["Extra Strong"]	[blue ts. + black ink + pc.]	ts. draft + rev.
328	0	HRC 1	9	"23"	ls. + clip left top + clip right top	["Extra Strong"]	[blue ts. + black ink + pc.]	ts. cover sheet + add.
329	45	HRC 1	9	[1] + "24"	yellow ls. + clip left top	[lily]	[black ts. + black ink + pc.]	ts. draft + rev.
330	45	HRC 1	9	"2" + "25"	yellow ls. + clip left top	[lily]	[black ts. + black ink + pc.]	ts. draft + rev.

Item	Canto	Box	Folder	Sheet	Paper/Sheet Properties	Watermark	Writing	Contents
331	45	HRC 1	9	"3" + "26"	yellow ls. + clip left top	[lily]	[black ts. + black ink + pc.]	ts. draft + rev.
332	46	HRC 1	9	[1] + "27"	yellow ls. + clip left top	[lily]	[black ts. + black ink + black pc. + red pc.	ts. cc. + rev.
333	46	HRC 1	9	"2" + "28"	yellow ls. + clip left top	[lily]	[black ts. + black ink + pc.]	ts. cc. + rev.
334	46	HRC 1	9	"3" + "29"	yellow ls. + clip left top	[lily]	[black ts. + black ink + pc.]	ts. cc. + rev.
335	46	HRC 1	9	"4" + "30"	yellow ls. + clip left top	[lily]	[black ts. + black ink + pc.]	ts. cc. + rev.
336	46	HRC 1	9	"5" + "31"	yellow ls. + clip left top	[lily]	[black ts. + black ink + pc.]	ts. cc. + rev.
337	46	HRC 1	9	"6" + "32"	yellow ls. + clip left top	[lily]	[black ts. + black ink + pc.]	ts. cc. + rev.
338	47	HRC 1	9	[1] + "33"	yellow ls. + clip left top	[lily]	[black ts. + black ink + pc.]	ts. draft + rev.
339	47	HRC 1	9	"2" + "34"	yellow ls. + clip left top	[lily]	[black ts. + black ink + pc.]	ts. draft + rev.
340	47	HRC 1	9	"3" + "35"	yellow ls. + clip left top	[lily]	[black ts. + black ink + pc.]	ts. draft + rev.
341	47	HRC 1	9	"4" + "36"	yellow ls. + clip left top	[lily]	[black ts. + black ink + pc.]	ts. draft + rev.
342	47	HRC 1	9	"5" + 37	yellow ls. + clip left top	[lily]	[black ts. + black ink + pc.]	ts. draft + rev.
343	48	HRC 1	9	[1] + "38"	yellow ls. + clip left top	[lily]	[black ts. + black ink + pc.]	ts. draft + rev.
344	48	HRC 1	9	"2" + "39"	yellow ls. + clip left top	[lily]	[black ts. + black ink + pc.]	ts. draft + rev.
345	48	HRC 1	9	"3" + "40"	yellow ls. + clip left top	[lily]	[black ts. + black ink + pc.]	ts. draft + rev.

Item	Canto	Box	Folder	Sheet	Paper/Sheet Properties	Watermark	Writing	Contents
346	48	HRC 1	9	"4" + "41"	yellow ls. + clip left top	[lily]	[black ts. + black ink + pc.]	ts. draft + rev.
347	48	HRC 1	9	"5" + "42"	yellow ls. + clip left top	[lily]	[black ts. + black ink + pc.]	ts. draft + rev.
348	48	HRC 1	9	"6" + "43"	yellow ls. + clip left top	[lily]	[black ts. + black ink + pc.]	ts. draft + rev.
349	49	HRC 1	9	[1] + "44"	yellow ls. + clip left top	[lily]	[black ts. + black ink + pc.]	ts. draft + rev.
350	49	HRC 1	9	"2" + "45"	yellow ls. + clip left top	[lily]	[black ts. + black ink + pc.]	ts. draft + rev.
351	49	HRC 1	9	"3" + "46"	yellow ls. + clip left top	[lily]	[black ts. + black ink + pc.]	ts. draft + rev.
352	50	HRC 1	9	[1] + "47"	ls. + clip top left	[Extra Strong]	[blue ts. + black ink + black pc. + red pc.]	ts. draft + rev.
353	50	HRC 1	9	"2" + "48"	ls. + clip top left	[Extra Strong]	[blue ts. + black ink + pc.]	ts. draft + rev.
354	50	HRC 1	9	"3" + "49"	ls. + clip top left	[Extra Strong]	[blue ts. + black ink + pc.]	ts. draft + rev.
355	50	HRC 1	9	"4" + "50"	ls. + clip top left	[Extra Strong]	[blue ts. + black ink + pc.]	ts. draft + rev.
356	50	HRC 1	9	[5] + "51"	ls. + clip top left	[Extra Strong]	[blue ts. + black ink + pc.]	ts. draft + rev.
357	51	HRC 1	9	[1] + "52"	yellow ls. + clip left top	[lily]	[black ts. + black ink + pc.]	ts. draft + rev.
358	51	HRC 1	9	"2" + "53"	yellow ls. + clip left top	[lily]	[black ts. + black ink + pc.]	ts. draft + rev.
359	51	HRC 1	9	"3" + "54"	yellow ls. + clip left top	[lily]	[black ts. + black ink + pc.]	ts. draft + rev.